RULEMAKING BY THE EUROPEAN COMMISSION

Rulemaking by the European Commission

The New System for Delegation of Powers

Edited by
CARL FREDRIK BERGSTRÖM
Professor of European Law, Uppsala University
and
DOMINIQUE RITLENG
Professor of Public Law, Strasbourg University

OXFORD
UNIVERSITY PRESS

OXFORD
UNIVERSITY PRESS

Great Clarendon Street, Oxford, OX2 6DP,
United Kingdom

Oxford University Press is a department of the University of Oxford.
It furthers the University's objective of excellence in research, scholarship,
and education by publishing worldwide. Oxford is a registered trade mark of
Oxford University Press in the UK and in certain other countries

First Edition published in 2016

Published in the United States of America by Oxford University Press
198 Madison Avenue, New York, NY 10016, United States of America

British Library Cataloguing in Publication Data
Data available

Library of Congress Control Number: 2015956794

ISBN 978–0–19–870323–5

Preface

Like so many good things, this book started with a meeting between friends. The meeting took place at the Uppsala University Law Faculty in the autumn of 2012. Since then much time has passed and much has happened to the topic which brought us together. The patterns of EU rulemaking behaviour after the reform introduced by the Lisbon Treaty have become visible and the rulemaking institutions have been given time to position themselves. Perhaps most importantly, the Court of Justice of the EU has also been given opportunity to clarify the law and to construct a legal meaning of the new system for delegation of powers. Having allowed ourselves to await the first important stages of that development we now present our assessment. We hope that it will encourage other scholars to deepen the understanding of EU rulemaking. At the same time, we know from before that the story will continue to happen and that there will be no lack of new reasons for us to meet again.

Many thanks are due to the participants of the 2012 workshop at Uppsala University who encouraged our interaction and shared their views. Most specifically grateful acknowledgement is made to Anna Jonsson-Cornell and Anna Michalski, who helped us to secure the generous funding from Uppsala Forum for Peace, Democracy and Justice that made our meeting possible, to Love Rönnelid for his priceless work with the translation of the chapter written by Jean Paul Jacqué, and to Frida-Louise Göransson and Matilda Rotkirch, whose professional commitments did not allow them to contribute to our book but who still helped us to improve its quality by providing invaluable comments and insights. Finally, we are deeply indebted for the support we have received from Oxford University Press, first and foremost from Elinor Shields and Gayathri Viswanathan.

Carl Fredrik Bergström
Dominique Ritleng

Uppsala and Strasbourg
10 September 2015

Contents

Table of Cases xi
Table of Legal Acts xv
Table of Official Documents xix
List of Abbreviations xxiii
List of Contributors xxv

1. **Introduction** 1
Carl Fredrik Bergström
1.1 The Distinction Between Legislative and Non-legislative Acts 1
1.2 The Development of a Doctrine of Delegation of Powers 4
1.3 The New Preconditions in Primary Law 9
1.4 The Aim of the Book and its Delimitations 11

PART I. THE INSTITUTIONAL EXPERIENCE

2. **The Evolution of the Approach to Executive Rulemaking in the EU** 21
Jean Paul Jacqué
2.1 Introduction 21
2.2 The Holder of Executive Power 22
2.3 Defining the Concept of Implementation 27
2.4 The Adoption of Measures of Implementation 32
2.5 Conclusion 35

3. **The Reform of Comitology and Delegated Acts: An Executive's View** 37
Paolo Ponzano
3.1 Introduction 37
3.2 Some Examples of Acts Adopted under Comitology Procedures 38
3.3 A Brief History of Comitology Procedures 40
3.4 The Regulatory Regime Established by the Lisbon Treaty 43
3.5 The New Comitology Procedures 45
3.6 The Delineation between Delegated and Implementing Acts 47
3.7 The Ruling of the Court of Justice in *Biocides* 48
3.8 The Modification of the Common Understanding 50
3.9 Conclusion 51

4. **Delegation of Powers in the European Union: Political Problems, Legal Solutions?** 55
Kieran Bradley

4.1 Introduction: Parliamentary Participation in Second-level Policy-making 55
4.2 Delegation and Conferral: Some General Issues 58
4.3 The European Parliament and Delegated Acts 63
4.4 The European Parliament and Implementing Acts 70
4.5 The Borderline between Delegating and Implementing Acts 77
4.6 The Future of Delegation: Balancing Eggs? 81

PART II. AN EMPIRICAL ASSESSMENT

5. **Interinstitutional Tensions in the New System for Delegation of Powers** 87
Thomas Christiansen and Mathias Dobbels

5.1 Introduction 87
5.2 Interinstitutional Tensions and Delegation: Potential Sites of Conflict 88
5.3 Interinstitutional Tensions and Delegation: the Legislative Process 91
5.4 The Role of 'Expert Groups' in the Preparation of Delegated Acts—Comitology Reinvented 94
5.5 Scrutiny by the EU Legislator: Revocation of Powers and Objections to Drafts 98
5.6 Scrutiny by the Member States: Introducing the Appeal Committee 99
5.7 Conclusion 102

6. **The Contest for Power in Delegated Rulemaking** 105
Adrienne Héritier, Catherine Moury, and Katarzyna Granat

6.1 Introduction 105
6.2 The Theoretical Argument 105
6.3 Incomplete Institutional Rules: Articles 290 and 291 107
6.4 Empirical Cases 109
6.5 Conclusion 126

PART III. THE LEGAL EVALUATION

7. **The Reserved Domain of the Legislature: The Notion of 'Essential Elements of an Area'** 133
Dominique Ritleng

7.1 Introduction 133
7.2 Origin: Going Back to the *Köster* Jurisprudence 137

7.3 Function: Defining the Legislature's Domain and Opening a Wide Scope for Delegation 139
7.4 Scope: a Limit to Legislative Delegation Only? 142
7.5 Content: To Be or Not To Be Essential, That Is a Tricky Question 149

8. Is There a Hierarchy of Legislative, Delegated, and Implementing Acts? 157
Jürgen Bast

8.1 Introduction 157
8.2 The Commission's Delegated and Implementing Powers: two Distinctive Regimes of Control 159
8.3 The Relationship between Delegated and Implementing Acts: neither Exclusivity nor Subordination 165
8.4 Conclusion 171

9. Comitology, Rulemaking, and the Lisbon Settlement: Tensions and Strains 173
Paul Craig

9.1 Introduction 173
9.2 The Lisbon Model: Core Assumptions 174
9.3 Analytical and Temporal: the Fragile Divide between Articles 290 and 291 177
9.4 Constitutional: Politics and Constitutional Architecture 187
9.5 Institutional: Agencies, Conferral, Delegated Acts, and Implementing Acts 194
9.6 Legal Form: Hard Law, Soft Law, and Articles 290 and 291 199
9.7 Conceptual: Rulemaking and Adjudication 200
9.8 Conclusion 201

PART IV. A PARTICIPATORY DIMENSION

10. Judicial Protection for Private Parties in European Commission Rulemaking 205
Maria Bergström

10.1 Introduction 205
10.2 A Systematic Analysis of Articles 263, 290, and 291 213
10.3 Main Obstacles and Remaining Incoherencies 228

11. The Making of Delegated and Implementing Acts: Legitimacy beyond Institutional Balance 233
Joana Mendes

11.1 Introduction 233
11.2 Controls and Democratic Legitimacy 235

11.3 A Matter of Institutional Collaboration Only? 241
11.4 Procedures and Democratic Legitimacy 246
11.5 Conclusion 253

PART V. THE GENERAL CONCLUSIONS

12. Patterns and Findings: Five Central Themes 257
Carl Fredrik Bergström and Dominique Ritleng

12.1 The Constitutional Narrative 257
12.2 The Practical Operation 259
12.3 The Institutional Implications 261
12.4 The Unsolved Problems 262
12.5 The Judicial Development 264
12.6 A New System? 266

Bibliography 271
Index 279

Table of Cases

JUDICIAL RULINGS

EU Court of Justice

Case 9/56 *Meroni v High Authority*, EU:C:1958:7 .... 15, 61, 65, 148, 195
Joined Cases 16-17/62 *Fruit and Vegetables Cases*, EU:C:1962:47 214–215
Case 25/62 *Plaumann v Commission*, EU:C:1963:17 .... 214, 223–224
Case 41/69 *ACF Chemiefarma v Commission*, EU:C:1970:71 .... 141, 147, 153, 159
Case 22/70 *Commission v Council*, EU:C:1971:32 31
Case 25/70 *EVGF v Köster, Berodt & Co*, EU:C:1970:115 .... 4, 11, 59, 136–140, 159, 212, 266, 269
Case 30/70 *Otto Scheer*, EU:C:1970:117 .... 4, 137, 140
Joined Cases 41-44/70 *International Fruit Company v Commission*, EU:C:1971:53 223
Case 62/70 *Bock v Commission*, EU:C:1971:108 221
Case 5/73 *Balkan-Import-Export*, EU:C:1973:109 168
Case 23/75 *Rey Soda*, EU:C:1975:142 141
Case 230/78 *Eridania*, EU:C:1979:216 .... 137–138, 141, 143
Cases 789 and 790/79 *Calpak v Commission*, EU:C:1980:159 215
Joined Cases 188–190/80 *France v Commission*, EU:C:1982:257 159
Case 60/81 *IBM v Commission*, EU:C:1981:264 215
Case 307/81 *Alusuisse v Council and Commission*, EU:C:1982:337 215
Case 11/82 *Piraiki-Patraiki v Commission*, EU:C:1985:18 .... 220–221, 223
Joined cases 205 to 215/82 *Deutsche Milchkontor GmbH v Germany*, EU:C:1983:163 25
Case 121/83 *Zuckerfabrik Franken*, EU:C:1984:175 141
Case 294/83 *Les Verts v Parliament*, EU:C:1986:166 .... 220, 222, 226
Case 222/84 *Johnston*, EU:C:1986:206 226
Joined cases 279, 280, 285 and 286/84 *Rau v Commission*, EU:C:1987:119 141
Case 333/85 *Mannesmann-Röhrenwerke v Council*, EU:C:1987:134 221
Case 26/86 *Deutz & Geldermann v Commission*, EU:C:1987:102 214–215
Case 45/86 *Commission v Council*, EU:C:1987:163 168
Case 46/86 *Albert Romkes v OJDZ*, EU:C:1987:287 .... 59, 137, 143, 159
Case 291/86 *Central Import Münster*, EU:C:1988:361 142
Case 265/87 *Schräder*, EU:C:1989:303 152
Case 302/87 *Parliament v Council*, EU:C:1988:461 .... 22, 71
Case 16/88 *Commission v Council*, EU:C:1989:397 .... 22, 73–74, 141, 159
Case 22/88 *Vreugdenhil and van der Kolk*, EU:C:1989:277 140
Case 160/88 *FEDESA v Council*, EU:C:1988:397 215
Case 167/88 *Association générale des producteurs de blé*, EU:C:1989:234 140
Case C-366/88 *France v Commission*, EU:C:1990:348 215
Case C-298/89 *Government of Gibraltar v Council*, EU:C:1993:267 215–216
Case C-309/89 *Codorniu v Council*, EU:C:1994:197 .... 215, 220
Case C-358/89 *Extramet Industrie v Council*, EU:C:1991:214 .... 215, 220
Case C-63/90 *Portugal and Spain v Council*, EU:C:1992:381 137
Case C-240/90 *Germany v Commission*, EU:C:1992:408 .... 7, 31, 59, 137–138, 141–142, 150, 267
Case C-65/93 *Parliament v Council*, EU:C:1995:91 62
Case C-156/93 *Parliament v Commission*, EU:C:1995:238 .... 7, 137, 143, 267
Joined Cases C-296/93 and C-307/93 *France and Ireland v Commission*, EU:C:1996:65 .... 143, 149, 154
Case C-417/93 *Parliament v Council*, EU:C:1995:127 .... 7, 60, 138, 141–142, 154, 159

Case C-478/93 *Netherlands v Commission*, EU:C:1995:324 141
Case C-200/94 P *Buralux SA v Council*, EU:C:1998:82 224
Joined Cases C-254, 255 and 269/94 *Fattoria Autonoma Tabacchi*, EU:C:1996:320....................152
Case C-285/94 *Italy v Commission*, EU:C:1997:313 141
Case C-303/94 *Parliament v Council*, EU:C:1996:238 ....57, 137, 143, 154
Joined Cases C-9/95, C-23/95 and C-156/95, *Belgium and Germany v Commission*, EU:C:1997:50 141
Case C-10/95 P *Asocarne v Council*, EU:C:1995:406 215
Case C-30/95 *SCPA v Commission*, EU:C:1998:148 221
Case C-57/95 *France v Commission*, EU:C:1997:164 216
Case C-241/95 *Accrington Beef*, EU:C:1996:496....................141
Case C-259/95 *Parliament v Council*, EU:C:1997:454 ....7, 23
Case C-321/95 P *Stichting Greenpeace v Commission*, EU:C:1998:153 224
Case 408/95 *Eurotunnel v Sea France*, EU:C:1997:532....................215
Case C-159/96 *Portugal v Commission*, EU:C:1998:550....................141, 145
Case C-386/96 P *Société Louis Dreyfus & Cie v Commission*, EU:C:1998:193....................222
Case C-104/97 P *Atlanta AG*, EU:C:1999:498 ....142, 154
Case C-356/97 *Molkereigenossenschaft Wiedergeltingen*, EU:C:2000:364 ....137–138, 150
Case C-48/98 *Söhl & Söhlke*, EU:C:1999:548....................137–138, 141, 143, 150
Case C-163/99 *Portugal v Commission*, EU:C:2001:189....................168
Case C-50/00 P *Unión de Pequeños Agricultores v Council*, EU:C:2002:462....................218, 222, 225–228
Case C-298/00 P *Italy v Commission*, EU:C:2004:240 ....223, 225
Case C-378/00 *Commission v Parliament and Council*, EU:C:2003:42 ....8, 142, 169
Case C-491/01 *British American Tobacco (Investments) and Imperial Tobacco*, EU:C:2002:741 ....208, 219, 230
Joined Cases C-37/02 and 38/02 *Di Leonardo Adriano Srl*, EU:C:2004:443 141
Case C-263/02 P *Commission v Jégo-Quéré & Cie SA*, EU:C:2004:210....................218, 226
Case C-131/03 P *Reynolds Tobacco and Others v Commission*, EU:C:2006:541 ....222, 227
Case C-171/03 *Toeters et Verbek*, EU:C:2004:714....................152
Case 66/04 *United Kingdom v Parliament and Council*, EU:C:2005:743 ....137–138, 140, 142–143, 155
Case C-122/04 *Commission v Parliament and Council*, EU:C:2006:134 141
Joined Cases C-154/04 and C-155/04 *Alliance for National Health*, EU:C:2005:449 ....138, 142, 148, 155
Case C-229/05 P *PKK and KNK v Council*, EU:C:2007:32. 226
Joined Cases C-402/05 P and C-415/05 P *Kadi and Al Barakaat v Council and Commission*, EU:C:2008:461 16
Case C-403/05 *Parliament v Commission*, EU:C:2007:624....................141
Case C-443/05 P *Common Market Fertilizers*, EU:C:2007:511 141
Joined Cases C-14/06 and C-295/06 *Parliament and Denmark v Commission*, EU:C:2008:176 ....57, 60, 141
Case C-125/06 P *Commission v Infront WM*, EU:C:2008:159....................225
Case C-133/06 *Parliament v Council*, EU:C:2008:257 ....72–73, 136–138, 159
Case C-521/06 P *Athinaïki Techniki v Commission*, EU:C:2008:422 215
Case C-58/08 Ex parte *Vodafone and others*, EU:C:2010:321 80
Case 407/08 P *Knauf Gips*, EU:C:2010:389....................153
Joined Cases C-71/09 P, C-73/09 P and C-76/09 P *Comitato 'Venezia vuole vivere'*, EU:C:2011:368 223
Joined Cases C-92/09 and C-93/09 *Volker and Markus Schecke*, EU:C:2010:662 153
Case C-221/09 *AJD Tuna Ltd*, EU:C:2011:153 152
Case C-322/09 P *NDSHT v Commission*, EU:C:2010:701....................215
Case C-70/10 *Scarlet Extended SA*, EU:C:2011:255 153

Case C-355/10 *Parliament v Council*, EU:C:2012:516 ......32, 49, 59, 62, 137, 143, 149–154, 237, 265
Joined Cases C-463/10 P and C-475/10 P *Deutsche Post v Commission*, EU:C:2011:656 ......215, 220, 222
Case C-617/10 *Åkerberg Fransson*, EU:C:2013:105 226
Case C-59/11 *Association Kokopelli*, EU:C:2012:447 ......222, 227
Case C-399/11 *Melloni*, EU:C:2013:107 226
Case C-583/11 P *Inuit Tapiriit Kanatami v Parliament and Council*, EU:C:2013:625 ......2–3, 72, 158, 210, 215, 217, 221
Case C-132/12 P *Stichting Woonpunt v Commission*, EU:C:2014:100 ......217, 220, 224–225
Case C-133/12 P *Stichting Woonlinie v Commission*, EU:C:2013:336 ......218, 221, 229
Case C-270/12 *United Kingdom v Parliament and Council*, EU:C:2014:18 ......14–16, 141, 144, 148, 151, 162, 176, 178, 194–195, 265
Case C-274/12 P *Telefónica SA v Commission*, EU:C:2013:852 ......71, 217, 219–222, 225, 227
Case C-293/12 *Digital Rights Ireland*, EU:C:2013:845 153
Case C-370/12 *Pringle v Ireland*, EU:C:2012:756 3
Joined Cases C-404/12 and 405/12 P *Council v Stichting natuur en Milieu*, EU:C:2014:309 138
Case C-409/12 *Council v Commission*, EU:C:2015:217 209
Case C-427/12 *Commission v Parliament and Council*, EU:C:2014:170 ......7, 16–17, 30, 44, 48–49, 60, 79–81, 102, 138, 143–144, 159, 167–168, 179–180, 212, 235, 237, 267
Case C-65/13 *Parliament v Commission*, EU:C:2014:2289 ......7, 63, 81, 138, 161, 168–169, 264
Joined Cases C-317/13 and C-679/13, *Parliament v Council*, EU:C:2015:223 72
Case C-357/13 *Drukarnia Multipress sp zo.o v Minister Finansów*, EU:C:2015:253 3
Case C-409/13 *Council v Commission*, EU:C:2015:217 61
Case C-540/13 *Parliament v Council*, EU:C:2015:224 72
Case C-88/14 *Commission v Parliament and Council*, OJ 2014 C135/24 ......81, 212
Case C-574/14 ex parte *Philip Morris et al*, OJ 2015 C 89/2 62

EU General Court

Case T-435/93 *ASPEC v Commission*, EU:T:1995:79 220
Case T-442/93 *AAC v Commission*, EU:T:1995:80. 220
Case T-480 and 483/93 *Antillean Rice Mills v Commission*, EU:T:1995:162 214
Case T-188/97 *Rothmans International v Commission*, EU:T:1999:156 82
Case T-177/01 *Jégo-Quéré & Cie SA v Commission*, EU:T:2002:112 225
Case T-167/02 *Établissements Toulorge v Parliament and Council*, EU:T:2006:193 226
Case T-231/02 *Piero Gonnelli and AIFO v Commission*, EU:T:2004:105 226
Case T-292/02 *Confservizi v Commission*, EU:T:2009:188 226
Case T-429/05 *Artedogan*, EU:T:2010:60 152
Case T-18/10 *Inuit Tapiriit Kanatami v Parliament and Council*, EU:T:2011:419 158
Case T-164/10 *Pioneer Hi-Bred International v Commission*, EU:T:2013:503 ......40, 76
Case T-240/10 *Hungary v Commission*, EU:T:2013:645 40
Case T-262/10 *Microban v Commission*, EU:T:2011:623 ......217, 220
Case T-367/10 *Bloufin Touna Ellas Naftiki Etaireia*, EU:T:2013:97 152
Case T-301/12 *Laboratoires CTRS v Commission*, EU:T:2013:346 ......40, 101

European Court of Human Rights

App No 6289/73 *Airey v Ireland*, Judgment of 9 October 1979 228
App No 6538/74 *Sunday Times*, Judgment of 26 April 1979 153
App No 37971/97 *Société Colas Est*, Judgment of 16 April 2002 153
App No 45036/98 *Bosphorus*, Judgment of 30 June 2005 226

US Supreme Court

New York v United States, 505 US 144 (1992) 24
Prinz v United States, 521 US 898 (1997) 24
US Terms Limits Inc v Thornton, 514 US 779 (1995) 24

French Conseil Constitutionnel

Decision 2009-592 DC of 19 November 2009 135
Decision 1998-401 DC of 10 June 1998 135

French Conseil d'Etat

Opinion of the French Conseil d'Etat n° 60.497 (1953) Revue du droit public 170 135

Table of Legal Acts

REGULATIONS

Regulation (EC) 2001/1049 of the European Parliament and of the Council, regarding public access to European Parliament, Council and Commission documents, OJ 2001 L 145/43 240

Regulation (EC) 2006/562 of the European Parliament and of the Council of 15 March 2006 establishing a Community Code on the rules governing the movement of persons across borders (Schengen Borders Code), OJ 2006 L 105/1 .... 59, 151, 182

Regulation (EC) 2006/1905 of the European Parliament and of the Council of 18 December 2006 establishing a financing instrument for development cooperation, OJ 2006 L 378/41 78

Regulation (EC) 2009/1070 of the European Parliament and of the Council of 21 October 2009 amending Regulations (EC) 2004/549, (EC) 2004/550, (EC) 2004/551 and (EC) 2004/552 in order to improve the performance and sustainability of the European aviation system, OJ 2009 L 300/34. 184

Regulation (EU) 2010/438 of the European Parliament and of the Council of 19 May 2010 amending Regulation (EC) 2003/998 on the animal health requirements applicable to the non-commercial movement of pet animals, OJ 2010 L 132/3 67

Regulation (EU) 2010/1093 of the European Parliament and of the Council of 24 November 2010 establishing a European Supervisory Authority (European Banking Authority), OJ 2010 L 331/12 .... 69–70, 195–196, 198, 201

Regulation (EU) 2010/1094 of the European Parliament and of the Council of 24 November 2010 establishing a European Supervisory Authority (European Insurance and Occupational Pensions Authority), OJ 2010 L 331/48 .... 69, 195

Regulation (EU) 2010/1095 of the European Parliament and of the Council of 24 November 2010 establishing a European Supervisory Authority (European Securities and Markets Authority), OJ 2010 L 331/84 .... 69, 195

Regulation (EU) 2011/182 of the European Parliament and of the Council of 16 February 2011 laying down the rules and general principles concerning mechanisms for control by Member States of the Commission's exercise of implementing powers, OJ 2011 L 55/13 .... 12, 33–35, 45, 70, 74–76, 82, 87, 91, 139, 144–145, 176, 185–186, 192–193, 213, 219, 238–239, 242

Regulation (EU) 2011/1173 of the European Parliament and of the Council of 16 November 2011 on the effective enforcement of budgetary surveillance in the euro area, OJ 2011 L 306/1 111

Regulation (EU) 2011/1174 of the European Parliament and of the Council of 16 November 2011 on enforcement measures to correct excessive macroeconomic imbalances in the euro area, OJ 2011 L 306/8 109

Regulation (EU) 2011/1176 of the European Parliament and of the Council of 16 November 2011 on the prevention and correction of macroeconomic imbalances, OJ 2011 L 306/25 109

Regulation (EU) 2011/1340 of the European Parliament and of the Council of 13 December 2011 amending Regulation (EC) No 1889/2006 on establishing a financing instrument for the promotion of democracy and

human rights worldwide, OJ 2011 L347/34 78
Regulation (EU) 2012/236 of the European Parliament and of the Council of 14 March 2012 on short selling and certain aspects of credit default swaps, OJ 2012 L 86/1....... 178, 184, 194–195
Regulation (EU) 2012/528/EU of the European Parliament and of the Council of 22 May 2012 concerning the making available on the market and use of biocidal products, OJ 2012 L 127/1 .... 48, 50, 79
Regulation (EU) 2012/530 of the European Parliament and of the Council of 13 June 2012 on the accelerated phasing-in of double-hull or equivalent design requirements for single-hull oil tankers, OJ 2012 L 172/3....... 92–93
Regulation (EU) 2012/648 of the European Parliament and of the Council of 4 July 2012 on OTC derivatives, central counterparties and trade repositories, OJ 2012 L 201/1....... 184
Regulation (EU; Euratom) 2012/966 of the European Parliament and of the Council of 25 October 2012 on the financial rules applicable to the general budget of the Union, OJ 2012 L 298/1....... 92–93, 182
Regulation (EU) 2013/576 of the European Parliament and of the Council of 12 June 2013 on the non-commercial movement of pet animals and repealing Regulation (EC) 2003/998, OJ 2013 L 178/1 67
Regulation (EU) 2013/610 of the European Parliament and of the Council of 26 June 2013 amending Regulation (EC) 2006/562 of the European Parliament and of the Council establishing a Community Code on the rules governing the movement of persons across borders (Schengen Borders Code), OJ 2013 L 182/1....... 182
Regulation (EU) 2013/1289 of the European Parliament and of the Council of 11 December 2013 amending Council Regulation (EC) 2001/539 listing the third countries whose nationals must be in possession of visas when crossing the external borders and those whose nationals are exempt from that requirement, OJ 2013 L 347/74 81
Regulation (EU) 2014/231 of the European Parliament and of the Council of 11 March 2014 establishing an Instrument for Pre-accession Assistance (IPA II), OJ 2014 L 196/1 114
Regulation (EU) 2014/233 of the European Parliament and of the Council of 11 March 2014 establishing a financing instrument for development cooperation for the period 2014–2020, OJ 2014 L77/44....... 78
Regulation (EU) 2014/806 of the European Parliament and of the Council of 15 July 2014 establishing uniform rules and a uniform procedure for the resolution of credit institutions and certain investment firms in the framework of a Single Resolution Mechanism and a Single Resolution Fund, OJ 2014 L 225/1...... 73
Council Regulation (EC) 1997/820 of 21 April 1997 establishing a system for the identification and registration of bovine animals and regarding the labelling of beef and beef products, OJ 1997 L 117/1 .... 7, 39
Council Regulation (EC) 2001/467 of 6 March 2001 prohibiting the export of certain goods and services to Afghanistan, strengthening the flight ban and extending the freeze of funds and other financial resources in respect of the Taliban of Afghanistan, OJ 2001 L 67/1 .... 7–8, 44
Council Regulation (EC) 2003/1 of 16 December 2002 on the implementation of the rules on competition laid down in Articles 81 and 82 of the Treaty, OJ 2003, L 1/1....... 147, 183
Council Implementing Regulation (EU) 2015/81 of 19 December 2014 specifying uniform conditions of application of Regulation (EU) 2014/806 of the European

Parliament and of the Council with regard to ex ante contributions to the Single Resolution Fund, OJ 2015 L 15/1 73
Commission Regulation (EC) 1998/494 of 27 February 1998 laying down detailed rules for the implementation of Council Regulation (EC) 1997/820 as regards the application of minimum administrative sanctions in the framework of the system for the identification and registration of bovine animals, OJ 1998 L 60/78 ....7, 39
Commission Regulation (EC) 2001/2199 of 12 November 2001 amending, for the fourth time, Council Regulation (EC) 2001/467 prohibiting the export of certain goods and services to Afghanistan, strengthening the flight ban and extending the freeze of funds and other financial resources in respect of the Taliban of Afghanistan, OJ 2001 L 295/16 8
Commission Regulation (EU) 2014/1368 of 17 December 2014 amending Regulation (EC) 2009/987 of the Parliament and of the Council laying down the procedure for implementing Regulation (EC) 2004/883 on the coordination of social security systems, OJ 2014 L 366/15 170
Commission Delegated Regulation (EU) 2010/244 of 16 January 2012 supplementing Directive (EU) 2010/31 of the European Parliament and of the Council on the energy performance of buildings by establishing a comparative methodology framework for calculating cost-optimal levels of minimum energy performance requirements for buildings and building elements, OJ 2012 C 115/1 199
Commission Delegated Regulation (EU) 2012/918 of 5 July 2012 supplementing Regulation (EU) 2012/236 with regard to definitions, the calculation of net short positions, covered sovereign credit default swaps, notification thresholds, liquidity thresholds for suspending restrictions, significant falls in the value of financial instruments and adverse events, OJ 2012 L 274/1 ....178, 195
Commission Implementing Regulation (EU) 2003/17 of 14 January 2013 approving the active substance Trichoderma atroviride strain I-1237, in accordance with Regulation (EC) 2009/1107 of the European Parliament and of the Council concerning the placing of plant protection products on the market, and amending the Annex to Implementing Regulation (EU) 2011/540, OJ 2013 L 9/5 183
Commission Implementing Regulation (EU) 2013/22 of 15 January 2013 approving the active substance cyflumetofen, in accordance with Regulation (EC) 2009/1107 of the European Parliament and of the Council concerning the placing of plant protection products on the market, and amending the Annex to Commission Implementing Regulation (EU) 2011/540, OJ 2013 L 11/8 183
Commission Implementing Regulation (EU) 2013/390 of 3 May 2013 laying down a performance scheme for air navigation services and network functions, OJ 2013 L 300/34. 185

DIRECTIVES

Directive (EC) 2001/18 of the European Parliament and of the Council of 12 March 2001 on the deliberate release into the environment of genetically modified organisms, OJ 2001 L106/1 76
Directive (EC) 2009/43 of the European Parliament and of the Council of 6 May 2009 simplifying terms and conditions of transfers of defence-related products, OJ 2009 L 146/1 ....13, 260
Directive (EU) 2010/30, of the European Parliament and the Council (labelling of energy consumption), OJ 2010 L 153/1 244

Directive (EU) 2012/19 of the European Parliament and of the Council of 4 July 2012 on waste electrical and electronic equipment, OJ 2012 L 197/38 .... 92, 94
Directive (EU) 2013/34 of the European Parliament and of the Council of 26 June 2013 on the annual financial statements, consolidated financial statements and related reports of certain types of undertakings, amending Directive (EC) 2006/43/EC of the European Parliament and of the Council, OJ 2013 L 182/19 .... 182, 184, 188
Directive (EU) 2014/40 of the European Parliament and of the Council of 3 April 2014 on the approximation of the laws, regulations and administrative provisions of the Member States concerning the manufacture, presentation and sale of tobacco and related products and repealing Directive (EC) 2001/37, OJ 2014 L 127/1 .... 62, 120
Council Directive (EEC) 1969/349 of 6 October 1969 amending the Directive of 26 June 1964 on health problems affecting intra-community trade in fresh meat, OJ 1969 L 256/5 41
Commission Directive (EU) 2014/18 of 29 January 2014 amending Directive (EC) 2009/43 of the European Parliament and of the Council as regards the list of defence-related products, OJ 2014 L 40/20 .... 13, 260

DECISIONS

Council Decision (EEC) 1987/373 of 13 July 1987 laying down the procedures for the exercise of implementing powers conferred on the Commission, OJ 1987 L 197/33 .... 6, 141
Council Decision (EC) 1999/468 of 28 June 1999 laying down the procedures for the exercise of implementing powers conferred on the Commission, OJ 1999 L 184/23 .... 6, 9, 76, 138, 142, 160, 175, 186, 190
Council Decision (EC) 2006/512 of 17 July 2006 amending, OJ 2006 L 200/11 .... 9, 139, 160, 190
Council Decision (EU) 2013/755 of 25 November 2013 on the association of the overseas countries and territories with the European Union (Overseas Association Decision), OJ 2013 L 344/1 238
Commission Implementing Decision (EU) 2012/766 of 7 December 2012 amending Part A of Annex XI to Council Directive (EC) 2003/85 as regards the list of national laboratories authorised to handle live foot-and-mouth disease virus, OJ 2012 L 337/5 170

Table of Official Documents

EUROPEAN COMMISSION

Commission Communication of 20 April 1978, The Transitional Period and the Institutional Implications of Enlargement, Bulletin EC Supplement 2-1978 5

Commission Communication of 12 November 1982, Problems of Enlargement—Taking Stock and Proposals (The Inventory Report), COM(1982) 757 final 5

Commission Communication of 1 March 1983, Institutional Implications of Enlargement: More Flexibility in Decision-Making (The Fresco II Report), COM(1983) 116 final 5

Commission Communication of 25 July 2001, European governance—A white paper, COM(2001) 428 final 6, 175

Commission Communication of 4 December 2002, The Institutional Architecture—For the European Union: Peace, Freedom, Solidarity, COM(2002) 728 final 6, 175

Commission Communication of 11 December 2002, The operating framework for the European Regulatory Agencies, COM(2002)718 final 14

Commission Communication of 9 December 2009, Implementation of Article 290 of the Treaty on the Functioning of the European Union, COM(2009) 673 final 29, 67, 77, 187, 240, 242–243

Commission Communication of 29 June 2011, A Budget for Europe 2020, COM(2011) 500 final 78

Commission Communication of 25 January 2012, Safeguarding Privacy in a Connected World - A European Data Protection Framework for the 21st Century, COM(2012) 9 final 118

Commission Communication of 19 May 2015 Proposal for an Interinstitutional Agreement on Better Regulation, COM(2015) 216 final 268

Commission Proposal to the IGC 1985, in Bulletin EC 9-1985 5

Commission Proposal of 11 December 2002 for a Council Decision amending Decision (EC) 1999/468, COM (2002) 719 final 175

Commission Proposal of 9 February 2010 for a Regulation of the European Parliament and the Council laying down the rules and general principles concerning mechanisms for control by Member States of the Commission's exercise of implementing powers COM(2010) 83 final 74, 192–193

Commission Proposal of 25 January 2012 for a directive of the European Parliament and the Council on the protection of individuals with regard to the processing of personal data by competent authorities for the purposes of prevention, investigation, detection or prosecution of criminal offences or the execution of criminal penalties, and the free movement of such data, COM(2012) 10 final 118

Commission Proposal of 25 January 2012 for a regulation of the European Parliament and the Council on the protection of individuals with regard to the processing of personal data and on the free movement of such data, COM(2012) 11 final 118

Commission Proposal of 19 December 2012 for a directive of the European Parliament and of the Council on the approximation of the laws, regulations and administrative provisions of the Member States concerning the manufacture, presentation and sale of tobacco and related products, COM(2012) 788 final 120, 122

Commission Proposal of 27 June 2013 for a regulation of the European Parliament and of the Council adapting to Article 290 and 291 of the Treaty on the Functioning of the European Union a number of legal acts providing for the use of the regulatory procedure with scrutiny, COM(2013) 451 final, COM(2013) 452 final and COM(2013) 751 final..186

Commission Proposal of 6 November 2013 for a Council decision concerning the placing on the market for cultivation of a maize product genetically modified for resistance to certain lepidopteran pests, COM(2013) 758 final..............268

Commission President Romano Prodi's Feasibility Study 'Penelope' of 4 December 2002.........................14, 150

Note from the Legal Service of the European Commission on 24 June 2011, Delegated Acts—Guidelines for the services of the Commission, SEC(2011) 855..............95

Commission Staff Working Document of 12 December 2012, Review of the Commission Consultation Policy, SWD(2012) 422 final........................249

Secretary General of the Commission 14 September 2012, Note for the Attention of Directors General and Heads of Service on Delegated and Implementing acts—further guidance, SEC(2012) 537..........................237, 244

Letter from M Šefčovič, Vice-President of the European Commission, 17 March 2014, enclosed in Cover Note, Initiative to complement the Common Understanding on Delegated Acts as regards the consultation of expert, 7792 2014 INIT................................244

EUROPEAN PARLIAMENT

Report of 3 August 1998 drawn up on behalf of the Committee on Institutional Affairs on the modification of the procedures for the exercise of implementing powers conferred on the Commission—'commitology' (rapporteur: M A Aglietta), EP Doc A4-292/1998..................................8

Report of 29 April 2003 on the proposal for a Council Decision on amending Decision (EC) 1999/468 laying down the procedures for the exercise of implementing powers conferred on the Commission (rapporteur: R Corbett), EP Doc A5-128/2003...9

Report of 23 March 2010 drawn up on behalf of the Committee on Legal Affairs Institutional Affairs on the power of legislative delegation (rapporteur: J Szajer), EP Doc A7-110/2010..................64, 83, 191

Report of 24 July 2013 drawn up on behalf of the Committee on the Environment, Public Health and Food Safety on the proposal for a directive of the European Parliament and of the Council on the approximation of the laws, regulations and administrative provisions of the Member States concerning the manufacture, presentation and sale of tobacco and related products (rapporteur: L McAvan), EP Doc A7-276/2013................................62

Report of 4 December 2013 drawn up on behalf of the Committee on Legal Affairs Institutional Affairs on follow up on delegation of legislative powers and control by Member States of the Commission's exercise of implementing powers (rapporteur: J Szajer), EP Doc A7-435/2013.......................51, 177

Report of 12 February 2014 drawn up on behalf of Committee on Constitutional Affairs on the implementation of the Lisbon Treaty with respect to the European Parliament (rapporteur: P Rangel) EP Doc A7-120/2014........................253

Resolution of 8 July 1987 on the Council Decision of 22 June 1987 on the implementing powers of the Commission, B2-724/87......................22

Resolution of 29 January 2003 on the Typology of Acts and the

Hierarchy of Legislation in the European Union, CONV 517/03......... 14
Resolution of 5 May 2010 on the power of legislative delegation (2010/2021 (INI)), OJ 2011 C 81E/6...68
Resolutions of 19 January 2012, P7_TA(2012)0009 and P7_TA(2012)0010..............................78
Resolution of 15 January 2013 with recommendations to the Commission on a Law of Administrative Procedure of the European Union (2012/2024(INI)) 234, 251, 253
Resolution of 12 September 2013 on the Central African Republic, P7_TA(2013)0389.....................123–125
Resolution of 16 January 2014, P7_TA-PROV(2014)0036...................76
Resolution of 5 February 2014 on the proposal for a Directive on explosives for civil use, EP Doc P7_TA-PROV (2014)0085..68
Resolution of 25 February 2014 on follow up on the delegation of legislative powers and control by Member States of the Commission's exercise of implementing powers (2012/2323(INI)...............................234
Resolution of 26 February 2014 on the proposal for a directive of the European Parliament and of the Council on the approximation of the laws, regulations and administrative provisions of the Member States concerning the manufacture, presentation and sale of tobacco and related products, P7_TA(2014)0160.............................121
Resolution of 13 March 2014 on the implementation of the Lisbon Treaty with respect to the European Parliament, 2013/2130(INI) 236
Amendments adopted by the European Parliament on 8 October 2013 on the proposal for a directive of the European Parliament and of the Council on the approximation of the laws, regulations and administrative provisions of the Member States concerning the manufacture, presentation and sale of tobacco and related products (P7_TA-PROV(2013)0398).................62
European Parliament, Amendment 112, P7_TA-PROV(2014)0212.................119
European Parliament, Amendment 200, P7_TA-PROV(2014)0212.................119
European Parliament, Amendments, P7_TA(2013)0389....................124–125
European Parliament, Minutes of the sitting of 25 March 2010, OJ 2010 C132 E/33.............................64
European Parliament, Manufacture, presentation and sale of tobacco and related products (debate), 8 October 2013.................................123
European Parliament, Protection of individuals with regard to the processing of personal data—Processing of personal data for the purposes of crime prevention (debate), 11 March 2014...................119
J Sjájer, debate on own-initiative report of the Committee on Legal Affairs on the power of legislative delegation (A7-0110/2010), verbatim report of EP proceedings of 19 April 2010...... 64
Motion for a resolution pursuant to Rule 87a(3) of the Rules of Procedure on the Commission delegated regulation of 12 December 2013 amending Regulation (EU) 2011/1169 of the European Parliament and of the Council on the provision of food information to consumers as regards the definition of 'engineered nanomaterials' (C(2013)08887—2013/2997(DEA)) 97
European Parliament, Completing the scoreboard for the Macroeconomic Imbalance Procedure (debate), 18 April 2013, contribution by MEP S Bowles..........111
G Pitella et al, *Activity Report on Codecision and Conciliation 14 July 2009–30 June 2014*, EP doc. DV\1031024EN.doc, 25........66
Press release at http://www.europarl.europa.eu/news/en/newsroom/content/20150109IPR06319/html/European-Ombudsman-transparency-a-key-concern-for-citizens-in-2013).............235

COUNCIL OF THE EU

Declarations on Council Decision 1999/468/EC of 28 June 1999 laying down the procedures for the exercise of implementing powers conferred on the Commission (Statement ad Article 5), OJ 1999 C203/1 76
Council Doc 11218/07 of 26 June 2007 2
Council Doc 17477/09 of 11 December 2009 187
Council Doc 16976/10 of 30 November 2010 193
Council Doc 16442/10 ADD1 REV1 of 10 December 2010 78
Council Doc 8753/1/11 of 14 April 2011 (Common Understanding on Delegated Acts) 12, 67, 163, 176, 188, 259
Council Doc 11483/13 of 24 June 2013 .... 120, 123–125
Council Doc 17727/13 of 17 December 2013 .... 120, 124–125
Council Doc 6774/14 of 21 February 2014 (Initiative to complement the Common Understanding on Delegated Acts as regards the consultation of experts) 50, 81, 97, 99, 165, 188–190, 234
Council Doc 7792/14 of 17 March 2014 188
Council Doc 11028/1 of 30 June 2014 119
Council Doc 6773/15 of 3 March 2015 81
Council Press Release 7763/14 120

EUROPEAN CONVENTION

Final Report of Working Group V on Complementary Competences of 4 November 2002, CONV 375/1/02 14
Final Report of Working Group IX on Simplification of 29 November 2002, CONV 424/02 .... 3, 55, 138, 175, 233, 258
Final Report of the Discussion Circle on the Court of Justice of 25 March 2003, CONV 636/03 .... 14, 220, 227
Summary Report on the plenary session on 5 and 6 December 2002, CONV 449/02 14

OTHER

House of Commons, 13th Report of the European Scrutiny Committee, Documents considered by the Committee on 4 September 2013 124
House of Lords Select Committee on the European Communities, Delegation of Powers to the Commission, Session 1986–7, 3rd Report 5
House of Lords Select Committee on the European Communities, Delegation of Powers to the Commission: Reforming Comitology, Session 1986–7, 3rd Report 6
Interinstitutional Agreement of 20 November 2010—Framework Agreement on the relations between the European Parliament and the European Commission, OJ 2010 L 304/47 244
Memorandum submitted by the French Government during the 1965-66 empty chairs crisis, Bulletin EEC 3-1966 5
Non-Paper of Denmark, Germany and the United Kingdom (unpublished paper from December 2011) 95
Report of 5 December 1995 from the Chairman of the Reflection Group of the 1996 IGC—a Strategy for Europe, Office for Official Publications 1995 6
Report of 25 February 2009 from the High Level Group on Financial Supervision in the EU chaired by J de Larosiere, at http://ec.europa.eu/finance/general-policy/docs/de_larosiere_report_en.pdf 198
Report of 31 July 2013 from the European Economic and Social Committee (Section for the Single Market, Production and Consumption), Better Regulation: Implementing acts and delegated acts (rapporteur: P Liz) 237
Rules of Procedure of the Appeal Committee, OJ 2011 C 183/13 75

List of Abbreviations

GENERAL

chap(s)	chapter(s)
ed(s)	editor(s)
edn	edition
n(n)	footnote(s)
p(p)	page(s)
para(s)	paragraph(s)
CJEU	Court of Justice of the European Union
Coreper	Committee of Permanent Representatives in the EU
CPVO	Community Plant Variety Office
EASA	European Aviation Safety Agency
EBA	European Banking Authority
EC	European Community
ECHR	European Convention on Human Rights
ECtHR	European Court of Human Rights
EEC	European Economic Community
EIOPA	European Insurance and Occupational Pensions Authority
EIPA	European Institute of Public Administration
EPSCO	Employment, Social Policy, Health and Consumer Affairs Council configuration
ESA	European Supervisory Authority
ESMA	European Security Markets Authority
IPAII	Instrument for Pre-accession Assistance
IPS	Instrument contributing to Stability and Peace
LGDJ	Librairie générale de droit et de jurisprudence
MEP	Member of the European Parliament
MFF	Multiannual Financial Framework
OHIM	Office for Harmonization in the Internal Market
PRAC	Procédure de Réglementation avec Contrôle (regulatory procedure with scrutiny)
RFDA	Revue Française de Droit Administratif
RTS	regulatory technical standards
SME(s)	small and medium-sized enterprise(s)
TEU	Treaty on European Union
TFEU	Treaty on the Functioning of the European Union

JOURNALS

CMLRev	Common Market Law Review
ECLR	European Competition Law Review
EIoP	European Integration Online Papers
ELJ	European Law Journal
ELRev	European Law Review
EuConst	European Constitutional Law Review
HarvLRev	Harvard Law Review

ICLQ	International & Comparative Law Quarterly
JCMS	Journal of Common Market Studies
JEPP	Journal of European Public Policy
MLR	Modern Law Review
PL	Public Law
RTDEur	Revue trimestrielle de droit européen
UPaLRev	University of Pennsylvania Law Review
YEL	Yearbook of European Law

List of Contributors

Jürgen Bast is Professor of Public Law and European Law at Justus Liebig University Giessen. He was previously Professor of International and European Law at Radboud University Nijmegen and before that Senior Research Fellow at the Max Planck Institute for Comparative Public Law and International Law in Heidelberg. His areas of interest are EU constitutional and administrative law, in particular institutions and legal instruments; migration law and policy; international institutional law; political theory.

Carl Fredrik Bergström is Professor of European Law at Uppsala University. He has a background as researcher at the European University Institute in Florence, lecturer at Stockholm University and Head of Legal Research, later Director, at SIEPS, the Swedish Institute for European Policy Studies. His primary areas of expertise are EU constitutional law and inter-relationship to national constitutional law, EU fundamental principles and system of norms, EU regulatory behaviour and legal method.

Maria Bergström is Associate Professor of European Law and Senior Lecturer in EU Law at Uppsala University. She holds a doctorate in Law from the European University Institute in Florence. Her research interests and publications include judicial protection of private parties, public and private partnerships, EU criminal law and procedure in the Area of Freedom, Security, and Justice, and methods of interpretation.

Kieran Bradley is Judge at the Civil Service Tribunal of the EU and President of its Second Chamber. He was previously an administrator on the secretariat of the European Parliament's Committee on Legal Affairs, then Head of Unit and latterly Director in the European Parliament Legal Service. He has also served as a judicial advisor (*référendaire*) at the European Court of Justice. In 2003–4, he was a member of the groups of legal experts who advised the European Convention and the Intergovernmental Conference on the drafting of the Constitution for Europe. He has published extensively in a number of areas of EU law, particularly institutional law, and has taught and lectured at various universities and third-level institutes, including Harvard Law School, Cambridge University, the College of Europe (Bruges) and SciencesPo (Paris).

Thomas Christiansen holds a Chair in European Institutional Politics and is Professor (part-time) at the Robert Schuman Centre of the European University Institute. He is Executive Editor (with Simon Duke) of the *Journal of European Integration*, co-editor (with S.Vanhoonacker) of the European Administration Governance book series at Palgrave Macmillan, and a member of the Board of the Research Committee on European Unification of the International Political Science Association. He has published widely on various aspects of European integration and EU politics.

Paul Craig is Professor of English Law at St John's College, Oxford. His research interests cover constitutional law, administrative law, comparative public law, and EU law. He is on the editorial board of Public Law, Public Law Review and European Constitutional Law Review. He is general editor of the Clarendon Law Series, and co-editor, with Grainne de Burca, of the Oxford Studies in European Law. Paul Craig is also alternate member for the UK of the Venice Commission on Law and Democracy.

Mathias Dobbels holds a PhD from Maastricht University which was funded by the Marie Curie research project. The thesis was a qualitative case study on inter-institutional negotiations with a focus on the European Parliament. His wider research deals with the European institutions, comitology, the role of civil servants and the concept of power in negotiations. He is currently Deputy Head of Cabinet for the Brussels Minister of Transport, and has previously worked at the Belgian Permanent Representation, including during the Belgian Presidency of the Council.

Katarzyna Granat is Junior Research Fellow and Marie Curie Fellow at Durham University Law School. Prior to this position she was 2014–2015 Emile Noël Fellow at the New York University Jean Monnet Centre. She completed her PhD at the European University Institute in Florence. Her research interests lie in the fields of EU legislative process, EU fundamental rights, and the Eurozone crisis as well as parliamentarism and comparative constitutional law.

Adrienne Héritier is Emeritus Professor of political science in the Department of Political and Social Science and the Roberts Schuman Centre for Advanced Studies at the European University Institute in Florence. Her research extends to theories of institutional change, institutional changes in the EU, comparative public policy, European policy-making, Europeanization, regulation, and new modes of governance.

Jean Paul Jacqué is Emeritus Professor at the University of Strasbourg, where he held a chair from 1978. He is also Professor at the *Collège d'Europe de Bruges* and at the *Institut d'Études européennes* of the *Université libre de Bruxelles*. He was Director of the Legal Service of the Council of the European Union from 1992 to 2008 and is presently Honorary Director General of the Council of the European Union.

Joana Mendes is Associate Professor at the University of Amsterdam. Her work has focused on public authority in the EU, also in relation to global regulatory regimes, with the aim to develop normative solutions to problems raised by executive power as exercised in the EU. She completed her doctoral thesis at the European University Institute in Florence. She is currently working on a research project on administrative discretion in the EU funded by the Netherlands Organisation for Scientific Research.

Catherine Moury is Assistant Professor at the FCSH-NOVA University of Lisbon. Her research focuses on institutional change in the EU and comparative policy-making. She has published in journals such as European Journal of Public Policy, West European Politics and Party Politics. She is the author of *Coalition Government and Party Mandate: How Coalition Agreements Constrain Ministerial Action* (Routledge 2013) and *Changing Rules of Delegation: A Contest of Power for Comitology* (with A Héritier, C Bisschoff and C F Bergström, Oxford University Press 2013).

Paolo Ponzano is Senior Fellow at the Robert Schuman Centre for Advanced Studies of the European University Institute in Florence and Special Adviser to the Vice-President of the European Commission He obtained a political science degree in 1967 and has spent most of his career in the Secretariat-General of the Commission. From 1995 to 2001, he also represented the Commission in the Committee of Permanent Representatives. After that, he served as Director for Institutional Affairs and 'Better Regulation'. In 2002 and 2003 he served as an alternate member of the European Convention.

Dominique Ritleng is a Professor of European Law at the University of Strasbourg, where he is Director of the Master of EU Law Programme and Deputy Director of the *Centre d'études internationales et européennes* (CEIE). He is also Visiting Professor at Uppsala University. He has been a Legal Clerk at the European Court of Justice, in the cabinets of Advocate General Poiares Maduro and Judge Safjan, and before that Professor at the University of Nancy II.

The life cycle of the committee is so basic to our knowledge of current affairs that it is surprising more attention has not been paid to the science of comitology. The first and most elementary principle of this science is that a committee is organic rather than mechanical in its nature. It is not a structure but a plant. It takes root and grows, it flowers, wilts, and dies, scattering the seed from which other committees will bloom in their turn.

Cyril Northcote Parkinson*

* C Northcote Parkinson, *Parkinson's Law or The Pursuit of Progress* (John Murray 1958), at p 31.

1
Introduction

Carl Fredrik Bergström

1.1 The Distinction Between Legislative and Non-legislative Acts

The primary law of the EU comprises the most fundamental instruments which establish what it shall do and how: the treaties concluded between its Member States, the protocols which are annexed to the treaties, and the EU Charter of Fundamental Rights. Even if the characteristics of these instruments differ in many respects they all have the same legal status.[1] The primary law provides the basis for the secondary law: the preconditions and procedures subject to which it may be adopted. Therefore, within the modern EU legal system, the primary law is seen to constitute the highest level in a hierarchy of norms, similar to the constitution within the legal system of most Member States. The secondary law of the EU encompasses a range of unilateral 'legal acts'—both legally binding and not—but also different forms of multilateral agreements (international and inter-institutional). If the content of a provision of secondary law is incompatible with the content of a provision of primary law, the latter shall prevail. This can be seen in the judicial review mechanisms required by the treaties and, in particular, Article 263 of the Treaty on the Functioning of the European Union (TFEU), where the grounds are set out for assessment of the illegality of legal acts.

A general framework in primary law for legal acts is established in Articles 288–92 TFEU. Essentially these provisions were all introduced by the 2009 Lisbon Treaty. The most central feature of the new framework can be found in a conceptual distinction between legal acts classified as either 'legislative' or 'non-legislative' acts. It is not their form or denomination which is decisive for that distinction—whether they are binding or not and if they are, for example, 'directives'—but the nature of the procedure subject to which the individual legal acts have been adopted. This means that there are some directives which are classified as legislative acts and other directives which are classified as non-legislative acts (and this is true for all types of legal acts).

[1] See most notably Articles 1, 6.1, and 51 of the Treaty on European Union (TEU).

In a more immediate sense, the origins of the conceptual distinction between legislative and non-legislative acts can be found in the 2003 Draft Treaty establishing a Constitution for Europe that was produced by the European Convention.[2] Later, when the idea of a constitutional treaty was abandoned, the same distinction 'between what is legislative and what is not and its consequences' was something which those responsible for integrating the innovations of the European Convention into existing treaties were instructed to maintain.[3] The content of the resulting provisions is largely identical to that of the corresponding provisions in the Draft Treaty establishing a Constitution for Europe (save for the denominations of binding legal acts). But even if it is still present, the conceptual distinction between legislative and non-legislative acts is less visible.[4]

It now follows from Article 289 TFEU that '[l]egal acts adopted by legislative procedure shall constitute legislative acts' and that a procedure is legislative only in those instances where that is expressly stated in the treaties. At the other end of the same logic are all those legal acts adopted by another procedure, which constitute non-legislative acts. Today, explicit recognition of the term 'non-legislative' within the general framework for legal acts can only be found in Article 290 TFEU. It can also be found in Article 297 TFEU, which establishes the requirements for publication of legal acts. In compliance with those requirements, the structure of a modern issue of the EU Official Journal is such that it presents the daily output of regulations, directives, and decisions under the headings of 'legislative' or 'non-legislative' acts (L-series).[5]

The classification of legal acts as either legislative or non-legislative has important practical consequences. One example can be found in the formal conditions for national parliaments' subsidiarity control of draft legislative acts, which does not extend to non-legislative acts.[6] Another example can be found in the criteria for individuals' standing in direct actions for judicial review, which are less generous when legislative acts are challenged.[7]

The conceptual distinction between legislative and non-legislative acts has far-reaching theoretical implications. Its focus is set on the question of *who* should pass 'legislation' in the EU (and *why*) and an answer to this question which reflects thinking in terms of separation of powers. Unambiguous expressions of that can be found in the *travaux préparatoires* of Articles 288–92 TFEU and, most clearly,

[2] Articles I-33 ('legislative acts') and I-34 ('non-legislative acts') of the 2003 Draft Treaty establishing a Constitution for Europe (in the 2004 Treaty on a Constitution for Europe the same provisions were numbered Articles I-34 and I-35).

[3] Mandate for the 2007 Intergovernmental Conference, based on the stipulations of the European Council of 21 and 22 June 2007 and reproduced in full in Council Doc 11218/07 of 26 June 2007 (point 19 v).

[4] This is most obviously so because no provision has been included which is equivalent to Article I-34 ('non-legislative acts') of the 2003 Draft Treaty establishing a Constitution for Europe. Cf. n 2.

[5] See http://publications.europa.eu/code/en/en-110200.htm.

[6] Article 3 of the Protocol on the application of the principles of subsidiarity and proportionality, OJ 2012 C 326/203.

[7] Article 263 TFEU, para 4, and the notion of 'regulatory' acts as clarified by the Court of Justice in Case C-583/11 P *Inuit Tapiriit Kanatami and Others v Parliament and Council*, EU:C:2013:625.

in the Final Report of the European Convention Working Group which prepared the new framework for legal acts:[8]

> The Union's system as we know it is not very clear or comprehensible to its citizens. However, ability to criticise the system is a key factor of democracy. Citizens must be able to understand the system so that they can identify its problems, criticise it, and ultimately control it.
>
> To simplify therefore firstly means "to make comprehensible", but also to provide a guarantee that acts with the same legal/political force have the same foundation in terms of democratic legitimacy. The democratic legitimacy of the Union is founded on its States and peoples, and consequently an act of a legislative nature must always come from the bodies which represent those States and peoples, namely the Council and the Parliament. Procedures must therefore be reviewed to ensure that they respect this simple principle: acts which have the same nature and the same legal effect must be produced by the same democratic procedure.
>
> This brings us directly to a clearer hierarchy of legislation, which is the consequence of a better separation of powers. This is not with the aim of paying tribute to Montesquieu, but out of concern for democracy.

Today, the straight-forward answer to the question of *who* may make legislation for the EU is its 'legislator'—but exactly what that legislator looks like depends on the relevant field of competence and the precise legal basis in primary law. Most typically the legislator is defined as the Council and the European Parliament acting jointly, within an 'ordinary legislative procedure' (Articles 289.1 and 294 TFEU). Exceptions to this are found where use is to be made instead of one of several forms of a 'special legislative procedure' (Article 289.2 TFEU). In those instances the relative involvement of the Council or the European Parliament will be different and the interests they each represent therefore have a stronger or weaker influence.

All legal acts which are the result of a procedure which, in primary law, is not expressly designated 'legislative' are non-legislative acts. Perhaps most obviously this includes those legal acts—often 'decisions'—which the treaties authorize the Council to adopt outside its legislative guise, notably within the field of common foreign and security policy and the field of economic policy.[9] But there are also numerous situations in which the treaties assign other institutions with a direct responsibility to adopt binding legal acts which are non-legislative acts.[10]

Another type of non-legislative acts—the object of study in this book—is made up of those regulations, directives, and decisions which have in common that their immediate legal basis is found, not in primary law and a provision of the treaties but in secondary law. Typically, such non-legislative acts are the result of a

[8] Final Report of Working Group IX on Simplification of 29 November 2002, CONV 424/02 (at http://european-convention.europa.eu), at pp 1–2. For confirmation of the legal value of this type of *travaux préparatoires* and a historical interpretation of provisions of EU law see, in particular, Case C-583/11 P (n 7), paras 50, 59, and 66; Case C-370/12 *Pringle v Ireland*, EU:C:2012:756, para 135; and Case C-357/13 *Drukarnia Multipress sp zo.o v Minister Finansów*, EU:C:2015:253, para 22.

[9] See, e.g. Article 28 TEU and Article 122.2 TFEU.

[10] See, e.g. Article 108.4 TFEU (Commission) and Article 132.1 TFEU (European Central Bank). Cf. below n 45.

delegation of powers from the legislator, explicitly provided for in legislative acts. A basic point of departure in EU law for this type of non-legislative acts can be found in the early ruling in *Köster*. Here the Court of Justice explained that 'the legislative system'—and an already consistent practice at that time —established a conceptual distinction between, on the one hand, acts directly based on the treaties which lay down 'the basic elements of the matter to be dealt with' and, on the other hand, derived acts intended to ensure their 'implementation' (cf. French *execution* and German *Durchführung*).[11] According to the Court, the legislative system it had in mind and the legal preconditions for such a 'delegation of powers' was reflected by Article 155 EEC (later renumbered Article 211 EC), stating that the Commission should exercise the powers of implementation which the Council conferred upon it in its legal acts. And that, said the Court, also permitted the Council to determine any requirements which it would want to subject such delegation of powers to the Commission.

1.2 The Development of a Doctrine of Delegation of Powers

It is noteworthy that the doctrine of delegation of powers introduced by the Court in *Köster* had first been advocated in a report from the European Parliament, and there can be no doubt that the Court used that report to phrase its findings.[12] But in sharp contrast to the report from the European Parliament, the Court was willing to accept a much wider interpretation of the notion of implementation (which would not 'have the effect of disturbing the harmonious functioning of the system' established in the basic legislative act).[13] Since then, such delegation of powers to the Commission has become a precious tool for the governments of the EU, to manage their own inability to agree within the Council and secure rulemaking outside—and to some extent independent from—the legislative process.

In the context of the political paralysis from which the EU suffered during the 1970s, the potential usefulness of delegation of powers had already crystallized as a key feature in the debate on the need for a reform of the treaties (eventually manifested by the entry into force of the Single European Act). Focusing on what was perceived as a pressing need to avoid legislative deadlocks in the Council, a series of proposals was presented, all based on the conclusion that it

[11] Case 25/70 *Einfuhr- und Vorratsstelle für Getreide und Futtermittel v Köster, Berodt & Co*, EU:C:1970:115, paras 6 and 9. Cf. also paras 13–19 and the Court's assessment of the question relating to 'the delegation of powers' to the Commission.

[12] This indeed is emphasized by Advocate General Dutheillet de Lamothe, in his Joint Opinion in Cases 11, 25, 26, and 30/70, EU:C:1970:100, at pp 1142–3. For an assessment of the context in which this ruling was given and, in particular, its links to the findings in the so-called Jozeau-Marigné Report of the European Parliament's Legal Committee, see C F Bergström, *Comitology—Delegation of Powers in the European Union and the Committee System* (Oxford University Press 2005), at pp 88–104.

[13] See in particular paras 16 and 17 of the Judgment.

was necessary to 'seek to distinguish between major and minor issues so as to make it possible to distribute the burden to others'.[14]

Most significantly it was asserted that the Council in its legislative role had 'become increasingly reluctant to give the Commission the powers it needs' and was all too often trying to deal itself with matters of implementation.[15] The solution suggested by the Commission was to let it be 'unfettered' from existing constraints and to replace its conditional powers resulting from a case-by-case delegation from the 'legislator'—the Council—by general powers of implementation with a firm basis in primary law. To secure this, the Commission argued, an amendment should be made to Article 155 EEC which declared its genuine right to exercise 'executive' powers.[16]

The governments had previously manifested a conviction that a 'delegation of powers must not imply that the tasks entrusted to the Commission will then be outside the purview of the Council',[17] and that conviction only grew stronger. Unsurprisingly, therefore, when they discussed the proposals relating to the exercise of powers of implementation, agreement was reached on a more cautious construction. This meant that the idea of an amendment to Article 155 EEC which would change the nature of the powers granted to the Commission was rejected and that an amendment was made, instead, to Article 145 EEC (later renumbered Article 202 EC) which emphasized that the Council had a responsibility to confer powers of implementation on the Commission. Importantly, that amendment—which was inserted by the Single European Act—also clarified that any 'requirements' in respect of the exercise of such powers had to be consonant with 'principles and rules' which the Council should lay down in advance.[18] The underlying reason for this was that a great variety of requirements had emerged over the years—different variants of procedures for consultation of so-called comitology committees with experts representing the national administrations—and that political disagreement over the design of such requirements had become a major problem.

[14] See in particular Report on European Institutions of 8 November 1979 presented by the Committee of Three to the European Council (The Three Wise Men Report), Office for Official Publications 1979, at pp 46–7. For a close study see C F Bergström (n 12), at pp 133–62.

[15] Commission Proposal to the IGC 1985, in Bulletin EC 9-1985, point 1.1.16 and Oral Evidence given by C-D Ehlermann in House of Lords Select Committee on the European Communities, Delegation of Powers to the Commission (final report), Session 1986–7, 3rd Report (16 December 1986), at pp 18–19.

[16] Commission Proposal to the IGC 1985, in Bulletin EC 9-1985, point 1, and Commission Communication of 20 April 1978, The Transitional Period and the Institutional Implications of Enlargement (The Fresco Report), Bulletin EC Supplement 2-1978, at p 16. Cf. also Commission Communication of 12 November 1982, Problems of Enlargement—Taking Stock and Proposals (The Inventory Report), COM(1982) 757 final, and Commission Communication of 1 March 1983, Institutional Implications of Enlargement: More Flexibility in Decision-Making (The Fresco II Report), COM(1983) 116 final.

[17] Quotation from the memorandum submitted by the French Government during the 1965–6 'empty chairs crisis', in Bulletin EEC 3-1966, at pp 6–7. See further C F Bergström (n 12), at pp 57–78.

[18] Through the 1985 Single European Act.

Parallel to the introduction of the refined rule on delegation of powers in primary law, a legislative decision was adopted in secondary law in which the principles and rules were established for the requirements in respect of the exercise of powers of implementation. This came to be known as the first Comitology Decision (Council Decision 1987/373). Essentially, it introduced a coherent system for post-delegation supervision based on a limited number of fixed procedures for consultation of existing committees which the Council could compel the Commission to comply with when preparing and adopting its measures of implementation.[19]

The refined rule in primary law remained unchanged until a new framework for legal acts was introduced by the Lisbon Treaty. But this does not imply that there was a lack of debate or, indeed, criticism. In particular, the idea that an amendment ought to be made to the treaties which would replace the rule for delegation of powers by a genuine right for the Commission to exercise truly 'executive' powers was considered several times.[20] The same idea was also repeatedly rejected by many governments who refuted the logic which they felt had too much in common with that of separation of powers within a state.[21] Those relatively minor adjustments on which agreements could be reached were made instead in secondary law, through the adoption of a second Comitology Decision (Council Decision 1999/468) and some later amendments.[22] It is noteworthy that such adjustments were not intended to satisfy the wishes of the Commission but to meet the increasingly more forceful demands from the European Parliament. Parallel to the development in secondary law a series of attempts were also made to come to terms with those demands through informal arrangements.[23]

Throughout the entire period leading up to the Lisbon Treaty, the Court of Justice upheld the doctrine of delegation of powers which it had already established in *Köster*, and that doctrine continued to shape the understanding of delegation

[19] Council Decision (EEC) 1987/373 of 13 July 1987 laying down the procedures for the exercise of implementing powers conferred on the Commission, OJ 1987 L 197/33.

[20] See, e.g. the Report from the Chairman of the Reflection Group of the 1996 IGC of 5 December 1995—a Strategy for Europe (The Westerdorp Report), Office for Official Publications 1995, at pp 30, 35–6, and Commission Communication of 25 July 2001, European Governance—A White Paper, COM(2001) 428 final, at pp 31–4. See also Commission Communication of 4 December 2002, The Institutional Architecture—For the European Union: Peace, Freedom, Solidarity, COM(2002) 728 final and the Explanatory Memorandum of Commission Proposal of 11 December 2002 for a Council Decision amending Decision (EC) 1999/468.

[21] See e.g. the Report from the Chairman of the Reflection Group of the 1996 IGC (n 20), at p 35. Cf. the UK House of Lords, which has (often) emphasized that '[t]he Treaty does not follow or impose any rigid doctrine of the formal separation of powers' and insisted, therefore, that the substantive scope of 'implementation' should remain flexible. See UK House of Lords, Delegation of Powers to the Commission: Reforming Comitology (3rd Report, Session 1998–9, HL Paper 23), at paras 163–4.

[22] Council Decision (EC) 1999/468 of 28 June 1999 laying down the procedures for the exercise of implementing powers conferred on the Commission, OJ 1999 L 184/23. For later amendments see below n 34.

[23] Most notably the so-called *Modus Vivendi*, the agreements between Plumb-Delors, Klepsch-Millan, Samland-Williamson, and Fontaine-Prodi, and the 'Peace Declaration'. See n 63 in Chapter 4.

of powers which was reflected in the choices made by the legislator and, indeed, in the reasoning of those responsible for reform of the treaties. As before, the Court, in return, confirmed its readiness to accept the manner in which the legislator—for most of that period the Council alone—put the doctrine of delegation of powers into practice and made active use of an increasingly wider notion of implementation.[24]

The development could be observed, clearly, in a number of rulings from the mid-1990s. First, the Court inferred from 'the legislative system' of the treaties that the Council 'may delegate to the Commission general implementing power without having to specify the essential components of the delegated power' (and that this may extend to a power to impose penalties).[25] Then it accepted an understanding of implementation which enabled substantive changes to be made in a legislative act without any legislative procedure. Perhaps most notably, in that respect, the Court explained that only some elements of a legislative act can be considered basic or 'essential' for the matter dealt with. The remaining non-essential elements, of the same legislative act, are 'merely part of the arrangements for implementing' and it is therefore also possible to decide upon them in a non-legislative act resulting from a delegation of powers.[26] This understanding of implementation did not only mean that a non-legislative act could be used to provide extensive detail within the framework of a legislative act but that it could also be used to *supplement* that framework and even *amend* the text of the legislative act (its non-essential elements).[27]

Two well-known examples of how the legislator, at the time, made active use of the generous discretion left to it with regard to delegation of powers and the notion of implementation can be found in Council Regulation 1997/820 establishing a system for the identification of bovine animals and Council Regulation 2001/467 extending the freeze of financial resources in respect of the Taliban of Afghanistan. In the first of these acts a delegation clause was included whereby the Commission was empowered 'to adopt detailed rules' on the application of administrative sanctions.[28] This was later used for the adoption of acts such as Commission Regulation 1998/494, which instructed national veterinary authorities that bovine animals 'shall be destroyed without delay' if their keeper cannot prove their identification within two working days, and without any right to compensation.[29] In the second of the two acts a delegation clause was included

[24] See e.g. C F Bergström (n 12), at pp 319–20.

[25] Case C-240/90 *Germany v Commission*, EU:C:1992:408, paras 35–42.

[26] Case C-417/93 *Parliament v Council*, EU:C:1995:127, paras 30–3. For another example see Case C-156/93 *Parliament v Commission*, EU:C:1995:238, paras 18–24. Cf. Case C-259/95 *Parliament v Council*, EU:C:1997:454, paras 24–6.

[27] Cf. Case C-427/12 below n 58, para 39, and Case C-65/13 *Parliament v Commission (EURES)*, EU:C:2014:2289, para 43.

[28] Article 10 of Council Regulation (EC) 1997/820 of 21 April 1997 establishing a system for the identification and registration of bovine animals and regarding the labelling of beef and beef products, OJ 1997 L 117/1.

[29] Article 1.1 of Commission Regulation (EC) 1998/494 of 27 February 1998 laying down detailed rules for the implementation of Council Regulation (EC) 1997/820 as regards the application

whereby the Commission was empowered 'to amend or supplement' a list in that act (Annex) over persons, entities, and bodies whose financial resources should be frozen and unavailable.[30] This delegation was later used to adopt acts such as Commission Regulation 2001/2199, which added new names and addresses to the existing list.[31]

Parallel to the step-by-step establishment in primary law of a co-decision legislative procedure, the Council's harmonious relationship to the Court's doctrine of delegation of powers and their wide interpretation of the notion of implementation—corresponding to a narrow understanding of those 'essential elements' that must be reserved for legislative acts—became a major problem for the European Parliament. Even if its role in the legislative procedure was now becoming equal to that of the Council, the European Parliament had still not been granted any formal right to influence the system for post-delegation supervision (the procedures for consultation of comitology committees). This was confirmed by the Court in 2003, when it explained that the rule in Article 145 EEC (now renumbered Article 202 EC) did not only apply to the shrinking category of legal acts adopted by the Council but also to the new category of legal acts adopted by the Council jointly with the European Parliament. At the same time the adoption of the 'principles and rules' for requirements in respect of the exercise of powers of implementation remained a responsibility for the Council alone.[32]

Essentially, the objection of the European Parliament was that the existing system for supervision functioned too well—for the Council—since it was often making generous delegations of powers accompanied by requirements for a ('regulatory') committee procedure which left the Commission little margin of discretion. The fundamental fear was that such behaviour would gradually undermine the co-decision legislative procedure, restricting its scope to adoption of legal acts with a very general nature. Therefore, what the European Parliament asked for was not only 'real equality' with regard to the responsibility for supervision of powers of implementation but also 'full respect for the legislative procedure in order to prevent a legislative act from being adopted as an implementing measure'.[33] Pending

of minimum administrative sanctions in the framework of the system for the identification and registration of bovine animals, OJ 1998 L 60/78.

[30] Article 10 of Council Regulation (EC) 2001/467 of 6 March 2001 prohibiting the export of certain goods and services to Afghanistan, strengthening the flight ban and extending the freeze of funds and other financial resources in respect of the Taliban of Afghanistan, OJ 2001 L 67/1. See further below n 60.

[31] Article 1 of Commission Regulation (EC) 2001/2199 of 12 November 2001 amending, for the fourth time, Council Regulation (EC) 2001/467 prohibiting the export of certain goods and services to Afghanistan, strengthening the flight ban and extending the freeze of funds and other financial resources in respect of the Taliban of Afghanistan, OJ 2001 L 295/16.

[32] Case C-378/00 *Commission v Parliament and Council*, EU:C:2003:42, para 40. Cf. J P Jacqué, 'Implementing Powers and Comitology', in C Joerges and E Vos (eds), *EU Committees: Social Regulation, Law and Politics* (Hart Publishing 1999), at p 62.

[33] Report of 3 August 1998 drawn up on behalf of the Committee on Institutional Affairs on the modification of the procedures for the exercise of implementing powers conferred on the Commission—'commitology' (rapporteur: M A Aglietta), EP Doc A4-292/1998. For another

the upcoming reform of the treaties—eventually manifested by the entry into force of the Lisbon Treaty—provisional improvements of the system for supervision were secured in secondary law, through amendments of the Comitology Decision (Council Decision 2006/512).[34] Most notably, these amendments gave birth to a new type of committee procedure: the 'regulatory procedure with scrutiny' (PRAC, after its French acronym). This enabled both branches of the legislature of the EU—both the Council and the European Parliament—to oppose, individually, the adoption—by the Commission—of an implementing act 'of general scope designed to amend non-essential elements' in a legislative act for going beyond the scope, aim, or content of their delegation.

1.3 The New Preconditions in Primary Law

It is against the background of the development outlined above—characterized in particular by the increasing emphasis on a systematic use of delegation of powers for rather divergent purposes (to ease the process for adoption of legislation but also to provide uniform conditions for national application) and the unavoidable demand for an adjustment of the rule in primary law—that the general framework for legal acts introduced by the Lisbon Treaty should be approached. The new preconditions for delegation of powers follow from an exercise in two stages, first repealing Article 202 EC (originally numbered Article 145 EEC) and, then, inserting two specific provisions in its place which establish new sub-categories of those non-legislative acts which result from a delegation of powers: Article 290 TFEU on 'delegated acts' (cf. French *actes délégués* and German *delegierten Rechtsakte*) and Article 291 TFEU on 'implementing acts' (cf. French *actes d'exécution*, German *Durchführungsrechtsakter*).

Article 290

1. A legislative act may delegate to the Commission the power to adopt non-legislative acts of general application to supplement or amend certain non-essential elements of the legislative act.

   The objectives, content, scope and duration of the delegation of power shall be explicitly defined in the legislative acts. The essential elements of an area shall be reserved for the legislative act and accordingly shall not be the subject of a delegation of power.

example see Report of 29 April 2003 on the proposal for a Council Decision on amending Decision (EC) 1999/468 laying down the procedures for the exercise of implementing powers conferred on the Commission (rapporteur: R Corbett), EP Doc A5-128/2003.

[34] Council Decision (EC) 2006/512 of 17 July 2006 amending Decision (EC) 1999/468 laying down the procedures for the exercise of implementing powers conferred on the Commission, OJ 2006 L 200/11, and in particular the new Article 5a inserted into the second Comitology Decision. In adopting this Decision, the Council was merely applying a supervisory scheme on which intergovernmental agreement had already been reached in the 2004 Treaty establishing a Constitution for Europe (Article I-36), and which was later integrated into the amendment introduced by the Lisbon Treaty (Article 290 TFEU). Cf. n 7 in Chapter 4.

2. Legislative acts shall explicitly lay down the conditions to which the delegation is subject; these conditions may be as follows:
   (a) the European Parliament or the Council may decide to revoke the delegation;
   (b) the delegated act may enter into force only if no objection has been expressed by the European Parliament or the Council within a period set by the legislative act.

   For the purposes of (a) and (b), the European Parliament shall act by a majority of its component members, and the Council by a qualified majority.
3. The adjective 'delegated' shall be inserted in the title of delegated acts.

Article 291

1. Member States shall adopt all measures of national law necessary to implement legally binding Union acts.
2. Where uniform conditions for implementing legally binding Union acts are needed, those acts shall confer implementing powers on the Commission, or, in duly justified specific cases and in the cases provided for in Articles 24 and 26 of the Treaty on European Union, on the Council.
3. For the purposes of paragraph 2, the European Parliament and the Council, acting by means of regulations in accordance with the ordinary legislative procedure, shall lay down in advance the rules and general principles concerning mechanisms for control by Member States of the Commission's exercise of implementing powers.
4. The word 'implementing' shall be inserted in the title of implementing acts.

The reasoning underlying the new preconditions for delegation of powers is explained, most notably, in the Final Report of the European Convention Working Group mentioned earlier. Here the basic observation was made with respect to the legislative system of the EU that it was 'difficult to make a crystal-clear distinction, as is done in national systems, between matters falling to the legislative arm and those falling to the executive'.[35] Against the background of that observation, the Working Group set out to make, not a perfect, but a clearer distinction than that which existed before. The result was presented as a three-level system of legal acts.

Firstly there were the 'legislative' acts which should contain 'the essential elements and the fundamental policy choices in a certain field'. Then there were the 'delegated' acts, which would permit the Commission to flesh out the detail or amend certain elements of a legislative act. The idea was that such acts should 'encourage the legislator to look solely to the essential elements of an act and to delegate the more technical aspects to the executive, provided that it had the guarantee that it would be able to retrieve, as it were, its power to legislate'. Finally, there were the 'implementing' acts which could be used by the Commission (and exceptionally the Council) for the implementation of legislative acts (and also for the implementation of delegated acts or non-legislative acts directly based on the treaties).

It is noteworthy, that the notion of implementation was not discussed in the light of the legal and political development that had already taken place. And in the light of that development it is also noteworthy that the supervision of 'implementation' was more or less automatically perceived as something over which the national administrations—rather than the legislature of the EU—should claim

[35] Final Report of Working Group IX (n 8), at pp 8–12.

responsibility (through the continuous use of committee procedures). No attempt was made to establish any substantive distinction between delegated and implementing acts. Instead it was said that the EU legislator should determine on a case-by-case basis—in its legislative acts—whether and to what extent it was necessary to have recourse to delegated acts or implementing acts and, then, what their scope would be.

1.4 The Aim of the Book and its Delimitations

The general framework for legal acts introduced by the Lisbon Treaty established new preconditions for delegation of powers and for post-delegation supervision of the exercise of these powers. Considering how central the rulemaking role of the European Commission has become to the EU machinery, it is not surprising that the reform has attracted much attention and that a relative mass of academic literature has already been produced on the topic. But much time has been needed to bring the system resulting from the changes in primary law into motion and it is only now that the full contours are starting to become visible.

The aim of this book is to examine the expectations on the new system for delegations of powers in the light of the experience after its first few years of operations and to provide a balanced assessment of its legal implications. At the centre of that aim lies the general question of whether the new system has really affected the old doctrine of delegation of powers and, if so, how? A wide range of more specific questions will be addressed. Have the objectives of the reform been achieved and what were these objectives? How does the new system for delegations of powers affect the division of functions between the institutions of the EU and the institutional balance? How does the new system affect the relationship between the EU and its Member States and does it concern the citizens? What matters may be dealt with in rulemaking by the European Commission and how important or 'essential' may that be? What is the room for overlap between different forms of delegation of powers and how shall the distinction be made between 'delegated' and 'implementing' acts? How new are the new preconditions for post-delegation supervision and, importantly, what is the role of national experts?

A first important delimitation which should be stated clearly concerns the type of rulemaking which is the object of our study. This is focused on the adoption of binding legal acts of general application (regulations, directives, and decisions[36]) on the basis, not of a provision in the treaties (primary law), but of a provision in another legal act (secondary law). This means that the resulting legal acts are 'derived' from 'acts directly based on the treaties'.[37]

During the initial years, after entry into force of the general framework introduced by the Lisbon Treaty, the institutional machinery for adoption of binding legal acts was not proceeding at normal speed. Even if the new provisions

[36] Article 288 TFEU. [37] Case 25/70 (n 11), paras 6 and 9.

in primary law were now in place the negotiations went on for numerous practical arrangements. It was not until 2011 that the 'rules and general principles' were adopted which were to constitute the system for supervision of implementing acts (European Parliament and Council Regulation 2011/182).[38] Parallel to that an informal 'common understanding' was presented with the ambition of settling the routines for delegated acts.[39] More than anything else this managed to expose a profound lack of common understanding, in particular with regard to governments' insistence on procedures for consultation of experts representing the national administrations, and a need, therefore, to re-enter into negotiations.

A reflection of the problems which initially beset the institutional machinery can be found in the low number of legislative acts adopted subject to the ordinary legislative procedure. During 2010, the first year after the reform, only 35 regulations, 16 directives and 8 decisions were adopted under this procedure.[40] Four years later, in 2014, the numbers were 88 regulations, 47 directives, and 13 decisions. An even more striking illustration can be found in the number of non-legislative acts resulting from delegation of powers. During 2010, there were no implementing acts or delegated acts adopted by the Commission (but 45 implementing acts adopted by the Council).[41] The year after, in 2011, there were 975 implementing acts (790 regulations, 21 directives, and 164 decisions) and 3 delegated acts (3 regulations) adopted by the Commission. Over the following years the numbers rose steadily and in 2014 there were 1032 implementing acts (703 regulations, 13 directives, and 316 decisions) and 138 delegated acts (111 regulations, 26 directives, and 1 decision) adopted by the Commission.[42]

Importantly, the low number of implementing and delegated acts adopted during the first years after the reform—and the increase—must be seen in the light of all those non-legislative acts which were simultaneously being adopted by the Commission in exercise of powers conferred upon it in legislative acts adopted before the entry into force of the Lisbon Treaty. In 2010 these were altogether 1495 acts (1123 regulations, 68 directives, and 304 decisions). This means that the regulatory productivity was not low during 2010, only that the new system for delegation of powers had not yet entered into operation (to compare with 2008, when the number of non-legislative acts adopted by the Commission in exercise of powers conferred upon it in legislative acts was 1139 regulations, 54 directives, and 374 decisions).[43]

[38] Regulation (EU) 2011/182 of the European Parliament and of the Council of 16 February 2011 laying down the rules and general principles concerning mechanisms for control by Member States of the Commission's exercise of implementing powers, OJ 2011 L 55/13.

[39] Common Understanding on Delegated Acts, Council Doc 8753/1/11 of 14 April 2011.

[40] All numbers presented in this section are based on the year of publication of the legal acts in the EU Official Journal (and not their year of adoption), excluding so-called *corrigenda*. Most numbers are retrieved directly from the electronic edition of the EU Official Journal (which is the only authentic source). The requirements for publication of legal acts can be found in Article 297 TFEU.

[41] The implementing acts adopted by the Council in 2010 were composed of 36 regulations and 9 decisions.

[42] The implementing acts adopted by the Council in 2014 were composed of 39 regulations and 43 decisions.

[43] The implementing acts adopted by the Council in 2008 were composed of 75 regulations and 49 decisions.

It should be observed that a relatively large proportion of non-legislative acts are still being adopted by the Commission in exercise of powers conferred upon it in legislative acts adopted before the entry into force of the Lisbon Treaty, that is, under the rules of the old system. In 2014 there were 243 such regulations and 21 such directives. A closer look at those non-legislative acts reveals that they are often the result of a delegation of powers to *supplement* or *amend* the content of legislative acts, combined with binding requirements for consultation of comitology committees (typically PRAC).[44] After the reform, when a delegation of such powers is made, it falls within the field of application of Article 290 TFEU. This means that the resulting acts will be designated delegated acts (and that it is not possible to uphold the old requirements for consultation of comitology committees).

Finally a few comments may be made with respect to the number of non-legislative acts which have their basis directly in primary law (and are not, therefore the result of any delegation of powers). Firstly, the number of such non-legislative acts adopted by the Commission is relatively small. During 2014 not more than 3 regulations, 0 directives and 39 decisions were adopted.[45] Secondly, the number of such non-legislative acts adopted by the Council is remarkably high.[46] In 2014 these totalled 58 regulations, 0 directives, and 331 decisions (to compare with 88 regulations, 48 directives and 22 decisions adopted as legislative acts, of which all but 1 directive and 9 decisions were subject to the ordinary legislative procedure).

A second important delimitation which should be stated clearly concerns the type of delegation of powers which is the object of our study. Here our assessment will focus only on delegation of powers from the legislature of the EU to the Commission and exclude, most obviously, delegation of powers from that legislature to 'agencies' (or 'offices' and 'bodies'[47]). This is not intended to suggest that the legal development with respect to agencies is not important for our understanding of the new system for delegation of powers. The topic will be touched upon briefly in the chapters by Dominique Ritleng and Paul Craig and a few more words should be said here as well.

During the last two decades, the legislature of the EU has assigned significant responsibilities to an increasing number of 'agencies' of which all but a few are located outside Brussels. According to the Official Directory of the EU there are today 35 such agencies in operation and new ones are being installed.[48] These agencies are not 'institutions' in the formal sense[49] but can be identified as bodies

[44] For an example see Commission Directive (EU) 2014/18 of 29 January 2014 amending Directive (EC) 2009/43 of the European Parliament and of the Council as regards the list of defence-related products, OJ 2014 L 40/20, with a legal basis in Article 10 of Directive (EC) 2009/43 of the European Parliament and of the Council of 6 May 2009 simplifying terms and conditions of transfers of defence-related products, OJ 2009 L 146/1.

[45] All 3 regulations and 27 decisions had their legal basis in Article 108 TFEU (State Aid), 9 decisions had their legal basis in Article 249 TFEU (Commission Rules of Procedure), 2 decisions had their legal basis in Article 328(1) and/or Article 331(1) TFEU (Enhanced Cooperation) and 1 decision, finally, had its legal basis in Protocol (36) on Transitional Provisions.

[46] Cf. n 9.

[47] See e.g. Article 263 TFEU and the passage quoted below in n 50.

[48] See http://europa.eu/whoiswho/whoiswho.html.

[49] Cf. Article 13 TEU.

with a legal personality of their own which have been set up to accomplish technical, scientific, or managerial tasks. Even if they have fundamental similarities there are also several differences, in particular with regard to their specific tasks and the type of action they may take.

Many agencies, but not all, have been subject to a formal delegation of powers to adopt binding legal acts (which for some of them may extend to acts of general application). At the same time it is unclear how legal acts adopted by these agencies fit into the general framework for legal acts in primary law. Not only does Article 288 TFEU define legal acts as acts adopted by 'institutions' but the impression that they are also reserved for institutions is supported by the requirements for a statement of reason in Article 296 TFEU and for publication in Article 297 TFEU.

In the European Convention a number of questions relating to the role of agencies were discussed. The most obvious result can be found in the amendments which were eventually made to EU judicial review mechanisms.[50] But parallel to that, a need was also addressed to clarify the role of agencies in the institutional structure and the nature of their powers. Perhaps most notably, in the Commission contribution to the European Convention the proposal was made for a new provision in primary law setting out general criteria and conditions for the establishment, running and monitoring of agencies.[51] In the end no such provision on agencies was introduced. Even if the reasons for that are not entirely clear, it is apparent that there were conflicting political positions—not the least between the institutions—and a fundamental fear within the Commission that agencies' autonomy would pose a threat to its responsibility for 'the unity and integrity of the executive function' of the EU.[52] The unfortunate asymmetry caused by this gap in primary law was left to be dealt with by the Court of Justice.

The central response from the Court can be found in its ruling in *Short Selling*.[53] Here the question which the Court had to answer was how the lack of a provision in primary law on delegation of powers to agencies should be understood, while at

[50] See in particular Article 263 TFEU, now stating the Court's duty to 'review the legality of acts of bodies, offices or agencies of the Union intended to produce legal effects vis-à-vis third parties' and Article 277 TFEU, now stating a party's right to invoke the inapplicability of 'an act of general application adopted by an institution, body, office or agency of the Union' in the proceedings. Cf. also Articles 265 and 267 TFEU.

[51] Commission Communication of 4 December 2002 (n 20), at p 13. There were also proposals along those lines in the Final Reports of several European Convention Working Groups. See most importantly Final Report of Working Group V on Complementary Competences of 4 November 2002, CONV 375/1/02; Final Report of Working Group IX (n 8); and Final Report of the Discussion Circle on the Court of Justice of 25 March 2003, CONV 636/03. See also the Summary Report on the Plenary Session on 5 and 6 December 2002, CONV 449/02, at p 3, where it was pointed out that provision would need to be made for 'implementing acts' to be adopted by agencies.

[52] See, e.g. Commission Communication of 11 December 2002, The operating framework for the European Regulatory Agencies, COM(2002)718 final (quotation from p 6) and Commission President Romano Prodi's Feasibility Study 'Penelope' of 4 December 2002 (Articles 71 and 79). For a contrasting political position see Resolution of 29 January 2003 on the Typology of Acts and the Hierarchy of Legislation in the European Union, CONV 517/03.

[53] Case C-270/12 *United Kingdom v Parliament and Council*, EU:C:2014:18. For an extensive comment see CF Bergström, 'Shaping the new system for delegation of powers to EU agencies: *United Kingdom* v. *European Parliament and Council (Short Selling)*' (2015) 52 CMLRev 219.

the same time the capacity of agencies to exercise those powers—to adopt binding legal acts—is envisaged by the judicial review mechanisms. The way in which the Advocate General approached this dilemma was to focus on the new system for delegation of powers to the Commission and argue for an extensive interpretation *contra legem* of Article 291 TFEU to the end that agencies were also permitted to adopt implementing acts.[54] But in contrast to that solution, what the Court opted for was the invention of an invisible provision which could fill the hole in primary law: an analogous regime on delegation of powers to agencies which will exist in parallel to Articles 290 and 291 TFEU.

This analogous regime permits the legislature to make a delegation of powers to agencies that enables them to adopt legal acts which can not only be binding on those to whom they are addressed but also be binding in general. Like a delegation of powers under Articles 290 and 291 TFEU, the analogous regime also requires that a legal basis can be found in the treaties—one enabling provision or several—where an appropriate competence with respect to the subject-matter in question has been conferred on the EU and its legislature. Presumably, a delegation of powers to agencies—as an alternative or, more typically, a complement to a delegation of powers to the Commission under Articles 290 or 291 TFEU—should be motivated by special needs, such as a higher degree of professional expertise and an ability to respond more swiftly (in interaction with corresponding national authorities).

Importantly, the analogous regime only permits the legislature to make a delegation of powers to agencies if the scope of those powers is circumscribed by 'criteria and conditions' which will ensure that the powers and their exercise are precisely delineated and amenable to judicial review. This basic rule follows from the principle established by the Court in its early ruling in *Meroni*.[55] Here the possibility was acknowledged of a delegation of powers to non-institutional bodies with a 'distinct legal personality' but that possibility was strictly limited, said the Court, with respect both to the manner in which the delegation had to be made and the scope of the powers it could involve.

Firstly, the delegation had to be made in a way which could ensure that all legal rules restricting the exercise of powers would continue to apply (and rules relating to judicial review and the duty to state reasons were specifically emphasized). Then, as to the scope of the powers, the Court explained that it could only permit a delegation if it involved 'clearly defined executive powers' (the exercise of which would be open to review 'in the light of objective criteria' established by the delegating authority). To go further than that and permit a delegation of discretionary powers to 'bodies other than those which the Treaty has established to effect and supervise the exercise of such power each within the limits of its own authority' would undermine a fundamental guarantee of constitutional nature (stemming from the concept of an 'institutional balance of powers').[56]

[54] Opinion of A G Jääskinen in Case C-270/12, EU:C:2013:562, in particular paras 86–7.
[55] Case 9/56 *Meroni v High Authority*, EU:C:1958:7, in particular pp 149–54.
[56] At p 152. Cf. the original version in French (at p 43).

According to the reasoning of the Advocate General in *Short Selling* the narrow scope for delegation of powers to agencies which could be permitted was premised on a 'sharp conceptual distinction' between 'normative' delegated acts and 'executive' implementing acts.[57] But the Court did not pick up the suggestion that any sharp conceptual distinction could be made with respect to agencies' powers.[58] It did not discuss any distinction between Articles 290 and 291 TFEU or, indeed, between notions of normative or executive acts. Nor did it discuss the nature of the powers that may be subject to a delegation to the Commission under those provisions in relation to the nature of the powers which may be subject to a delegation of powers to agencies under the analogous regime.

For these reasons one must be cautious about using the terminology in Articles 290 and 291 TFEU for analyses of the powers which may or may not be involved in a delegation to agencies under the analogous regime. Logically, the reasoning of the Court in *Short Selling* does not exclude a delegation of powers to agencies which, if it was made to the Commission, would involve not only powers to *implement* legislative acts (Article 291 TFEU) but also powers to *supplement* or *amend* them (Article 290 TFEU). The decisive factor for agencies would be found instead in the principle established in *Meroni* and the resulting prohibition against any delegation which, irrespective of the nature of the powers involved, would permit the exercise of a large freedom of appreciation or a 'wide margin of discretion' which may translate into an actual policy.[59] It should be recalled, in this context, that the expression 'amend or supplement' is not, in itself, premised on the exercise of any discretion. An illustration of that point can be found in the regulatory framework challenged before the Court in *Kadi and Al Barakaat*. Here the Commission was empowered to 'amend or supplement' a legislative act in application of prior determinations from the UN Security Council, an arrangement characterized by the perceived need for expediency and a striking lack of latitude.[60]

Until it has been clarified by the Court, it cannot be taken for granted that the notion of 'executive powers' which is used in *Meroni*—and therefore also in *Short Selling* is identical to the notion of executive or, more precisely, 'implementing' powers in Article 291 TFEU. This would in particular be so considering that at the time of *Meroni* and during the remaining period before the entry into force of the amendments introduced by Lisbon Treaty, the notion of executive or 'implementing' powers also covered powers to adopt 'acts which supplement or

[57] Opinion (n 54), paras 60, 75–7, and 81. According to A G Jääskinen, '[a] clear demarcation between these two phenomena was proposed by the European Convention and it was included in the Treaty establishing a Constitution for Europe' (para 75).

[58] See also Case C-427/12 *European Commission v European Parliament and Council (Biocides)*, EU:C:2014:170. Here the Court was called upon to rule on the difference between the powers which may be subject to a delegation to the Commission under Articles 290 and 291 TFEU. For an extensive comment see D Ritleng, 'The Dividing Line between Delegated and Implementing Acts: the Court of Justice Sidesteps the Difficulty in *Commission* v. *Parliament and Council (Biocides)*' (2015) 52 CMLRev 243.

[59] See that test by the Court in Case C-270/12 (n 53), paras 44–53.

[60] Joined Cases C-402/05 P and C-415/05 P *Kadi and Al Barakaat v Council and Commission*, EU:C:2008:461, paras 27–33 and 280. See also n 31.

amend certain non-essential elements of a legislative act'.[61] Having said all this, it would still make sense if the Court should seek to bring the different expressions of executive and implementing powers together. Irrespective of that, it remains to be seen how the development with regard to agencies will interrelate to the operation of Articles 290 and 291 TFEU, and how that development will affect the way in which the legislature of the EU uses its discretion to choose between different forms of delegation of powers.

The book is divided into four main parts:

Part I: *The Institutional Experience:* In this part the wider context—political and historical—in which the rulemaking takes place will be examined with special emphasis on the inter-relationship between the Council, the European Parliament, and the European Commission. A central ambition is to identify driving forces behind reform and reactions, patterns in behaviour, strategic considerations, and competing agendas.

Part II: *An Empirical Assessment:* In this part the operation of the system for delegation of powers to the European Commission after the reform is examined with a focus on institutional practices and interinstitutional relations. It is of particular interest to identify changes in the pattern of behaviour, the reasons for such changes, and, indeed, the consequences of such changes for the system for delegation of powers and for the institutional balance of powers.

Part III: *The Legal Evaluation:* In this part there will be a detailed assessment of the legal substance of the new framework for rulemaking by the European Commission and the emerging case law from the Court of Justice of the EU. The assessment will clarify the content of the new treaty provisions and the measures which have been adopted to implement them. But most importantly it will examine the relevance, after the reform, of pre-existing notions and the meaning of new concepts and, in particular, identify the matters which are likely to be addressed in judicial proceedings.

Part IV: *A Participatory Dimension:* In this part the focus will be on the procedural dimension and in particular the legal preconditions for private actors to participate in rulemaking by the European Commission. It is of particular interest to assess to what extent existing rights to participate in such rulemaking and the possibility to initiate judicial review could be considered to constitute a complementary source of democratic legitimacy of delegated and implementing rulemaking.

In addition to these parts there are, finally, some general conclusions where the striking patterns observed in the preceding parts of the book are set out and the most forceful findings.

[61] Case C-427/12 (n 58), para 36.

PART I

THE INSTITUTIONAL EXPERIENCE

2

The Evolution of the Approach to Executive Rulemaking in the EU

*Jean Paul Jacqué**

2.1 Introduction

This contribution is aimed at tracing the evolution of the approach to executive rulemaking in the European Union, without dealing in depth with the legal and technical aspects that are the object of profound analysis in the other contributions. Since the Union started to legislate, the distinction between legislative and executive acts has caused recurring debates concerning who is the holder of the executive power and what control the Parliament can exercise over that entity. These questions took a conflictual turn when the co-decision procedure entered into force, because the Parliament took advantage of its shared legislative power to claim a shared executive power. The Commission has always played an ambiguous role in these debates, since its aim, above all, has been to be recognized as the final holder of the executive power. One of the reasons for the incessant discussions about the concept of execution[1] is perhaps that the problem has always been treated as a power struggle, without genuine reflection on the origins of the debate.[2]

The debate in effect started off between the Council and the Commission about whether the former could exercise a control over the latter concerning its adoption of measures of execution. Then the Parliament intervened in the discussions, emphasizing its hostility to the comitology, but before Maastricht it did so mostly

* The author wishes to acknowledge the invaluable support from Doctoral Candidate Love Rönnelid at the Uppsala University Law Faculty, with translation of the text from French to English.

[1] Note that the French expression *exécution*, extends, in English, to both 'execution' and 'implementation' (depending on the context). In cases referring to the treaty provisions on 'implementation' that expression has been used; otherwise, the expression 'execution' has been preferred.

[2] Perhaps with the exception of K Lenaerts and A Verhoeven, 'Towards a Legal Framework for Executive Rulemaking in the EU? The Contribution of the New Comitology Decision' (2000) 37 CMLRev 645. For a recent vision that excludes any constitutional perspective, see J Bering Liisberg, 'The EU Constitutional Treaty and its distinction between legislative et non-legislative acts—Oranges into apples?' Jean Monnet Working Paper 01/06 NYU School of Law.

by supporting the prerogatives of the Commission. That in turn created the first situation where the Parliament claimed its right to standing before the Court in order to annul the first Comitology Decision,[3] which, according to the Parliament, led to a paralysis of the decisions taken by the Commission.[4]

The founding treaties did not ignore the existence of measures of execution, since they conferred on the Council the power to delegate the adoption of such measures to the Commission. They therefore recognized the existence of an executive power distinct from the legislative power. The treaties did not contain explicit criteria for discerning the two categories. This situation gave rise to suggestions about the establishment of a hierarchy of norms in Community law. This meant that Community law, as it stood before the entry into force of the Lisbon Treaty, recognized a certain kind of hierarchy of norms. Clearly, secondary law was subordinate to primary law and the measures of execution had to take their authority from an enabling provision in secondary law. The system thus contained three legislative levels arranged hierarchically. Each act had its specified place in the Community legal order and had to conform to superior norms. There was a distinction between legislation and measures of execution but the criterion was not an organic one, since the legislator, for most of that period the Council alone, could keep for itself the power to adopt measures of execution. The Commission's implementing powers rested on an empowerment granted by the legislator.

2.2 The Holder of Executive Power

There is hardly any discussion about the holder of the power to take measures for implementation of Union acts. The Union is based on a system of indirect administration and the material application of measures taken by it falls within the competencies of the Member States. It is essentially only where the intervention by the Union is limited to granting financing within the confines of programmes that it is possible to conceive of an intervention by the Commission under its executive budget powers (Article 317 TFEU). That intervention can, if necessary, be controlled by a comitology procedure.[5] At stake in the debate is thus essentially the determination of which organ holds the power to adopt normative executive measures. The discussions on this subject are frequently inspired by ideas about horizontal separation of powers but have overlooked any consideration of vertical separation of powers.[6]

[3] Case 302/87 *Parliament v Council*, EU:C:1988:461.

[4] Resolution of 8 July 1987 on the Council Decision of 22 June 1987 on the implementing powers of the Commission, B2-724/87.

[5] Case 16/88 *Commission v Council*, EU:C:1989:397.

[6] The expression 'horizontal separation of powers' is used to indicate the classical vision of a separation of the executive, the legislator, and the judiciary. The expression 'vertical separation of powers' refers to the division of competencies between the Union and the Member States.

2.2.1 Horizontal separation of powers and the conferral of powers on the Commission

In this respect, the traditional positions have suffered from a crippling flaw. Because of their state-centred nature, these positions have been blind to the particular characteristics of the Union. Founded on the traditional theory of separation of powers, these positions were rooted in the idea that the executive power must be the privilege of the institution that fills the role of a government in the Union; that is the Commission. This vision presupposed that the Union was based on a classical conception of separation of powers, which was not the case in the founding treaties.

Right or wrong, the drafters of the treaties wanted to make the Council the holder of the executive power. The formulation of Article 155 EEC (which became 211 EC) before the Single European Act was without ambiguity in this regard. The Commission only exercised the executive power that it was afforded by the Council. The Single European Act did not change Article 155 EEC, it simply added a paragraph to Article 145 EC (which became Article 202 EC), that adopted the principle of delegation to the Commission, but with the Council having the possibility to retain the powers for itself in specific cases. Thus, the Commission did not hold its own powers in the matter. It could definitely wield executive power, but it was not the original holder of such power. It was merely the beneficiary of a delegation.

Did this power belong to the Council alone? This was not even in question at the time when the Council was the sole legislator. But has the situation changed with the advent of the co-decision procedure? The Court had held that in cases where the treaty referred to the Council this must be understood as a reference to the Council and the Parliament in cases where the legal basis indicated a co-decision procedure.[7] Therefore, the reference to the Council in Article 202 EC had to be understood as referring to the Parliament and the Council when the legal basis required recourse to co-decision. Nevertheless, the formulation of Article 202 EC could have been more clearly worded. It had not been modified, although the holder of the legislative power was no longer solely the Council since Maastricht. The discussion had gone on and on concerning which organ was the original holder of the executive power. However, in fact, and since the executive power was conferred in legislative acts, the legislator (the Council alone or jointly with the European Parliament) had the power to decide both the extent and the modalities of measures of implementation. Accordingly, the Commission only exercised such power on the basis of a delegation and could not be the original holder of such power.

The Lisbon Treaty has confirmed this situation by entrusting the Commission with the power to adopt implementing acts only where the legislator has delegated such power. In principle the Commission thus holds an executive power, but only where it is prescribed by law. The Council can exercise such power, according to

[7] Case C-259/95 *Parliament v Council*, EU:C:1997:454.

Article 291, on the basis of legislative authorization that can be accorded only in duly justified specific cases. It is unlikely, for political reasons, that this situation will occur outside situations where the Council is the sole legislator. Therefore, the Lisbon Treaty fundamentally modifies the situation, since the Commission becomes the holder of the executive power from the moment it receives a legislative delegation.

2.2.2 Taking vertical separation of powers into account

The fact that the Council, which represents the Member States, has been the holder of the executive power according to the founding treaties, must be examined in close connection with the question of the division of powers between the Union and the Member States. This is not a situation that is specific to the Union, since every federal state faces similar questions. In fact, in a federal system it is to be determined if the allocation of competences provided for by the constitution applies to the legislative level as well as to the executive level.

The United States have given an affirmative answer to that question. The federal power extends equally far when it comes to adopting laws as to measures of implementation. Thus, the federal power 'may not commandeer the States' legislative processes by directly compelling them to enact and enforce a federal regulatory program'.[8] The allocation of competences covers the legislative as well as the executive, which explains the existence of a federal administration on the totality of the territory in order to ensure the implementation of federal law. Judge Kennedy gave an account of this situation when he held that the constitution establishes 'a legal system unprecedented in form and design, establishing two orders of government, each with its own direct relationship, its own privity, its own set of mutual rights and obligations to the people who sustain it and are governed by it'.[9]

The situation in the Federal Republic of Germany is different. According to Article 80 of the Basic Law, the Federal Government, a Federal Minister, or the *Land governments* can be authorized by law to adopt regulations. In such a case the *Bundesrat*, which represents the *Länder*, is often called upon to intervene in order to approve these regulations. On the other hand the popular assembly—the *Bundestag*—is excluded from this process. According to Article 83 of the Basic Law, the power to execute federal laws belongs to the *Länder* in their own right. The *Länder* can also, if it is prescribed by federal law, implement it on delegation from the Federation. In such circumstances, if the Government wishes to adopt general administrative rules for how to apply a federal law, it has to obtain the consent of the *Bundesrat*. Of course, the federation disposes of a oversight power over the *Länder* that can lead to an acknowledgment by the *Bundesrat* of a violation of the federal law by the *Land* (Article 84 of the Basic Law). Apart

[8] The Supreme Court of the United States of America, in *New York v US*, 505 US 144 (1992). The same idea can be found in *Prinz v United States*, 521 US 898 (1997).

[9] Individual opinion in *US Terms Limits, Inc v Thornton*, 514 US 779, 838 (1995).

from these technical dispositions, the overarching structure is simple. It rests in the area of federal competences, on a distinction between legislative measures that are adopted on the federal level and measures of implementation that are in principle incumbent upon the *Länder*. When the Federal Government is authorized by the Basic Law or a law to take executive measures, the *Bundesrat* (which represents the States) intervenes in most cases.

The measures adopted by the European Union often leave a considerable margin of appreciation to the national authorities, and even offer them the choice between several implementing solutions. Under such circumstances, national authorities are under a duty to adopt normative measures of implementation, so that the Union is similar to a system of executive federalism. However, that does not solve the question of who is the holder of the executive competence. Do the national authorities act on delegation of the Union, or do they exercise a competence of their own within the limits set by the legislative act? The founding treaties do not provide any evidence for an exclusive executive competence for the Union, which has prompted debates among the institutions on the question.

The case law on the principle of sincere cooperation in Article 5 EEC (now in Article 4(3) TEU) could contribute to a solution. It is true that two readings of that Article were possible. The more restrictive, which has been supported by the Commission, resulted in the conclusion that the only function of Article 5 EEC was to impose on the Member States an obligation to take all measures to execute Community law. This was no doubt one of the objectives of the Article. But it also had another purpose, which was to express the idea that execution of Community law fell within the responsibility of the Member States. That is the conclusion one could draw from the reasoning of the Court, which was expressed clearly in *Deutsche Milchkontor*:[10]

> According to the general principles on which the institutional system of the Community is based and which govern the relations between the Community and the Member States, it is for the Member States, by virtue of Article 5 of the Treaty, to ensure that Community regulations, particularly those concerning the common agricultural policy, are implemented within their territory. In so far as Community law, including its general principles, does not include common rules to this effect...

If these words are to have any meaning,[11] the ruling recognized the executive competence of the Member States. Admittedly, the jurisprudence of the Court generally focused more on the obligation to implement that stems from the principle of sincere cooperation than on the competence, but this was only due to the fact that the type of cases the Court was seized of related to this aspect.

The Lisbon Treaty has put an end to the controversy in favour of executive federalism. According to Article 291(1) TFEU: 'Member States shall adopt all measures of national law necessary to implement legally binding Union acts'. This does not

[10] Joined cases 205 to 215/82 *Deutsche Milchkontor GmbH v Germany*, EU:C:1983:163.

[11] The wording 'it is for' [('*il appartient*' in French)] clearly reflects the idea that this is a competence of the Member States, and not only the existence of an obligation to execute.

mean that there is no possibility for adopting norms of execution at the Union level. It is in fact not even excluded that norms at the Union level could be indispensible to assure uniform application of the law in order to avoid discrimination between Union citizens or distortion of the competition. In such circumstances, the Union shall intervene. This again is the formulation in the Lisbon Treaty, which indicates that implementing powers are conferred on the Commission '[w]here uniform conditions for implementing legally binding Union acts are needed'. This implies that execution at the Union level is only subsidiary in case of specific circumstances that have to be motivated in the legislative act.

In case of implementation at the Union level, the practice then embedded in the Treaty, confirmed by case law, has been to involve the Member States in the elaboration of implementing norms. Where the Union is exercising a power of execution, which in principle is granted to the Member States, it appears logical to institute a close collaboration between them and the Union, when presented with a situation where they cannot, because of a Union intervention, exercise that competence on a national level. This collaboration has developed into a supervision of the Commission by committees with Member States' representatives in charge of giving opinions on the proposals for measures of implementation prepared by the Commission. A negative opinion, and even the absence of an opinion, can lead to the question being referred back to the Council. This system is generally known as the 'comitology'. It serves two functions.

Firstly, it permits Member States, which are more familiar than the Commission with administrative specificities, to advise the Commission in order to avoid concrete difficulties of implementation. Secondly, and above all, it permits Member States to participate in the exercise of a power that normally belongs to them, but which now is exercised at Union level. The Lisbon Treaty modifies the situation by indicating that the control of the implementation, when it is entrusted to the Commission, should be performed by the Member States, meaning that the Council, as an institution, is excluded from a process where it could earlier be called upon to play a major role.

The European Parliament has not, from the outset, wanted to maintain this situation. From the emergence of the co-decision procedure, it has wanted to share the power to execute legislation with the Council. That is the reason why the Parliament has been opposed to legislation where it has not received guarantees on this point. For this reason, it refused in 1994 to adopt the common position of the Council concerning voice telephony. In order to overcome this blockage, an interinstitutional *modus vivendi* was reached after negotiations. That foresaw that the Parliament was provided with information and the possibility for it to address a motivated opinion to the Council when the latter was seized. The text also indicated that the next intergovernmental conference should return to the question. That conference, however, limited itself to indicating in a declaration that the Commission should make a new proposal for a comitology decision. The Comitology Decision from 1999 maintained the procedure requiring that information be provided to the Parliament and accorded it a possibility to address a motivated opinion to the Commission when it assessed that the measures of implementation exceeded the competences delegated by the legislator. Thus, the Parliament did not acquire any competence concerning the measures of implementation themselves, but only the right to preserve the powers of the legislator against all encroachment by the Commission. The power to control the execution rested in the hands of the Council.

The Lisbon Treaty definitely clarifies the situation by substituting the control by the Council with a control by the Member States. The implementation is thus a question for the Member States, or the Member States and the Commission. The logic of the system thus excludes all parliamentary involvement, even though it is natural that the Parliament is informed. The only real power it possesses is therefore the possibility to contest the legality of an implementing measure that would be contrary to the legislative act from which it arises. For its part, the Parliament has abandoned its demands, in exchange for the creation of the delegated act.

The present model of implementation rests on the priority given to a decentralized system. If, on the Union level, the executive power level belongs without dispute to the Commission, it only exercises that power within the framework of the comitology: that is, in close association with the Member States.

2.3 Defining the Concept of Implementation

The demands by the Parliament and the Commission that have fuelled the debate for a long time are clearly based on different conceptions. For the Commission, the question was about being seen as the holder of the executive power, and freeing itself from the supervision of the committees as well as from the right of evocation of the Council. For the Parliament, the rationale has been different and based on the desire to be seen as an equal to the Council in the comitology process, at least in areas of co-decision. In both cases the outcome has been a challenge to the balance set by the Treaties and a refusal of vertical separation of powers. In the course of the discussions, it has seemed to the Council that the parliamentary critique was the result of the ambiguities of the system and that its clarification would make it possible to meet the concerns of the Parliament. In reality the executive procedure was applied to two different operations that have, because of this, been subject to the same parliamentary reprobation: implementation and delegation. One of the important innovations of the Lisbon Treaty has been to distinguish these two cases.

2.3.1 Delegated acts and measures of implementation

Under the guise of implementation, the Commission has frequently been able to carry out modifications of the very legislative text. It was a commonly used procedure to update the countless technical annexes that contained (the substance of) the regulations and directives. On a practical level, it was evident that the use of the legislative procedure for adding, for example, a product on a list of dangerous substances was disproportionate, because it was both administratively cumbersome and time-consuming, while the adoption was a matter of certain urgency. Could one abstain from placing such provisions in the legislation and leave the whole matter to the executive power, since these annexes do not constitute essential elements of the act? That would run counter to the wishes of the legislator, which demanded that, at the time of its adoption, a concrete meaning be given to the text and called for such annexes. Under such conditions, the most efficient procedure was to entrust the Commission with updating them within a comitology procedure.

That meant granting the holder of the executive power the capacity to modify an act adopted by the legislator. Therefore, it was hardly surprising that the Parliament, when the matter fell under the co-decision procedure, demanded the right to inspect the measures. The most common demand was the formulation of a right to call back, which, when expressed within a certain period of time, would refer the matter back to the legislator. A concern of similar nature was expressed about the legislation on financial services. The Lamfalussy Report on the implementation of the legislation concerning financial services advocated that the legislator should limit itself to issuing very broad framework policies measures and that the details of the regulation should be adopted through the comitology procedure. The fear of the Parliament was that the executive power might in this way intrude upon its prerogatives. It therefore wanted to include a sunset clause in the authorization, which would permit Parliament to put an end to it on the basis of later findings; it also wanted to ensure that the Commission has to consult it concerning envisaged measures and take its view into account. Such a procedure was not, in itself, contrary to Article 202 EC, since the legislator could always limit an authorization in time and there was nothing to prohibit the Commission from informing the Parliament about its proposals and to take its views into account. However, it testified to the reluctance of the Parliament to accept situations where the role of the executive is supplementing the legislation rather than implementing it.

It thus appeared that the Parliament could be satisfied by distinguishing between executive acts and acts that amend non-essential elements of a legislative act. The Parliament would abandon its demands on the first category in exchange for a control power concerning the latter. The idea was developed in an article published under a pseudonym by a member of the legal service of the Council,[12] and which later was taken up without success by the Austrian presidency during the elaboration of the Comitology Decision of 1999. However, within the Union, few are the ideas that have triumphed at first attempt. But the debate was launched.

Accordingly, it seemed important to distinguish pure execution from delegation accorded in order to modify a legislative act. If one was to remain faithful to the jurisprudence of the Court, the delegation should not concern the essential elements of the act, which should remain within the exclusive power of the legislator. For the other non-essential elements of the act, it was clear that, when the purpose was to modify them, the technique of delegation should be used. The difficulty lay

[12] Justus Lipsius, 'The 1996 Intergovernmental Conference' (1995) 20 ELRev 235.

in the definition of the criterion to be used for distinguishing the delegated power from the executive power. This criterion could only be a material one, which meant that every formula was subject to interpretation and presented risks of litigation.

It appeared difficult to obtain absolute precision in this domain, but a formula that combined the possibility of modifying the non-essential elements of the act with the possibility of complementing them could, even though it could not avoid litigation, serve as a basis for a judicial interpretation. On a procedural plane, different solutions were proposed: tacit acceptance by the Parliament and the Council after the expiry of a period of time, the possibility for revocation of a delegated regulation by the Parliament or the Council, automatic expiry of a regulation after a fixed time of authorization unless it has been expressly renewed. Due to the obstacles to the entry into force of the Constitution, the discussions about a revision of the Comitology Decision restarted in the Council. Those discussions resulted in a formulation close to that in the Constitution: that is, the regulatory procedure with scrutiny. However, the Council succeeded in limiting parliamentary control in cases where the proposed measures 1) exceed the competences foreseen by the delegation, 2) are not compatible with the purpose and content of the legislative act, or 3) are contrary to the principles of subsidiarity or proportionality. The entry into force of the Lisbon Treaty should put an end to the use of this specific procedure and replace it by the procedure of delegated acts provided for in Article 290 TFEU, without taking into account the limits imposed on the intervention of the Parliament.

The regime for delegated acts is set forth in its entirety in Article 290 TFEU and the institutions agreed that no implementing provisions were necessary. Nevertheless, the Commission has outlined its vision of the situation in a communication.[13] The delegated acts are of general scope, which excludes use of the procedure for individual authorizations. It can only concern non-essential parts of legislative acts, but, as recourse to the procedure is optional, the legislator is never obliged to use it and can choose to pronounce itself on the matter, when it is about amending or supplementing non-essential elements of a legislative act. Last, its object is to supplement or amend the legislative act. If the notion of amendment is clear, the notion of supplementation is less so. The risk is great that a wide interpretation of the supplementing action will suppress every possibility of resort to the classic measures of implementation, since every implementing measure supplements the legislative act it implements. The Parliament could be even more tempted by such an interpretation since it can exercise a right of veto on delegated acts whereas it has no such possibility to prevent the enactment of implementing acts. Under the regulatory procedure with scrutiny, which established the same conditions, an agreement had been reached between the institutions on the margin of appreciation left to the Commission by the legislative act. If the Commission was left a very large margin that was not limited by precise

[13] Commission Communication of 9 December 2009—Implementation of Article 290 of the Treaty on the Functioning of the European Union, COM(2009) 673 final.

criteria set in the legislative act, it was agreed that supplementation of the legislative act was at stake. The Commission's communication proposes to keep this solution: 'The Commission believes that in order to determine whether a measure "supplements" the basic instrument, the legislator should assess whether the future measure specifically adds new non-essential rules which change the framework of the legislative act, leaving a margin of discretion to the Commission. If it does, the measure could be deemed to "supplement" the basic instrument. Conversely, measures intended only to give effect to the existing rules of the basic instrument should not be deemed to be supplementary measures'.[14] The ruling of the Court in *Biocides* does not depart fundamentally from that vision.[15]

Article 290 TFEU provides two methods of oversight by the legislator of the use made of the legislative delegation. The Parliament and/or the Council can oppose the entry into force of the delegated act. Furthermore, the Parliament and/or the Council can revoke the delegation. The authorization granted by the legislator can include any of the methods, but the institutions have agreed that they do not exclude each other, and that they can be used simultaneously. However, the Commission takes the position that the use of sunset clauses (that is, delegations accorded for a limited amount of time) must disappear, since the legislator has the possibility to revoke the delegation. Nevertheless, the Parliament retains this possibility by providing for, if need be, a tacit renewal of the delegation. The opposition of the Council or the Parliament to a delegated act must be formulated within a specified time limit. The Commission proposes a two-month period, which can be prolonged by one month, with the possibility for shorter time limits for urgent matters.

The position of the Commission has to a large extent been accepted by the Council and the discussion has only been on the question of a possible intervention of the Member States. According to its communication, the Commission was willing to consult the committees of representatives of the Member States before the adoption of a delegated act. It needs to take their position into account in order to ensure that the delegated act will be well implemented, but also in order to prevent a possible veto by the Council.

At present, the situation thus appears as follows. The exclusive legislative domain concerns the essential elements of an act. Nothing prevents the legislator from going further than this and it is, in such a case, accorded the right to delegate to the Commission the power to amend or supplement the non-essential elements subject to control by the Parliament and/or the Council. The Commission is thus given the right to adopt delegated acts under the condition that the two legislative branches do not oppose it. Of course, this will mean that it will have to take the positions of the Parliament and, above all, the Council, into account when

[14] Ibid.

[15] Case C-427/12 *Commission v Parliament and Council (Biocides)*, EU:C:2014:170. For an extensive comment see D Ritleng, 'The Dividing Line between Delegated and Implementing Acts: the Court of Justice Sidesteps the Difficulty in *Commission* v. *Parliament and Council (Biocides)*' (2015) 52 CMLRev 243. For assessments of that ruling in this volume see the chapters by Paolo Ponzano (Section 3.7), Kieran Bradley (Section 4.5.3), Jürgen Bast (Section 8.3.1), and Paul Craig (Section 9.3.1).

elaborating the acts, the latter insisting on consultation of national experts. The situation has not yet stabilized and the institutions are considering ways to solve the recurring conflicts about the choice of the procedure at the moment of the adoption of the legislative acts, but the disagreements between them remain strong.

2.3.2 The preservation of the essential elements of the legislative text

It is for the EU legislator to legislate concerning the essential elements of a matter. As the Court underscored in its ruling in *Köster*:[16]

> It cannot therefore be a requirement that all the details of the regulations concerning the common agricultural policy be drawn up by the Council according to the procedure in Article 43. It is sufficient for the purposes of that provision that the basic elements of the matter to be dealt with have been adopted in accordance with the procedure laid down by that provision.

It follows that the legislation has to lay down the essential elements of the matter and that no implementing power (cf. French *compétence d'exécution* and German *Durchführungsbefugnisse*) concerning such questions can be delegated. But this does not mean that the competence of the legislator is limited to these essential elements. The legislator is free to regulate all elements of the subject matter without leaving any place for the executive power. If there is a domain reserved for the legislator, there is none reserved for the executive.

The obligation to legislate on the essential elements is intended to preserve the institutional balance. The legislator does not have the right to renounce its power to legislate by delegating it to the Commission. Furthermore, by proceeding in this manner in a domain where the Parliament has a power to participate in the legislative procedure, the use of measures of implementation would deprive it of the possibility to exercise its prerogatives. That would be especially undesirable for the Parliament in the domains subject to consultation since it would be deprived of that right without having consented to it. In the past, however, the Court has interpreted the notion of essential elements very restrictively. In *Germany v Commission* it pronounced that essential rules are rules that are intended to give concrete shape to the fundamental guidelines of Community policy, which left a wide space for the executive power.[17] Yet, the power to impose penalties, such as the exclusion of farmers who had given false information, was at stake and the authorization was silent on the issue. For the Court, a general authorization was sufficient and there was no need (though the Comitology Decision required it) to prescribe the essential elements of the measures of implementation to be taken:[18]

> 41. It is clear from the aforementioned K[ö]ster judgment that since the Council has laid down in its basic regulation the essential rules governing the matter in question, it may

[16] Case 22/70 *Commission v Council*, EU:C:1971:32.
[17] Case C-240/90 *Germany v Commission*, EU:C:1992:408.
[18] Case C-240/90, ibid, paras 41 and 42.

delegate to the Commission general implementing power without having to specify the essential components of the delegated power; for that purpose, a provision drafted in general terms provides a sufficient basis for the authority to act.
42. That principle is not affected by the aforementioned decision. As a measure of secondary law it cannot add to the rules of the Treaty, which do not require the Council to specify the essential components of the implementing powers delegated to the Commission.

At that time, the scope of the executive competence was interpreted very broadly. Admittedly, it concerned the agricultural domain, where the Council was both the sole legislator and the holder of the executive power.

After the Lisbon Treaty, the interpretation of the scope of the executive power will be much stricter, as can be seen in the ruling in *Schengen Borders Code*. For the Court, the notion of essential elements is intended to protect the legislator's own responsibility and refers to political choices that only the legislator should make. The notion, thus, has to be interpreted on a case-by-case basis, depending on the matter at hand, and is to be assessed in the light of objective criteria. It cannot be left to the sole legislator's political appreciation. In *Schengen* the granting of coercive powers to border guards demands an assessment and political choices that have to be performed within the framework of the legislative procedure.[19]

2.4 The Adoption of Measures of Implementation

The Single European Act formalized the adoption of measures of implementation within the so-called comitology procedures. During the elaboration of these measures, the Commission was required to take the opinions of committees composed of Member State representatives into account. In the event of a negative opinion of these committees or even in the absence of an opinion, the measure was referred to the Council.

Within the advisory procedure, the committee gave the Commission an opinion about the proposed measures of implementation. Afterwards, the Commission took its decision freely. The management procedure—which was to be used for the management of agricultural and fishing policies, and also for the management of financial programs—provided that the committee should give an opinion to the Commission by qualified majority. If the opinion was favourable or there were no opinion, the Commission adopted the proposed measures. When the opinion was negative, the Council was seized and could adopt a different text with qualified majority. If no decision was taken by the Council, typically because no qualified majority could be brought together, the Commission adopted its proposal.

[19] See Case C-355/10 *Parliament v Council (Schengen Borders Code)*, EU:C:2012:516, paras 76 and 77.

The regulatory procedure would take place in cases of implementation of essential elements of a legislative act or for modification of non-essential elements of such an act. Here the committee worked according to the same procedure, but the referral to the Council did not only occur where the opinion was negative, but also where there was no opinion. Under such circumstances, the Commission submitted a proposal to the Council which, according to the general rule on modifications of proposals of the Commission, meant that it could only be modified by the Council unanimously. If the Council adopted the proposal—modified or not—it was applied as an implementing measure. Otherwise, the Commission took the decision of the measures of implementation itself unless the Council opposed it with qualified majority. In such a case, no implementing measure was adopted and the procedure either had to be restarted from the beginning or to take the legislative route.

The Lisbon Treaty has kept the comitology procedure, but excluded the direct intervention of the Council through the reference in Article 291 TFEU to 'mechanisms for control by Member States', which forbids the intervention of an institution such as the Council. The Treaty prescribes that a decision concerning the comitology should be taken by the Parliament and the Council, whereas it was to be taken by the Council alone under the previous treaties. One could have expected the interinstitutional discussion to be difficult, but it was not, since the agreement on the proposal presented by the Commission was reached quickly in December 2010, that is, one year after the entry into force of the Lisbon Treaty, which is a short period of time for such a much-debated question.[20]

The proposal of the Commission was aimed at limiting, as far as possible, the binding character of the intervention of Member States, by limiting the types of committees and by imposing strict criteria for recourse to a certain type of committee. It replaced the three types of committees that had existed up until that time with two new ones: firstly, the advisory committee, whose opinion was not binding on the Commission, even though (according to the proposal) it had to be afforded 'the greatest account', and secondly, the examination committee, where only a negative opinion stopped the Commission from adopting measures of implementation. Recourse to the examination committee could only take place under specific circumstances of adoption of measures of implementation of general scope or other measures concerning agriculture or fishery, the environment, security and safety, or protection of the health or security of persons, animals, or plants, and common commercial policy.

At the end of the discussions, the structure proposed by the Commission was accepted, but the changes introduced by the Council and accepted by the Parliament are profound. They concern both the type of committee and the procedure, paying special attention to the procedure concerning adoption of commercial measures.

[20] Regulation (EU) 2011/182 of the European Parliament and of the Council of 16 February 2011 laying down the rules and general principles concerning mechanisms for control by Member States of the Commission's exercise of implementing powers, OJ 2011 L 55/13.

During the debates concerning the previous Comitology Decision, the Council had already refused to establish binding criteria for the choice of procedure. It has not changed its opinion, and, by adding the expression 'in particular' before the enumeration of cases where use will be made of the examination procedure, the authors of the regulation have given the legislator the possibility to choose this procedure at any time, as long as its choice is motivated. The list proposed by the Commission submitted in particular measures of general scope to this procedure, which gave it a very broad application. The regulation retains the list proposed by the Commission, but further adds measures of implementation concerning programs with substantial implications. This addition was important for the Member States, which have always wanted to control the way in which the Commission allocates the funds foreseen in the funding programs, while the Commission itself has tried to keep its managerial independence. Nevertheless, in order to keep a certain flexibility, the domains enumerated in Article 2(2) do not fall within the exclusive remit of the examination procedure. They can, in duly justified cases, be subject to the advisory procedure. Thus, the rigidity that the Commission wanted has disappeared.

On the procedural plane, the proposal concerning the advisory procedure has not been amended. The opinion of the committee is adopted by a simple majority and the Commission has to take the utmost account of it. By contrast, the examination procedure proposed by the Commission has been profoundly changed. According to a standard pattern, a favourable opinion by the committee (which decides by qualified majority) as well as the absence of an opinion opens the way for the measures proposed by the Commission, while a negative opinion closes that possibility. In the event of a negative opinion, the Commission can present a modified proposal to the committee. The previous Comitology Decision provided an appeal to the Council in the event of a negative opinion in the management procedure. In the regulatory procedure, the question was in addition referred to the Council in the absence of opinion by the committee. Relying rightly on the wording of Article 291 TFEU, which only refers to the intervention of the representatives of Member States, the proposal of the Commission had excluded every recourse to the Council, which is an institution.

The Council was not ready to accept such a solution and instituted, with the agreement of the Parliament, an instance superior to the examination committee—the Appeal Committee. In this committee, the Member States are represented at an appropriate level, which leaves open the possibility of permanent representatives and even ministers.[21] The difference compared to the previous solution is that the chairmanship of the Appeal Committee is assured by the Commission. The Appeal

[21] Article 3(7) of Regulation (EU) 2011/182 of the European Parliament and of the Council of 16 February 2011 laying down the rules and general principles concerning mechanisms for control by Member States of the Commission's exercise of implementing powers, OJ 2011 L 55/13.

Committee is convened in the event of a negative opinion by the examination committee, but also in the absence of an opinion where the basic act so provides, when a simple majority is opposed to the act in the examination committee, and when the acts concern 'taxation, financial services, protection of the health or security of persons, animals or plants, or definitive safeguard measures'.[22] One finds in this enumeration the principal cases where recourse was made to the regulatory procedure. A negative opinion by the Appeal Committee stops the adoption of the act. The absence of an opinion permits the Commission to adopt the act, but it is not obliged to do so, which leaves it a certain degree of flexibility. The appeal procedure thus groups together the old management and regulatory procedures, but permits the retention of some of their specificities when the basic act so permits.

During the discussions, the Parliament seems to have admitted that, since the implementation is in principle a matter for the Member States, it should not intervene directly in the implementation procedure at Union level. It is possible that the question is not of major importance to the Parliament, since it estimates that most of the measures will fall under the procedure of delegated acts, where its role is decisive.

After the adoption of this text, the question of executive rulemaking, which has been the object of incessant discussions between the Parliament and the Council, seems to be definitively settled and the legislative discussion should be simplified. However, the choice between the use of delegated acts and implementing acts will remain a delicate question in every case.

2.5 Conclusion

It has taken more than fifty years to reach a stable situation concerning the Union's executive rulemaking. This situation seems to be due to the pragmatism that the institutions have shown. The comitology was born from practical demands, was later streamlined, and lastly progressively adapted to the evolution of the institutional balance. What was at the heart of these technical debates was the question of how much liberty could be left to the Commission in the adoption of delegated acts and implementing acts. From the beginning, the Commission conducted an unending combat in order to obtain the recognition of a wide executive power. Admittedly, the Commission has not obtained what it demanded and, at least concerning measures of implementation, the present situation is not fundamentally different from the situation earlier. On their side, the Member States have been able to maintain their position. But beyond the procedural discussions, there have been very few disputes in the past and it is exceptional that the Commission has been stopped from adopting an implementing measure because of the opposition

[22] Article 5(4) of Regulation (EU) 2011/182/EU, Ibid.

of the Member States. The only recent disputes have concerned authorizing genetically modified organisms. The Commission is an executive under control, but under a control that does not hinder its action. However, the technical debates have altogether overshadowed a real constitutional question: the question of the Union's 'federative' nature. Perhaps, a constitutional reflection on this question earlier on would have saved us from this long process of trial and error.

3

The Reform of Comitology and Delegated Acts

An Executive's View

Paolo Ponzano

3.1 Introduction

Clearly 'comitology' is one of the most bandied-about words in Brussels jargon, but also one of the least understood in the Member States of the European Union. The word comitology does not in fact mean, as its etymology would seem to suggest, the study or the science of committees, but rather the procedure whereby the executive of the EU (in principle the European Commission) adopts the implementing acts of the Union—in other words those acts which allow the legislative acts to be applied (i.e. the regulations, directives, and decisions adopted by the EU legislator). The reference to committees can be explained by the fact that the Commission is assisted in exercising its executive function by a large number of committees (around 260) made up of representatives of the Member States. Indeed, the EU Treaties stipulate that in principle it is the responsibility of the Member States to implement EU law, except when EU legislative acts require the adoption of measures that are harmonized at Union level to ensure that they are applied uniformly and without discrimination in all Member States. In this case it is, in principle, the responsibility of the Commission to adopt such measures of implementation with the assistance of committees made up of representatives of the Member States (given that it is then down to the national administrations to effectively apply EU rules).

For example, the application of EU agricultural regulations in the Member States requires national agricultural producer organizations to be set up which can act as contact points for the Commission and can implement the obligations provided for by EU law. It is therefore incumbent on the Member States to create these organizations in line with national practices while complying with EU regulations. On the other hand, it is the Commission, assisted by committees made up of national officials, which is responsible for setting the level of export refunds (subsidies) that farmers receive for agricultural products, because the refunds must be granted in a harmonized way at European level so as to avoid any discrimination between farmers from different Member States. Consequently, EU measures of implementation in principle correspond to ministerial decrees adopted by national governments (in practice by the competent minister in each Member State), to implement the laws passed by the national legislator.

As will be seen later, the EU legislator (the Council of Ministers between 1957 and 1993, the Council and the European Parliament legislating by common agreement for certain matters after 1993) gradually began extending the scope of measures of implementation in the 1970s to cover measures adapting EU legislative acts to economic, scientific, and technical progress. This scope included the Commission—still assisted by committees made up of national officials—updating European rules that required rapid adaptation to new scientific and technical data without having to go through the onerous procedure of amending the initial legislative act. Consequently, the Commission received the EU legislator's authorization—not initially provided for by the Treaties—to supplement and even amend the substance of the initial legislative act. By way of example, EU regulations on foodstuffs make provision for either a positive list of authorized ingredients that can be included in products, or a negative list of ingredients that are prohibited because they would be harmful to consumers' health. The initial lists defined by the legislator can be supplemented or amended by the Commission after consultation with scientific experts and with a committee made up of representatives of the Member States.

In the 1990s this delegation of powers to the Commission for the amendment of legislative acts was further extended, in particular in the financial services sector, so as to allow the Commission to supplement EU regulations in that area more easily and quickly than the legislator could have done. Consequently, the so-called comitology procedure, initially intended for the adoption of implementing acts equivalent to ministerial decrees at national level, was used for the adoption of legal acts which exist in several Member States (for example France, Belgium, Greece, Spain, and Italy), but which involve greater political responsibility on the parts of governments vis-à-vis the legislator, because in these cases the government does not act in its own sphere of competence but in that of the legislator. In French law, such acts are called '*ordonnances*' (in Italian law '*decreti legislativi*') and not ministerial decrees. As will be seen later, it was not until the Lisbon Treaty that this legal 'anomaly' which had been introduced into the practices of the EU institutions in the 1970s was resolved.

3.2 Some Examples of Acts Adopted under Comitology Procedures

Before giving a brief history of comitology, it is appropriate to provide some specific examples of acts adopted according to the comitology procedure so as to properly grasp the content of such measures, which, in practice, differ greatly from one another. It is useful first to distinguish between the measures of implementation themselves, that is, those which roughly correspond to ministerial decrees in the Member States (it should be highlighted that these measures are adopted in principle by the competent minister without involving the government's collegiate responsibility):

1) measures taken on the basis of *factual findings* allowing almost no room for discretion. This covers cases where the Commission is authorized to ban *imports of a product* or to *prohibit fishing* in a defined area as soon as the said imports reach a level set in advance by the legislator or as soon as catches reach a threshold determined by scientific advice. In these cases, the Commission has practically no margin of discretion. As soon as the levels are reached, it *must* adopt the implementing measure. A similar scenario applies when the Commission is supposed to apply an anti-dumping duty on imports of a product from a third country that is priced lower than the cost price. In this case, the Commission has a small margin of discretion, but it would undoubtedly be punished by the Court of Justice if it did not comply with the criteria set in the basic regulatory instrument.
2) measures aimed at programming or granting *financial support* to the beneficiaries of an EU financial instrument. In such cases, the Commission is responsible for allocating the money provided for by an EU funding programme (for example the Erasmus or Media programmes, the Social Fund and others financial programmes) among the potential beneficiaries of that programme (e.g. universities, audiovisual producers, national organizations). When allocating the funding, the Commission is required to comply with the criteria set in the basic regulatory instruments (demographic criteria, cultural criteria, or criteria relating to the financial reliability of the applicant organizations). Consequently, even though the Commission has a certain margin of discretion, it is not completely free to choose the bodies or individuals that benefit from EU funding. The same applies when the Commission sets the level of refunds for agricultural exports, always in line with the criteria predetermined by the legislator. Of course, the decision-making procedure can play an important role in the allocation of funding because the need to obtain the agreement of a qualified majority of Member States could lead the Commission to make provision for a certain 'fair return' in the choice of beneficiaries or in the size of the funding awarded (see Section 3.5).
3) measures aimed at *implementing* in a harmonized way the legislative acts in the field of common policies (especially in the field of agricultural policy, such as Council Regulation 1997/820 establishing a system for the identification and registration of bovine animals which has been implemented by the Commission Regulation 1998/494 laying down detailed rules for the implementation of the previous Council regulation as regards the application of minimum administrative sanctions (cf. Section 1.2). Some rulings of the Court of Justice have underlined that the Commission is authorized to

adopt all the measures which are necessary or appropriate for the implementation of the basic regulation, provided that they are not contrary to it.

4) measures aimed at *authorizing* or *prohibiting* the placing on the market of a certain product (or authorizing or refusing a safeguard clause requested by a Member State). This category of measures can cover a vast range of situations. For example, the Commission can prohibit the use of aeroplanes included on a blacklist of machines that would not meet the safety standards established by the legislator. Likewise, the Commission can authorize or prohibit the marketing of a genetically modified (GM) product on the basis of scientific advice and criteria set by the legislator. In such cases too, the Commission has a very limited margin of discretion, or none at all, because it is difficult to see how it could depart from such advice and criteria without risking the measure being quashed by the Court of Justice.[1] These measures—which have been delegated by the EU legislator to the Commission for the first time in the 1970s—would today be named delegated acts or implementing acts, according to whether the basic act is amended or not (see Section 3.7). However, a distinction should be made in relation to the measures of general application which could be adopted by the legislator but which are in fact delegated by it (both within the EU and in the Member States) to the executive (Commission or national government as appropriate) so as to avoid the legislative act being too cumbersome or quite simply in the interests of speed. These measures differ from the previous ones because the executive in this case does have a true margin of discretion in establishing them. For example, they may consist in setting general criteria which *supplement* the legislative act and on the basis of which the executive will then be able to adopt the authorization or prohibition measures which turn out to be necessary. Therefore, this category of measures should be qualified as 'quasi-legislative' acts and not as true implementing acts. The Lisbon Treaty took up this distinction, as will be seen later, even though it did not establish a very clear dividing line between these two categories of measures, a division which does however exist in several Member States (see *ordonnances* in French law or *decreti legislativi* in Italian law as opposed to ministerial decrees).

3.3 A Brief History of Comitology Procedures

The first management committees were set up in 1962 at the time of the adoption by the Council of the first basic regulations concerning a certain number of agricultural products (cereals, meat, etc.). The management committee procedure

[1] See, e.g., Case T-301/12 *Laboratoires CTRS*, EU:T:2013:346; Case T-164/10 *Pioneer Hi-Bred International v Commission*, EU:T:2013:503; T-240/10 *Hungary v Commission*, EU:T:2013:645.

allowed the Commission to take agricultural management measures quickly, except in cases where a qualified majority of Member State representatives were opposed to the Commission's draft measure. In that case, the Commission's draft would be referred on appeal to the Council of Ministers, which could amend it by a qualified majority. The committees system was gradually extended to other fields (e.g. customs union, commercial policy, transport policy, and internal market) with the procedural variant of the regulatory committee, according to which the Commission had to find a favourable qualified majority within the committee, failing which the draft measure would be referred on appeal to the Council, which could adopt it within a time frame of three months. In the absence of a Council decision within three months, the Commission would itself adopt the proposed measure (known as the *safety net* procedure). In 1968, the Council created the *veterinary committee*, which, due to its political sensitivity (public health protection measures), had an additional procedure provided for it, granting the Council the power to oppose the adoption of the measure planned by the Commission by a simple majority (referred to as the *double safety net* procedure as opposed to the *safety net* procedure).

These procedures worked well in the vast majority of cases because, as far as management and regulatory committees were concerned, the responsible Commission departments almost always mustered the necessary votes enabling their draft measures to be adopted within the committees, meaning that the Commission's draft measures were only on very rare occasions referred on appeal to the Council for amendment (less than one per cent of cases). Moreover, even in the cases that were referred on appeal to the Council, the Commission's approach was to amend its draft measure to allow the Council to find the necessary qualified majority (according to the statistics drawn up by the Commission's services, it opposed a qualified majority obtained within the Council against its draft implementing measure on only three occasions). In an equivalent—similarly small—number of cases, the Council rejected the Commission's draft measure in the veterinary and plant health field by a simple majority. Between 1970 and 1986, the committee procedures introduced by the Council in legislative acts multiplied to such an extent that the Commission under Jacques Delors proposed in 1986 to limit the number of procedures to three formats: advisory, management, and regulatory committees. In the meantime, some cases of conflicts intervened between Commission and Council.[2]

The Council adopted its first 'comitology' decision on 13 July 1987, in which it reduced to five the number of procedures that could be used, while maintaining

[2] The first case of conflict was in 1971, the so-called Jacquemart Accident (from the name of the official involved), when the Commission adopted a reduction of customs duties for the spare parts of aircraft with the support only of Luxembourg and a vote against from five other Member States. This 'accident' later led the Commission to make its so-called Aerosol Statement in 1974, in which it made a commitment to avoid, as far as possible, to adopt a measure against a predominant majority of Member States. Cf. the introduction, for the first time, of the 'double safety net' procedure (cf. French *contre-filet*) in Council Directive (EEC) 1969/349 of 6 October 1969 amending the Directive of 26 June 1964 on health problems affecting intra-community trade in fresh meat, OJ 1969 L 256/5.

the regulatory committee procedure with the '*double safety net*', which does not guarantee that the decision is taken within a set time frame. In the meantime, the Council's decisions to make the exercise of the Commission's executive powers subject to committee procedures had sparked off a conflict with the European Parliament, insofar as some of these procedures (in particular the regulatory committee procedure, especially in its *double safety net* variant) did not allow the Parliament to exercise its political scrutiny over the Commission's executive activity. The European Parliament's opposition to comitology's procedures grew even stronger after the Maastricht Treaty granted the Parliament the right to 'co-decide' with the Council on around half of all legislative acts, and consequently the right to delegate new implementing powers to the Commission. After a long series of guerrilla tactics undertaken by the Parliament (ranging from rejecting particular legislative acts to blocking funding for committee meetings), the Council agreed to amend the Comitology Decision on 28 June 1999. This resulted in the European Parliament being granted a '*right of scrutiny*' over measures of implementation arising from co-decided legislative acts, allowing it to contest the Commission's excessive powers. The Commission, on the other hand, secured the reduction to three committee procedures and the withdrawal of the '*double safety net*' variant in the regulatory committee procedure (this concession being compensated by the Council's power to oppose the Commission's proposal by a qualified majority instead of by unanimity as was previously the case).

Nevertheless, this second Comitology Decision only secured a *temporary truce* because the European Parliament quickly noticed that the influence it could exercise over the Commission's implementing measures was only very slight, while at the same time the Commission's implementing powers were to be extended further in the sphere of financial services because of the new 'Lamfalussy' procedure. The need for speedy adoption of regulatory measures in a sector where market conditions change very quickly was used to justify the Commission being granted very broad powers aimed at *supplementing* primary legislation, which had to remain relatively succinct. On the other hand, the European Parliament's right of scrutiny enabled it to modify the measures proposed by the Commission in only one or two cases out of the five thousand or so draft measures presented by the Commission pursuant to co-decided acts. Meanwhile, the Constitutional Treaty signed in Rome on 29 October 2004 for the first time introduced into EU primary legislation the notion of *delegated legislation*, by recognizing the distinction existing in several Member States between measures of implementation falling under the executive's own responsibility and delegated measures exercised by the executive upon specific delegation by the legislator or for reasons of urgency (see earlier). Once again, the European Parliament adopted its institutional guerrilla tactics aimed at securing joint scrutiny with the Council over measures of implementation arising from co-decided acts, or at least over those measures aiming to supplement or amend legislative acts. In July 2006, this new offensive by the European Parliament led the Council to adopt an amendment to the (second) Comitology Decision, for the first time granting the European Parliament a real *right of veto* over the substance of the draft measures drawn up by the Commission that can be qualified as *quasi-legislative* (measures of general application intended to amend non-essential elements of a basic act adopted by co-decision).

3.4 The Regulatory Regime Established by the Lisbon Treaty

Adapting to developments, the Lisbon Treaty for the first time introduced the distinction between *legislative delegation* and *executive delegation.* In this way, the Lisbon Treaty aligned the European Union's primary legislation with the practices of the national legal systems, which recognize three different legal situations: a) cases where the legislator acts in its own sphere of competence (legislative acts); b) cases where the executive acts in its own sphere of competence (ministerial decrees); c) cases where the executive acts in the legislator's sphere of competence (either by virtue of an explicit delegation of powers, or on its own initiative in urgent cases): in the French legal system, these acts are called '*ordonnances*' (in Italian *decreti legislativi* or *decreti-legge*).[3] The Lisbon Treaty recognizes therefore that it is inappropriate to equate the executive amending the existing legal framework with that same executive simply implementing EU legislation. For this reason, the Treaty introduced a category of delegated acts that the Commission is responsible for adopting under the direct scrutiny of the EU legislator (Council and European Parliament) without any comitology procedure.

The limits of this article do not allow us to examine in detail the questions debated on the subject of delegated acts. Suffice it to say that delegated acts are defined by the Treaty as non-legislative acts of *general application* which *supplement or amend* certain non-essential elements of a legislative act (regardless of whether or not the act was adopted jointly by the European Parliament and the Council, or by the Council alone). While it should normally be easy to check whether a delegated act *amends* the basic act, it can be more difficult to judge whether it *supplements* the basic act. Nevertheless, a planned measure can be considered to be a delegated act if it specifically adds *new non-essential rules* which change the legal framework of the basic legislative act, leaving a broad margin of discretion to the Commission. By way of example, if a legislative act were to grant the Commission the power to establish or amend the criteria according to which a genetically modified product could be authorized or prohibited on the market, this would clearly be a delegated act. If, on the other hand, the Commission were to receive the power to authorize or prohibit a genetically modified product on the basis of the criteria contained in the delegated act, this would be an implementing act.

However, a specific problem arises when the EU legislator gives to the Commission the power to amend the annexes of a basic regulation in conformity

[3] It seems pointless to refer to the absolute power of the legislator ('the legislator can do everything, except changing a man into a woman', as it used to be said about the UK Parliament) because, in practice, the EU legislator could not stop imports from China, stop fishing in the Baltic Sea, or grant money to one NGO rather than to another.

with new scientific advice or a decision of an international forum (for instance, the UN Security Council). In this case, the Commission has no margin of discretion at all in amending the basic regulation because it should follow entirely the content of the scientific advice or the decision of the international forum (cf. Council Regulation 2001/467, discussed in Section 1.2).

In any event, it is up to the EU legislator to decide on a case-by-case basis, whenever it adopts a basic legislative act, to specify which measures should be subject to delegated acts and which to implementing acts. This position has been supported in principle by the Court of Justice in its ruling in *Biocides*,[4] while the Commission's position was that the delimitation between Articles 290 and 291 TFEU is only a legal question, with respect to which the legislator enjoys no discretion. In reality, the European Parliament may be inclined to seek to enlarge the category of delegated acts, while the Council may seek to reduce it because it can benefit from the Member States' scrutiny of implementing acts (see Section 3.6). A 'Common Understanding' between the institutions was adopted in 2011 in order to facilitate the negotiations on each legislative act. However, this Common Understanding has not been respected in practice because the institutions (especially the Council and the European Parliament) have a tendency to depart from the provisions of the Common Understanding in individual cases or tried to interpret the new provisions in a way more favourable for them (see Section 3.6).

As already indicated, the Commission will no longer need to refer to committees made up of representatives of the Member States and to find variable majorities according to the current procedures before adopting a delegated act. Nevertheless, the Commission has decided to systematically consult the national experts in order to benefit from the expertise of the national authorities which will be responsible for implementing the delegated acts (just as it consults those same experts before proposing a legislative act). As will be explained later, the Member States have asked for a modification of the Common Understanding in order to improve the consultation of experts before the adoption of delegated acts (see Section 3.8).

The second important innovation introduced by the Lisbon Treaty concerns implementing acts and the comitology procedure itself. First of all, the Treaty abolishes the Council's general responsibility for delegating implementing powers to the Commission (ex Articles 202 and 211 EC). The Council will still be able to hold certain implementing powers, but only in the area of foreign policy or in specific duly justified cases (limiting that power, in practice, to around 10% of the overall legislative acts which will be adopted by the Council alone in accordance with the special legislative procedure). Secondly, the so-called Comitology Regulation was adopted in 2011 and has replaced the previous Comitology Decision (cf. Section 3.3 above). Moreover, this Comitology Regulation has been adopted jointly by the European Parliament and the Council, whereas the old Decision was adopted by the Council alone, acting unanimously. Finally, it is expressly stipulated that the Commission's executive activity shall be scrutinized

[4] Case C-427/12 *Commission v Parliament and Council (Biocides)*, EU:C:2014:170.

by the Member States and not by the legislator nor, *a fortiori*, by the Council alone. Consequently, the Lisbon Treaty aims to put the legislator's two branches on an equal footing, both in terms of the power to adopt measures under the new comitology and in terms of the absence of scrutiny over the Commission's executive activity.

3.5 The New Comitology Procedures

The innovations brought about by the Lisbon Treaty required the adoption of the new Comitology Regulation to replace the previous (second) Comitology Decision. That is why in March 2010 the Commission submitted a proposal for a regulation to the European Parliament and the Council as provided for by Article 291(3) TFEU. The Commission's proposal was essentially aimed at abolishing the scrutiny of the Council as such over implementing acts in favour of the Member States alone, simplifying committee procedures by reducing the number of procedures to two (including for common commercial policy measures which were subject to special procedures) and maintaining the basic principle of the old comitology according to which, as a general rule, only a qualified majority of Member States objecting to a draft measure from the Commission could prevent it from adopting and implementing the proposed measure.

The negotiations on the Commission's proposal took place under a tight schedule throughout the whole of 2010, both within the Council and at the European Parliament. The European Parliament, which for the first time had joint legislative power with the Council for the adoption of the new comitology, did not hesitate to use this power to safeguard its own rights and prevent the Council from retaining its former powers of scrutiny over the Commission. The Council, on the other hand, after initially having tried to interpret restrictively the new provisions of the Treaty, ended up agreeing to compromise solutions compatible with the Treaty on the basis of the position adopted by the European Parliament at first reading. This culminated in the adoption of the Comitology Regulation in February 2011, which came into force on 1 March 2011 and repeals the previous Comitology Decision (except for transitional provisions and the provisional maintenance in force of the old regulatory procedure with scrutiny).[5] It would be too complicated to explain in detail all the procedural steps of the committee procedures as provided for by the new rules. Here are the key points:

1) The four procedures of the old system (advisory, management, regulatory, and safeguard) have been replaced by two procedures (advisory and examination). In addition, the Commission has the option of adopting emergency measures without first consulting a committee, on condition that in the

[5] Regulation 2011/182/EU of the European Parliament and of the Council of 16 February 2011 laying down the rules and general principles concerning mechanisms for control by Member States of the Commission's exercise of implementing powers, OJ 2011 L 55/13.

event of a negative opinion being issued *ex post*, the Commission should immediately repeal the adopted implementing act.

2) Scrutiny of the Commission's measures of implementation is exercised solely by the Member States and no longer by the Council (or the European Parliament). In the event of a negative committee opinion (and, in certain cases, in the absence of an opinion), the Commission may submit its draft measure to an appeal committee for further deliberation. The appeal committee will be made up of representatives of the Member States (undoubtedly at a higher level), but it will also be chaired by a Commission representative and not by a national official. It is not therefore a committee of permanent representatives (Coreper) in disguise, since only the Commission remains authorized to adopt the implementing measure.

3) The management committee procedure (used above all for agricultural management and financial support measures) disappears under the new system, replaced by the new examination committee procedure (which also replaces the previous regulatory committee procedure). Under this new procedure, the Commission must obtain a qualified majority in favour in order to adopt the implementing act (as in the former regulatory committee procedure). Nonetheless, the Commission may also adopt the act in the absence of an examination committee opinion, except, essentially, when the proposed act concerns particular sensitive sectors (financial services, taxation, human health and safety, or trade protection measures) or when a simple majority of Member States opposes it. This last clause is intended in particular to prevent the Commission authorizing the marketing of genetically modified products against the wishes of a simple majority of Member States, as has often been the case. In the event of a negative examination committee opinion, the Commission may not adopt the act except under exceptional circumstances, and must either submit an amended draft, or refer to the Appeal Committee. However, it may, in exceptional cases, adopt the act in order to prevent significant disruption of agricultural markets or a risk for the financial interests of the Union (even if it means subsequently repealing the act should the Appeal Committee confirm its negative opinion).

4) A 'right of scrutiny' over the Commission potentially exceeding its powers (*ultra vires*) is recognized both for the European Parliament (which has had this right since 1999) and for the Council. However, this 'right of scrutiny' does not involve the automatic suspension of the procedure; instead, the Commission is required to review its draft and inform the legislator's two branches of its conclusions.

5) The common commercial policy is included in the scope of comitology, whereas it always used to be subject to special procedures. Trade protection measures (anti-dumping or compensatory measures) must comply with the standard rules, subject to certain specific procedural obligations and a short transitional period. All *provisional* trade measures can be adopted by the

Commission in urgent cases, while *definitive* anti-dumping or compensatory measures are subject to an exemption.

6) The new comitology procedures grant the Commission greater flexibility on whether or not to adopt an implementing measure, in particular when the committee has not issued an opinion (whereas under the old procedure the Commission was required to adopt the act). On the other hand, it imposes an obligation on the Chair of the Committees (i.e. on the Commission) to seek the broadest possible consensus on the content of the measures and 'codifies' the Commission's commitment (made for the first time in 1974) not to proceed if there is prevailing opposition in the Member States against an implementing measure.

3.6 The Delineation between Delegated and Implementing Acts

The introduction of a new nomenclature of the EU legal acts has generated some difficulties in its application as far as there could be in some cases a 'grey zone' between two categories of acts and it could be difficult to draw a precise borderline between *delegated* and *implementing acts* (while, in the view of the Commission, there can be no such grey zone). From a theoretical point of view, it should be quite easy to distinguish between measures which *change* the *legal framework* of *a* legislative act (by amending formally one or several provisions of the act or by supplementing it with other provisions that the legislator could have adopted at the same time) and measures aiming only to *implement* the same act. For the purpose of this distinction, it seems futile and useless to refer to the situation before Lisbon Treaty (in which the measures of implementation adopted through comitology procedure had covered a very large spectrum of provisions) or to the old case law (which took a broad view of the term 'implementation' with the aim to legitimate delegation of power to the Commission). Now, there are two categories of acts (delegated and implementing acts) and the two categories are, in principle, mutually exclusive.

Of course, nobody could expect that the theoretical distinction between the two categories of acts would be applied in practice without difficulties. As the choice of a delegated or an implementing act involves a shift in the respective powers of the institutions (the Commission, the European Parliament, and the Council), it could happen that each institution tried to interpret and to apply the new provisions in a way more favourable for them (even if the Commission has declared that it has no institutional bias for delegated or implementing acts, as it is guided only by legal criteria of the Treaty). Moreover, the Commission has published (while the European Parliament and the Council did not) its internal guidelines on delegated acts where it explains in all transparency its views on the delineation between Articles 290 and 291 TFEU.

Without reviewing all problems of interpretation, let's examine the more important of them. The dividing line between delegated and implementing acts should be decided by the legislator on the basis of political bargaining or on the basis of objective criteria amenable to judicial review. The first cases of legislative acts adopted by the European Parliament and Council after the entry into force of the Lisbon Treaty seem to substantiate the opinion that the EU legislator is favourable to a large freedom of the latter in choosing between delegated and implementing acts when it confers new delegation of powers on the Commission. While it could be imagined that the European Parliament would have requested the use of delegated acts instead of implementing acts in all cases in which the legislator is placed within the 'grey zone' of competences, this has not been the case. In some legislative acts, the European Parliament has given up its priority to obtain some concessions from the Council on the substance of the act in exchange for accepting the Council's request for granting implementing powers to the Commission under comitology procedure. An example can be found in European Parliament and Council Regulation 2012/528 concerning the placing on the market and use of biocides products.[6]

3.7 The Ruling of the Court of Justice in *Biocides*

Shortly after the adoption of European Parliament and Council Regulation 2012/528 concerning the placing on the market and use of biocides products, in September 2012, the European Commission initiated a proceeding against the European Parliament and Council for the annulment of Article 80(1), in so far as that provides for the adoption of measures setting the fees payable to the European Chemicals Agency by an act based on Article 291(2) TFEU ('implementing act'), and not—as had been proposed by the Commission—by an act adopted under Article 290(1) TFEU ('delegated act'). In the opinion of the Commission, since those measures are designed to supplement non-essential elements of the Regulation, they should be adopted by a delegated act under Article 290 TFEU.

The reasoning of the Commission is based on the fact that the challenged provision of the Regulation gives to the Commission the power to fix, 'upstream' of the implementation of the Regulation, a consistent set of rules and more specific criteria of general application, whose aim is to *supplement* the non-essential elements of the legislative act (leaving the Commission a margin of discretion). From a legal point of view, the Commission considers that the demarcation between Articles 290 and 291 TFEU is not for the legislator alone and cannot be a matter of political bargaining but 'must be based on objective factors amenable to judicial review'. The last sentence refers to the consistent case law with respect to the choice of legal basis of legislative acts, confirmed by analogy in the Court's ruling in *Schengen Borders Code* with regard to the 'essential elements' of

[6] Regulation 2012/528/EU of the European Parliament and of the Council of 22 May 2012 concerning the making available on the market and use of biocidal products, OJ 2012 L 127/1, and in particular the clause in Article 80(1), which was contested in Case C-427/12 (n 4).

a legislative act.[7] On the contrary, the EU legislator (both European Parliament and Council) seems to consider, at least in its recent legislative practice, that the respective scope of the Articles 290 and 291 TFEU overlap and that a provision may be a matter for a delegated act or for an implementing one following its drafting, without reference to objective criteria submitted to judicial review. Therefore, the judgment of the Court in this case would have been important for establishing the dividing line between delegated and implementing acts.

The Court of Justice gave its judgment in *Biocides* on 18 March 2014 and dismissed the action by the Commission as unfounded.[8] The ruling does not provide for clear and easily applicable criteria for the delimitation between delegated and implementing acts. Nevertheless, some first conclusions can be drawn:

1) Firstly, the Court does not appear to question that Articles 290 and 291 TFEU each have their own scope with no overlap between them. This can be deduced in particular from paragraph 35 of the judgment, according to which 'the concept of an implementing act within the meaning of Article 291 TFEU must be assessed in relation to the concept of a delegated act, as derived from Article 290 TFEU'.
2) Secondly, the criteria of the Court used to distinguish between delegated acts and implementing acts seem largely inspired by the language of Articles 290 and 291 TFEU, and notably by the distinction between 'supplementing' and 'implementing' the basic act. At the same time, the Court states that an implementing act may 'provide further detail in relation to the content of a legislative act, in order to ensure that it is implemented under uniform conditions'. It might be argued that with this reasoning, the Court effectively allows an implementing act to complete the legislative act by adding more specific rules on matters of detail, and thereby enlarges the notion of implementing act to the detriment of that of delegated acts. However, at the same time, the Court stated that it considered that the legislative act at issue laid down 'a complete legal framework'. Therefore, whereas the Court applied the notion of 'implementation' in the specific case differently from how the Commission interpreted it, it does not appear that the Court held generally that an implementing act can supplement the legal framework.
3) Thirdly, the Court recognizes that the legislator has a margin of discretion when it decides to confer a delegated power on the Commission pursuant to Article 290(1) TFEU or an implementing power pursuant to Article 291(2) TFEU. As a consequence, the Court finds that 'judicial review is limited to

[7] Case C-355/10 *Parliament v Council (Schengen Borders Code)*, EU:C:2012:516. Also discussed in Section 7.5.2.

[8] Case C-427/12 *Commission v Parliament and Council (Biocides)*, EU:C:2014:170. Here the Court was called upon to rule on the difference between the powers which may be subject to a delegation to the Commission under Articles 290 and 291 TFEU. For an extensive comment see D Ritleng, 'The Dividing Line between Delegated and Implementing Acts: the Court of Justice Sidesteps the Difficulty in *Commission* v. *Parliament and Council (Biocides)*' (2015) 52 CMLRev 243.

> manifest errors of assessment as to whether the EU legislator could reasonably have taken the view, first, that, in order to be implemented, the legal framework which it laid down regarding the system of fees referred to in Article 80(1) of Regulation 2012/528 needs only the addition of further detail, without its non-essential elements having to be amended or supplemented and, secondly, that the provisions of Regulation 2012/528 relating to that system require uniform conditions for implementation'.

This pronouncement is not in line with the views defended by the Commission. The Court also does not indicate what could constitute a manifest error of assessment regarding the delimitation between Articles 290 and 291 TFEU. However, it is noteworthy that the Court subsequently engages in an extensive discussion of the arguments regarding the delimitation between Articles 290 and 291 TFEU. A risk of invalidity in future cases for manifest error of assessment regarding delimitation can therefore not be excluded.

Said in short terms, the limited role of jurisdictional control by the Court of Justice in defining the distinction between 'supplementing' in the meaning of Article 290 TFEU and 'implementing' in the meaning of Article 291 TFEU entails the recognition of a margin of discretion of the EU legislator regarding the choice between delegated and implementing acts. This means that the delimitation does become to a certain extent—that is, within the limits of the manifest error of assessment—a matter of political choice. The main consequence of this judgment will be that the Commission's services may take into account questions of political opportunity in the negotiations on future proposals, provided that the changes made by the legislator remain within the limits of its discretion.

3.8 The Modification of the Common Understanding

While awaiting the ruling from the Court of Justice in *Biocides*, the three institutions tried to define a new common understanding in order to avoid as much as possible the conflicting situations that occurred in the past in the legislative procedure. However, as of the present time, the three institutions have not reached an agreement because the Council proposed some changes to the procedural issues not acceptable for the European Commission—especially on the consultation of national experts by the Commission before the adoption of a delegated act—and the European Parliament has preferred to adopt a new report before taking a definitive position.

On 21 February 2014, the Council took the initiative to complement the Common Understanding on Delegated Acts of 2011 as regards the consultation of experts.[9] The Member States (at the initiative of French and German delegations) considered that the Commission should systematically carry out

[9] Initiative to complement the Common Understanding on Delegated Acts as regards the consultation of experts, Council Doc 6774/14 of 21 February 2014.

appropriate and transparent consultations well in advance of the adoption of a delegated act, including with groups composed of experts designated by all the Member States. Moreover, when adopting a delegated act, the Commission was asked to take the utmost account of the opinion delivered by the expert group, without being bound by it. To this end, the Commission should submit its draft delegated act to the relevant expert group. This group should in principle adopt an opinion on the draft by consensus; if the group votes, it would do so by simple majority. Furthermore, the Commission should operate a comprehensive register containing the draft acts, the opinions delivered by expert groups and the final delegated acts adopted.

The Vice-President of the European Commission, Maros Sefcovic, answered on 12 March 2014 that it was of course ready to discuss ways for improving the consultation process and making it more transparent. However, the Commission could not accept a 'mandatory consultation procedure essentially similar to the advisory procedure under comitology framework, as it would not be compatible with the Treaty'. In other words, the 'red line' for the Commission is the restoration of 'surrogate' comitology procedures not provided for by the Lisbon Treaty for the delegated acts.

In the meantime the European Parliament has adopted its Szajer report.[10] This contains a number of criteria for the application of Articles 290 and 291 TFEU in order to provide the European Parliament rapporteurs with some practical guidelines when dealing with delegated and implementing acts. These criteria should avoid that the negotiators of the European Parliament in a legislative procedure accept 'ad hoc solutions' for delegated or implementing acts in an overall deal with the Council on the substance of the basic act. Concerning in particular the problem of the 'authorizations' of individual products, the European Parliament considers that, if the Commission's decision to authorize a specific substance is fully based on criteria contained in the basic act, this decision could be an implementing act; where, however, the criteria still allow the Commission to make further policy choices, such authorization should be a delegated act.

3.9 Conclusion

The Lisbon Treaty put an end to an anomaly in the comitology system which allowed the European Commission to supplement or even amend a legislative act without the agreement of the legislature. Contrary to the opinion of some commentators, the distinction between delegated acts and purely implementing acts has made the Union system more democratic and more in keeping with the

[10] Report of 4 December 2013 drawn up on behalf of the Committee on Legal Affairs on follow up on delegation of legislative powers and control by Member States of the Commission's exercise of implementing powers (rapporteur: J Szajer), EP Doc A7-435/2013.

distribution of powers between 'the legislature' and 'the executive'. The new system provides for a more democratic legitimacy giving more rights to the European Parliament in the legislative procedure. It had become politically impossible to pursue a system in which the EU legislator granted large delegation of powers to the Commission through the comitology procedure (for instance following the Lamfalussy procedure for the sector of financial services) without providing for new powers of control to the European Parliament.

Moreover, the new system provides for a better 'separation of powers' through a clearer delineation between matters that should fall to the legislative arm of government and those that should fall within the province of the executive. Finally, the new system allows to the legislator the faculty to reduce the content of the legislative act because it retains the control on the definition by the Commission of some 'non-essential' elements of the legislative act. Admittedly the system of delegated acts does not draw a sufficiently precise dividing line separating it from the implementing acts regime, meaning that it falls to the EU legislator to decide, on a case-by-case basis, which measures provided for by a legislative act will be subject to a delegated act and which an implementing act. As expected, the ruling from the Court of Justice in *Biocides* has not defined with accuracy the boundary between the two categories of acts. As the members of the European Parliament will be interested rather in the substance of acts than in the choice between the two categories, the delineation between delegated and implementing acts will continue to depend above all on the interest shown by the two arms of the EU legislature in the substance concerned.

On the other hand, the new Comitology Regulation simplifies the existing procedures (two instead of four), while retaining the basic elements of the old system (partnership between the Commission and the Member States within the committees and transparency with respect to the legislator). However, unlike the system that was in force for about thirty-seven years (until 1999), the Commission will no longer be able to impose its draft implementing measure on a qualified majority of Member States (although, in practice, it made use of this power on just three occasions, of which only two measures came into force). Even the management committees system, which allowed the Commission to get its draft through thanks to a 'blocking minority' of Member States (91 votes out of 345), has been abolished in the new comitology. Admittedly, the Commission could still adopt measures in the absence of a committee opinion, but it will no longer be able to do this against the wishes of a qualified majority of Member States. Incidentally, the Comitology Regulation has provided a derogation allowing the legislator to prevent the Commission from adopting an implementing act, when 'no-opinion' is delivered by the Examination Committee, where a basic legislative act explicitly states it. In an interesting recent trend, the EU legislator has been invoking this exception more and more (see CAP reform, CO^2 car emissions, tobacco products, and food information to consumers).

On another hand, a derogation clause has been planned for some exceptional cases of urgency provided that there is not a negative opinion of the Appeal

Committee (in which case the Commission must repeal its act immediately). Likewise, the Commission will be required to negotiate more with the Member States within the committees on measures for the allocation of financial support because, as a general rule, it will have to muster a far greater number of votes than the ninety-one votes of the blocking minority (which previously allowed it, for example, to allocate 50% of financial support under the MEDIA programme to the audiovisual projects of two or three Member States). In conclusion, while on the one hand the new system of delegated acts has increased the Union's democratic legitimacy, on the other hand the new comitology has created a stricter framework for the Commission's executive powers.

What conclusions can be drawn from this evolution from the point of view of the shift of the powers? The comitology procedure has been restricted to the implementing measures *stricto sensu*, leaving any formal or substantial change of the legal framework of a legislative act to the political control of the legislator (European Parliament and Council). The fact that the European Parliament and Council cannot amend the delegated act does not prevent the Commission from taking into account the possible objections of the two institutions in drafting the text of the delegated act.[11] Moreover, the European Parliament has succeeded in its long fight to obtain both the right to control the exercise of the delegation of competences to the Commission and an equal footing with the Council when powers had been delegated to the Commission under ordinary legislative procedure. On the other hand, the powers initially granted to the Commission for adopting measures of implementation (including some 'quasi-legislative' measures, named after the Lisbon Treaty delegated acts), even against the will of a majority of Member States, has been progressively restricted by supplementary constraints or new procedures (the Aerosol Statement in 1974, the double safety net procedure, the new Comitology Regulation).

However, despite this institutional fight for power between the institutions and its poor democratic legitimacy, the comitology system has proved a significant efficiency from the point of view of the results obtained. The fact that in more than 99% of cases the committees approve the Commission's proposals can be seen, on the one hand, as a sign of the efficiency with which the Commission's departments manage comitology business and, on the other hand, as a proof of their successful collaboration with Member States representatives. The additional fact that disagreements between the Commission and the EU legislator for the delegated acts remain exceptional confirms this conclusion (see Section 5.7)

Of course, from the point of view of political accountability, it is up to the EU legislature (and especially the European Parliament) to exercise at best its

[11] As underlined by a researcher from the Bruges College of Europe, the experience shows that 'the Commission, as a general rule, takes into account the objections made by the Member States and the European Parliament. The EU legislator enjoys therefore a de facto power to make amendments, because the Commission has no interest to engage in a political fight; it would lose on the ground of democratic legitimacy'.

political control on the Commission's delegated acts. The recent developments (the rulings of the Court of Justice as well as the requests for a better consultation before the adoption of delegated acts) could push in the direction of a more consensual practice between the institutions for the adoption of both delegated and implementing acts.

4

Delegation of Powers in the European Union

Political Problems, Legal Solutions?

*Kieran Bradley**

4.1 Introduction: Parliamentary Participation in Second-level Policy-making

4.1.1 And the winner is...

The European Parliament has regularly been described as having emerged a 'winner'[1] from the Lisbon Treaty reforms, particularly as regards the arrangements concerning delegated and implementing acts[2] governed by Articles 290 and 291 TFEU respectively. Apart from the fact that Parliament was not really a 'player' in the drafting of the relevant provisions—remarkably, alone amongst the four major Union institutions, Parliament was not invited to make expert submissions on the delegation and conferral of powers to the relevant European Convention working group[3]—and

* The text is written in a private capacity and the views expressed may not be attributed to any of the institutions with which the author is or has been associated, nor do they prejudice any position he may be required to take in his professional capacity. Best thanks are due to María Gómez-Leal, Anders Neergaard, and Els Vandenbosch for their very helpful comments; responsibility for any errors is, of course, entirely that of the author.

1 See, e.g. T Christiansen and M Dobbels, 'Comitology and delegated acts after Lisbon: How the European Parliament lost the implementation game' (2012) 16 European Integration online Papers (EIoP) Article 13, (http://eiop.or.at/eiop/texte/2012-013a.htm); W Voermans, 'Delegation is a matter of confidence' (2011) European Public Law 313, 314; as regards delegated acts, P Craig, *The Lisbon Treaty* (Oxford University Press 2010), at p 58.

2 For convenience, these are henceforth referred to collectively as 'secondary normative acts'; they may not accurately be described as either 'sub-legislative' or 'non-legislative' acts, as the Lisbon Treaty makes a clear (formal) distinction between measures adopted by 'legislative' procedure ('legislative acts') and other normative measures which are not legislative, including those based directly on the Treaty (adopted by 'innominate non-legislative procedures'); both of these may give rise to secondary normative acts (see generally K Bradley, 'Legislating in the European Union', in C Barnard and S Peers (eds), *European Union Law* (Oxford University Press 2014) 97, at pp 118–23). The verb 'confer' is used to designate the attribution to the Commission of implementing powers (see Article 291(2) TFEU).

3 Final Report of Working Group IX on Simplification of 29 November 2002, CONV 424/02 (at http://european-convention.europa.eu), at p 24; Parliament was, of course, represented in the working group itself.

therefore can neither take much credit for their virtues nor blame for their flaws, it would be difficult to subscribe unreservedly to this rose-tinted assessment. Moreover, though intended to take the controversial matters of the adoption and supervision of secondary normative acts off the agenda of the Union institutions, at least within a relatively short time frame, these provisions contain within them the seeds of conflict, as Parliament and the Council appear to agree.[4] However, as the application of the new Treaty provisions requires the agreement of the two branches of the legislature,[5] the intervention of a third party would in practice be necessary for the interpretation of these provisions to be referred to the Court for authoritative guidance. It follows that, in order fully to enjoy the fruits of its 'victory', Parliament will thus require a certain amount of assistance from the Union's institutional 'referee'.

That said, in two rather obvious senses the description of Parliament as a 'winner', or at least a major institutional beneficiary of the Lisbon Treaty in this area, is appropriate. In the first place, Articles 290 and 291 TFEU grant Parliament powers in relation to the supervision of delegated acts and the design of arrangements for the adoption of implementing acts which it did not enjoy under old-style comitology. Secondly, the very fact that its role in the adoption of certain categories of secondary normative measures is recognized in the Treaty itself, as opposed to being left to the good graces of the Council and/or the Commission, is in itself a significant gain for Parliament, and in the long run for the other institutions too. Parliament's exclusion from the process for adopting comitology arrangements, and for supervising the exercise of secondary normative powers, was long a source of interinstitutional strife; it took various strong-arm political tactics from the parliamentary institution, on the legislative, budgetary, and litigation fronts, before the Council rather grudgingly granted it a supervisory role in the adoption of a single, albeit important, category of secondary normative acts under the regulatory procedure with scrutiny.[6] In so doing, the Council was, moreover, merely applying a supervisory scheme on which the governments of the Member States had already agreed in the Treaty establishing a Constitution for Europe in 2004, and which was finally integrated into primary law with the Lisbon Treaty.[7]

[4] See Section 4.6.

[5] Unlike, e.g. the European Parliament, the Court of Justice prefers 'legislat*ure*' to 'legislat*or*', presumably on the grounds that while the former is the collective body, the latter is an individual member of such a body; the Court's terminology will henceforth be used throughout in preference to Parliament's.

[6] See e.g. K Bradley, 'Halfway House: The 2006 Comitology Reforms and the European Parliament', in D Curtin and M Egeberg (eds), *Towards a New Executive Order in Europe?* (Routledge 2009), at pp 199, 210–12, and the literature cited.

[7] Article I-36 on 'delegated European regulations', is the precursor of both the regulatory procedure with scrutiny and Article 290 TFEU; on the genesis of these provisions, see in particular G Garzón Clariana, 'Les actes délégués dans le système des sources du droit de l'Union Européenne' (2011) 12 ERA Forum 105.

4.1.2 Parliamentary participation before Lisbon: Justus lip service?

The new Treaty provisions on delegated and implementing acts are based on the notion that both branches of the legislature should supervise the exercise of at least certain forms of secondary normative powers. This may be seen as a vindication of Parliament's long-held view that the various comitology arrangements previously adopted fell short of what the institutional system of the Union required, particularly since the inauguration of the co-decision, now ordinary legislative, procedure by the Maastricht Treaty. Thus, for example, in the guise of 'improv[ing] the involvement of the European Parliament' where implementing powers were granted in an act adopted under co-decision, Article 8 of the 1999 Council decision allowed Parliament to adopt a resolution—which the Commission could subsequently ignore[8]—explaining why a draft implementing measure was *ultra vires* the basic act.[9] This concession was a hollow gesture at best, which added nothing of substance to prerogatives Parliament already enjoyed under the Treaty, prerogatives which, moreover, were not restricted to acts implementing legislation adopted under a particular procedure. The real intention behind Article 8 of the 1999 decision appears therefore to have been either to reduce the risks of such litigation in the future, where the Commission gives Parliament's views some credence, or to put the adopting institution on notice of possible future such proceedings, the better to defend itself in Court. Indeed, the Council may have been at least partly influenced in this regard by the annulment, at Parliament's behest, of one of its own implementing directives in the ruling in *Pesticides*.[10] The avoidance of litigation is, of course, a perfectly valid objective, but it is curious that the Council should present the Article 8 resolution as a substantive improvement of Parliament's position in regard to the adoption and supervision of comitology measures.

The regulatory procedure with scrutiny went one step forward, in allowing Parliament to prevent the adoption of implementing measures, though only if its objection was putatively based on one of three legal grounds. It has been suggested, somewhat fancifully, that 'Parliament as a whole failed to fully grasp and understand the potential of the [regulatory procedure with scrutiny]'; this analysis is partly founded on the fact that over a three-year period 'Parliament successfully objected to only three [proposed implementing measures] in plenary'.[11] It is not, however, necessary for each and every individual member of Parliament to 'get acquainted with this highly technical and complex EU decision-making

[8] See, e.g., the facts of Joined Cases C-14/06 and C-295/06 *Parliament and Denmark v Commission*, EU:C:2008:176.

[9] The expression *ultra vires* is legal shorthand for the concept that a secondary measure exceeds the powers conferred by the basic act. The other 'improvements' to Parliament's position under comitology, regarding for example the provision of information and documents, may be considered modest but useful.

[10] Case C-303/94 *Parliament v Council* (*Pesticides*), EU:C:1996:238.

[11] M Kaeding and A Hardacre, 'The European Parliament and the Future of Comitology after Lisbon' (2013) 19 ELJ 382, at p 396; though they proffer this analysis as an explanation of 'why there have been so few objections by the Parliament', the authors acknowledge that 'having more knowledgeable and experienced MEPs would not automatically lead to more objections' (loc. cit.).

instrument'; that said, failing any evidence to the contrary, one might be entitled to assume that even the least procedure-savvy of MEPs could grasp the difference between a procedure which allows Parliament to huff and to puff, and one which allows it to blow the Commission's house down. In the unlikely event that this task proves to be beyond the capacities of one or other elected member, (s)he will have available an army of lawyers, committee officials, political group advisors, assistants, and, in some cases, lobbyists who will between them be able to provide the necessary level of comprehension to allow her/him to come to an informed judgement.

Furthermore, the 'successful' vetoing by Parliament of a proposed implementing measure which the Commission and, possibly, the regulatory committee, had considered necessary and appropriate, is not some sort of political objective, but indicates rather a significant breakdown in the process for the adoption of such acts. The paucity of such vetoes[12] may reflect the greater willingness of the Commission to take account of Parliament's known views at the drafting stage, just as Parliament has always suspected the Commission anticipated the views of the national administrations in formulating implementing measures under comitology. In any case, in this area, as in legislating generally, Parliament has always had to operate a trade-off between protecting its institutional prerogatives and achieving its substantive policy objectives;[13] clearly the electorate is—and should be—more interested in common policies than comitology.

4.2 Delegation and Conferral: Some General Issues

4.2.1 Why do essential elements matter?

The first question which must be resolved in evaluating the possible delegation (or conferral)[14] of powers is whether the powers in question only concern matters which are 'non-essential'.[15] This verification is required not only because the delegation of powers to regulate essential elements would be illegal, but because the formal degree of influence of each of the respective institutional actors,[16] including Parliament, on the content of the resulting measures varies dramatically in function of the procedure for their adoption, whatever the influence a particular institution or Member State may in fact wield in a given case. To this end, the parliamentary committee responsible for scrutinizing a basic act containing a delegation of power must, in effect, ensure its compliance with Article 290 TFEU, and

[12] For more complete figures, see Section 4.3.3.

[13] See e.g. Parliament's apparent volte-face in relation to the tobacco products directive and facts of the Biocides regulation, Sections 4.2.2 and 4.5.2.

[14] Only Article 290(1) TFEU refers to 'non-essential elements', though the conferral of the power to deal with essential elements in an implementing act is also excluded.

[15] See the very helpful contribution of Dominique Ritleng to this debate (Chapter 7 in this volume).

[16] That is, the EU political institutions and the Member States.

in case of doubt may request an opinion of the committee on legal affairs; the legal committee may also take up the matter on its own initiative.[17]

The rule that secondary normative measures may only concern non-essential elements was originally formulated by the Court in *Köster* with a view, inter alia, to protecting the prerogatives of the European Parliament;[18] the Advocate General's positive assessment in that case of the legality of the management committee procedure was heavily influenced by a resolution Parliament had adopted two years previously approving that procedure and indeed the comitology system in general.[19] Relying on the 'legislative scheme of the Treaty' and the 'consistent practice of the… institutions', the Court found a distinction between 'measures directly based on the Treaty itself and derived law intended to ensure their implementation'; it was 'sufficient for the purposes of [the Treaty] that the basic elements of the matter to be dealt with' be adopted under the legislative procedure. In *Romkes I*, the Court went out of its way to stress that an implementing regulation adopted without any parliamentary consultation 'must respect the basic elements laid down in the basic regulation… after consultation of the European Parliament'.[20] It later held that the classification as 'essential to the subject-matter… must be reserved for provisions which are intended to give concrete shape to the fundamental guidelines of [Union] policy'.[21]

The introduction of the regulatory procedure with scrutiny gave a new edge to the distinction between essential and non-essential elements; that the implementing measure be restricted to non-essential elements was one of the criteria for recourse to that procedure, which was, moreover, obligatory where the conditions laid down by the 2006 Comitology Decision were fulfilled. In *Schengen Borders Code*, where the regulatory procedure with scrutiny had in fact been applied,[22] the European Parliament challenged an implementing decision (by the Council) on the ground that it illegally extended to essential elements of the basic legislative act.[23] The most important issue before the Court was that of who decides what

[17] Rule 37a, EP Rules of Procedure; see e.g. the legal committee's opinion on delegation in the proposed tobacco products directive (Section 4.2.2).

[18] Case 25/70 *Einfuhr- und Vorratsstelle für Getreide und Futtermittel v Köster and Berodt & Co.*, EU:C:1970:115.

[19] Opinion of A G Dutheillet de Lamothe in Case 25/70, EU:C:1970:100. The resolution in question was not, however, a definitive statement of Parliament's views on the matter, which continued to evolve in a direction critical of comitology; K Bradley, 'The European Parliament and Comitology: On the Road to Nowhere?' (1997) 3 ELJ 230.

[20] Case 46/86 *Albert Romkes v Officier van Justitie for the District of Zwolle*, EU:C:1987:287, para 16; the protection of Parliament's prerogatives had not been adverted to by either the parties or the Advocate General.

[21] Case C-240/90 *Germany v Commission* (*German sheepmeat*), EU:C:1992:408, paras 36–7.

[22] See Article 12(5) of Regulation (EC) 2006/562 of the European Parliament and of the Council of 15 March 2006 establishing a Community Code on the rules governing the movement of persons across borders (Schengen Borders Code), OJ 2006 L 105/1. The contested decision was adopted after the Lisbon Treaty had come into force, but under a regulatory procedure with scrutiny which was still in force.

[23] Case C-355/10 *Parliament v Council*, EU:C:2012:516, in particular paras 65–7. See in general M den Heijer and E Tauschinsky, 'Where Human Rights Meet Administrative Law: Essential Elements and Limits to Delegation' (2013) 10 EuConst 513; and M Chamon, 'How the concept of essential elements of a legislative act continues to elude the Court' (2013) 50 CMLRev 849.

is 'essential' and 'non-essential'. Both the Council and the Commission argued, in effect, that the legislature enjoyed untrammelled freedom to decide whether a particular aspect of the basic legislative act constituted an 'essential element', which could only be modified in accordance with the legislative procedure, or a 'non-essential element' the power to modify which could be delegated to the Commission (or, exceptionally, the Council). The Court noted that 'provisions [whose adoption] require[s] political choices falling within the responsibilities of the European Union legislature cannot be delegated'. Moreover, it continued, '[ascertaining] which elements of a matter must be categorised as essential is not... for the assessment of the European Union legislature alone, but must be based on objective factors amenable to judicial review'.

In so holding, the Court applied the same test as obtains for the choice of the legal basis of primary legislation,[24] and for essentially the same reasons, that is, the fact that the choice of procedure is decisive for the degree of influence of each of the institutions; as a result, it falls to the Court to ensure the relevant legal rules are respected in the making of such choice, or, in a hallowed phrase, that the 'institutional balance' is maintained.[25] The ruling established, or at the very least confirmed,[26] that the Court would exercise full legal review of respect of the 'essential elements' restriction; that this was not a foregone conclusion is witnessed by the fact that two of the major political institutions argued for a contrary position, and the Court itself took quite a different approach to the issue of the legislature's discretion to delegate or confer powers in its ruling in *Biocides*.[27] On the other hand, the Court refused to be drawn on what 'essential elements' are, noting only, as it had in *German sheepmeat*, that they entail 'political choices'.[28]

4.2.2 How to spot an 'essential' element

The reference to the criteria for the choice of legal basis in *Schengen Borders Code* may provide one possible avenue for seizing the elusive notion of 'essential elements'. In adopting legislative acts, the legislature must take account of a certain number of objectives, policy considerations, and in some cases *modi operandi*, identified in the legal basis of the act; Article 39(1) TFEU, for example, lays down no fewer than five objectives of the common agricultural policy, and Article 39(2) TFEU a further three matters of which the legislature must take account, to say nothing of

[24] See generally K Bradley, 'Powers and Procedures in the EU Constitution: Legal Bases and the Court', in P Craig and G de Burca (eds), *The Evolution of EU Law*, 2nd edn (Oxford University Press 2011), at pp 85–109.

[25] In the context of the choice of committee procedure under the 1987 comitology regime, see Case C-417/93 *Parliament v Council (TACIS)*, EU:C:1995:127, para 25.

[26] See e.g. Joined Cases C-14/06 and C-295/06 (n 8).

[27] Case C-427/12 *Commission v European Parliament and Council (Biocides)*, EU:C:2014:170; see further Section 4.5.3.

[28] In this regard, the criticism of M Chamon (n 23, 859), that the Court 'missed an opportunity to shed greater light on the dividing line between essential and non-essential elements', appears to be based on a rather optative notion of the role of the Court in constitutional litigation.

the choice of forms of market organization allowed by Article 40(1) TFEU, as well as any applicable general principles of Union law. As the Court noted in *Meroni*, only the legislature is empowered to 'reconcile any conflict which may be implied by... objectives [laid down in a legal basis] when considered individually and... grant such priority to one or other of the objectives... as appears necessary'. The reconciliation of objectives 'implies a real discretion involving difficult choices, based on a consideration of the economic facts and circumstances in the light of which those choices are made'. It followed that the delegation of a discretionary power, 'implying a wide margin of discretion which may... make possible the execution of actual economic policy' was illegal.[29]

By the same token, where the legislature has identified the particular objective(s) of a legislative act, the legal and policy considerations which it deems relevant, and the means by which those objectives are to be achieved and those considerations are to be taken into account, these are 'political choices' and hence essential elements, the power to regulate or modify which may not be delegated. In reviewing the delegation of powers in a basic act, or the exercise of such powers in a delegated act, the Court would therefore be able to rely on these political choices in order to determine whether the delegation or the delegated act, as the case may be, is valid.

In practice, the issue of whether the regulation of particular matters entails such choices does not appear to give rise to major difficulties, *Schengen Borders Code* being a truly exceptional example of a measure adopted by one branch of the legislature which in the view of the other branch overstepped the line. In *Schengen Borders Code*, Parliament had argued that 'the concept of "essential elements" includes the definitions laid down by the basic legislation which delimit its material scope and... sets the framework within which that legislation applies'.[30] Without using the term 'framework', the Court upheld Parliament's view that the contested decision contained such essential elements.

Furthermore, in case of doubt, or disagreement between its two branches on the question, the legislature will always have the relatively safe option of regulating the matter in the legislative act.[31] In this context, Parliament has on occasion relied on the 'essential elements' requirement to reject what it sees as an excess of zeal on the part of the Commission to consign certain matters to the realm of secondary normative acts. In its first reading position on the new tobacco products directive, for example, Parliament deleted a series of provisions delegating powers to the Commission on the grounds that the matters dealt with were in fact essential elements, and that such measures should be dealt with either in the instant directive or in future legislative

[29] Case 9/56 *Meroni v High Authority*, EU:C:1958:7, at pp 151–2.

[30] The locus of the legal dispute was whether an implementing act could modify 'the definitions laid down by the basic legislation which delimit its material scope and... set[] the framework within which that legislation applies'; the Decision allowed border guards to take certain measures against persons or ships which did not come within the notion of 'surveillance' (paras 44 and 69–73).

[31] Though the Commission may not agree with this course of action, and may even withdraw its proposal in these circumstances: see Case C-409/13 *Council v Commission*, EU:C:2015:217.

measures.[32] At the end of the day, Parliament came round to the view that a significant number of provisions of the directive should delegate powers to the Commission; the validity of most of these delegating provisions has now been challenged in *Philip Morris*.[33]

4.2.3 Delegation and judicial review

The Court's judgment in *Schengen Borders Code* clarified a further point of general importance, that is, that an institution may challenge the legality of a measure whose adoption it could have prevented under the applicable procedure; the apparent contradiction between the institution's political and legal positions does not constitute a procedural obstacle to such annulment proceedings. In this case, though entitled to do so, Parliament had not objected that the draft measure would be *ultra vires*. It nonetheless took proceedings for the annulment of the subsequent decision.[34]

Significantly, the alleged inadmissibility of Parliament's action was the Council's principal ground of defence.[35] It argued that Parliament had no interest in bringing annulment proceedings or any right to challenge the decision: 'if ... Parliament had doubts as to the legality of the contested decision, it ought to have opposed it'. The Court held that, in common with the other political actors of the Union, Parliament does not need to demonstrate a subjective interest in the outcome of legal proceedings in order to be able to initiate an annulment action. Its right to do so was not contingent on any position it had taken during the course of the adoption process, such as its decision not to oppose the draft Council Decision under the regulatory procedure with scrutiny.[36] In particular, the Court firmly rejected the Council's somewhat surprising suggestion that Parliament's scrutiny power could be considered in some way as a substitute for judicial review.

While this does not appear explicitly from the judgment, the Court may have taken the view that Parliament's decision not to prevent the adoption of the draft decision under the comitology procedure could, in the circumstances, be seen as a fully rational one, rather than the MEPs blowing legally hot and politically cold.[37] There was widespread agreement that the proposed Union rules on border surveillance should be put in place by Summer 2010, which would almost certainly not

[32] The amendments were adopted on 8 October 2013 (P7_TA-PROV(2013)0398), on the basis of an opinion of the legal affairs committee attached to the McAvan report (A7-276/2013).

[33] Dir 2014/40/EU, OJ 2014 L127/1; Case C-574/14 *ex parte Philip Morris et al*, pending.

[34] Case C-355/10 (n 23); under the applicable procedure, the power to adopt the decision passed to the Council where, as here, the comitology committee was unable to adopt the Commission draft.

[35] Ibid, para 33: '[t]he Council primarily argues that the Parliament's action is inadmissible'; this is an unusual tactic in a dispute of this importance, when the institutions have a shared interest in obtaining judicial guidance on a substantive point of law.

[36] For a somewhat different approach, see Case C-65/93 *Parliament v Council (1993 GSP)*, EU:C:1995:91.

[37] Opinion of Advocate General Mengozzi in Case C-355/10, EU:C:2012:207, para 20 and note 13.

have been possible had the contested decision been blocked by Parliament the previous Spring. It was presumably for this reason too that, exceptionally for an applicant party, Parliament requested that the Court maintain the effects of the contested decision until it had been replaced; the Court accepted the request, adding that the replacement should be effected 'within a reasonable time'. The Court was thus able to reconcile the fundamental desirability of access to judicial review with a healthy respect for the exercise of political discretion.

4.2.4 The implementing act based on a delegated act: an institutional chimera

It has been suggested in some quarters, presumably on the basis of a rather literal reading of Article 291 TFEU ('legally binding Union acts'), that the Commission could adopt an implementing act on the basis of a delegated act. Such an act would be a veritable institutional chimera. It presupposes either that the Commission would impose a neo-comitology procedure on itself—but to what end, if it already has the power to adopt the necessary measures without such a procedure?—or that the legislature would do so in specifying the content and scope of the delegation. In the latter case, Parliament and the Council would presumably be able to supervise the adoption of the relevant implementing acts using the mechanisms for control of the delegated acts, notwithstanding the fact that Article 291(3) TFEU provides that the exercise of implementing powers is subject to the control of the Member States, rather than the institutions. While under a delegated power the Commission may 'supplement or amend' the basic legislative act, it may not do so by means of an implementing act;[38] so what exactly would these implementing measures do? Given that the Commission would be acting on the basis of a delegation even when adopting such measures, in order to comply with Articles 290(3) and 291(4) TFEU, would they need to be called 'delegated implementing acts'? The legal mind boggles.

4.3 The European Parliament and Delegated Acts

4.3.1 Introduction: parity at last

This is the area of secondary normative activity where the affirmation of Parliament's role is most palpable. Where the ordinary legislative procedure applies, the two branches of the legislature are, as Parliament had long claimed they should be, on an equal footing. The fact that in order to revoke a delegation or object to a delegated act Parliament must act by a majority of its component members, as distinct from a (simple) majority of members participating in the vote, while

[38] Case C-65/13 *Parliament v Commission (EURES)*, EU:C:2014:2289, para 45; see also Section 4.5.3 *in fine*.

the Council need only garner a qualified majority, does not necessarily grant the Council a 'slight preference... in enforcing the limits of delegation'.[39] Though the special voting requirement may on occasion prevent Parliament exercising its supervisory powers under Article 290(2) TFEU,[40] in everyday practice is it often just as easy, if not easier, for Parliament, with its handful of mainly well-disciplined political groups,[41] to achieve the higher voting threshold,[42] than for the Council to achieve a qualified majority of the twenty-eight delegations which participate in its deliberations.

Parliament's right of revocation and objection are no longer restricted, as was its right of objection under the regulatory procedure with scrutiny, to a set of predetermined grounds of an essentially legal character, and extends to delegation under almost all normative measures based on the Treaty. Parliament's own rapporteur on the delegation of powers called the Article 290 TFEU 'perhaps the most important and yet often neglected innovation in the Lisbon Treaty' and 'one of the most significant expansions of Parliament's jurisdiction',[43] though this expansion could be seen as being at least partly a by-product of the generalization of the ordinary legislative procedure.

4.3.2 Parliament's general approach to delegation

On the eve of the 2014 elections, Parliament took stock of four years of 'the delegation of legislative powers and control by Member States of the Commission's exercise of implementing powers'.[44] Though based on a report by Parliament's committee on legal affairs, the resolution may be considered first and foremost the statement of a political position, or even the first draft of a negotiating position for an agreement on improving the functioning of delegation and the conferral of implementing powers, rather than being an exclusively legal analysis of the relevant Treaty provisions and their application. In Parliament's view, 'delegation is a delicate operation whereby the Commission is instructed to exercise a power which is intrinsic to the legislature's own role'. As the relevant Treaty provisions seek to 'guarantee a sufficient level of democratic legitimacy', they must be correctly applied, and therefore 'the starting-point in examining the issue of delegation must always be the freedom of the legislature'.

[39] R Schütze, '"Delegated" Legislation in the (New) European Union: A Constitutional Analysis' (2011) 74 MLR 661, at p 685.

[40] This was in fact the case in Case C-355/10 (n 23), where the majority in favour of the draft resolution blocking the adoption of the contested Council decision, while significant (336 for, 253 against, 30 abstentions), fell a few dozen votes short of the required figure: OJ 2010 C132 E/33.

[41] See K Bradley, 'The European Parliament', in T Tridimas and R Schütze (eds), *Oxford Principles of European Union Law* (Oxford University Press, forthcoming), section IV(e).

[42] A qualified parliamentary majority is in any case required at various stages of the ordinary legislative procedure, notably in second reading (Article 294(7)(b) and (c) TFEU).

[43] J Sjájer, debate on own-initiative report of the committee on legal affairs on the power of legislative delegation (A7-110/2010), verbatim report of EP proceedings of 19 April 2010, item 16.

[44] Resolution of 25 February 2014, P7_TA-PROV(2014)0127.

This statement represents an ambitious, if only partially successful, attempt to summarize a number of complex interlocking ideas. On its own, the phrase 'intrinsic to the legislature's own role' might be considered ambiguous; clearly, it cannot refer to matters on which only the legislature may decide, being 'essential elements' which cannot be delegated, as indeed the resolution explicitly acknowledges. That said, this formulation has the merit of seeking to capture in a single phrase the notion that the matters on which the regulatory power can be delegated to the Commission are those which fall in principle within the legislature's decisional ambit, and that in these circumstances delegation is a choice and not a duty; delegation may be justified 'where flexibility and efficiency are needed and cannot be delivered by means of the ordinary legislative procedure'.[45] It is 'intrinsic' in the character of delegated powers that delegation is an exception and that, as the Court established two generations ago in *Meroni*, a delegation may not be presumed.[46]

Parliament also opined that 'the decision to confer delegated... powers must be based on objective factors which must permit judicial review of the solution adopted'.[47] Given that, unlike Article 291 TFEU in respect of implementing powers, Article 290 TFEU does not lay down any substantive limits on the legislature's discretion to delegate, it is difficult to see on what 'objective grounds' such a decision could be challenged other than for respect of the 'essential elements' reservation and the formal requirements laid down in this latter provision.

4.3.3 What are 'delegated acts'?

In its resolution, Parliament sought to lay down a number of practical guidelines as to what measures may be adopted as 'delegated acts', which must be read along with those it adopted on the scope of implementing powers. Certain of these guidelines appear merely to paraphrase Articles 290 and 291 TFEU, such as its injunction that '[the] Commission may only amend legislative acts [including annexes to such acts] by means of delegated acts', to which Parliament appended a warning that '[a]nnexes are not to be added or deleted with the aim of triggering or avoiding the use of delegated acts'.

More concretely, Parliament considers that 'Union lists or registers of authorised products or substances... should remain... an integral part of the basic act', and hence that the power to adopt these may not be delegated. In its view, the following may be adopted as delegated acts:

(a) measures 'intended to further define the exact content of the obligations spelt out in the legislative act', as these supplement the basic act;

[45] Ibid, Para D; of course, acts adopted by a special legislative procedure can also provide for implementing powers (n 2).

[46] Case 9/56 *Meroni v High Authority*, (n 29) at p 151.

[47] The Court adopted a somewhat different position in Case C-427/12 (n 27); see further Section 4.5.3.

(b) measures 'designed to lay down [further] conditions, criteria or requirements to be met', as these 'will, by definition, alter the content of the legislation and add new rules of general application';
(c) 'additional binding rules of general scope that affect in substance the rights or obligations laid down in the basic act;
(d) measures laying down 'specific technical matters, strategic interests, objectives, expected results' of financial programmes;
(e) measures determining 'the type of information to be provided under the basic act (i.e. the exact content of the information)' insofar as it supplements the obligation to provide information;
(f) depending on the 'content, context and the nature of the provisions set out in the basic act' measures laying down a procedure (defined as 'a way of performing of giving effect to something') involving 'further non-essential policy choices';
(g) 'decisions concerning the authorisation or prohibition of the inclusion of a specific substance in food, cosmetics etc', except in so far as 'the Commission decision is fully based on criteria contained in the basic act', in which case an implementing act would be acceptable.

Parliament's classification as delegated acts of 'measures leading to a choice of priorities, objectives or expected results', where these are not reserved to the basic act, could prove difficult to apply in practice, in so far as such choices may constitute essential elements.[48]

During the 2009–14 legislative period, Parliament only objected to a delegated act once—the same rate as the Council—while one proposed objection was rejected by the plenary, and two others were withdrawn; on several other occasions, delegated acts were discussed in detail in the relevant committee, without an objection being lodged.[49] Recourse to the so-called 'early non-objection' procedure, whereby Parliament signals it has no objections to the draft text without waiting for the expiry of the deadline,[50] was rather more frequent, with seven cases. On the other hand, Parliament prevented the adoption of measures under the regulatory procedure with scrutiny on four occasions during the same period, while a further four motions for objection were considered but not adopted; on nine occasions, Parliament signalled its early non-objection to draft acts proposed under this latter procedure.

4.3.4 Systematic consultation of national experts: comitology by the back door?

Parliament also has concerns on a number of issues which are either are not dealt with, or are papered over, in the 2011 Common Understanding on Delegated

48 At least according to the approach to identifying 'essential elements' suggested above (Section 4.2.2).

49 G Pitella et al, *Activity Report on Codecision and Conciliation 14 July 2009–30 June 2014*, EP doc. DV\1031024EN.doc, 25.

50 Rule 105, EP Rules of Procedure.

Acts.[51] The first of these concerns, both temporally and in importance, relates to the participation of national experts in the work of the Commission in preparing delegated acts.

In its Communication on Article 290 TFEU, the Commission went out of its way to emphasize what it considered to be fundamental differences between delegated and implementing acts.[52] It must therefore have come as an unpleasant surprise, bordering on provocation, for Parliament to learn from the same document of the Commission's intention 'systematically to consult experts from the national authorities of all the Member States' during the course of preparing draft delegated acts.[53] Granted, the Commission is under a Treaty obligation to 'carry out broad consultations with parties concerned in order to ensure the Union's actions are coherent and transparent',[54] including actions in the form of delegated acts; common sense dictates that it must be able to take good advice where it can find it. On the other hand, a self-imposed obligation systematically to consult experts merely because they happen to hail from a particular Member State, rather than because their contributions are likely to be useful in the formulation of the delegated act, might be considered to go beyond what is required by the Treaty and the Commission's undoubted prerogative to organize its work as it sees fit. Moreover, given that the Commission's resources are limited, will it give priority to ensuring that *all* the Member States have been consulted over getting access to the best and most pertinent expertise?

Not unnaturally, Parliament saw this as comitology by the back door, and at the first opportunity set its face firmly against the inclusion of such a provision, when examining a proposal for a regulation on the free movement of domestic pets. The preamble of the Regulation subsequently adopted reflects the compromise text it agreed with the Council, to the effect that it was 'of particular importance that the Commission carry out appropriate consultations during its preparatory work, including at expert level',[55] a compromise which was in turn taken up in the Common Understanding.

In clause 15 of the 2010 Framework Agreement between the two institutions, the Commission undertook to keep Parliament fully informed of 'its meetings with national experts within the framework of its work on the preparation and implementation of Union legislation, including' (sic) 'soft law and

[51] Common Understanding on Delegated Acts, Council Doc 8753/1/11 of 14 April 2011 (PE164, INST 195).

[52] Commission Communication of 9 December 2009, Implementation of Article 290 of the Treaty on the Functioning of the European Union, COM(2009) 673 final.

[53] Ibid, Para 4.2

[54] Article 11(3) TEU.

[55] Regulation (EU) 2010/438 of the European Parliament and of the Council of 19 May 2010 amending Regulation (EC) 2003/998 on the animal health requirements applicable to the non-commercial movement of pet animals, OJ 2010 L 132/3. The same formulation is now used in para 30 of the preamble to the revised regulation, Regulation (EU) 2013/576 of the European Parliament and of the Council of 12 June 2013 on the non-commercial movement of pet animals and repealing Regulation (EC) 2003/998, OJ 2013 L 178/1.

delegated acts'.[56] This implies some sort of acceptance by Parliament of the principle that the Commission may convene such meetings, the *quid pro quo* being that 'the Commission may...invite Parliament's experts to attend those meetings' if Parliament so requests, though the Commission appears to be under no obligation to do so. The annex to the Agreement identifies which meetings are concerned, and specifies that it does not apply to meetings of comitology committees, subject to any arrangements concerning the provision of information to Parliament in the exercise of the Commission's implementing powers. In Parliament's view, clause 15 applies to all the activities of Commission meetings with national experts, except the actual discussion of draft implementing acts.[57] The practice as regards attendance at such meetings varies from one parliamentary committee to another and often depends in part on the political importance of the matter under consideration. In general, it is committee staff, rather than MEPs, who attend.

4.3.5 Revocation and objection OK, but is there a third way?

In providing that the conditions to which delegation is subject 'may be' the two mechanisms set out in that provision, revocation and objection, Article 290(2) TFEU does not indicate whether any other mechanisms are permitted or whether they are in principle excluded.[58] It has been suggested that the most plausible interpretation of this provision is that this is merely an indication, rather than a restriction, of the mechanisms which can be used, and that the legislative history bears out this interpretation.[59] For its part, Parliament has interpreted it as meaning that these two mechanisms are 'purely illustrative', and that the freedom of manoeuvre of the legislature would allow recourse to other mechanisms, such as a requirement that the Commission seek prior approval for individual delegated acts, or the possibility for either branch of the legislature to repeal delegated acts already in force.[60] The Common Understanding, on the other hand, 'builds further on [the Commission] communication', and does not mention the possibility of a third way to supervise the exercise of

[56] The Agreement is published as Annex XIV to Parliament's Rules of Procedure (http://www.europarl.europa.eu/sides/getDoc.do?pubRef=-//EP//TEXT+RULES-EP+20140310+ANN-14+DOC+XML+V0//EN&language=EN&navigationBar=YES). Neither soft law nor delegated acts can be considered 'legislation' properly so called.

[57] See the statement annexed to its legislative resolution of 5 February 2014 on the proposal for a Directive on explosives for civil use (EP Doc P7_TA-PROV (2014)0085).

[58] The wording appears to originate in the report of the European Convention's working group on simplification, which was not tasked with drafting the necessary provisions; it was subsequently taken up in the Treaty establishing a Constitution for Europe at Article I-36(2) and hence in Article 290(2) TFEU.

[59] G Garzón Clariana (n 7), at p 127.

[60] Resolution of 5 May 2010 on the power of legislative delegation (2010/2021 (INI)), OJ 2011 C 81E/6; for R Schütze, any element of 'free choice beyond the control mechanisms expressly mentioned would be a serious constitutional retrogression' (loc. cit. (n 39), at note 149).

delegated powers, though it stops short of precluding other forms of supervisory mechanism.

While its somewhat laconic drafting might be regretted, Article 290(2) TFEU rightly envisages the possibility of other mechanisms than those specified, at the very least in order to take account of the fact that 'legislative acts' may be adopted under a special legislative procedure by either Parliament or the Council acting alone in each case, and the idea that in general the delegator is entitled to supervise the exercise of the powers it delegates. Thus where the Council is acting alone under such a procedure, Article 290 TFEU would allow it to supervise the exercise of delegated powers alone too; by the same token, for the few legislative acts that the European Parliament adopts, it should be allowed to exclude Council supervision of any delegated acts.

That said, such exclusion should not be automatic. The principal characteristic of a 'legislative' procedure, whether ordinary or special, is that Parliament and the Council both participate in the adoption of the legislative act, albeit not on equal terms where a special legislative procedure applies. From the text of Article 290(2) TFEU, it follows that *any* legislative act, whether adopted by the ordinary or a special legislative procedure, may provide for supervision by both Parliament and the Council; it would therefore be perfectly permissible for an act adopted by the Council or Parliament under a special legislative procedure to provide for supervision by both branches of the legislature. Thus, for example, the adoption by the Council of 'action to combat discrimination' on grounds other than nationality under Article 19(1) TFEU requires Parliament's consent; in theory, Parliament could withhold its consent unless it is allowed some say in the supervision of any delegated acts. Conversely, the adoption by Parliament of 'regulations and general conditions governing the performance of the duties its members' requires the Council's consent, by unanimity where taxation is concerned. Again, allowing the Council jointly to supervise the exercise of powers Parliament has delegated to the Commission, particularly where tax matters are concerned, would not a priori be entirely illogical.

Other constraints on the Commission's freedom to exercise delegated powers may be laid down in legislation, such as European Parliament and Council Regulation 2010/1093 setting up the European Banking Authority, which provides for a specific procedure for the adoption of 'regulatory technical standards' (RTS) in this field.[61] Such RTS 'shall be technical, shall not imply strategic decisions or policy choices, and their content shall be delimited by the legislative acts on which

[61] Regulation (EU) 2010/1093 of the European Parliament and of the Council of 24 November 2010 establishing a European Supervisory Authority (European Banking Authority), OJ 2010 L 331/12; similar arrangements apply in the fields of insurance and financial services: Regulation (EU) 2010/1094 of the European Parliament and of the Council of 24 November 2010 establishing a European Supervisory Authority (European Insurance and Occupational Pensions Authority), OJ 2010 L 331/48; Regulation (EU) 2010/1095 of the European Parliament and of the Council of 24 November 2010 establishing a European Supervisory Authority (European Securities and Markets Authority), OJ 2010 L 331/84. See also Declaration 39 to the Final Act of the Lisbon Intergovernmental Conference.

they are based'. The draft RTS are prepared by the Authority, for endorsement by the Commission as delegated acts; the Commission may, in coordination with the Authority, amend the Authority's draft, though 'only in very restricted and extraordinary circumstances', and it may only take the initiative to adopt an RTS as a delegated act where the Authority has not submitted a draft RTS within the relevant time limit. In each case, the draft RTS is subject to a public consultation procedure and the consultation of the Banking Stakeholder Group. The revocation and objection procedures of Article 290 TFEU also apply to RTS.[62]

4.4 The European Parliament and Implementing Acts

4.4.1 Introduction: second place or consolation prize?

Here Parliament's 'victory', if such it were, was significantly more mitigated. Certainly it achieved parity with the Council, at least on paper, in the sense that in theory neither is allowed to interfere with the exercise of the implementing powers conferred on the Commission. Yet both Article 291 TFEU and the neo-comitology regulation of 2011, the first formal legal instrument on the supervision of secondary normative activity adopted jointly by Parliament and the Council,[63] not only fail in certain respects to address some of Parliament's historic concerns with the design and structure of the comitology system but they add a number of features to the pre-existing situation which Parliament might find objectionable.

4.4.2 The 'implementation' of EU law: Article 291(3) TFEU and the palace revolution

It should be noted at the outset that the text of Article 291 TFEU itself seeks to resolve the question of principle, as old as comitology itself, of where responsibility for supervising the exercise of implementing powers actually lies. On the basis of the EEC Treaty as it stood in the early 1960s, Parliament had argued that it alone was entitled to supervise such exercise, on the grounds that under the Treaty implementing powers could only be conferred on the Commission, that the necessary supervisory powers were vested exclusively in the parliamentary institution, and that these could not, in effect, be transferred to the administrations of

[62] Para 23 of the preamble, and Articles 10, 12, and 13 of Regulation (EU) 2010/1093.

[63] Regulation (EU) 2011/182 of the European Parliament and of the Council of 16 February 2011 laying down the rules and general principles concerning mechanisms for control by Member States of the Commission's exercise of implementing powers, OJ 2011 L 55/13. The 1999 (second) Comitology Decision and the 2006 amending decision were each accompanied by interinstitutional agreements, known respectively as the *modus vivendi* and the 'ceasefire'/'peace declaration'. See further K Bradley, 'Institutional Aspects of Comitology: Scenes from the Cutting Room Floor', in C Joerges and E Vos (eds), *EU Committees: Social Regulation, Law and Politics* (Hart Publishing, 1999), at pp 71, 71–6, and K Bradley (n 6), at pp 210–12.

the Member States.[64] Furthermore, review of such implementing acts would have been amongst the most important 'supervisory powers' Parliament was called upon to exercise in accordance with Article 149 EEC.[65]

Article 291(1) TFEU affirms the obligation of the Member States to implement legally binding Union acts. In itself, this affirmation is unexceptionable, in so far as it is merely a manifestation of the more general duties of sincere cooperation of the Member States with respect to the Union, in particular to 'ensure fulfilment of [their Treaty] obligations [and to] facilitate the achievement of the Union's tasks'.[66] It is Article 291(3) TFEU which effects a palace revolution, in specifying that responsibility for supervising the exercise of the Commission's implementing powers is to be confided in the Member States alone, to the exclusion of Parliament and, at least formally, of the Council. This is little more than a *coup de force* by the Treaty authors, which contravenes the logic underlying the constitutional and institutional structures of the Union.[67] The 'implementation' of Union law by the Member States under Article 291(1) TFEU is quite different in character from the 'implementation' by the Commission under Article 291(2) and (3) TFEU. In the former, the national authorities give effect in their national legal and administrative orders to measures adopted at the Union level; these authorities are not vested with any powers of political supervision regarding the adoption of the Union measure which they are charged with implementing, though they may, and should, supervise the adoption of the necessary national measures. This may, for convenience, be dubbed 'national implementation', political and judicial review of which falls primarily within the jurisdiction of the national courts, subject to the possibility of a preliminary reference or infringement proceedings.

The 'implementation' governed by Article 291(2) and (3) TFEU, by contrast, is an activity which takes place purely at the Union level ('Union implementation'). In this case, one Union institution adopts measures to implement Union acts (normally legislative in character) adopted by another Union institution or institutions;[68] here judicial review of the implementing act falls primarily within the jurisdiction of the Union Courts, as it does for the basic (Union) legislation, albeit that review can also be effected via the preliminary ruling procedure.[69] The Lisbon Treaty even opened a new head of annulment jurisdiction at the suit of individuals or companies to challenge 'a regulatory act which is of direct concern to them and

[64] K Bradley, 'The European Parliament and Comitology ' (n 19), at pp 231–2.

[65] With a fine sense of irony, in the 'comitology case' (which is not in fact about comitology at all), the Court relied inter alia on Parliament's rather puny supervisory powers as grounds for ruling that it should not enjoy the possibility of initiating annulment proceedings: Case 302/87 *Parliament v Council*, EU:C:1988:461, para 12.

[66] Article 4(3) TEU.

[67] Cf. the view of C F Bergström, for whom this was a 'rather minor attempt to bring about conceptual clarification'; *Comitology—Delegation of Powers to the Commission and the Committee System* (Oxford University Press 2005), at p 349.

[68] Different scenarios are possible: implementing powers may be conferred on the Commission or, in limited circumstances, on the Council, by basic acts adopted by Parliament and the Council, or by each of these acting alone.

[69] See Case C-274/12 P *Telefónica v Commission*, EU:C:2013:862, para 29.

does not entail implementing measures', including in principle implementing acts within the meaning of Article 291 TFEU.[70]

In accordance with this scheme, the political supervision of Union implementation should also fall to the Union institutions. This is not, however, the case under Article 291(3) TFEU; by conflating two distinct concepts of 'implementation', the Treaty authors have taken away supervisory functions heretofore vested in the Union's political institutions and transferred these to the Member States. While it is true that the national administrations may have a certain influence on the content of such implementing measures, particularly where the examination procedure is applied, the implementing act will nonetheless be adopted by the Commission,[71] which is answerable to Parliament and not the Member State governments. As noted in respect of delegated acts,[72] the Commission is obliged to consult broadly before formulating draft implementing rules and decisions, and in this regard the input of the national administrations is no doubt invaluable. However, neither this, nor the fact that it falls to the national administrations to apply such rules in concrete situations, justifies bestowing on them a monopoly of political supervision of the adoption of such rules, when the measures are formally adopted under the responsibility of the Union institutions. Be that as it may, *Roma locuta est, causa finita est.*

4.4.3 The mechanics of auto-conferral

In one other respect too, Article 291 TFEU may be said to have confounded Parliament's expectations, by allowing the Council to exercise implementing powers which it has conferred on itself. Under the pre-Lisbon regime, the Court had rejected a widely-practised technique, generally referred to as the inclusion in a legislative act of a 'secondary legal basis', whereby the Council granted itself the power to adopt a secondary normative act outside the confines of the comitology regime, under a procedure which allowed it to escape the requirements laid down by the legal basis of the basic legislation, notably the participation of the European Parliament or even the necessity for a Commission proposal. In *Refugee Procedures*, the Court held that the establishment of 'secondary legal bases, whether for the purpose of strengthening or easing the detailed rules for the adoption of an act, is tantamount to according that institution a legislative power which exceeds that provided for by the Treaty'.[73]

Now Article 291(2) TFEU permits the conferral of implementing powers on the Council 'in duly justified specific cases', and in the area of the common foreign and security policy. Given the predominant role of the Council and concomitantly modest functions vested in the Commission in foreign and security policy, the

[70] See Case C-583/11 P *Inuit Tapiriit Kanatami v Parliament and Council*, EU:C:2013:625.

[71] Except where these are conferred on the Council.

[72] See Section 4.3.4.

[73] Case C-133/06 *Parliament v Council*, EU:C:2008:257, para 56; see also Joined Cases C-317/13 and C-679/13, and Case C-540/13 *Parliament v Council*, EU:C:2015:223 and EU:C:2015:224 respectively.

latter possibility is amply justified. On the other hand, it is difficult to see why the Council should be entitled to exercise implementing powers outside that area. In practical terms, it is unlikely that, in an act adopted under an ordinary legislative procedure (or a special legislative procedure which provides for parliamentary consent), the European Parliament will be willing to countenance such auto-conferral other than very exceptionally.[74] It follows that in the vast majority of such cases, the Council acting under a special legislative procedure or an innominate non-legislative procedure will be permitted to confer implementing powers on itself, thereby in effect by-passing the material and procedural requirements of the Treaty legal basis.

The phrase 'duly justified specific cases' which qualifies the possibility for the Council to exercise implementing powers directly is clearly inspired by the Court's interpretation of the equivalent Treaty provision after the Single Act reforms, Article 145 EEC: 'the Council may reserve the right to exercise implementing powers directly only in specific cases, and it must state in detail the grounds for such a decision'.[75] This was generally taken to refer to the various scenarios under the 1987 Comitology Decision whereby the power to adopt a implementing act reverted to the Council, acting essentially in an executive, rather than a legislative, capacity.[76] While some argued that such a case should be considered sufficiently 'specific', in that reversion only arose when the committee voted in a particular manner, in general neither the recourse to the committee procedure nor the exercise by the Council of implementing powers was accompanied by any detailed statement of the reasons justifying this course of action.

The Court's phrase was then taken up in Article 1 of the 1999 Comitology Decision, which declared that the Council could only exercise implementing powers 'in specific and substantiated cases where the basic instrument [so provided]', that is, under the management or regulatory procedure and, following the 2006 reforms, the regulatory procedure with scrutiny. In *Refugee Procedures*, the Court not only confirmed the legitimacy of that limited form of conferral of implementing powers on the Council, it even invited the Council to defend the conferral provision at issue by 'requalifying' it as implementation *à la* comitology, rather than insisting that it was a secondary legal basis, an invitation which the Council refused.[77]

[74] And yet such conferrals exist; see e.g. Article 70(7) of Regulation (EU) 2014/806 of the European Parliament and of the Council of 15 July 2014 establishing uniform rules and a uniform procedure for the resolution of credit institutions and certain investment firms in the framework of a Single Resolution Mechanism and a Single Resolution Fund, OJ 2014 L 225/1, and Council Implementing Regulation (EU) 2015/81 of 19 December 2014 specifying uniform conditions of application of Regulation (EU) 2014/806 of the European Parliament and of the Council with regard to ex ante contributions to the Single Resolution Fund, OJ 2015 L 15/1.

[75] Case 16/88 *Commission v Council*, EU:C:1989:397, para 10.

[76] See generally K Bradley, 'Comitology and the Law: Through a Glass, Darkly' (1992) 29 CMLRev 693, at pp 714–17.

[77] Case C-133/06 (n 73), paras 45–51.

The wording of Article 291(3) TFEU appears prima facie to be somewhat more restrictive than the Court's formulation in *Commission v Council*;[78] it could be argued that it is notably not enough that the reservation be supported by a detailed statement of reasons, but the reasons themselves must stand up to substantive scrutiny, should the Court be called upon to review such a conferral. Remarkably, the Court does not appear ever to have had the occasion to apply the strictures it laid down in its 1989 judgment, possibly because those who challenged the conferral or exercise of such powers were only interested in an annulment on substantive, rather than procedural, grounds.

4.4.4 The Council in neo-comitology procedures: Now you see me...

One of Parliament's long-standing criticisms of the comitology system was that in effect it allowed the Council to control the entire process; under this analysis, comitology committees, being national officials operating under Council voting rules, were for all intents and purposes the same as the Council. This is, of course, a legal analysis of the system, which does not purport to take account of how such committees operate in daily practice. An alternative view of the situation pre-Lisbon posited the notion that 'in run of the mill cases, the "Committees" composed of mid-ranking officials have long lost their allegiance to their controllers and work very much within their own universe for what they perceive as their function and task'.[79]

In its proposal for the neo-comitology regulation, the Commission was at great pains to stress that there was no role for the Council in supervising the exercise by the Commission of its implementing powers.[80] The Regulation as adopted, however, provides for the participation of an 'appeal committee' which looks suspiciously like the Council writ (not particularly) small. The appeal committee intervenes in a small number of circumstances, to break the deadlock between the examination committee and the Commission, notably where the committee delivers a negative opinion but an implementing act is nonetheless deemed necessary, or for certain types of trade defence measures, or emergency measures required to protect the organization of the agricultural market or the Union's financial interests.[81]

The neo-comitology regulation says very little about the composition of the appeal committee, beyond noting somewhat redundantly in the preamble that it 'should meet at the appropriate level'. More candidly, the rules of procedure of the

[78] See Case 16/88 *Commission v Council*, EU:C:1989:397.

[79] J H H Weiler, 'Epilogue: "Comitology" as Revolution-Infranationalism, Constitutionalism and Democracy', in C Joerges and E Vos (eds) (n 63), at pp 339, 342.

[80] Commission Proposal of 9 February 2010 for a Regulation of the European Parliament and the Council laying down the rules and general principles concerning mechanisms for control by Member States of the Commission's exercise of implementing powers COM(2010) 83 final, section 1.

[81] Regulation (EU) 2011/182 (n 63), Articles 5(3), 5(5), second subparagraph, and 7, second paragraph.

appeal committee provide that the 'level of representation... should be of a sufficiently high and horizontal nature, including at Ministerial level [and as] a general rule... not below the level of members of [Coreper]'.[82] While it is true that the appeal committee is chaired by a Commission representative, it is also true that the chair does not take part in the committee vote; an appeal committee 'at Ministerial level' could arguably be seen as the Council in all but name, old-style comitology by the side door, as it were.

It is true that, unlike the Council under the pre-Lisbon comitology arrangements, the appeal committee does not enjoy any formal right to adopt implementing measures. Appeal committee members may nonetheless suggest amendments to the draft implementing act, and the Commission must 'endeavour to find solutions which command the widest possible support within the appeal committee', and report back to the committee on how their discussions and proposed amendments have been taken into account, 'in particular as regards suggestions for amendments which have been largely supported within the appeal committee'. A negative opinion of the appeal committee prevents the adoption of the Commission's draft implementing act; in the absence of an opinion, the Commission may adopt the act, while a positive opinion obliges it to do so.[83]

The practical impact of the participation of the appeal committee on Commission decision-making thus depends on a number of factors: the extent to which the Commission is prepared to defend its own draft acts, or whether it will formulate its draft implementing acts in the light of the known views of the examination and appeal committees, and whether the members of the appeal committee are prepared to reconsider the draft act on its merits, or merely reflect the opinions previously formulated by their respective national administrations. However, appeal committee members are unlikely to have 'lost allegiance to their controllers', as they are either the Permanent Representatives of the Member States, who are as close as this to the Ministers, or are themselves the controllers. The Commission's stated desire to keep the Council out of the implementation process has been significantly undermined by the addition of the appeal committee, it must be acknowledged, with Parliament's approval.

4.4.5 Implementation in practice: the return of Transgenic Maize

As Oscar Wilde might have said,[84] to lose one GMO stand-off with the Commission may be regarded as a misfortune; to lose two looks like carelessness. Yet this appears to be precisely what the legislature runs the risk of doing in incidents almost two decades, and several rounds of comitology reform, apart. The story of the adoption, against the opposition of a large majority of the Member State governments and of the European Parliament, of Commission Decision 1997/98, which allowed

82 Rules of Procedure of the Appeal Committee, OJ 2011 C 183/13.
83 Article 6 of Regulation (EU) 2011/182 (n 63).
84 Lady Bracknell to Mr Worthing, Act I, 'The Importance of Being Earnest' (1895).

the marketing of a line of maize genetically modified to resist corn borer and to tolerate a particular herbicide, has already been told.[85] If press reports are to be believed, history seems about to repeat itself, should the Commission carry out its intention to push ahead with the adoption of another genetically-modified maize product, in the teeth of the opposition of the European Parliament and the majority of the Member States which took a position on the matter.[86]

On the occasion of the adoption of the 1999 Comitology Decision, the Commission undertook, inter alia, in reviewing proposals in 'particularly sensitive sectors', to 'act in such a way as to avoid going against any predominant position which might emerge within the Council against the appropriateness of an implementing measure' under a regulatory procedure.[87] In the present case, the Commission's draft authorizing decision had not been adopted by the competent regulatory committee in early 2009; only six Member States, representing 91 votes (out of a total of 345 votes), favoured the measure, which was then submitted to the Council for approval.[88] Unsurprisingly, the Council was unable to adopt or reject the proposal, as either course of action would have required a qualified majority. In such circumstances, the relevant comitology provision stipulates that 'the proposed implementing act shall be adopted by the Commission'.[89]

A similar situation under the examination procedure, where the committee is unable to provide a negative or a positive opinion, would lead to a somewhat similar result, in that the Commission would be able to adopt the implementing act. Here, however, a simple majority of the component members of the committee (at present, fifteen Member State representatives), would be sufficient to prevent the adoption of the measure proposed. That said, if it considered the implementing act to be 'necessary', the Commission could either submit an amended draft to the committee or submit the original draft to the appeal committee, which would in turn be entitled to propose amendments or even block the adoption of the measure.[90]

[85] K Bradley, 'Alien Corn, or the Transgenic Procedural Maze', in R van Schendelen (ed), *EU Committees as Influential Policymakers* (Ashgate 1998), at p 207.

[86] For details of the procedure leading up to the proposal for a Council Decision authorising cultivation of 'Pioneer 1507' see Commission Proposal of 6 November 2013 for a Council decision concerning the placing on the market for cultivation of a maize product genetically modified for resistance to certain lepidopteran pests COM(2013) 758 final; the European Parliament opposed the proposal by resolution of 16 January 2014, P7_TA-PROV(2014)0036.

[87] Statement ad Article 5, OJ 1999 C 203/1.

[88] 12 Member States (127 votes) voted against the draft decision, while 9 Member States (127 votes) either abstained or did not participate in the vote which under a qualified majority procedure is tantamount to expressing opposition.

[89] Article 5(6), subpara 3, of the 1999 (second) Comitology Decision, Council Decision (EC) 1999/468 of 28 June 1999 laying down the procedures for the exercise of implementing powers conferred on the Commission, OJ 1999 L 184/23, applicable by virtue of Article 30(3) of Directive (EC) 2001/18 of the European Parliament and of the Council of 12 March 2001 on the deliberate release into the environment of genetically modified organisms, OJ 2001 L106/1; see also Case T-164/10 *Pioneer Hi-Bred International v Commission*, EU:T:2013:503.

[90] Article 5(4) of Regulation (EU) 2011/182 (n 63).

4.5 The Borderline between Delegating and Implementing Acts

4.5.1 Bright lines and grey zones

The most contentious issue which arises out of the new Treaty arrangements for the delegation of powers is that of the borderline between delegating and implementing acts. According to the Commission, there can be no overlap between these two types of instrument: '[an] act cannot be classified under two different headings at the same time...The authors of the new Treaty clearly intended the two articles to be mutually exclusive and indeed the resulting acts have different legal names'.[91] This ringing declaration does not assist in resolving the question of whether, and if so the extent to which, the legislature enjoys a discretion in classifying particular measures as delegated acts as opposed to implementing acts, or whether it is obliged, by the application of legal criteria, to opt for one and exclude the other.

In this regard, it has been noted that, whereas the Treaty defines a 'delegated act' in terms of its content ('non-legislative acts of general application [which] supplement or amend certain non-essential elements of the legislative act'), it identifies an 'implementing act' in terms of its rationale, that is, the necessity to lay down 'uniform conditions for implementing legally binding Union acts'.[92] It therefore becomes at least possible to imagine a secondary measure which is a delegated act as to its content, but an implementing act as to its *raison d'être*. To compound an already difficult situation, the near-exclusion of parliamentary supervision over the exercise of implementing powers *à la* Article 291 TFEU means that the European Parliament has a clear interest in favouring delegated acts over implementing acts, while the involvement of national officials, right up to 'Ministerial level', in the neo-comitology system provides the Council with a further incentive to opt for implementing acts. In this regard, the suggestion that, as the Commission is the principal beneficiary of the conferral of implementing powers, the Council would join with Parliament in preferring delegated acts seems somewhat improbable in principle and is not borne out in practice.[93]

4.5.2 Some examples from practice: principle vs politics

The divergence of interests and the ambiguity of the Treaty provisions are a recipe for interinstitutional friction, which has occasionally risen. One such *casus belli* was the classification of strategy papers for the geographical and thematic programmes the Commission adopts on the basis of the regulation on a financial instrument for

[91] COM(2009) 673 final (n 52), section 2.2, 3.

[92] See e.g. T Christiansen and M Dobbels (n 1).

[93] C Blumann, 'Actes législatives et mesures d'exécution dans le projet de Constitution pour l'Europe', in J Andriantsimbazovina et al, *Les dynamiques du droit européen en début de siècle: études en l'honneur de Jean Claude Gautron* (Editions A Pedone 2004), at pp 249 and 263.

development cooperation,[94] and the multiannual indicative programmes which are based on the strategy papers. A geographic 'strategy paper' sets out 'a coherent framework for cooperation between the [Union] and the partner country or region concerned'; multiannual indicative programmes 'set out the priority areas selected for [Union] financing, the specific objectives, the expected results and the performance indicators'. A 'thematic strategy paper' is the equivalent document for a 'theme', that is, a Union activity in which the shared interest of the partner countries is not determined by geography.

In the debates on the revision of this regulation in 2011, Parliament took the view that these papers and programmes were guidelines of general application which supplement the basic act, and should thus be classed as delegated acts. For its part, the Council considered that the strategy papers and programmes were not of general scope, because they were addressed to third countries, and were in any case not binding; in consequence, they should be considered implementing acts.[95] The 2011 amendments to the Regulation reflect the Council's view, in that all the strategy papers and multiannual programmes, as well as any reviews of these instruments and any accompanying measures, are to be adopted as implementing measures,[96] though the Commission undertook to 'propose the extensive use of delegated acts' in this area in the future.[97]

A similar row blew up regarding secondary measures to give effect to two environmental measures, the revised WEEE directive and the biocidal products regulation, which the Council again insisted were implementing acts, again successfully. On this occasion too, Parliament preferred not to sacrifice the substantive measure in order to make an institutional point, though adopting a statement to the effect that the measures adopted were 'the result of a delicate compromise, which in some cases departs from Parliament's position in first reading... Parliament has accepted implementing acts instead of delegated acts in certain specific cases'. In true Magrittian style, Parliament declared in each case that 'these provisions shall not be taken or used as a precedent'.[98]

4.5.3 The *Biocides* judgment: Delphic or pragmatic?

The matter does not end there, however. In what looks like a rare act of institutional altruism,[99] the Commission initiated proceedings for the annulment of

[94] Regulation (EC) 2006/1905 of the European Parliament and of the Council of 18 December 2006 establishing a financing instrument for development cooperation, OJ 2006 L 378/41.

[95] Council first reading position, 10 December 2010, Doc 16442/10 ADD1 REV1.

[96] Article 21 of Regulation (EC) 2006/1905 (n 94) (as amended by Regulation (EU) 2011/1340, OJ 2011 L347/34).

[97] Commission Communication of 29 June 2011, A Budget for Europe 2020, COM(2011) 500 final, at p 24; see now Regulation (EU) 2014/233 of the European Parliament and of the Council of 11 March 2014 establishing a financing instrument for development cooperation for the period 2014–20, OJ 2014 L77/44.

[98] Legislative resolutions of 19 January 2012, P7_TA(2012)0009 and P7_TA(2012)0010.

[99] The Commission's position is in principle much more comfortable under a comitology procedure than under delegation.

Article 80 of the Biocides regulation,[100] which classifies as an implementing act the regulation the Commission adopts regarding the fees and charges payable to the European Chemical Agency for a Union authorization. The Commission argued that in reality Article 80 attributes delegated powers by allowing it to supplement the basic regulation in several respects: the coordination of the sources of Agency financing, the definition of exceptions to the principle that fees must be proportionate to the service provided, of the circumstances justifying waiver of the fee, and of the conditions of payment, and the establishment of criteria for fee reductions in favour of small and medium-sized enterprises (SMEs). The Court rejected the Commission's challenge, holding that the Regulation provided a 'complete legal framework' as regards the matters raised by the Commission.

The Court held that in the absence of a definition of 'implementing act' in Article 291 TFEU, this concept must be interpreted together with that of 'delegated act' as defined in Article 290 TFEU. Whereas a delegated act contains 'rules coming within the regulatory framework as defined by the basic legislative act', an implementing act is designed 'to provide further detail in relation to the content of a legislative act,[101] in order to ensure that it is implemented under uniform conditions in all Member States'. Having established this distinction, which it described as a 'contrast', between these two forms of act, the Court went on to hold that 'the EU legislature has discretion when it decides to confer a delegated power…or an implementing power…Consequently, judicial review is limited to manifest errors of assessment as to whether the EU legislature could reasonably have taken the view, first, that the legal framework…needs only the addition of further detail, without its non-essential elements having to be amended or supplemented and, secondly, that the provisions of the [basic act] require uniform conditions for implementation'.[102]

The Court's reluctance to lay down any brightline test for distinguishing between the scope of application of delegated and implementing powers has been criticized, particularly in the light of an 'emerging consensus' in favour of the margin of discretion left to the Commission as a criterion.[103] The extent of the Commission's discretion could, however, prove unworkable in practice. It is difficult to imagine any act, delegated or implementing, which would leave the Commission with *no* margin of discretion, so then the question is what margin of discretion would tip the balance in favour of a delegated act as opposed to an implementing act? Would a 'considerable amount of discretion' do the job? Is this the same as a 'significant

[100] Regulation (EU) 2012/528 of the European Parliament and of the Council of 22 May 2012 concerning the making available on the market and use of biocidal products, OJ 2012 L 127/1; Case C-427/12 (n 27).

[101] Strictly speaking 'an act based directly on the Treaty'; acts adopted by an innominate non-legislative procedure (n 2) may also provide for implementing, though not delegated, acts.

[102] Case C-427/12 (n 27), para 40.

[103] D Ritleng, 'The dividing line between delegated and implementing acts: The Court of Justice sidesteps the difficulty in *Commission* v. *Parliament and Council (Biocides)*' (2015) 52 CMLRev 243, 253–4.

amount', or would the Commission only be able to adopt implementing measures where its discretion was 'insignificant' in extent?

Moreover, the Court's holding in this regard reflects the absence of Treaty rules constraining the legislature's choice. In effect, the Court held that the assessment of which type of act is appropriate for a particular secondary normative measure is a policy choice; in line with the established case law on judicial review of policy decisions, the Court will only interfere with such legislative assessments in very limited circumstances, such as a manifest error or abuse of power or procedure.[104] The Court did not take up the Commission's invitation to focus on 'the nature and the purpose of the powers conferred on the Commission',[105] preferring instead to exercise marginal review of whether the legislature had laid down a complete legal framework. Having carried out a prima facie examination of the different elements on which the Commission relied to demonstrate its powers were delegated rather than implementing, the Court concluded that the legislature had not committed any manifest error of appreciation or other abuse, in considering the basic regulation complied with this standard. It does not, of course, follow from the judgment that the institutions have any discretion not to comply with the criteria laid down by Articles 290 and 291 TFEU for recourse to each type of secondary act.[106]

This aspect of the judgment has been criticized on the ground that 'there is no foundation for adopting a different solution' in the case of delegated and implementing acts to that adopted for demarcating essential and non-essential elements.[107] The dividing line between these two types of act is, however, not obviously a question 'of similar nature' to that between legislative and non-legislative measures. As the legislature chooses the form of secondary act and the supervisory arrangements under which the delegated or implementing powers are exercised, whichever type of measure it opts for, it will have fully discharged the duties imposed on it by the Treaty. On the other hand, if the Commission were to be empowered by a legislative act to adopt the essential elements of the matter to be regulated, the legislature would not have fulfilled its legal or democratic obligations in respect of those elements.[108]

The suggestion that in *Biocides* the Court concluded that 'the more specific the "criteria and conditions" established by the EU legislature... the more reasonable a delegation of implementing powers'[109] appears to be predicated on the notion that the legality of a choice of secondary act is in some way a matter of degree. To succeed under the 'manifest error' test, however, the party challenging the choice of secondary act must demonstrate that the error or abuse is obvious; here the Commission had not been able to establish that the legislative framework was manifestly incomplete. The suggestion that 'the Court did

104 Case C-58/08 *Ex parte Vodafone and others*, EU:C:2010:321, para 52.
105 Case C-427/12 (n 27), para 23. 106 Ibid, para 41.
107 D Ritleng (n 103), at p 254.
108 See the discussion on the ruling in *Schengen Borders Code*, Section 4.2.2.
109 C F Bergström, 'Shaping the New System for Delegation of Powers to EU Agencies: *United Kingdom* v. *European Parliament and Council (Short selling)*' (2015) 52 CMLRev 219, 239.

actually, under the veil of a control limited to manifest errors of assessment, exercise full review' of the legality of the choice of an implementing act is also unconvincing.[110] The number of paragraphs the Court required to establish the absence of any such errors reflects the completeness of the Commission's arguments and the thoroughness of the Court's reasoning, rather than the putative soundness of the arguments in question. Thus, to take the Commission's submissions concerning its duty to take account of the specific needs of SMEs as an example, the mere fact that the basic regulation provided that the fees must be set at a level which ensures that the Agency's costs are covered and takes account of the specific features of SMEs, and that SMEs may pay by instalments, was adjudged to comprise a 'complete legal framework' in this regard.[111] This appears to fall some way short of 'full review'.

The Court has subsequently clarified, if the matter were in any doubt, that an implementing act may not amend or supplement the non-essential elements of a basic legislative act.[112] This analysis is clearly in line with the idea that Articles 290 and 291 TFEU establish a hierarchy of norms, with delegated acts coming above implementing acts in that hierarchy, as the working group on simplification of the European Convention had intended when it proposed 'three levels with regard to the adoption of acts within the framework of the European Union'.[113] More recently, the Court has upheld the validity of a 'cascade' system of Commission actions, whereby it first adopts an implementing act, then if this does not have the desired effect, a delegated act, and finally a legislative proposal.[114]

4.6 The Future of Delegation: Balancing Eggs?

At the time of writing, the modification of the current arrangements for the adoption of delegated acts is under active consideration, on the basis of Parliament's resolution of 25 February 2014[115] and the Council's 'initiative to complement the Common Understanding on Delegated Acts as regards the consultation of experts', which it transmitted officially to Parliament in February 2014 and again in March 2015.[116] Perhaps old habits die hard, but one might be forgiven for thinking that the institutions concerned were dealing with two completely different problems;

[110] D Ritleng (n 103), at p 254. [111] Case C-427/12 (n 27), para 52.

[112] Case C-65/13 (n 38), para 46.

[113] Final Report of Working Group IX on Simplification of 29 November 2002 (n 3), at p 9.

[114] Regulation (EU) 2013/1289 of the European Parliament and of the Council of 11 December 2013 amending Council Regulation (EC) 2001/539 listing the third countries whose nationals must be in possession of visas when crossing the external borders and those whose nationals are exempt from that requirement, OJ 2013 L 347/74; Case C-88/14 *Commission v Parliament and Council*, EU:C:2015:499.

[115] N 44 and Sections 4.3.2 and 4.3.3.

[116] Initiative to complement the Common Understanding on Delegated Acts as regards the consultation of experts, Council Doc 6774/14 of 21 February 2014; See also Council Doc 6773/15 of 3 March 2015 which is essentially a covering note, though it is not lacking in substantive interest.

though they identify in essentially similar terms the difficulties which they had encountered in the first four years of the application of the Lisbon Treaty, the solutions they propose are miles apart, and indeed each proposes the amendment of a different interinstitutional agreement.[117]

The Council's analysis is that 'many of the difficulties experienced are due to insufficient guarantees about a proper consultation of experts during the preparation of delegated acts', a concern it claims is shared by Parliament;[118] the failure to address this matter 'was the main reason for the Council's... first objection to a delegated act'. Its proposed solution is Member State experts, more Member States experts, and yet more Member State experts. In particular, the Commission should systematically consult groups of such experts before proposing delegated acts, 'endeavour to find solutions which command the widest possible support within [the group and]... inform [the group] of the manner in which its discussions and suggestions for amendments have been taken into account, in particular as regards those suggestions which have been largely supported within' the group. When adopting a delegated act, 'the Commission shall take the utmost account of the opinion delivered by' the group.

In case this sounds somewhat familiar, the suggested provisions are a copy-paste of the provisions of the neo-comitology regulation governing the powers and duties of either the examination procedure (as regards expert group amendments) or the advisory procedure ('utmost account').[119] Not without a certain dry humour, the Council notes in the explanatory note to its initiative that 'the purpose of the [expert group] procedure is not to establish a mechanism for control by Member States of the Commission's exercise of the power to adopt delegated acts' but merely 'to assist the Commission through an ex-ante consultation in its preparatory work'.[120] Folk with longer memories will recall that under the 1987 and 1999 decisions the task of comitology committees also purported to be that of 'assisting' the Commission,[121] while commentators of more recent vintage will note that precisely the same provisions as the Council is now proposing are, in the context of Article 291(3) TFEU, described as 'mechanisms for control by Member

[117] Parliament proposes the revision of the Agreement on Better Law-making (resolution of 25 February 2014, para 2 (n 44)), while the Council's initiative concerns the Common Understanding on Delegated Acts (n 51).

[118] The Council initiative, which was adopted on 19 February 2014, cited the report of Parliament's legal affairs committee, rather than awaiting the adoption by Parliament of the text of the resolution, the content of which it may have hoped in vain to influence.

[119] See Articles 3(4), 2nd subpara, and 4, Regulation (EU) 2011/182 (n 63).

[120] Council initiative (n 116), at p 5.

[121] In *Rothmans International* the then Court of First Instance relied on the fact that a comitology committee 'assisted' the Commission in order to hold that the documents of such committees are to be considered Commission documents (see Case T-188/97 *Rothmans International v Commission*, EU:T:1999:156, para 58). It was noted at the time that 'blocking the adoption by the Commission of [its proposed measure], or causing its referral to the Council... is the kind of "assistance" the Commission might prefer to do without': K Bradley, 'The Institutional Law of the European Union in 1999' (2000) 19 YEL 547, at p 555.

States of the exercise of implementing powers'. In short, in the domain of delegated powers the Council is proposing comitology by the front door.

That the insufficient consultation of national experts should be the root cause of the legislature's difficulties in deciding on the delegation of powers over the first four years of the Lisbon regime, and the further implication of such experts in this process a panacea, might come as news for the European Parliament. In the eight and a half pages of its resolution of 25 February 2014, such experts are mentioned just twice; once where Parliament calls on the Commission to keep it informed of the scheduled meetings of expert groups, and once where it urges the Commission to simplify the procedure for the invitation of Parliament's experts to such meetings. This less than ringing endorsement of the Council's analysis should also be read in the light of the view of Parliament's legal affairs committee in March 2010 that '[c]ontrol of power delegated by the Legislator should in all logic remain the preserve of the Legislator... In particular, Member States and *a fortiori* committees composed of experts from the Member States, have no role to play in this area'.[122]

In the third season of *House of Cards (US)*, Frank Underwood attempts to balance an egg on his desk; his failure to do so prompts a radical rethink in his strategy, seeking to exploit, rather than attempt to fight, political developments he cannot prevent. Warding off the participation of national experts in the preparation of delegated acts may prove as futile as balancing eggs, and Parliament too might have an interest in adopting a more strategic approach to the matter. After all, there appears to be much good sense in what the Council says. Proper prior consultation is widely considered the foundation of sound policy-making, as is recognized by the Treaty-imposed obligation on the Commission to 'carry out broad consultations'; it is also true that 'the Member States' authorities will be responsible for implementing or transposing delegated acts'.[123] Moreover, if bringing groups of Member States' experts in on the act is the price to pay to persuade the Council to resort more freely to delegated acts as opposed to implementing acts,[124] it may prove to be a bargain; in exchange, Parliament could insist, for example, on having the right to revoke individual delegated acts, at least in areas in which it distrusts the policy line likely to be pursued by the Commission,[125] and on imposing the same degree of transparency on the work of such groups as currently obtains for comitology committees. There is also no particular reason, at a time when the human resources of the Union institutions are being squeezed until the pips squeak, that Parliament and its committees should not seek to benefit from

[122] Section 7, EP Doc A-7-110/2010.

[123] Respectively Article 11(3) TEU and Council initiative (n 116), at p 3.

[124] Where this is not 'manifestly erroneous' in the terms of the judgment in *Biocides* (Section 4.5.3), or otherwise illegal.

[125] For example in relation to the authorization of the cultivation of genetically-modified plants (see Section 4.4.5).

the expertise of the Member State administrations, as they already do from the Commission and representatives of civil society.[126] How ironic it would be if the application of comitology to delegated acts were to be the occasion of greater interinstitutional cooperation and efficiency after more than fifty years of strife and waste.

[126] The balance of evidence would suggest that parliamentary committees do not currently receive information from comitology committees, and have not done so in the past to any discernible extent.

PART II

AN EMPIRICAL ASSESSMENT

5

Interinstitutional Tensions in the New System for Delegation of Powers

*Thomas Christiansen and Mathias Dobbels**

5.1 Introduction

The Lisbon Treaty established a new legal basis for the comitology procedures and creates two new instruments: delegated and implementing acts.[1] Article 290 TFEU provides for the possibility to delegate the power to adopt non-legislative delegated acts that are of 'general application', and 'supplement or amend non-essential' elements of the basic legal act to the Commission. The article also provides for post hoc control to be exercised by the European Parliament and the Council, either through the right to revoke the delegation or the right to object to the adoption of a specific delegated act within a time limit set by the basic legal act. Article 291 TFEU, on the other hand, confers the right to implement legislation to the Member States. However, where there are uniform conditions for implementation, it shall in principle be conferred to the Commission. In these cases, however, neither the Council nor the European Parliament has the right to substantially control the Commission's exercise of these implementing powers, which is the prerogative of the Member States. They exercise this *ex ante* right of control through specialized committees composed of Member State representatives that scrutinize and discuss draft implementing acts before they are adopted by the Commission. As set out in the Comitology Regulation, the standard rule in this control procedure is that Member States can stop a Commission act from being adopted by qualified majority, while also providing for an advisory procedure that facilitates the provision of non-binding opinions.[2]

* The authors gratefully acknowledge the research assistance provided by Lana Damm, Carmen Esser, Natascha Spörle, and Dustin Williams.

[1] Notwithstanding the formal distinction introduced by the Lisbon Treaty between 'delegated acts' (Article 290 TFEU) and 'implementing acts' (Article 291 TFEU), in this chapter we will consider both types of acts of implementation in the broader sense of the word, i.e. as acts whose purpose it is to implement a previously enacted basic act (cf. the original notion of 'implementation' in Section 1.2).

[2] Regulation (EU) 2011/182 of the European Parliament and of the Council of 16 February 2011 laying down the rules and general principles concerning mechanisms for control by Member States of the Commission's exercise of implementing powers, OJ 2011 L 55/13.

While important aspects of this round of reform are the changes to the formal procedures and the legal questions the new framework throws up—not least the quandary of the 'choice' that the EU legislator now has between the Article 290 and the Article 291 procedures—another dimension concerns the impact that these changes have had on the actual practice of legislative implementation. After all, the Lisbon reform had been agreed in the context of a simplification of the system, while the recognition of the role of the European Parliament in the scrutiny of delegated acts also promised a greater degree of democratic legitimacy for this traditionally technocratic part of EU decision-making. However, as we have discussed elsewhere, it is arguable that the reform did not really achieve these objectives.[3] At the same time, there have been concerns that the reform, with the introduction of the European Parliament as a new veto-player, might make decision-making more cumbersome, create more lengthy interinstitutional negotiations, and as a result reduce the efficiency of a system that until then had worked very well considering the history of interinstitutional tensions.

Following these considerations, the starting point for the analysis advanced in this chapter is the question as to how the Lisbon Treaty reform has impacted in practice on interinstitutional relations and on the adoption of delegated and implementing acts. In particular, we look at a number of areas of potential conflict and examine if and how the new system has improved or worsened the efficiency of decision-making, in order to be able to provide an assessment as to how the delegation of powers works.

5.2 Interinstitutional Tensions and Delegation: Potential Sites of Conflict

In the EU's system of administrative governance, the adoption of implementing acts relies on the effective and continuous cooperation of the three legislative institutions of Parliament, Council, and Commission (as well as the Member States represented in other bodies involved in the process). Traditionally, there has been considerable tension, if not outright conflict, between these institutions concerning the setting of the underlying 'rules of the game',[4] a state of affairs demonstrated not least by a significant body of case law that has accumulated over the past decades.[5]

[3] T Christiansen and M Dobbels, 'Delegated Powers and Inter-Institutional Relations in the EU after Lisbon : A Normative Assessment' (2013) 36 West European Politics 1159.

[4] M Alfe and T Christiansen, 'Institutional Tensions in the Evolution of Comitology', in T Christiansen and B Vaccari (eds), *21st Century Comitology: The Role of Implementation Committees in the Wider European Union* (EIPA 2009), at pp 37–51.

[5] A Türk 'The Development of Case Law in the Area of Comitology', in T Christiansen and B Vaccari (eds), *21st Century Comitology: The Role of Implementation Committees in the Wider European Union* (EIPA 2009), at pp 52–70.

However, while these disputes have traditionally been about constitutional or meta-legislative questions—the principles underpinning the choice of correct procedures, each institution's formal prerogatives, the provision of information or rights of scrutiny—the system has in practice operated rather smoothly, with actual problems in the application of the procedures or disagreements preventing the timely exercise of delegated powers being few and far between,[6] even if there have been continuing limitations concerning the access to documents.[7] Indeed, some observers have gone as far as suggesting that comitology, rather than being a tool for the control of the Commission by the Member States should rather be seen as a site of a fusion between the national and European administrative domains.[8]

It is therefore important in assessing the impact of the Lisbon reforms in this area to go beyond the wording of treaty articles, framework regulations, and interinstitutional agreements. While these foundational texts may well provide indications as to the latent conflict they incorporate, the proof is in the proverbial pudding, namely in the way in which these formal provisions are actually applied in the day-to-day practice of the Union. This chapter seeks to provide such an account of delegated powers in practice by identifying four sites of potential conflict, as detailed below, and analysing the degree to which interinstitutional tensions can be identified here in the period immediately after the coming into force of the Lisbon Treaty.

5.2.1 The adoption of legislative acts under the ordinary legislative procedure

The key decisions on the use of a particular procedure for implementation are being made in the legislative process, as it is at this point that European Parliament and Council must agreed on whether to make use Article 290 TFEU or Article 291 TFEU, and, in case it is the latter, choose between the advisory and the examination procedure. Similar choices between the various comitology procedures also had to be made previously—an area of occasionally serious disagreement between the institutions, as demonstrated by the relevant case law from the Court of Justice, but one could argue that the choice post-Lisbon is starker: now it concerns a rather fundamental choice between either including or excluding the European Parliament from the scrutiny over implementation.

[6] See M Alfé, G J Brandsma and T Christiansen, 'The Functioning of Comitology Committees in Practice', in T Christiansen and B Vaccari (eds), *21st Century Comitology: The Role of Implementation Committees in the Wider European Union* (EIPA 2009), at pp 95–105.

[7] See G J Brandsma, D Curtin, and A Meijer, 'How Transparent are EU "Comitology" Committees in Practice?' (2008) 14 ELJ 819.

[8] See W Wessels, 'Comitology: fusion in action. Politico-administrative trends in the EU system' (1998) 5 JEPP 209; T Christiansen, 'Administrative Fusion in the European Union—Reviewing 10 Years of Comitology Reform', in U Diedrichs, A Faber, F Tekin, and G Umbach (eds), *Europe Reloaded: Differentiation or Fusion?* (Nomos 2010).

The situation is aggravated by the fact that the treaty does not provide a clear-cut answer to the question of which article should be applied to which kind of implementing measure, opening the possibility that disagreements over this choice might add to the time it takes to reach agreement under the ordinary legislative procedure.

5.2.2 The introduction of expert groups in the area of delegated acts

The procedure to be followed under Article 290 TFEU does away with the requirement on the Commission to submit its draft implementing acts to comitology committees, but nevertheless the Common Understanding that was adopted by European Parliament, Council, and Commission in 2011 did foresee the establishment of groups of national experts that the Commission would consult on proposed delegated acts. This also constitutes a site of potential interinstitutional conflict: while these expert groups can be seen as filling the void after the discontinuation of the use of the relevant comitology committees, the Commission has been adamant that—in line with the wording of the treaty—it would not need the approval of such expert groups before adopting the act and that the deliberations of these experts groups would be entirely non-binding. The European Parliament, for its part, has insisted that it should also have the right to be involved in this consultative process—something which could be interpreted as a demand to participate in the work of these expert groups.

5.2.3 The EU legislator(s) objecting to delegated acts or revoking delegated powers

While the adoption of delegated acts may have been streamlined in that the Commission in this area does not have to contend with comitology committees, the shifting of the control function to the *ex post* stage means that now both legislative institutions have the right to object to Commission acts—a situation which brings with it a degree of uncertainty (perhaps alleviated by the above-mentioned expert groups) and the potential for delays in the adoption of delegated acts as the Commission faces—possibly repeated—objections from either the Council or the European Parliament. The absence of a dedicated dispute settlement process (as provided for in the remaining area of 'comitology proper' discussed in the next section) heightens this concern and creates pressure on all parties involved to set up viable channels of communication to liaise about the reasons for possible or actual objections. Still more damaging to the efficiency of the process could be the unilateral right of either legislative institution to revoke the delegated powers entirely, thereby creating the need for the adoption of an entirely new legislative act with a different mode of implementing it—a potentially time-consuming process that would imply a temporary block on implementation altogether.

5.2.4 The role of the Appeal Committee set up under the Comitology Regulation

The first Comitology Regulation adopted under Article 291 TFEU created a new appeal process to address the situation in which the Commission failed to receive the required majority in the comitology committee. When previously such referrals would have landed at the door of the Council, this avenue was foreclosed post-Lisbon in recognition that the Council, as a legislative institution, would have to share any role it had in the process with the European Parliament. Instead, in recognition of the wording of the treaty under which it is the *Member States* rather than the Council that exercise scrutiny rights under Article 291 TFEU, the Regulation established the legal base for a new committee composed of Member State representatives, that would hear appeals arising from lack of agreements in the comitology system. However, the new Appeal Committee is not a formal institution of the Union, and as such not empowered to adopt any measures itself, but merely to issue opinions on the Commission's proposed acts, which is why the new procedure requires the Commission to enter into a kind of 'conversation' with the Appeal Committee before it can adopt an implementing act that is acceptable to the Member States.

In the following sections, we examine empirically in some detail developments in each of these areas, charting the introduction of new procedures and institutional arrangements following the coming into force of the Lisbon Treaty. This analysis is based on data covering the immediate period after the new regime for delegated acts became fully operational, following the interinstitutional agreement on a Common Understanding regarding Article 290 TFEU and the adoption of the Comitology Regulation.[9] In the final conclusion, this chapter will then draw some overarching conclusions on the impact that the Lisbon Treaty reforms have had on interinstitutional relations in the area of delegated acts. As we will show in the empirical analysis, while there is considerable *potential* for conflict among the three main institutions, this has so far not led to a significant slowdown in activity—the efficiency of the system appears to have been maintained for the time being.

5.3 Interinstitutional Tensions and Delegation: the Legislative Process

The first and arguably most important question mark concerning the efficiency of the reformed system has been whether the choice between Articles 290 and Article 291 TFEU that the Lisbon Treaty opened up would become a problem in the legislative process—whether bargaining between Parliament and Council might delay the adoption of the basic acts and thereby make legislative decision-making

[9] See Regulation (EU) 2011/182 (n 2).

more difficult than it would otherwise have been. While this is inherently difficult to study, considering the hypothetical nature of the question, one way of attempting an answer is to go through all basic acts adopted in a particular year and identify any instances in the course of the legislative procedure that could be shown to have impacted on the time frame for their adoption. We have conducted such an analysis for basic acts adopted in 2012, and while this year was still early days for the new system and might therefore not turn out to be representative of subsequent practice, the data does shine an interesting light on interinstitutional bargaining over the choice between delegating powers via Article 290 and Article 291 TFEU—or rather, the absence of such bargaining.

In the course of 2012, a total of seventy-three basic acts were adopted (forty-seven Regulations, eighteen Directives, and eight Decisions). While about half (51%) of these did not contain any provisions for the delegation of powers, the remainder did involve reference to either Article 290 TFEU (nine acts/11%) or Article 291 TFEU (eleven acts/12%) or both (sixteen acts/22%). This simple distinction indicates that potential problems over the choice of the procedure would be limited to about half of all acts being adopted, and that about equal use is being made use of delegated acts and implementing acts as modes of delegating powers to the Commission.

Looking in detail at the passage of each individual act through the decision-making process of the ordinary legislative procedure indicates that only in a very small number of cases did the inclusion of delegated powers in the basic act become an issue for either of the legislative institutions. Among the basic acts adopted in 2012 that make reference to Article 290 TFEU, there were only three cases in which the choice of the procedure became a matter of interinstitutional bargaining and could therefore be classified as a cause of legislative delays (see Table 5.1). Thus the number of acts in which at least some of the time in negotiations between Parliament and Council was taken up with discussions about delegated powers was comparatively small: the number of three basic acts equates to 12% of all acts in which reference to Article 290 TFEU was made, and just 4.11% of all basic acts adopted in 2012.[10]

[10] These were: Regulation (EU) 2012/530 of the European Parliament and of the Council of 13 June 2012 on the accelerated phasing-in of double-hull or equivalent design requirements for single-hull oil tankers, OJ 2012 L 172/3; Regulation (EU) 2012/966 of the European Parliament and of the Council of 25 October 2012 on the financial rules applicable to the general budget of the Union and repealing Council Regulation (EC) 2002/1605, OJ 2012 L 298/1; and Directive (EU) 2012/19 of the European Parliament and of the Council of 4 July 2012 on waste electrical and electronic equipment, OJ 2012 L 197/38. In each of these cases, the statements attached by the European Parliament to the amendments adopted refer to the search for compromise between it and the Council concerning the matter of Delegated Acts. The difficulty these decisions posed are most apparent in the case of Directive (EU) 2012/19 where the European Parliament declared that it had given in to the Council on the issue of the choice between delegated and implementing acts. While the Commission proposal contained the use of Article 290 TFEU across the board, something also insisted on by the European Parliament in its first reading position, it did accept, in its second reading agreement, that in certain cases the Commission could use implementing acts instead—thereby accepting the demands of the Council. It added, however, that this agreement ought not to set a precedent for regulating similar matters in future legal acts.

Table 5.1 Observed difficulties and/or delays with delegated powers in the negotiation of basic acts in 2012

	Regulations	Directives	Decisions	all
Total number of Basic Acts (2012)	47	18	8	73
Distribution of Art.290 provisions	17	8	0	25
Percentage of all acts	68%	32%	0	100%
Distribution of Art.291 provisions	17	8	2	27
Percentage of all acts	62, 96%	29, 63%	7, 41%	100%
Delay, difficulties with Art.290 provisions	2	1	0	3
Percentage of all acts with Art.290 provisions	8%	4%	n/a	12%
Percentage of all basic acts	2, 74%	1, 40%	n/a	4, 14%
Delay, difficulties with Art.291 provisions	0	1	0	1
Percentage of all acts with Art.291 provisions	n/a	3, 70%	n/a	3, 70%
Percentage of all basic acts	n/a	1, 37%	–	1, 37%

Source: Data compiled by the authors

With regard to the use of Article 291 procedures, the picture is even more stark: there was only a single case among the twenty-seven basic acts making reference to 'comitology proper', the equivalent of 3.70% of all such acts, or 1.34% of all basic acts.[11] And given the fact that this one problematic act for Article 291 inclusion was already included in the list of difficulties encountered regarding Article 290, there was in fact a sum total of three out of the total seventy-three acts where the use of delegated powers became an issue, that is, in just over 4% of all acts.

It is impossible to say without more detailed research how long the actual 'delay' was in each of these cases,[12] as other matters, potentially more salient to the decision-makers in either institution, were also raised in the course of the negotiations. Be that as it may, the fact that these acts were after all adopted despite interinstitutional disagreements about the question of delegated powers demonstrates that this question did not constitute a 'deal-breaker' that would have prevented an ultimate agreement.[13]

[11] Directive (EU) 2012/19, ibid, containing references to both Article 290 TFEU and Article 291 TFEU.

[12] The time between the publication of the legislative proposal and the adoption of the act was 8 months in the case of Regulation (EU) 2012/530, 22 months in the case of Regulation (EU) 2012/966, and 43 months in the case of Directive (EU) 2012/19. Consequently, the timely adoption of the latter two acts was also affected by the coming into force of the Lisbon Treaty during the legislative procedure, changing the circumstances concerning the choice of the implementing procedure as a result.

[13] It needs to be recognized that by selecting only *adopted* acts, i.e. by looking only at legislative procedures that have produced a positive result, we have not considered in our sample any failed attempts to adopt basic acts, including those that might have failed due to disagreements over the use of delegated powers. Such hypothetical failures are, however, difficult to research and to our knowledge there have been no such cases in the period under investigation.

The quantitative measure of counting the number of basic acts in which problems with the use of delegated powers were encountered is also rather rudimentary and potentially misleading, assuming as it does that all basic acts are of equal relevance. In practice, some basic acts are clearly more important than others, and thus the assessment of legislative delays should take into account the relative significance of the act concerned. Again, this would require further research into the substance of, and intensity of interests at stake in, each of these basic acts.

However, notwithstanding these limitations, the impression left after a superficial analysis of the legislative record of the first year of the new system in action indicates that the negative impact has been rather minimal, with less than 5% of the total number of basic acts affected in some way by disputes over the nature and extent of the Commission's delegated powers. In each of these cases, agreement was ultimately reached and therefore did not prevent the adoption of the act. On the face of it, this data suggests that EU lawmaking after Lisbon has been barely affected by the greater complexity of delegated powers and the potential for interinstitutional dispute. The idea that legislative decision-making might be bogged down by disagreements about procedural matters between the European Parliament and the Council is certainly not supported by the analysis of developments in 2012.

5.4 The Role of 'Expert Groups' in the Preparation of Delegated Acts—Comitology Reinvented

The main differences in terms of control between the two new instruments are the timing of control (*ex ante* with implementing acts and *post hoc* with delegated acts) and the fact that the institutions are excluded from the control on implementing acts. Analysis of the negotiations on the establishment of the procedures governing the two new instruments after the ratification of the Lisbon Treaty already indicated this could develop into a source of conflict.[14] Member States were shown to be sceptical about the use of delegated acts as it only implied *post hoc* control rights and could potentially give much freedom to the Commission in fulfilling the powers that were delegated. The Commission eventually accepted the introduction of a standard recital that had to be inserted in every basic legal act that delegated powers to the Commission saying that it would consult experts when expertise was needed in the preparation of delegated acts. Important to know is that the Member States had demanded that *national* experts be consulted,

[14] T Christiansen and M Dobbels, 'Comitology and delegated acts after Lisbon: How the European Parliament lost the implementation game' (2012) 16 European Integration online Papers (EIoP) Article 13; G J Brandsma and J Blom-Hansen, 'Negotiating the Post-Lisbon Comitology System: Institutional Battles over Delegated Decision-Making' (2012) 50 JCMS 939.

Table 5.2 Distribution of Expert Groups by Sector

Directorate-General (Aug 2014)	Number of Expert Groups
AGRI	4
BUDG	1
CLIMA	1
ENTR	2
ENV	3
MARE	1
MARKT	3
MOVE	5
REGIO	1
SANCO	9
TRADE	1

but that on the insistence of the European Parliament the word 'national' was deleted. This implies that external experts or those appointed by the European Parliament should be consulted as well. Table 5.2 above shows the range of experts appointed since 2011.

Previous research has shown that the fact that the recital fails to define how these consultations should be organized is a source of tension between the institutions.[15] A number of Member States demanded the formalization of the preparation of delegated acts by pleading for formal agendas for discussions with experts from national authorities.[16] In addition, the Commission was asked to give national experts the opportunity to comment on changes in the draft proposal *before* it is adopted by the Commission. Finally, the Commission was also asked to give privileged access to national experts in that they are allowed to comment *after* the suggestions from civil society organizations are included. The Commission refused to further formalize the preparation phase of delegated acts, arguing it would anger the European Parliament, bring in *ex ante* control by the Member States, and go against the provisions of the Treaty.

In its guidelines to its services, the General Secretariat of the Commission acknowledges that consultations are necessary to ensure efficient implementation but argues that the legislator cannot impose compulsory consultations of national experts and that these experts have 'no institutional role in the decision-making process'.[17] That said, the General Secretariat does call

[15] T Christiansen and M Dobbels, 'Non-Legislative Rule Making after the Lisbon Treaty: Implementing the New System of Comitology and Delegated Acts' (2013) 19 ELJ 42.

[16] Non-Paper of Denmark, Germany and the United Kingdom (unpublished paper, December 2011).

[17] Delegated Acts—Guidelines for the services of the Commission, Note from the Legal Service of the European Commission on 24 June 2011, SEC(2011) 855.

upon its services to systematically consult experts, including from all twenty-eight Member States, where expertise is necessary. In addition, it asks the Directorates-General that consultations are carried out in a timely manner, possibly by using existing expert groups or by creating new ones. Under no circumstance, however, can a comitology committee be asked to prepare a delegated act, and under no circumstances can a vote take place as there is no requirement for a formal opinion. Most remarkably, the guidelines state that European Parliament experts may be invited, if requested by the European Parliament, but that Directorates-General are not legally obliged to comply with this request. They are, however, warned about the political consequences of refusal.

Primary research of available records carried out in the third year after the establishment of the instrument of delegated acts shows that at least eleven Directorates-General of the European Commission tasked their expert groups with the preparation of delegated acts. Of the thirty-one expert groups used for preparing delegated acts, twenty-four are composed of experts sent by the Member States. Six expert groups also include corporations or agencies. One expert group does not include any experts sent by Member States (the European ITS Advisory Group). Fifty-five delegated acts had been adopted up until the end of March 2013 and in all cases except three where no expertise was needed, all Member States were consulted.

The European Parliament has had little opportunity and limited resources to actually scrutinize implementing acts before their adoption in the past. Now, following the Lisbon changes, there is the possibility for doing so, at least when it comes to delegated acts. This requires considerable resources, given the technical expertise the Commission's services (and their expert committees) as well as Member State administrations can muster. This not only goes for the rights of objection and revocation, which will be discussed in the following section, but also for the consultation phase.

The European Parliament has demanded to be present in any such consultation meetings, and its representatives are now participating in meetings of expert groups that are consulted on delegated acts, albeit only as observers. This creates a kind of symbolic presence, but actually provides the European Parliament with very little if any input into the process. European Parliament officials from the staff of committee secretariats devote their limited time to attending such expert group meetings without having the opportunity—due to their lack of detailed expertise—or the capacity to influence proceedings. In addition, it has also been necessary to set up a circuit among officials working for the various European Parliament committees in order to exchange practices and develop a common strategy. All of this requires time and resources which are scarce in the Parliament.

The very fact that consultations happen more informally makes it more difficult for the European Parliament to understand what is being discussed and to influence the drafting process accordingly. Indeed, the working arrangements emerging for delegated acts remind one of the early years of comitology during which much of what happened in the system prior to adoption was 'in the dark'.

More recently, both Council and European Parliament have sought to formalize the process of early consultation. The European Parliament demanded a more simplified mechanism for involving its experts in the meetings of national experts groups,[18] while the Council has proposed a comprehensive review of the Common Understanding, specifically with a view to enhancing the involvement of national experts. In their proposal for a revised Common Understanding, the Council refers to 'expert consultation [as a] a cornerstone of good governance and better regulation' and complains that 'no satisfactory agreement could be reached until now about the systematic consultation of experts. And this despite the fact that Member States' authorities will be responsible for implementing or transposing delegated acts once they are adopted'.[19] The Council also identifies dissatisfaction among Member States with insufficient consultation of their experts as the main reason for the rejection of the Commission's delegated act on minimum standards for the so-called Galileo global navigation system.

Among the solutions to these problems proposed by Council are:

- requiring a 'systematic' consultation by the Commission, i.e. making consultation of expert groups obligatory;
- creating greater transparency of the consultative process by making all documents discussed in the experts groups available to European Parliament and Council, by creating a register containing all details about expert groups and their meetings, and through the publication of an annual report on expert group consultations;
- adopting a number of 'standard clauses' which could then be included in secondary legislation on a regular basis and thereby further clarify the respective rights and responsibilities of the three institutions.

While the Council here is linking its position to the more general discourse about good governance and expert groups in the EU, it also resonates with earlier efforts to systematize comitology in the 1990s. What is remarkable, though, in this context is that it is now the Council, rather than the European Parliament, that is at the forefront of pushing the Commission towards greater systematisation and transparency.[20] The Commission's response has been to present a series of proposals

[18] Motion for a resolution pursuant to Rule 87a(3) of the Rules of Procedure on the Commission delegated regulation of 12 December 2013 amending Regulation (EU) 2011/1169 of the European Parliament and of the Council on the provision of food information to consumers as regards the definition of 'engineered nanomaterials' (C(2013)08887—2013/2997(DEA)).

[19] Initiative to complement the Common Understanding on Delegated Acts as regards the consultation of experts, Council Doc 6774/14 of 21 February 2014.

[20] Cf. W Voermans, JMR Hartmann, and M Kaeding, 'The Quest for Legitimacy in EU Secondary Legislation' (2013) 2 The Theory and Practice of Legislation 5.

for further formalization of the provisions in the Common Understanding.[21] The proposals offer some clarity on the distinction between delegated and implementing acts as well as standard clauses for basic acts and transparency on the Commission's consultation of experts groups in the preparatory phase of drafting delegated acts. Even if the new move appears to match the demands from the Council, it remains to be seen, at the time of writing. Whether it would be agreeable to the EP, and whether an agreement could be found, as intended, by the end of 2015.

5.5 Scrutiny by the EU Legislator: Revocation of Powers and Objections to Drafts

Article 290 TFEU gives the Council and the European Parliament *post hoc* control rights, namely the right of objection and the right of revocation. These rights of control are in fact quite drastic as they only entail the 'nuclear option' of voting against a draft measure adopted by the Commission or revoking the delegation of powers altogether. Neither the Council nor the European Parliament is empowered to adopt an alternative decision to override the Commission's intended act. Therefore, the Member States in the Council have tried to find other ways of influencing the process of the adoption of delegated acts by focusing on the preparation stage, as discussed above.

The modalities for exercising the rights of objection and revocation are set out in a Common Understanding which was negotiated to streamline the practical arrangements for the adoption of delegated acts. Paragraph 10 of the Common Understanding sets out the practice for the right of objection. The period in which objection can be raised is defined on a case-by-case basis in each basic legal act, but should in principle be two months and certainly not less than that. These two months are extendable by another two months if either the Council or the European Parliament demands so.

The European Parliament already had to hire additional staff to deal with the growing workload under the previous revision of the comitology system, in 2006, and the scrutiny of delegated acts requires even greater resources. It also adds new demands to the agenda of European Parliament committees, which have to debate any motion to object to a draft delegated act prior to a vote in plenary, within the very restrictive timetable under which such objections can be made.

In the Council delegated acts are on the agenda at working party level. Specialized working groups, often the same that negotiated the basic legal act, scrutinize the acts put forward by the Commission. In the European Parliament the same is done in the committees. Each committee has a staff member who screens both delegated and implementing acts put forward, and most committees even have an MEP who is the designated politician to oversee this process. In 2012 18% of the delegated acts sent to Parliament were taken up by the committee for discussion, however no objections were raised.

Of the fifty-five delegated acts that were adopted up until the end of March 2013 no objections were raised, neither by the European Parliament, nor by the

[21] Commission Communication of 19 May 2015 Proposal for an Interinstitutional Agreement on Better Regulation, COM(2015) 216 final.

Council. On the Council side this is explained by the fact that the Commission engages with the Member States in proper consultations. Only once was an extension of the deadline requested. The European Parliament assigns the lack of objections more to the time constraints and the fact that one would need an absolute majority in plenary to stop an act from being adopted.

It seems that in this initial period after the coming into force of the Lisbon Treaty, the procedures worked well. Matters have been more difficult later, however, indicating that this early period may have been something of a 'honeymoon'. We already alluded above to the fact that the Council did object in late 2013 to a delegated act related to Galileo. Soon thereafter, the European Parliament in turn objected to a delegated act on the provision of food information to consumers as regards the definition of 'engineered nanomaterials'.[22] While these instances remain rare, given the large and rising number of delegated acts being adopted, they may point to a growing dissatisfaction of both legislative institutions with the way the Commission is handling its new powers. After all, there had been a rise also in vetoes issued under the old RPS procedure,[23] and significant problems in the realignment from the RPS procedure to Article 290 TFEU.[24]

It is evident that the European Parliament, which is traditionally disadvantaged vis-à-vis the other two institutions when it comes to both technical expertise and time, has to confront similar challenges again, despite having invested in additional resources to address these shortcomings. But also Member States have become restive, as the above-mentioned Council initiative on revising the Common Understanding has demonstrated. In that document, the Council highlights that on several occasions 'negotiations on key legislative packages…were blocked for considerable time due to disagreement over the issue of delegated acts. Only after lengthy discussions causing regrettable delays could these files be adopted'.[25] Thus, while our analysis has not shown up significant delays in the initial period after the Common Understanding was adopted, there is a sense that with time passing, and a higher volume of decision-making in this area, there is also more potential for disagreement and interinstitutional conflict.

5.6 Scrutiny by the Member States: Introducing the Appeal Committee

With the clearer distinction between the role of legislative institutions in the area of delegated acts and the Member States in the area of 'comitology proper' came the requirement to replace the possibility of comitology committee referrals to the

[22] European Parliament (2014).

[23] See M Kaeding and A Hardacre, 'The European Parliament and the Future of Comitology after Lisbon' (2013) 19 ELJ 382.

[24] D Gueguen, 'Unifying comitology—Omnibuses meet brick wall of Member State opposition', *Europolitics* (Brussels, 25 July 2014).

[25] Council of the European Union, Doc 6774/14, Initiative to complement the Common Understanding on delegated acts as regards the consultation of experts, Brussels, 21 February 2012.

Council to a new body that would not—at least not formally—be part of the EU level legislative process. The solution was found with the creation of an appeal committee which would be composed of senior civil servants from the Member States, and which would engage with the draft implementing acts that had not received the required majority in the relevant comitology committee. In practice, however, it did not change matters much compared to the pre-Lisbon experience: previously, when the 'Council' would have to deal with referrals, such dossiers were generally dealt with on the agenda of Coreper I, before ending up on the Council agenda as 'A items', with no further involvement of ministers themselves. The Appeal Committee, in the way in which its work evolved in the first year of its existence, met mainly in the composition of Deputy Permanent Representatives—in other words, it turned out to be a meeting of Coreper I under a different name. While formally this was now a body of 'Member State representatives', it is in practice still very much part of the Council machinery. The main difference to the status quo ante pertains to the chair: while Council/Coreper meetings are of course chaired by the Presidency, the Appeal Committee is presided over by the Commission—something both the European Parliament and the Commission itself had insisted on when the Comitology Regulation was adopted.

In fact, the composition of the committee was a matter of some debate among the Member States, with differences of opinion regarding the level of seniority of committee members. The Comitology Regulation only refers to an 'appropriate level of representation' which presumably implies more senior officials than those in the original comitology committee, but beyond that does not provide clear guidance. In order to ensure the body would have sufficient weight in order to engage, when necessary, with the Commission, some Member States sought a higher, possibly even political, level of representation, whereas for others senior administrators or diplomats were considered sufficient.

In practice, we have observed a gradual drop in the level of seniority in the composition of the committee, with an increasing number of Member States not even sending their Deputy Permanent Representative, but instead relying on attachés and counsellors. It should be noted that the general practice is to recruit attendees of the Appeal Committee from the staff of the PermReps, and to bring in officials from national ministries or agencies only on particular occasions when their expertise is pertinent to the dossier under discussion, and only in addition to the PermRep staff. In this context, it is also worth noting that there has been a rising number of abstentions in the votes of the committee: whereas in 2011 most votes involved all Member States, there have been significant numbers of votes withheld in the meetings in 2012—an indication that Member States increasingly do not attend meetings of the Appeal Committee, or, if representatives do attend, these are lacking a clear mandate for voting.

While the Appeal Committee has seen some confrontation between the Commission and the Member States, it is important to point out that by and large the relatively smooth cooperation between national and European administrators has continued post-Lisbon. In its first year of operation, the Appeal Committee was convened on seven occasions, and voted on a total of fourteen proposed implementing measures that had been referred to it from various examination committees. In view of the almost 1,800 comitology acts that were adopted by the Commission during this period, this amounts to less than 1% and as such is in line with the usual number of annual referrals to the Council prior to the Lisbon Treaty. This appears to be clear indication that the new procedures under Article 291 facilitated 'business as usual' in the area of comitology.

Furthermore, of the fourteen votes taken by the Appeal Committee between September 2011 and September 2012, eleven resulted in a 'no opinion', two in a 'positive opinion' and only one in a negative opinion. In other words, the vast majority of referrals from examination committees did not end up blocking the Commission, but rather permitted it to adopt its proposed measures after all.

The single negative opinion to arise from a vote in the Appeal Committee during its first year is therefore hardly representative of the kind of conflict that might ensue in this institutional context. Having said that, this particular vote—known as the 'Orphacol case'—was the cause of bitter disagreements between Member States and the Commission and eventually led to the first post-Lisbon case on comitology (before the General Court). Bearing in mind how exceptional this case is in the general context of comitology, it still warrants a more detailed look as it provides interesting insights into the potential complications that can arise in the post-Lisbon procedure.

This case concerned the authorization request for a pharmaceutical which the Commission proposed to deny. Having failed to reach a qualified majority in favour during the meeting of the relevant examination committee, the act was considered in the Appeal Committee on 8 November 2011 where a qualified majority of Member States voted against the Commission's proposals. In line with the procedure set out in the Comitology Regulation this initially blocked the Commission from adopting the decision, and instead obliged it to review its proposal and submit a new proposal to the original committee. In fact, the Commission submitted an essentially unchanged proposal to the committee on 8 May 2012 where the result of the renewed vote was 'no opinion'. This voting result permitted the Commission to adopt its proposed decision, which it did on 25 May 2012.

This decision, however, proved to be unusually contentious for a number of reasons: the Commission had gone against the initial scientific advice of the European Medicines Agency, it had ignored protests from some Member States about the scheduling of the comitology committee meeting on 8 May 2012—a public holiday in several Member States, and it had adopted its decision despite a case on the matter still pending in the General Court. In addition, through lobbying by the applicant and a corresponding media campaign, the European Parliament also became involved in this particular dossier and initiated a hearing with officials from the relevant DG of the European Commission.

Ultimately, in its ruling 4 July 2013 in *Orphacol*, the General Court annulled the Commission's decision, forcing it to table a new proposal permitting the market authorization for Orphacol which was finally approved unanimously by the Member States in the relevant comitology committee.[26] The Commission may have

[26] Case T-301/12 *Laboratoires CTRS v European Commission*, EU:T:2013:346.

'lost' in this particular case on the substantive matter under dispute—whether or not to allow the product onto the market—but to the frustration of many observers the Court did not enter into the procedural aspects pertaining to comitology.[27] As a result, the question as to whether the Commission violated the principle of loyal cooperation with the Member States by 'submitting the same draft decision to the comitology committee until receiving a positive or neutral opinion from the committee'[28] and insisting on convening committee meetings on dates that are known to be inconvenient to some Member States was not conclusively answered.

The political message from this particular case was clear, however: if the Commission is seen to be overstepping its mark by 'forcing through' certain decisions and unfairly exploiting its role of chair of the Appeal Committee, Member States are willing to defend their institutional prerogatives. This dispute also shows that individual decisions of this kind, however technocratic they may appear, have the potential for both politicization through the involvement of the media and political actors such as the European Parliament. It also drives home the fact that judicial review remains an important tool in the area of comitology, even if the Court failed in *Orphacol* (as well as in *Biocides*, which also related to comitology[29]), to resolve the ambiguities over different possible interpretations of the Lisbon Treaty provisions.[30]

Overall, the Appeal Committee has established itself as an essential part of the new comitology machinery and continues to work very much in the same vein as the Council did prior to Lisbon. Its impact on the day-to-day work of comitology is rather marginal, considering the low numbers of referrals and the even lower number of negative opinions. It certainly cannot be accused of having slowed down the pace of policy implementation by the Commission. If anything, the concern perhaps needs to be the opposite, namely whether it can effectively fulfil the role of scrutinizing the Commission's execution of delegated powers. As experience of the *Orphacol* case shows, a Commission intent on pushing through its proposed decisions may well encounter only 'soft' resistance by the Member States, with the Court rather than the Appeal Committee limiting its power.

5.7 Conclusion

In this chapter, we have examined the track record of the Commission's delegated powers in the first few years after the coming into force of the post-Lisbon regime. In particular, we studied the way in which the Commission has interacted with

[27] D Gueguen, 'Court of Justice keeps low profile on secondary legislation', *Europolitics* (Brussels, 21 March 2014).

[28] Permanent Representation of the Federal Republic of Austria 2012.

[29] Case C-427/12 *European Commission v European Parliament and Council (Biocides)*, EU:C:2014:170. For an extensive comment see D Ritleng, 'The Dividing Line between Delegated and Implementing Acts: the Court of Justice Sidesteps the Difficulty in *Commission* v. *Parliament and Council (Biocides)*', 52 CMLRev (2015) 243.

[30] See D Gueguen, 'Court of Justice keeps low profile on secondary legislation', *Europolitics* (Brussels, 21 March 2014).

the European Parliament, the Council and the Member States across a number of crucial areas of interinstitutional relations: the duration of the legislative process, the possibility of objections to delegated acts and of revocations of delegated powers, the role of expert groups and of the Appeal Committee. The overall conclusion from looking in some detail at the administrative practice in these areas is that, even if interinstitutional agreement on the implementation of Articles 290 and 291 TFEU was fraught with some difficulty, the system, once operational, has worked remarkably well. The adoption of basic acts has not been slowed down in any noticeable way, there have not been any rejections of draft delegated acts by either Council or European Parliament, nor have there been any moves to recall delegated powers altogether. Expert groups (in the area of delegated acts) and Appeal Committee (in the area of implementing acts) have been, on the whole, cooperative venues for meetings between the Commission and the Member States.

There had been occasional disagreement in one or the other area, but any such conflict has been isolated and was exceptional in this early period. As a rule, delegated rulemaking after Lisbon worked smoothly and did not seem to differ fundamentally in practice from the pre-Lisbon arrangements. This does not mean, however, that there are no open questions raised by this analysis. Indeed, the low incidence of interinstitutional conflict was perhaps an indication that there are some deficiencies in the new set-up. One could ask, for example, whether the legislative institutions actually possess the capacity to control the Commission's delegated powers effectively. Council and European Parliament are, after all, fairly new to the business of Commission scrutiny in this area, and even though they fought hard battles to establish the constitutional right to be formally involved, having the administrative resources, the necessary time and the required political will to engage with matters of delegated rulemaking on a regular basis is another matter. This may be a question of institutional adaptation and of the need for further reform of the system, as indicated by the initiatives launched by all three institutions and the expectation on a new Interinstitutional Agreement on Better Regulation as proposed by the European Commission in May 2015.[31] Non-legislative rulemaking after Lisbon is still work in progress, and thus it is too soon for a conclusive assessment of the functioning of the post-Lisbon arrangements. The coming years will have to show whether this assessment of the practice of interinstitutional relations in the years after the Lisbon Treaty is turning out to be a permanent or a transitory state of affairs.

[31] Commission Communication of 19 May 2015 Proposal for an Interinstitutional Agreement on Better Regulation, COM(2015) 216 final.

6

The Contest for Power in Delegated Rulemaking

Adrienne Héritier, Catherine Moury, and Katarzyna Granat

6.1 Introduction

Ever since the Lisbon Treaty introduced the new provisions on delegated rulemaking under Articles 290 and 291 TFEU, the newly created institutional rules have undergone change. Some of the changes have occurred openly in the formal political arenas, and have been contested by the relevant actors, that is, Council, European Parliament, and Commission. By contrast, other changes have occurred in a more covert or invisible way, unfolding after the adoption of a formal rule in the course of its application, and may therefore be formalized at a later stage. We are focusing on the latter type of institutional change and its consequences and ask 'Under what circumstances does "interstitial" institutional change occur, what are its dynamics and its consequences?'

6.2 The Theoretical Argument

Building on Farrell and Héritier[1] and Héritier,[2] we define interstitial institutional change as informal institutional change which occurs between two formal rule revisions. For example, at time t_1 a committee may initially formally agree that all of its decisions will be made by a unanimous vote; progressively, and informally, it may then accept some delegation of decision-making powers to individual members; and finally, and formally, at time t_2 it may reconvene to discuss the decision-making rule it will follow. Interstitial institutional change is the second step in that sequence, that is, the informal step taken between t_1 and t_2. Clearly, what happens then may have an important impact on the decision at t_2. The study of this type of institutional change is therefore relevant from a theoretical point of view because it

[1] H Farrell and A Héritier, 'A Rationalist-institutionalist Explanation of Endogenous Regional Integration' (2005) 12 JEPP 273.

[2] A Héritier, *Explaining Institutional Change in Europe* (Oxford University Press 2007), at p 47.

informs the burgeoning literature on the nature of institutions and the conditions for institutional change. In addition, it is topical from a societal/democratic stance because, if interstitial institutional change carries the promise of flexibility and efficiency, it may also lead to severe limitations in the operation of formal checks and balances.

Our argument in this paper is that interstitial institutional changes are happening as a result of the application of Articles 290 and 291 TFEU. We build on the *theory of continuous institutional change* in order to capture interstitial institutional change.[3] It emphasizes the renegotiation or re-interpretation of incomplete institutional rules and policies. Institutional change emerges once a formal political decision of integration has been taken and this decision constitutes an incomplete contract. This offers the possibility of it being renegotiated and specified in the course of its application. The explanation is based on the assumptions of goal-oriented, boundedly rational actors, seeking to maximize their institutional power and thereby their power over policy outcomes. Answers as to why patterns of deepening integration appear may be derived from the pressure of external problems, specific institutional conditions, and the relative bargaining power of the actors involved when redefining incomplete institutional or policy rules.

Given problem pressure and a demand for coordinated policies, it is crucial whether decisions to coordinate at the higher level represent complete or incomplete contracts. If actors have similar preferences and agree on a detailed decision to upload competences to the higher level which also clearly circumscribes the power given to *supra*national actors, a limited transfer of powers has occurred in a complete contract and in an overt way in the main political arena. If, by contrast, Member States have diverse preferences on the desired policy solutions and appropriate limits of *supra*national power, the outcome of the decision process in the main arena is likely to be vaguely formulated (an incomplete contract) and/or at the lowest common denominator. An incomplete contract—for strategic reasons and reasons of substantive uncertainty[4]—leaves many details to be specified, and thereby opens the door for subsequent institutional and policy changes.[5] These changes often happen outside the formal political arena. The renegotiation may give rise to informal rules on the handling of powers emerging alongside the formal political arena. The outcome of the implicit re-bargaining of the

[3] A Héritier, 'Policy-making by Subterfuge: Interest Accommodation, Innovation and Substitute Democratic Legitimation in Europe—Perspectives from Distinctive Policy Areas' (1997) 4 JEPP 171; A Héritier (n 2); A Héritier, 'Institutional Change in Europe: Co-decision and Comitology Transformed' (2012) 50 JCMS 38; H Farrell and A Héritier, 'Formal and Informal Institutions Under Codecision: Continuous Constitution-Building in Europe' (2003) 16 Governance 577; H Farrell and A Héritier, 'Interorganizational Negotiation and Intraorganizational Power in Shared Decision Making' (2004) 37 Comparative Political Studies 1184; J Stacey and B Rittberger, 'Dynamics of Formal and Informal Institutional Change in the EU' (2003) 10 JEPP 858.

[4] A Cooley and H Spruyt, *Contracting States: Sovereign Transfers in International Relations* (Princeton University Press 2009).

[5] A Héritier (n 2); A Héritier 'Institutional Change in Europe: Co-decision and Comitology Transformed' (n 3).

incomplete contract will be determined by the most powerful actors (as defined by their fall-back position), the existing decision-making rule and exogenous events. When specifying the incomplete contract, *supra*national executive actors may form an alliance with judicial actors in interpreting the details of the contract and—through judicial rulings—make an inroad into competences previously not formally mandated.

In short, a deepening integration may result from the fact that—given external pressure—diverging preferences and consensus or unanimity rules make the formal political decision-makers commit themselves to only vaguely formulated institutional rules or policy goals. Given the ambiguity of the rule or policy mandate, implementing actors, that is, executive actors, and judicial actors, as well as political actors at the national level, are able to redefine the generally stated goal. Depending on the preferences and the relative power of the actors involved in the re-negotiation of the incomplete contract and given institutional restrictions, deepening integration may ensue.[6] This leads to the conjecture that '*an incomplete institutional rule or policy may lead to an institutional change in the course of its application. In the renegotiation of the incomplete institutional rule, the preferences of the most powerful actors will be reflected in the substance of the modified institutional rule*'.

6.3 Incomplete Institutional Rules: Articles 290 and 291

The Treaty on the Functioning of the European Union (TFEU) distinguishes between legislative delegation and executive delegation for the first time, and provides for two separate procedures for 'delegated acts' and 'implementing acts'.[7] Under Article 290 TFEU, the Commission—by legislation—may be delegated the power to adopt 'delegated acts' of general scope supplementing or amending certain non-essential elements of the legislation in question. The legislator must explicitly define the objective, content, scope, and duration of this delegation. It also can choose the mechanism(s) used to control the Commission when it applies these delegated powers: revocation and objection.[8] In the case of revocation, either the Council or the Parliament may revoke a delegation. Similarly, an objection on the part of either the Council or the Parliament would prevent an individual 'delegated act' from entering into force.[9]

The new provisions of the Lisbon Treaty leave open many questions as to how delegated acts (Article 290 TFEU) and implementing acts (Article 291 TFEU)

6 Ibid.

7 P Ponzano, 'La Nouvelle Comitologie et les Actes Délégués', Mscr, Workshop RSCAS, EUI, Florence, 11/12 February 2010. For the pre-Lisbon regime of delegation see, in particular, Chapter 1 by Carl Fredrik Bergström and Chapter 2 by Jean Paul Jacqué in this volume.

8 On the use of these mechanisms in practice and interinstitutional tensions in this regard see Chapter 5 by Thomas Christiansen and Mathias Dobbels in this volume.

9 See also J Blom-Hansen, 'The EU Comitology System: Taking Stock Before the New Lisbon Regime' (2011) 18 JEPP 607.

should be applied.[10] In other words, the provisions constitute an incomplete contract. We assume that actors seek to take full advantage of their institutional power in order to maximize their influence over policy outcomes; we further assume the following meta-preferences of the institutional actors involved: the Commission will in general prefer extensive delegation over delegation with minimal or no control by Member States and the European Parliament. The European Parliament will prefer legislation over delegation because it can wield more influence than under delegation (in particular in the case of implementing acts); if delegation has been chosen, it is assumed to prefer delegated acts over implementing acts. The Council will generally prefer delegation over legislation under co-decision since it has to share power with the European Parliament under co-decision; if delegation has been chosen, it will prefer implementing acts over delegated acts because it does not have to share power with the European Parliament and Member States can still wield influence in the committees under implementing acts. From these assumed preferences we conclude that when the Commission proposes a 'delegated act', as a rule a conflict ensues between the Parliament, the Council, and the Commission. The Council seeks to oppose it entirely or to reduce its scope, or to translate it into an implementing act. The European Parliament will welcome the use of a delegated act and conversely oppose the use of implementing acts. Given these conflicts[11] arise frequently, in order to come to an agreement packages are struck across various issues as to whether to use 'delegating' or implementing acts.[12]

Hence the guiding question we pose when scrutinizing four empirical cases is: How were the institutional rules on the application of delegated and implementing acts interpreted and renegotiated in these specific cases? Which issues were at stake and how were they resolved?

Methodologically, in our discussion of the four cases we do not claim to conduct a systematic empirical scrutiny but only seek to probe the plausibility of our general argument that '*an incomplete institutional rule may lead to an interstitial institutional change in the course of its application. In the renegotiation of the incomplete institutional rule, the preferences of the most powerful actors will be reflected in the substance of the new modified institutional rule*'.

The first part of the empirical analysis will focus on the strategic interaction between the Commission, the Council, and the European Parliament in renegotiating the ambiguous institutional rules governing delegation under the Lisbon Treaty. In the second part, an additional institutional player, the national parliaments, enters the stage to renegotiate the ambiguous institutional rules about how to apply delegated and implementing acts under the Lisbon Treaty.

[10] On the unclear divide between delegated and implementing acts see, in particular, Chapters 7, 8, and 9 in this volume by Dominique Ritleng, Jürgen Bast, and Paul Craig, respectively.

[11] A Héritier, C Moury, C S Bischoff, and C F Bergström, *Changing Rules of Delegation: A Contest for Power in Comitology* (Oxford University Press 2013).

[12] Interview Commission, January 2012.

6.4 Empirical Cases

6.4.1 The contest of power between Commission, Council, and Parliament

Case 1: The Regulation on the Prevention and Correction of Macroeconomic Imbalances

The first case focuses on the conflict between the Commission, the Council, and the European Parliament in the definition of the economic indicators under the scoreboard regime as part of the preventive arm of the Prevention and Correction of Macroeconomic Imbalances.[13] The conflict over the interpretation of the legal rules when deciding how to flesh out the scoreboard regime, that is, the indicators used to measure and monitor macroeconomic and macrofinancial imbalances, gave rise to a new informal rule (set out in the recital of the Regulation and not in the legal text), about how to specify the formal rule which, however, due to the political importance, became de facto binding.

The Macroeconomic Imbalances Procedure is based on two regulations that are part of the 'six-pack' of legislative measures strengthening the surveillance of fiscal and macroeconomic policies in the EU.[14] One regulation defines the details of the new surveillance procedure and covers all Member States. Another regulation, which introduces an enforcement mechanism and possible sanctions, is only applicable to the members of the euro area. Under the new surveillance procedure for the identification of possible imbalances, a two-step approach has been established. An alert mechanism seeks to provide early warning of signs in some Member States of macroeconomic imbalances which require in-depth investigation. 'The objective is to identify macroeconomic imbalances at the early stage of their emergence so that necessary policy actions can be taken in due time and thus prevent the development of severe imbalances which are damaging for the Member State concerned and risk jeopardizing the functioning of the euro area'.[15] The alert mechanism serves as an instrument of scrutiny, as a first step before a more in-depth inquiry which may then be followed by concrete policy recommendations.

More specifically, the alert mechanism provides for a scoreboard based on indicators complemented by an economic reading thereof presented in an annual Alert Mechanism Report. The economic reading of the scoreboard indicators implies that there is no automaticity involved and that other relevant information can be

[13] Regulation (EU) 2011/1176 of the European Parliament and of the Council of 16 November 2011 on the prevention and correction of macroeconomic imbalances, OJ 2011 L 306/25.

[14] Regulation (EU) 2011/1176, ibid, and Regulation (EU) 2011/1174 of the European Parliament and of the Council of 16 November 2011 on enforcement measures to correct excessive macroeconomic imbalances in the euro area, OJ 2011 L 306/8.

[15] P Bouwen and J Fischer, 'Towards a Stronger EU Surveillance of Macroeconomic Imbalances: rationale and design of the new procedure' (2012) 51 Reflets et perspectives de la vie économique 21, at p 25.

taken into account. The indicators in the scoreboard focus on the most relevant dimensions of macroeconomic imbalances and losses of competitiveness, with particular focus on the smooth functioning of the euro area. 'For this reason, the scoreboard consists of indicators which can monitor external balances, competitiveness positions, and internal imbalances, and encompass variables where both the economic literature and recent experiences suggest associations with economic crises'.[16] A wide range of policies are included when addressing the issue of imbalances, including fiscal policies, financial market regulation, or structural reforms. The latter are meant to increase the flexibility of product and labour markets, facilitating adjustments through changes in relative prices and wages together with the reallocation of labour and capital in the economy.[17]

The results of the Alert Mechanism Report are discussed in the Council and Euro Group and, if deemed necessary, the Commission is empowered to decide which countries require in-depth reviews. If a review reveals a macroeconomic imbalance, the Commission will propose policy recommendations for the Member State in question. In the preventive arm, these proposals are part of the recommendations under the European semester. If the Commission comes to the conclusion that there are severe imbalances, it will recommend an excessive imbalances procedure to the Council; this is part of the corrective arm of the new procedure.[18]

Some vague provisions were introduced in the Regulation on the Prevention and Correction of Macroeconomic Imbalances that needed specification through delegated legislation. In the interpretation of these incomplete institutional rules, a conflict emerged over the choice of either delegated acts (Article 290 TFEU) or implementing acts (Article 291 TFEU). When deciding how to flesh out the scoreboard regime, that is, the indicators used to measure and monitor macroeconomic and macrofinancial imbalances, the Commission first proposed to define these indicators on its own. Following resistance from both the Council and the European Parliament, the Commission and the European Parliament proposed 'delegated acts' (Article 290 TFEU) whilst the Council wished to use an implementing act (Article 291 TFEU). A deadlock ensued and after a round of negotiations this led to the use of an informal new type of procedure which is *neither* Article 290 TFEU *nor* Article 291 TFEU, the 'compromise'. The respective recital 12 of the Regulation says:

> The Commission should closely cooperate with the European Parliament and the Council when drawing up the scoreboard and the set of macroeconomic and macrofinancial indicators for Member States. The Commission should present suggestions for comments to the competent committees of the European Parliament and of the Council on plans to establish and adjust the indicators and threshold. The Commission should inform the European Parliament and the Council of any changes to the indicators and threshold and explain its reasons for suggesting such changes.

[16] The scoreboard (indicators and thresholds) includes a combination of stock and flow indicators which can capture both shorter-term rapid deteriorations as well as the longer-term gradual accumulation of imbalances. Bouwen and Fischer, ibid, at p 25.

[17] Ibid, at p 29.

[18] Ibid, at p 26.

Note the difference to the 'real' use of a delegated act used in another 'six-pack' regulation on the effective enforcement of budgetary surveillance in the euro area.[19] As prescribed in the Comitology Regulation, it states that the Commission shall be empowered to adopt 'delegated acts' regarding the criteria establishing fines and procedures for investigations (Article 8.4); that the Commission shall draw up a report in respect of the delegation of power; and that the delegation may be revoked at any time by the Parliament or by the Council (Article 11.2 and 3).

What is striking from our theoretical perspective of interstitial institutional change is that the existing formal rules constitute ambiguous terms of contract, which—in the situation of a decision stalemate—were re-bargained and transformed so as to overcome the impasse. By so doing, the power of the Commission was clearly strengthened.

However, renewed conflicts emerged in the further application of the transformed institutional rule. The European Parliament considers that the compromise solution does not work out well and it does not feel fairly treated by the Commission. It states in its resolution of 2013: the European Parliament '... notes with deep regret a lack of equal treatment of the co-legislators in this process, as the Commission reportedly consulted the relevant working group of the Council'. More specifically in November 2012 the Commission added a new financial sector indicator on the growth rate of financial sector liabilities to the original set of indicators. The European Parliament welcomed this addition and had in fact asked for it in December 2011. However, they accused the Commission of not having respected the 'six-pack' rules requiring that the Commission should propose suggestions for comment to the European Parliament and the Council when establishing and adjusting indicators and thresholds. The European Parliament argued that it had not been properly consulted.

To make matters worse, the European Parliament accused the Commission of having consulted the Council at the technical level through the EcoFin Council. In short, as the chair of the Economic and Monetary Affairs Committee of the European Parliament concluded in the Parliamentary Debate on this issue '... the message seems not to have quite trickled through yet to the relevant Commission services that Parliament has equal rights with the Council here'.[20] The Commission responded by affirming that it had acted in accordance with the relevant regulation and in pursuit of a political agreement with the Council and Parliament of 2011 for completion of a scoreboard with an eleventh indicator...: 'The Commission shall assess on a regular basis the appropriateness of the scoreboard, including the composition of indicators, the thresholds set and the methodology used, and it shall adjust or modify them where necessary'. It emphasized that there had been close cooperation with the Council and Parliament, as mentioned in the modified new institutional rule (Recital 12). It argued that the Commission had treated

[19] Regulation (EU) 2011/1173 of the European Parliament and of the Council of 16 November 2011 on the effective enforcement of budgetary surveillance in the euro area, OJ 2011 L 306/1. Cf. n 15.

[20] European Parliament, Completing the scoreboard for the Macroeconomic Imbalance Procedure (debate), 18 April 2013, contribution by MEP S Bowles.

the European Parliament and the Council in the same way and informed them at the same time since the Commission had taken into account the views provided by the European Parliament's Economic Policy Committee which has a mandate to 'provide advice to the Commission'.[21] This ongoing struggle about the correct application of the already modified institutional rule (Recital 12) shows that this interstitial rule, in turn, proves to be incomplete and offers opportunities for the actors involved to assert the relative institutional power over how to apply the modified rule in a specific case.

Case 2: Financial Instruments External Relations: Pre-accession IPA II

In December 2011, the European Commission published the 'Global Europe' Communication and a package of proposals for EU instruments for external action for the 2014–20 period. The instruments are set in the context of the recently agreed Multiannual Financial Framework (MFF) 2014–20, under its heading 4 with resources of €66.3 billion, or 6.12% of the total. This is a 3% increase on the previous MFF, but 16% less than the Commission's initial proposal. The main legal basis for the instruments for external action are Articles 209(1) TFEU (development cooperation programmes) and 212(2) TFEU (economic, financial, and technical cooperation with other third countries). The agreement on the MFF is applicable from 1 January 2014.

The legislative package comprises nine geographic and thematic instruments, and a horizontal regulation defining common implementing rules for six of them: Instrument for Pre-accession Assistance (IPA II); European Neighbourhood Instrument (ENI); Partnership Instrument for cooperation with third countries (PI); Development Cooperation Instrument (DCI); Instrument for the Promotion of Democracy and Human Rights (EIDHR); Instrument contributing to Stability and Peace (IPS).[22] Under the Lisbon Treaty, External Relations have been subject to the ordinary legislative procedure (co-decision) for the first time, hence implying new powers for the European Parliament. As a consequence, in negotiating the specifics of Articles 290 and 291 TFEU in their application to External Relations, all actors, that is, the Commission, the Council, or the Member States and the European Parliament were treading on institutionally new ground and very cautiously negotiated the specifics of the application of Articles 290 and 291 TFEU to the Financial Instruments of External Relations.[23] As we argued in the theoretical section: we assume that all actors are intent on maximizing their institutional power in order to have influence over policy outcomes. Hence we proposed that: '*An incomplete institutional rule may lead to an interstitial institutional change in the course of its application. In the renegotiation of the incomplete institutional rule, the preferences of the most powerful actors will be reflected in the substance of the newly modified institutional rule*'.

[21] Ibid, contribution by Commissioner C Malmström.

[22] As a result of the interinstitutional negotiations, Commission's original proposal for the title (Instrument for Stability, IPS) was changed to Instrument contributing to Stability and Peace (IPS).

[23] Interviews European Parliament, January–February 2014.

How is this proposition reflected in the empirical story[24] of the application of Articles 290 and 291 TFEU in the case of the financial instruments external relations?[25]

(a) The Common Implementing Rule

The Commission proposed a *common implementing regulation*, that is, a horizontal regulation defining common, simplified rules and procedures for all external action instruments. The Commission's financing decisions will take the form of action programmes based on multiannual programming documents. Moreover, the Commission may set specific rules for some instruments (e.g. IPA II). The regulation also sets out the conditions for access to assistance. The common regulation and each instrument will be reviewed at the end of 2017.

In the political decision-making process on the common implementing regulation, the Common Rule was negotiated at a high level among the Chair of Parliament's Foreign Affairs Committee, the Council presidency (Coreper ambassador), and the Commission. The Council proposed not to use delegated acts (Article 290 TFEU) while the European Parliament insisted they be used. In other words, it asked for all the Commission's strategic papers for individual countries (valid for seven years) to be subject to delegated acts under Article 290 TFEU. It argued that strategic choices on important objectives for specific countries would be defined in this implementation phase. This, the European Parliament argued, constitutes a political process in which the European Parliament (and the Council) should be involved. It further stressed that, given the seven-year commitment, the European Parliament and the Council as co-legislators should be able to make a mid-term reflection on these priorities, that is, after three and a half years. By this time, circumstances could have changed and therefore priorities would have to be reconsidered. It also argued that the outgoing European Parliament should not commit the future MEPs for seven years without allowing them to make an intermittent review.

Both the Commission and the Council rejected the European Parliament's request and the Commission emphasized that pure implementation issues were at stake. After one and a half years of negotiations, a compromise was struck at the end of 2013. The European Parliament had to renounce its request to use delegated acts for all strategic papers. But it was conceded that delegated acts can be used in the annexes or in the text of the instrument itself when thematic priorities should be changed. In a mid-term review in 2017, the Commission will need to inform the European Parliament and the Council on the state of affairs. And, crucially, any potential change of thematic priorities during the mid-term review will be subject to a so-called '*amending delegated act*' as opposed to a '*self-standing delegated act*'. In formulating such a decision and in accordance with the

[24] Ibid.

[25] We would like to thank Ricardo Rodrigues for collecting documentary materials on this case.

interinstitutional framework agreement, European Parliament representatives are invited by the Commission to informally give their views on the draft.

In conclusion, renewed negotiations took place in view of the ambiguity of how Articles 290 and 291 TFEU should be employed in the case of the Financial Instruments External Relations *Common Rule*. In these negotiations a compromise was struck between the Commission and Council on the one hand and the European Parliament on the other in which all involved actors made concessions. The outcome was the emergence of a new type of delegated act, that is, the '*amending delegated act*' in the mid-term review of the objectives/thematic priorities of individual beneficiary countries.

(b) Pre-accession Assistance (IPA II)

More specifically, Council Regulation 2006/1085 assistance expired at the end of 2013 in the case of the individual financial instrument Pre-accession Assistance IPA II which is part of the Budget for Europe 2020. The framework for planning and delivering external assistance, in this case of external assistance for enlargement, is to be continued in the future. This is dependent on specific conditions: an applicant state can only become a member when it meets the membership criteria agreed upon in Copenhagen in 1993. These criteria include the stability of democratic institutions, the rule of law, human rights and respect and protection of minorities, and the existence of a functioning market economy. Candidate status (as of February 2014) has been granted to Iceland, Montenegro, Macedonia, Turkey, and Serbia.

Assistance will be provided on the basis of country or multi-country indicative strategy papers of a duration of seven years as part of the multiannual framework (Article 6). Progress in the achievement of specific objectives will be monitored and assessed (Article 2). The Commission makes annual assessments of the implementation of the strategic papers, informs and, if deemed necessary, sends proposed revisions to the IPA II committee consisting of representatives of the Member States, chaired by the Commission (Articles 6 and 12). If considered necessary, there will also be a mid-term review and possibly revision of the strategic papers at mid-term (Article 6.4).

In order to take account of changes in beneficiary countries, the Commission was given the power to adopt acts under Article 290 TFEU so that the thematic priorities for assistance listed in Annex II can be adapted and updated.[26] The implementation of the Regulation will be exercised in accordance with the Comitology Regulation. They will be adopted through an examination procedure unless they are technical measures involving low-level finances (Article 11a).

The essential provisions of IPA II described above are the outcome of interinstitutional negotiations between the Commission, the Council, and the European Parliament; as pointed out above, for the first time this has been subject to the

[26] Article 10 of Regulation (EU) 2014/231 of the European Parliament and of the Council of 11 March 2014 establishing an Instrument for Pre-accession Assistance (IPA II), OJ 2014 L 196/1.

ordinary legislative procedure (co-decision).[27] Initially, the Commission proposed a common strategy framework for all types of action of assistance to all countries under pre-accession assistance which was to be subject to implementing acts under Article 291 TFEU. The European Parliament opposed this on the grounds that this common strategy framework should be subject to a stand-alone delegated act under Article 290 TFEU. The amendments of the European Parliament were rejected by both the Council and the Commission. In response, the European Parliament offered to renounce delegated acts in the case of individual strategic papers but insisted on their requirement under the common strategy framework. This request was also rejected by the Council. The resulting deadlock in the decision-making process was overcome by deleting the proposal of a common strategy framework altogether. As a result, IPA II has only two levels of rules and no middle layer: the Regulation itself and the strategic papers describing the actions for individual countries.

In the case of strategic papers for individual pre-accession countries, the European Parliament reintroduced its request to use delegated acts under Article 290 TFEU. The Council opposed the European Parliament's proposals to the very last and only made some concessions briefly before all instruments expired in December 2013.[28] There was considerable political pressure resting on all actors involved to come to an agreement before the expiry of the instruments as well as to ensure that programming in beneficiary countries could start on time (or continue). In the end, a compromise was found by introducing an 'amending delegated act' with regard to Annex II. More specifically, the European Parliament ensured that Annex II of the Regulation, which contains a list of overall thematic priorities, can be amended by a mid-term 'amending delegated act' if developments so require. In sum, the European Parliament had to renounce its request to use delegated acts for all strategic papers, that is, the common strategy paper, which was entirely dropped, but in return it was conceded that an 'amending delegated act' can be used in the redefinition of thematic priorities in Annex II.

Moreover, while the European Parliament had to renounce the use of stand-alone delegated acts with respect to strategic papers, it was also granted that a Strategic Dialogue be conducted with the Commission. This constitutes a *political (as opposed to legal) obligation* by the Commission. Under the Strategic Dialogue, in the preparation of strategic papers the Commission has the political obligation to take the European Parliament's position into account when it is engaged in the programming process with beneficiary countries. This should allow the European Parliament to hold the Commission accountable when formulating and implementing agreements with beneficiary countries.

> The Commission will conduct a strategic dialogue with the European Parliament prior to the programming of... (financial instrument external relations...)... (It) will present to

[27] Interviews European Parliament, January–February 2014.

[28] Heading 4 (external relations) under the multiannual financial framework was one of the last to be approved at the end of 2013.

the Parliament the relevant available documents on programming with indicative allocations foreseen per country/region ... The Commission will present to the Parliament the relevant available documents on programming with thematic priorities, possible results, choice of assessing modalities, and financial allocations for such priorities foreseen in thematic programmes. The Commission will take into account the position expressed by the European Parliament on the matter. The Commission conducts a strategic dialogue with the European Parliament in preparing the Mid Term Review and before any substantial revision of the programming documents during the period of validity of this Regulation.[29]

To conclude, in view of the ambiguity of how Articles 290 and 291 TFEU should be employed in the case of the Financial Instruments IPA II, a compromise was struck in the negotiation process between the Commission and both the Council and the European Parliament in which all actors involved made concessions. The institutional outcomes were the emergence of a new type of delegated act, that is, the 'amending delegated act' in the mid-term review of the thematic priorities of individual beneficiary countries and the introduction of the Strategic Dialogue between the Commission and the European Parliament.

6.4.2 The contest of power between the Commission and national parliaments

In the next two case studies, we focus not only on the Commission, the Council and the European Parliament, but also on additional institutional players, namely the national parliaments. This new actor became involved in the contest of how to apply delegated rulemaking through the subsidiarity review procedure in Protocol No 2 on the application of the principles of subsidiarity and proportionality. As part of this procedure, a national parliament may issue a reasoned opinion within eight weeks from the date of transmission of a draft legislative act, stating why it considers that the draft in question does not comply with the principle of subsidiarity.[30] Each national parliament is equipped with two votes; in the case of a bicameral parliament, each of the two chambers has one vote.[31] If the number of issued reasoned opinions represents at least one-third of all the votes allocated to the national parliaments, or one-fourth of these votes in case of proposals in the area of freedom, security and justice, the Commission has to review its proposal and may consequently decide to maintain, amend, or withdraw the proposal.[32] The jargon for this procedure is the 'yellow card'. Moreover, national parliaments may trigger an 'orange card' under the ordinary legislative procedure, if the reasoned opinions account for at least a simple majority of the votes allocated to national parliaments.[33] Again, the Commission reviews its proposal and may

[29] Commission Declaration to the European Parliament legislative Resolution of 11 December 2013 on the proposal for a regulation of the European Parliament and of the Council establishing a Partnership Instrument for cooperation with third countries, P7_TA(2013)0569.

[30] Article 6. The reasoned opinions are available at www.ipex.eu.

[31] Article 7(1).

[32] Article 7(2).

[33] Article 7(3).

decide to maintain, amend, or withdraw it. If it is maintained, the Council (55% majority) or the European Parliament (majority of the votes cast) may stop the legislative procedure.

The reasoned opinions of national parliaments not only assess the subsidiarity principle, but also other elements of the Commission proposals, and therefore go beyond the strict wording of Protocol No 2.[34] One of the elements of Commission proposals that national parliaments take into account in their reasoned opinions are the delegations to adopt delegated or implementing acts. Hence, in the following two case studies we analyse first the reaction of national parliaments to the delegations included in the Commission proposals for the new data protection legislation and new tobacco products directive. Next, we look at the willingness of the Commission to take the opinions of parliaments into account. Both case studies examine the preferences of the Commission, Council and the European Parliament for legislation or delegation of power, yet the legislative procedure in the case of the data protection proposal is still underway. Subsequently, within delegation, we look at the choice between delegated and implementing powers. We also inquire into the extent of delegation preferred by different actors. Finally, we identify the outcomes of the choice of rule, legislation or delegation, delegated act or implementing act, and compare them to the original preferences of the national parliaments.

Based on the assumption made above that actors choose the institutional rule that maximizes their institutional power in order to wield the highest possible influence on policy outcomes, we indicate the following situational preferences that actors hold in these cases. For the purpose of these case studies, we treat parliamentary chambers as unified actors with a preference for legislation, and if delegation is chosen, for delegated acts (Article 290 TFEU).

National parliaments will prefer legislation, because it allows for the greatest control over the outcome. More specifically, the Lisbon Treaty granted national parliaments new powers in the EU legislative procedure, but no competences under Articles 290 and 291 TFEU. These provisions empower the Commission to the greatest extent; hence, as argued above, we assume that the Commission's preference is for extensive delegation. The European Parliament will favour legislation over delegation as it can shape the basic legislative act more than delegated or implementing acts. Under delegation, it can only revoke or object to the delegation with regard to delegated acts. Finally, we assume that the Council will choose delegation, and in the context of delegation will prefer implementing acts, as it provides representatives of the Member States with influence in the committees.

Case 3: Data Protection Legislation

In January 2012, the Commission proposed a new legal framework for the protection of personal data in order to reinforce the individual's fundamental right

[34] F Fabbrini and K Granat, '"Yellow Card, but No Foul": The Role of the National Parliaments Under the Subsidiarity Protocol and the Commission Proposal for an EU Regulation on the Right to Strike' (2013) 50 CLMRev 115.

to data protection.[35] The proposal consists of a directive[36] and the General Data Protection Regulation.[37] Both draft acts contain a considerable number of delegations to adopt delegated and implementing acts.[38]

National parliaments scrutinized both proposals within the subsidiarity review procedure. As a result, the Belgian *Chambre des Représentants*, the French *Sénat*, and the *Italian Camera dei Deputati* issued a reasoned opinion on the proposed regulation, while the German *Bundesrat* and the Swedish *Riksdag* issued an opinion on both the regulation and the directive. Especially the reasoned opinions related to the draft regulation criticized the use of delegated and implementing acts by the Commission, among other issues.

The most important criticism concerned the large number of delegations[39] allowing for 'practically full authority to adopt delegated acts relating to almost every one of the most important elements' of the proposal.[40] In the view of the German *Bundesrat*, the amount of delegated acts goes beyond Article 16(2) TFEU, which provides that a comprehensive regulation of data protection can only be made by the EU legislator.[41] Along similar lines, the Swedish *Riksdag* argued that the consequence of the transferred powers is that the Commission has been given a legislative role replacing legislators and courts.[42] In the same vein, the Belgian *Chambre des Représentants* favoured a comprehensive regulation instead of the use of executive acts, in order to ensure the participation of all institutions, the Parliament, and the Council.[43] Finally, the French *Sénat* distinguished between issues which demand regulation by the EU legislator (e.g. 'the right to be forgotten' expressed in Article 17 of the proposal) and other issues to be decided at the national level.[44]

In line with the Commission's preference for delegation, it replied that delegations by means of delegated acts do not concern any essential element of the act proposed and that the duration of their validity is limited.[45] Moreover,

[35] Commission Communication of 25 January 2012, Safeguarding Privacy in a Connected World—A European Data Protection Framework for the 21st Century, COM(2012) 9 final.

[36] Proposal for a directive of the European Parliament and the Council on the protection of individuals with regard to the processing of personal data by competent authorities for the purposes of prevention, investigation, detection or prosecution of criminal offences or the execution of criminal penalties, and the free movement of such data, COM(2012) 10 final.

[37] Proposal for a regulation of the European Parliament and the Council on the protection of individuals with regard to the processing of personal data and on the free movement of such data, COM(2012) 11 final.

[38] Articles 56 and 57 of the draft directive and Articles 86 and 87 of the draft regulation.

[39] Reasoned opinion of the French Sénat on COM(2012) 11, 4 March 2012.

[40] Reasoned opinion of the Italian Camera dei Deputati on COM(2012) 11, 4 April 2012.

[41] Reasoned opinion of the German Bundesrat on COM(2012) 11, 30 March 2012, point 3.

[42] Reasoned opinion of the Swedish Riksdag on COM(2012) 11, 30 March 2012.

[43] Reasoned opinion of the Belgian Chambre des Représentants on COM(2012) 11, 6 April 2012, at p14. Criticism concerned Article 62 of the proposal setting the requirements for Commission implementing acts in the consistency mechanism.

[44] Reasoned opinion of the French Sénat on COM(2012) 11, 4 March 2012, at p 3.

[45] Commission reply to the German Bundesrat, 10 January 2013, point 4; Commission reply to the Belgian Chambre des Représentants, 7 May 2013, at p 3. For the explanation and limits of the

the Commission's reply to the German *Bundesrat* and the Belgian *Chambre des Représentants* also maintained that more detailed rules instead of delegated acts 'would result in an inflexible and unwieldy legal text which would not be open to innovation and new technologies'. In the Commission's view, the regulation was 'deliberately drafted as a technologically neutral legal instrument', 'to anticipate all technological developments of the next twenty years', so the regulation can be supplemented without resorting to a revision of the regulation itself in every case.[46] As to delegation under implementing acts, the Commission explained that it has been proposed for the technical and practical aspects which demand uniform implementation.[47]

During the first reading of the proposal, the European Parliament did not mention the points raised by national parliaments with regard to delegated rulemaking directly. For example, with regard to the delegated acts concerning the right to be forgotten, a problem raised by the French chamber, the European Parliament added that the Commission may adopt delegated acts in this respect, 'after requesting an opinion of the European Data Protection Board'.[48] A similar rule was included with regard to the adoption of implementing acts by the Commission expressed in Article 62 of the proposal on the consistency mechanism. Whilst during the debate on the proposal, only one MEP raised the issue of the number of delegated acts,[49] in line with the European Parliament's preference for legislation the European Parliament decreased the number of delegations by means of delegated acts in the proposal (out of twenty-six delegations six remained and a number of delegations by means of implementing acts were changed into delegations by delegated acts).[50] Also in line with the European Parliament's preference for delegated acts within the delegated rulemaking, the number of delegations to adopt implementing acts has been drastically decreased (out of twenty-two only one remained).

In its most recent position, the Council deleted delegation by means of delegated acts in the cases mentioned by national parliament's reasoned opinions; with regard to the right to be forgotten and some of the delegations by means of implementing acts in Article 62 of the proposal.[51] Yet the Council did not acknowledge any role of the reasoned opinions of national parliaments in this regard. In general, following its preference for delegation the Council's position left more of the dispositions for delegated and implementing acts than the first reading of the European Parliament (out of twenty-two delegations by means of implementing

notion of 'essential elements of an area' see, in particular, the contribution of Dominique Ritleng (Chapter 7 in this volume).

[46] Commission reply to the Italian Camera dei Deputati, 21 February 2013.

[47] Commission reply to the Belgian Chambre des Représentants of 7 May 2013, at p 3; Commission reply to the French Sénat of 14 November 2012, at p 2.

[48] European Parliament, Amendment 112, P7_TA-PROV(2014)0212.

[49] European Parliament, Protection of individuals with regard to the processing of personal data—Processing of personal data for the purposes of crime prevention (debate), 11 March 2014. See the contribution of MEP F Obermayr.

[50] European Parliament, Amendment 200, P7_TA-PROV(2014)0212.

[51] Council Doc 11028/14, 30 June 2014.

acts nine remained and out of twenty-six delegations by means of delegated acts six were left).

In conclusion, this case shows that national parliaments became new actors in delegated rulemaking due to the ambiguity in the application of Article 290 and 291 TFEU, and consequently attempted to influence delegation. However, national parliaments play a very limited role because they may only react within the subsidiarity review procedure. Moreover, under Protocol No 2, the Commission is not obliged to introduce changes in its proposal unless required by the European Parliament and the Council within the 'orange card' procedure. Finally, the preference of the Commission for delegation over legislation reduced the opportunities for national parliaments to be able to change the delegations. It seems however, that the concern of national parliaments about the total number of delegations is shared by the European Parliament and the Council and it remains to be seen whether the final act will maintain this approach.

Case 4: Tobacco Directive

The Tobacco Directive case focuses on a new tobacco products directive that updates and replaces the current legislation in this field.[52] The novelty of the Commission proposal concerns issues such as enlarging the size and the position of health warnings, prohibition of flavourings, ban on slim cigarettes, and the regulation of e-cigarettes.[53]

The legal basis of the proposal is Article 114 TFEU, which demands the ordinary legislative procedure for approximation of laws of Member States for the establishment and functioning of the internal market. Accordingly, in June 2013 the Council issued a general approach[54] and the European Parliament voted on the amendments to the proposal in October 2013.[55] After five trilogues, the institutions approved the text of the directive in December 2013 with a view to an agreement on this legislative proposal at first reading.[56] In March 2014 the Tobacco directive was finally adopted.[57]

The issue at stake is the large number of provisions empowering the Commission to adopt delegated (twenty-two) and implementing acts (four) incorporated in the

[52] Commission Proposal of 19 December 2012 Directive of the European Parliament and of the Council on the approximation of the laws, regulations and administrative provisions of the Member States concerning the manufacture, presentation and sale of tobacco and related products, COM(2012) 788 final.

[53] M J Elsmore and V Obolevich, 'Thank You for Not Smoking: the Commission's Proposal for a New Tobacco Products Directive—Legally Sound, But Does It Hit the Spot?' (2013) 38 ELRev 552.

[54] General approach, Council Doc 11483/13, 24 June 2013.

[55] Amendments adopted by the European Parliament on 8 October 2013, P7_TA(2013)0398.

[56] Council Doc 17727/13 of 17 December 2013 (analysis of the final compromise with the view to an agreement) and Council Doc 17727/13 of 20 December 2013 (after the agreement of the Permanent Representatives Committee).

[57] Directive (EU) 2014/40 of the European Parliament and of the Council of 3 April 2014 on the approximation of the laws, regulations and administrative provisions of the Member States concerning the manufacture, presentation and sale of tobacco and related products and repealing Directive (EC) 2001/37, OJ 2014 L 127/1. The European Parliament adopted its position at first reading on 26.02.2014 and the Council adopted the Tobacco Directive on 14 March 2014 (See Council Press Release 7763/14). In this chapter we refer mostly to the European Parliament and Council positions

Commission proposal.[58] The most important delegations based on delegated acts related to, firstly, the adaptation of standards for the maximum yields of ingredients and their measurement methods in accordance with scientific development and international standards. A second type of delegation aimed at setting maximum levels of additives that produce a characterizing flavour. The third type of delegation referred to adapting the wording and the form of health warnings to scientific and market developments. Finally, with regard to e-cigarettes, the proposal conferred the Commission with the power to update the quantities of nicotine and the health warnings on these products by means of delegated acts.

With regard to implementing acts, the Commission proposed delegations to set and update the format for the submission of information by manufacturers and producers on ingredients and emissions of tobacco products and the dissemination of this information by Member States. Moreover, the Commission was given power to adopt uniform rules by means of implementing acts to determine whether a tobacco product has a characterizing flavour and whether a tobacco product contains additives that increase its toxic or addictive effects at the stage of consumption.

Several national parliaments reacted critically to the Commission's directive proposal within the subsidiarity review procedure under Protocol No 2. Nine parliamentary chambers in total issued a reasoned opinion stating a violation of the subsidiarity principle: the Portuguese *Assembleia da República*, the Danish *Folketing*, the Hellenic *Vouli ton Ellinon*, the Swedish *Riksdag*, the Bulgarian *Narodno sabranie*, the Czech *Poslanecká sněmovna*, the Italian *Senato* and *Camera dei Deputati*, and the Romanian *Camera Deputaților*.[59]

Even though the procedure under Protocol No 2 concerns only the scrutiny of the subsidiarity principle, the ambiguity in the rules regarding the exercise of delegated powers enshrined in Article 290 TFEU prompted a strong reaction from national parliaments.[60] The implemented acts seemed less problematic;[61] this is due to the fact that the Commission is assisted in the shaping of implementing acts by the committees composed of representatives of the Member States. Therefore, the attention of national parliaments focused on delegated acts, under which the Council and the European Parliament have 'only' an *ex post* right of objection and revocation. The Greek *Vouli ton Ellinon*, the Italian *Senato*, the Czech *Poslanecká*

before reaching the agreement by these institutions at first reading, which allows for better following of their preferences. The shape of delegations reached in the compromise text was later reflected in the final text of the acts. See legislative Resolution of 26 February 2014 on the proposal for a directive of the European Parliament and of the Council on the approximation of the laws, regulations and administrative provisions of the Member States concerning the manufacture, presentation and sale of tobacco and related products, P7_TA(2014)0160.

[58] The numbers express the total number of delegations in the proposal as some of the provisions contained more than one delegation.

[59] These opinions represented together only 14 votes out of the 18 required to raise a yellow card (at least one-third of 56 votes).

[60] Except for Swedish and Portugal chambers and Italian Camera dei Deputati.

[61] The German Bundesrat, which replied to the Commission proposal within Barroso's 'political dialogue', was the only chamber that referred to the delegation to adopt the implementing acts.

sněmovna, and the Bulgarian *Narodno sabranie* claimed that the proposal empowers the Commission to adopt delegated acts with regard to essential elements of the proposal.[62] Thus, the Bulgarian parliament disputed the application of delegated acts concerning the maximum tar, nicotine, carbon monoxide, and other yields; regulation of ingredients; health warnings; and appearance and content of unit packets.[63] In addition to the points raised by the Bulgarian chamber, the Italian *Senato* criticized delegations with regard to the e-cigarette.

Besides the delegation of essential elements, national parliaments criticized the large number of empowerments to adopt delegated acts within *one* legislative act. The Czech, Hellenic, Romanian, and Italian chambers objected to the fact that the Commission proposal provided for such an extensive transfer of powers to the Commission to adopt non-legislative acts on substantial provisions within one act.[64] Additionally, the Bulgarian parliament and the Italian *Senato* objected to the unlimited duration of the empowerment to adopt delegated acts.

In their reasoned opinions, national parliaments underlined the consequences of such a power transfer to the Commission. Accordingly, the Danish *Folketing* considered the delegations of power to be a hurdle for national parliaments when seeking to monitor the compliance of proposals with the principle of subsidiarity and the consequences of the directive.[65] Additionally, the Italian *Senato* claimed 'an excessive and unjustified' conferral of power on the Commission that encroached on the competence of national parliaments by denying them the possibility to assess the subsidiarity and proportionality of the delegated acts.[66] Finally, in the view of the Bulgarian chamber, the approach presented in the proposed directive deprived the Member States of 'the opportunity to implement a policy tuned to their national specificities and societal and cultural differences, in accordance with national health policies'.[67]

In line with the Commission's preference for delegation, it gave a very succinct reply to the concerns of national parliaments rebutting all their arguments against the proposed delegated powers.[68] More specifically, the Commission defended the power to adopt delegated acts as necessary in order to make this directive 'fully operational in the view of technical, scientific, and international developments in the tobacco manufacture, consumption, and regulation'. The Commission further

[62] The Hungarian parliament and the Czech Senát raised similar issue within the Barroso 'political dialogue'.

[63] Similar points were also raised by the Hungarian parliament within the political dialogue.

[64] The Slovak Národná Rada raised this issue within the political dialogue.

[65] Reasoned opinion of the Danish Folketing on COM(2012) 788, 4 March 2013, at p 3.

[66] Reasoned opinion of the Italian Senato on COM(2012) 788, 30 January 2013, at pp 1–2; Reasoned opinion of Bulgarian Narodno sabranie on COM(2012) 788, 28 February 2013, point 3.

[67] Reasoned opinion of Bulgarian Narodno sabranie on COM(2012) 788, 28 February 2013, point 3.

[68] Reply of the Commission to the Italian Senato (25 June 2013) and the Camera dei Deputati (28 May 2013), the Greek parliament (25 June 2013), the Romanian Camera Deputaţilor (18 June 2013), the Bulgarian parliament (18 July 2013) the Danish Folketing (25 June 2013), the Czech Poslanecká sněmovna. The opinions issued in the political dialogue received a similar reply from the Commission.

maintained that the delegations of power provide for 'clear and concise criteria, giving limited discretion to the Commission'. Moreover, the Commission ensured involvement of the Member States in the preparation of the delegated acts and simultaneous transmission of relevant documents to the European Parliament and Council. In sum, due to the fact that the subsidiarity procedure does not empower national parliaments to block the legislative procedure, the Commission may unilaterally impose the conditions of delegation. Consequently, parliament's role in shaping delegated and implementing acts is limited even in cases when they trigger a 'yellow card'.

As to the contest between legislation or delegation, we argued earlier that *under the ordinary legislative procedure, the Commission and the Council will prefer delegated powers, whilst the Parliament will opt for legislation.* Accordingly, in the case of the directive on the tobacco products, the Commission proposed a large number of delegations which expressly empower the Commission. The Council also favoured delegations. The EPSCO Council's general approach shows that the Council reduced only two of the delegations by means of delegated acts[69] and added new provisions with delegations.[70]

In the European Parliament, a number of MEPs raised concerns during the plenary vote on amendments about the broad scope of delegated acts envisaged in the Commission proposal and underlined that the delegations concerned essential elements of the proposal.[71] As a result, the European Parliament upheld only less than a half of the delegated acts foreseen by the Commission, removing the controversial provisions on the characteristic flavourings, shape of unit packets, and nicotine-containing products.[72] With regard to one delegation, the European Parliament directly regulated details of text warnings for tobacco products in the legislative act.[73]

The final text of the directive shows that the opinions of national parliaments have not been shared by the Commission. The views of national parliaments did, however, find some support within the European Parliament and the Council in relation to the duration of the delegation. The EU legislator proposed that delegations should be limited to five years. As to the mode of delegation under delegated acts or implementing acts, only the delegated act on detailed rules for the shape and size of unit packets,[74] to which national parliaments objected, was deleted by both the European Parliament and the Council. Nonetheless, we cannot empirically ascertain the influence of national parliaments as neither the Council nor the

[69] Articles 9.3d and 13.3 of the proposal.

[70] Cf. Council Doc 11483/13 of 24 June 2013, Proposal for a Directive of the European Parliament and of the Council on the approximation of the laws, regulations and administrative provisions of the Member States concerning the manufacture, presentation and sale of tobacco and related products (First reading)—General Approach.

[71] European Parliament, Manufacture, presentation and sale of tobacco and related products (debate), 8 October 2013.

[72] European Parliament amendments, P7_TA(2013)0389.

[73] Article 8.3. Similar to the Council in General Approach.

[74] Article 13.3 of the proposal.

European Parliament referred directly to national parliaments as the source of influence for introducing these changes.

As to the high number of delegations, the European Parliament also opted to limit the number of delegations but did not directly invoke the arguments of national parliaments. This specific objection of national parliaments did not find support in the Council; the final legislative act contains a high number of delegations to adopt delegated acts. This might be due to the fact that Bulgaria, the Czech Republic, Poland, and Romania were in the opposing minority in the Council and hence their views were not taken into account in the general approach.[75]

In sum, the text of the directive remained closest to the Commission's and Council's preference for delegation, whereas the European Parliament's preference for legislation, expressed in the limits placed on the number of delegations, was not generally shared.[76]

Turning to the choice of a type of delegation that depended on the relative institutional power under the two forms of delegation, that is, delegated or implementing acts, we assumed that the European Parliament prefers delegated acts, whereas the Council prefers implementing acts. The general approach adopted in the Council introduced a number of amendments concerning delegated and implementing powers. As mentioned earlier, with regard to delegated acts, the Council removed only two delegations by means of delegated acts in their entirety[77] and moved another to the main body of the directive,[78] whilst limiting the scope of some other delegations. However, the Council did not introduce far-reaching limitations with regard to implementing acts. In fact, it advanced two new delegations to adopt implementing acts.[79] Additionally, as many as four delegations by means of delegated acts were replaced by implementing acts.[80] These changes confirm the Council's preference for implementing acts.

Whereas the European Parliament eliminated a very large number of delegations by means of delegated acts, it also added one new delegation of this type, namely on the procedure to obtain approval on additives by manufacturers and importers.[81] Meanwhile, it deleted all delegations to adopt implementing acts except for one.[82] These choices of the European Parliament confirm what we have argued earlier, namely that within delegation the European Parliament prefers delegated acts.

Finally, the agreed text of the directive is closest to the preferences of the Council and the Commission (for the implementing acts) in that the institutions

[75] House of Commons, 13th Report of the European Scrutiny Committee p 1.9, available at http://www.publications.parliament.uk/pa/cm201314/cmselect/cmeuleg/83-xiii/8302.htm.

[76] One exception exists. The EP's request for deletion of delegated act in Article 13(4) has been followed in order to finalize the agreement on the directive. Cf. Council Doc 17727/13 of 17 December 2013, Proposal for a Directive of the European Parliament and of the Council on the approximation of the laws, regulations and administrative provisions of the Member States concerning the manufacture, presentation and sale of tobacco and related products (first reading—legislative deliberation)—Analysis of the final compromise text with view to an agreement, p 2.

[77] Articles 9.3d and 13.3, Council Doc 11483/13.

[78] New Article 8.4a.

[79] New Articles 6.2b and 14.8a.

[80] Articles 9.4, 14.8b–c, and 14a.2.

[81] Article 6.10a, P7_TA(2013)0389.

[82] Article 5.3.

agreed to change some of the delegated acts into implementing ones, and added implementing acts proposed earlier by the Council and three new implementing delegations.[83] A particularly interesting instance concerns the procedure for the approval of additives by the Commission. In this regard, the European Parliament proposed in the amendments voted in October 2013 that this procedure would be established by the Commission by means of delegated acts.[84] However, the agreement reached by the institutions modified the procedure proposed by the European Parliament. The compromise solution provides that the Commission may set by means of implementing acts a 'priority list' of additives allowed in cigarettes and roll-your-own tobacco subjected to re-enforced reporting obligation by manufacturers or importers.[85]

As to the contest about the extent of delegation and as stated earlier, the Council indicates a preference for implementing acts whereas the European Parliament chooses delegated acts, thus conforming to their comparatively more far-reaching powers in each of the cases. Hence, the Council will be more willing to limit the scope of delegations by means of delegated acts and the European Parliament will prefer to limit the extent of delegations by means of implementing acts. In the Tobacco case, the Council has limited the scope of some delegations by means of delegated acts. For example, the Council decided in its general approach that with regard to the nicotine-containing products, the Commission may only adapt the wording of the health warnings, but not their position, format, layout, design, and rotation.[86] In sum, the Council followed its institutional preference for limitation of delegated acts as explained above.

In contrast to the Council, the European Parliament deleted most of the delegations under implementing acts. It was only with regard to the labelling of smokeless tobacco products that the European Parliament introduced limitations in the scope of delegation similarly to the Council.[87] Consequently, the expectation that the European Parliament will limit the extent of delegations based on implementing acts is confirmed by the fact that the European Parliament decided to almost completely eliminate them.

Finally, both the Council and the European Parliament proposed that the power to adopt delegated acts should be conferred on the Commission for a limited time period of five years, and demanded a report from the Commission in respect of the delegation of power nine months before that date. This amendment proposed by both institutions is in line with the Common Understanding. In sum, the changes in the scope of delegated acts introduced by the Council were largely followed in the agreement reached among the institutions.

To conclude, the existing formal rules in Articles 290 and 291 TFEU constitute ambiguous terms of contract and therefore trigger the scrutiny of national

[83] Article 5(1a) on additives, Article 8(6) on position of health warning in roll on tobacco and Article 18(11) on the notification format for the electronic cigarettes and refill containers, Council Doc 17727/13.

[84] Article 6.10a, P7_TA(2013)0389.

[85] Article 5.1a (new), Council Doc 17727/13.

[86] Article 18.5, Council Doc 11483/13.

[87] Article 11.3, P7_TA(2013)0389.

parliaments under Protocol No 2, originally directed at the review of the subsidiarity principle. Also in the Tobacco case, the Commission did not change the delegations in the basic act despite the opinions of national parliaments. In the subsequent bargaining over the Commission proposal under the co-decision procedure, the participating actors followed their institutional preferences. Given the choice between legislation and delegation, the Commission opted for delegations whereas the Council approved of delegation but limited the scope of delegated acts or proposed implementing acts. By contrast, the European Parliament opted for legislation, as manifested in the large amounts of deleted delegations. With regard to the choice between delegated acts and implementing acts, the Council chose implementing acts and the European Parliament showed a preference for delegated acts once delegation was decided upon. Finally, the European Parliament restricted the Commission's power in the remaining delegated acts by limiting the extent of these delegations in line with its preference for limiting delegation and using legislation. On the other hand, the Council limited delegation under delegated acts in favour of delegation under implementing acts. The agreement on the final text reached by the institutions shows that the Commission succeeded in keeping the majority of delegations intact. The Council succeeded in changing some of them into implementing acts and adding new ones. Compared with the other institutions, the European Parliament's preferences are less reflected in the decision outcomes.

Finally, as described above, the Commission did not follow the arguments stated in the reasoned opinions of national parliaments. In addition, the final text of the directive contains a large number of delegations criticized by national parliaments. However, the EU legislator decreased the duration of the empowerment to adopt delegated acts in line with the expectation of some of the parliaments. Similarly, one of the delegations by means of delegated acts to which the national parliaments objected was deleted. Nonetheless, as neither the European Parliament nor the Council mention the changes proposed by national parliaments, the role of national parliaments in shaping delegated legislation cannot be shown empirically.

6.5 Conclusion

Ever since the Lisbon Treaty introduced the new provisions on delegated rulemaking under Articles 290 and 291 TFEU, the newly created institutional rules have been subject to change. Some of the changes have occurred upfront in the formal political arenas, and have been contested by the relevant actors, that is, Council, European Parliament, and Commission as well as national parliaments. By contrast, other changes have occurred in a more covert or invisible way, unfolding after the adoption of a formal rule in the course of its application. We are focusing on the latter type of 'interstitial' institutional change and its consequences and ask 'Under what circumstances does "interstitial" institutional change occur after a formal rule has been adopted; what are its dynamics and its consequences?'

We define interstitial institutional change as informal institutional change which occurs between two formal rule revisions. Institutional change emerges once a formal political decision of integration has been taken that constitutes an incomplete contract. This offers the possibility of renegotiation and specification in the course of its application. The explanation is based on the assumptions of goal-oriented, boundedly rational actors, seeking to maximize their institutional power and thereby their power over policy outcomes. We hypothesize that '*an incomplete institutional rule or policy may lead to an interstitial institutional change in the course of its application. In the renegotiation of the incomplete institutional rule, the preferences of the most powerful actors will be reflected in the substance of the modified interstitial institutional rule*'. In order to show the plausibility of our argument, we discuss four cases of institutional change resulting from ambiguities in institutional rules under Articles 290 and 291 TFEU.

The Lisbon Treaty distinguishes between legislative delegation and executive delegation and provides for two separate procedures for 'delegated acts' and 'implementing acts'. Under Article 290 TFEU, the Commission—by legislation—may be delegated the power to adopt 'delegated acts' of general scope supplementing or amending certain non-essential elements of the legislation in question. The legislators must explicitly define the objective, content, scope, and duration of this delegation. They can also choose the mechanism(s) used to control the Commission when it applies these delegated powers: revocation and objection. However, the new provisions of the Lisbon Treaty leave unanswered many questions as to how delegated acts (Article 290 TFEU) and implementing acts (Article 291 TFEU) should be applied. In other words the provisions constitute an incomplete contract.

The first case focuses on the conflict between the Commission, the Council, and the European Parliament in the definition of the economic indicators under the scoreboard regime under the preventive arm of the Prevention and Correction of Macroeconomic Imbalances. Some vague provisions were introduced in the Regulation on the Prevention and Correction of Macroeconomic Imbalances that needed specification through delegated legislation. In the interpretation of these incomplete institutional rules, a conflict emerged over the choice of either delegated acts (Article 290 TFEU) or implementing acts (Article 291 TFEU). When deciding how to flesh out the scoreboard regime, that is, the indicators used to measure and monitor macro-economic and macro-financial imbalances, the Commission first proposed to define these indicators on its own. When there was resistance from both the Council and the European Parliament, the Commission proposed 'delegated acts' together with the European Parliament (Article 290 TFEU) whilst the Council wished to use an implementing act (Article 291 TFEU). A deadlock ensued which, after a round of negotiations, led to the use of an informal new type of procedure which is *neither* Article 290 TFEU nor Article 291 TFEU, the 'compromise'. What emerges from our theoretical perspective of interstitial institutional change is that the existing formal rules constitute ambiguous terms of contract, which in the situation of a decision stalemate—were re-bargained and transformed in such a way as to overcome the impasse. By so doing, the power of the Commission was clearly strengthened.

In the further application of the new institutional rule, it emerged however that the European Parliament did not feel fairly treated by the Commission. This ongoing struggle about the correct application of—in this case—already modified interstitial institutional rule (Recital 12) shows that the modified rule is in turn incomplete and offers opportunities to assert the relative institutional power of the actors involved, that is, about how to apply the modified rule in a specific case.

The second case, 'Financial Instruments External Relations: Pre-accession IPA II', refers to the issue that, under the Lisbon Treaty, External Relations were subject for the first time to the ordinary legislative procedure (previously the co-decision procedure), hence implying new powers for the European Parliament. Consequently, in negotiating the specifics of Articles 290 and 291 TFEU in their application to External Relations all actors, the Commission, the Council or the Member States and the European Parliament were treading on institutionally new territory and very cautiously negotiated the specifics of the application of Articles 290 and 291 TFEU to the Financial Instruments of External Relations. Renewed negotiations took place in view of the ambiguity of how Articles 290 and 291 TFEU should be employed in the case of the Financial Instruments External Relations Common Rule. The European Parliament wished to employ delegated acts, while the Commission and the Council opted for implementing acts. In these negotiations, a compromise was struck in which all involved actors made concessions. The outcome was the emergence of a new type of delegated act, that is, the '*amending delegated act*' in the mid-term review of the objectives/thematic priorities of individual beneficiary countries, as well as a strategic dialogue between the Commission and the European Parliament when defining strategic papers for individual Member States.

The third case concerns the legislation (one directive and one regulation) proposed by the Commission on data protection. The draft regulation in particular contained a large number of delegations that empowered the Commission. In view of the ambiguity in the application of Articles 290 and 291 TFEU, national parliaments became new actors in delegated rulemaking. Namely, national parliaments reacted to these proposals under the subsidiarity review mechanism introduced by Lisbon Treaty, overriding the strict wording of Protocol No 2 which demands a focus on the principle of subsidiarity violations. Their reasoned opinions highlighted the fact that the Commission proposals contain numerous delegations with far-reaching scope. Moreover, national parliaments signalled that these delegations grant the Commission far-reaching authority to adopt delegated acts with regard to the most important elements of this legislation.

As the number of opinions issued by national parliaments did not reach the 'yellow' or 'orange card' threshold, the Commission was not obliged to take any further steps to review its proposal. In its responses to national parliaments, the Commission rejected the arguments raised by national parliaments in line with its preference for delegation. In particular, the Commission replied that the delegations by means of delegated acts do not concern any essential element of the act proposed and that their period of validity is limited, allowing for more flexibility and openness to innovation and new technologies.

The fourth case concerns the new tobacco directive, and like the third case focuses on national parliaments as a new player in delegated rulemaking. With regard to the Commission proposal for a new tobacco directive, national parliaments criticized the large number of empowerments to adopt delegated acts within *one* legislative act, often concerning essential elements of the directive, as well as the unlimited duration of these delegations. However, as in the case of data protection, the Commission remained firm on its position and rebutted the arguments of national parliaments. In the subsequent bargaining over the Commission proposal under the co-decision procedure, the participating actors followed their institutional preferences. The preferences for delegation of the Commission and of the Council are taken most into account in the adopted text. The directive further contains a large number of delegations, which was one of the critical points raised by national parliaments. However, the EU legislator limited the duration of the empowerment to adopt delegated acts and deleted one of the delegations in accordance with the reasoned opinions of national parliaments. Hence, national parliaments have played some role in the delegated legislation in the tobacco case, but we cannot empirically show the impact of national parliaments as the European Parliament and the Council have not acknowledged it formally.

In conclusion, the comparison of the four cases shows that the European Parliament had real blocking power in the decision-making process in the first two cases and consequently was able to force the Commission and the Council to offer some concessions and obtain a modification of delegation rules in its favour.[88] Given the conflicting preferences of the other two institutional actors, it did not achieve what it requested, which was the use of delegation acts, but it attained modified institutional rules of delegation in each case: the *compromise rule* in the case of Excessive Macro Economic Imbalances, and the *amending delegated rule* in the case of external relations.

By contrast, the national parliaments had no formal blocking power of a Commission decision draft and did not obtain any concessions from the Commission. Only with the support of one of the other European level institutional actors could it have wielded more leverage, as in the case of some issues highlighted by national parliaments in the tobacco directive.

[88] In this respect see also Kieran Bradley's contribution to this volume (Chapter 4) on the 'winning' position of the European Parliament in the delegated rulemaking and the assistance of the Court of Justice.

PART III

THE LEGAL EVALUATION

7

The Reserved Domain of the Legislature

The Notion of 'Essential Elements of an Area'

Dominique Ritleng

7.1 Introduction

The notion of the 'essential elements of an area' included in Article 290 TFEU is designed to demarcate a material preserve of the legislature and relates therefore to the issue of delegation of powers. Legal assessments of delegation of powers are ambivalent.[1] In terms of principle, it is regarded with suspicion: *delegatus non potest delegare*. But the practical need to delegate is usually acknowledged: *sed delegare necesse est.*

Indeed, especially legislative delegations conflict with fundamental dogmas of the constitutional law theory. The democratic principle commands that legislation be adopted by the parliament composed of elected representatives of the people. To that end, the legislative power has been bestowed on the parliament and the latter cannot delegate it to another authority without colliding with the constitutional order of competences and the principles of democracy and separation of powers.[2] Accordingly, all rules of general application ('legislation' in the substantive sense) should be issued by the legislature.

But this ideal does not correspond to reality any longer, if ever it did. Even the most fervent proponents of Montesquieu's *trias politica* admit that the executive

[1] On this kind of schizophrenia, see G Tusseau, 'La législation déléguée', in M Troper and D Chagnollaud (eds), *Traité international de Droit constitutionnel*, Vol 2, (Dalloz 2012), 605, at pp 606–16.

[2] See the classical position defined by John Locke in *Second Treatise of Civil Government* (1690), Ch XI § 141 (available at http://www.constitution.org/jl/2ndtreat.htm): 'The legislative cannot transfer the power of making laws to any other hands: for it being but a delegated power from the people, they who have it cannot pass it over to others…And when the people have said, We will submit to rules, and be governed by laws made by such men, and in such forms, no body else can say other men shall make laws for them; nor can the people be bound by any laws, but such as are enacted by those whom they have chosen, and authorized to make laws for them. The power of the legislative, being derived from the people by a positive voluntary grant and institution, can be no other than what that positive grant conveyed, which being only to make laws, and not to make legislators, the legislative can have no power to transfer their authority of making laws, and place it in other hands.'

adopts norms of general application. The exigencies of modern states have led to a shift of lawmaking authority from the legislative to the executive branch. Modern parliaments lack both the time and the expertise to master technical details and adapt with sufficient speed to a changing environment. That is why most countries resort nowadays to the instrument of delegated legislation, whereby the legislator delegates its authority to issue generally binding rules to the government, in order to supplement or amend parliamentary legislation.

Nevertheless, because legislative delegation conflicts with several constitutional principles, conditions and limits are usually imposed on it.[3] One of the most important limits consists in assigning an exclusive domain to the legislature and in precluding consequently the legislator from delegating its power in this domain; in other words, in defining 'a substantive reserve of essential legislative power that parliament could not constitutionally shift to the executive'.[4] In Europe,[5] the concept of 'réserve de loi'[6] can be traced back to the beginning of the twentieth century in Germany. In its endeavour to clarify the division of power between the legislative and the executive within the constitutional framework of the second German empire, some scholars like Otto Mayer[7] posited that a legislative act was necessary for every regulation prejudicial to liberty and property, so as to ensure that limitations to fundamental rights are consented to by their holders or their representatives.

But this idea of a legislative domain did not imply at that time a non-delegation clause. It meant merely that the executive could not exert its normative power in the legislative domain without legislative authorization. It is only with the development of the review of constitutionality that the legislative domain became binding on the legislature and got its present meaning as an obligation for the legislature to exert its competence. So understood, the *réserve de loi* may be an absolute one and compel the legislature to entirely regulate a matter except the technical details; or a relative one and oblige the legislature to determine only the essential elements of a matter.[8] In both cases, the executive cannot intervene except in implementation

[3] For a survey with a comparative perspective see, apart from G Tusseau (n 1); H Pünder, 'Democratic Legitimation of Delegated Legislation—A Comparative View on the American, British and German law' (2009) 58 ICLQ 353; P L Lindseth, 'The Paradox of Parliamentary Supremacy: Delegation, Democracy and Dictatorship in Germany and France, 1920s–1950s' (2003–4) 13 Yale Law Journal 1341.

[4] P L Lindseth (n 3) at p 1352.

[5] For a brief account of the American non-delegation doctrine, see H Pünder (n 3); R Schütze, '"Delegated" Legislation in the (New) European Union: A Constitutional Analysis' (2011) 74 MLR 661, at pp 664–6.

[6] On this issue, see especially, J Tremeau, *La réserve de loi. Compétence législative et constitution*, Presses universitaires d'Aix-Marseille (1997).

[7] O Mayer, *Le droit administratif allemand*, Bibliothèque internationale de droit public, 4 Vols (Giard and Brière 1903–6).

[8] For examples of such a distinction, see the account of the Spanish and Italian constitutional laws given by J Tremeau (n 6), at pp 45–56. See also the wording of Article 34 of the French Constitution which distinguishes between the matters whose rules shall be determined by parliamentary laws and the matters of which parliamentary laws shall lay down the basic principles, but the jurisprudence has considerably mitigated this distinction.

of the legislation. However, *if* the legislature is forbidden from leaving the executive to use its own executive powers in the regulation of a matter that is part of the legislative domain, delegation of legislative power is not always prohibited.

For instance, in legislative matters that are listed mainly in Article 34 of the Constitution of 4 October 1958, the legislature is bound to legislate and to exhaust its competence, or it would commit what is called in French public law an 'incompétence négative'.[9] But Article 38 of the Constitution authorizes the parliament to accord to the government a legislative delegation.[10] Likewise, the Italian legislature is under an obligation to regulate substantially the matters belonging to the 'riserva di legge', unless it delegates the exercise of the legislative function in compliance with Article 76 of the Constitution of 27 December 1947.[11]

However, very often a delegation of legislative power can relate only to certain matters that form part of the legislature's domain. For example, Article 82 of the Spanish Constitution of 27 December 1978 excludes from the realm of a legislative delegation the adoption of organic laws pertaining to the implementation of fundamental rights and public liberties, those approving the Statutes of autonomy and the general electoral system and other laws provided for in the Constitution.[12] In a similar fashion, the Portuguese Constitution of 25 April 1976 distinguishes between matters of the legislative domain falling under the exclusive responsibility of the legislature (Article 164) and matters of the legislative domain that can be the object of a delegation of legislative power (Article 165). Also, in German constitutional law, according to the *Gesetzesvorbehalt* theory, there is an area reserved for the legislature, in which the executive is forbidden to act. This area is delimited in keeping with the *Wesentlichkeits* theory, according to which the adoption of essential rules—that is, norms restricting the exercise of fundamental rights or having an impact on some other fundamental aspect of public policy—must be reserved for the legislature.[13]

The same causes have produced the same effects in EU law. The phenomenon of delegation is widespread as well.[14] Admittedly, in the absence of an organic

[9] For some illustrations, see Conseil constitutionnel, Decision 2009-592 DC of 19 November 2009, 4–7; Decision 98-401 DC of 10 June 1998, paras 7–17. See also P Rrapi, 'L'incompétence négative dans la QPC: de la double négation à la double incompréhension' (2012) 34 Nouveaux Cahiers du Conseil constitutionnel 12; A Vidal-Naquet, 'L'état de la jurisprudence du Conseil constitutionnel sur l'incompétence négative' (2015) 46 Nouveaux Cahiers du Conseil constitutionnel 7.

[10] On the other hand, during the 4th French Republic, some matters were reserved to the legislature pursuant to the Constitution and the republican constitutional tradition without any possibility of legislative delegation. However, in these matters, the legislature could limit itself to the adoption of the essential rules and the executive power could be enabled to lay down the details (see Opinion of the French Conseil d'Etat n° 60.497 (1953) Revue du droit public, p 170).

[11] M Baudrez-Toucas, 'Italie. Les décrets législatifs' (1987) 3 RFDA 732.

[12] M Cano and J Mestre, 'Espagne. La délégation législative' (1987) 3 RFDA 725.

[13] H Maurer, *Droit administratif allemand* (LGDJ 1994), at pp 108–23; see also P L Lindseth, 'The "Law-Regulation Distinction" and European Law Integration: Reflections on the German Jurisprudence from the 1960s to the Present' (2010) 4 *Jus politicum*.

[14] For an in-depth analysis of the legal instrument of the delegation in European law, see Y Gautier, *La délégation en droit communautaire*, PhD thesis (University of Strasbourg III 1995).

separation of powers,[15] it could not be spoken of as a legislative power in a formal sense in the pre-Lisbon world.[16] Nonetheless the Council, which had also been granted the executive power at Community level,[17] had been originally vested with the power to enact primary legislation in the substantive meaning of the word, that is, measures of general application having their legal basis directly in the EC Treaty. And the treaty makers had anticipated that the Council would show itself unable to legislate on all matters falling within the scope of the Treaty. Though legislative delegation was not legally possible before the entry into force of the Lisbon Treaty,[18] the EC Treaty had provided for the possibility of a delegation of implementing powers from the Council to the Commission: Article 155 EEC (then renumbered Article 211 EC) entitled the Commission 'to exercise the powers conferred on it by the Council for the implementation of the rules laid down by the latter'. In the course of the years, the Council made an increasing use of it.

A study issued in 2004 showed that 62% of legal acts had been adopted on a secondary basis, and 89% of them by the Commission.[19] This intensive recourse to the mechanism of delegation has occurred despite the fact that delegation of powers must meet with some requirements to be legal in EU law as well. The Court of Justice has developed in particular a non-delegation doctrine,[20] whereby 'the European legislator is prohibited from delegating essential political choices to the executive'.[21] This non-delegation doctrine has been explicitly taken up in the Lisbon Treaty. Article 290 TFEU, which allows for the first time delegations of legislative power,[22] subjects them to a limit: 'the essential elements of an area shall be reserved for the legislative act and accordingly shall not be the subject of a delegation of power'.

The new legal context created by the Lisbon Treaty in which the legislature's domain takes place now may change its meaning. To assess whether it is the case, after a brief reminder of the origin of the notion of 'essential elements of an area', its function, scope, and content will be looked into.

[15] On, notwithstanding, the existence from the outset of a functional separation of powers, see K Lenaerts, 'Some Reflections on the Separation of Powers in the European Community' (1991) 28 CMLRev 11.

[16] D Ritleng, 'La loi', in J B Auby (ed), *L'influence du droit européen sur les catégories du droit public* (Dalloz 2010), at p 215.

[17] i.e. the power to adopt measures implementing EC basic acts.

[18] Indeed, in the absence of a treaty provision enabling the legislature to delegate its power, both principles of conferral and of institutional balance prohibited the use of secondary legal bases for the purpose of adopting legislative measures following a simplified procedure as opposed to that laid down by the Treaty. That is what the Court recalled in its ruling in Case C-133/06 *Parliament v Council*, EU:C:2008:257.

[19] A Von Bogdandy, F Arndt, and J Bast, 'Legal Instruments in European Union Law and their Reform: A Systematic Approach on an Empirical Basis' (2004) YEL 91, at pp 126–7.

[20] Case 25/70 *Einfuhr- und Vorratsstelle für Getreide und Futtermittel v Köster, Berodt & Co*, EU:C:1970:115, para 6.

[21] R Schütze, '"Delegated" Legislation in the (New) European Union: A Constitutional Analysis' (2011) 74 MLR 661, at p 662.

[22] R Schütze, ibid; B Driessen, 'Delegated legislation after the Lisbon Treaty: an analysis of Article 290 TFEU' (2010) 35 ELRev 837; D Ritleng, 'La délégation du pouvoir législatif de l'Union européenne', in *Mélanges J P Jacqué* (Dalloz 2010), at p 559.

7.2 Origin: Going Back to the *Köster* Jurisprudence

The ban made on the legislature to delegate its power to issue the rules concerning the essential elements of an area is not something new in EU law. The origin is to be found in the landmark ruling *Köster* handed down by the Court of Justice on 17 December 1970. In this judgment, the Court drew from 'the legislative scheme of the treaty... (and from) the legal concepts recognised in all the Members States'[23] a distinction between the measures directly based on the treaty itself and derived law intended to ensure their implementation. For the Court, it cannot be a requirement that all the details of a matter be drawn up according to the procedure laid down by the treaty for the purpose of complying with the institutional balance set by that procedure.[24] Only 'the basic elements of the matter to be dealt with' shall be reserved for basic regulations or directives. Implementing measures adopted according to a less cumbersome procedure, either by the Council itself or by the Commission acting on a delegation given in compliance with Article 155 EEC, may set out the remainder.[25]

The *Köster* solution became settled case law. Its statements have been repeated many times by the Court since then. Sometimes, the reminder was word for word the same,[26] sometimes the wording differed slightly: some rulings spoke about the 'rules (which are) essential to the subject-matter envisaged';[27] in some others, the 'basic elements of the matter to be dealt with' became 'the essential elements of the matter to be dealt with'[28] or 'the essential rules governing the matter in question'[29] or, more shortly, 'essential rules'.[30] In a judgment delivered in 2005, the Court of Justice stated that the Community legislature, acting on the basis of the then Article 95 EC, 'must determine in the basic act the essential elements of the harmonising measure in question',[31] adding that the legislative act 'may be limited to defining the provisions which are essential for the achievement of objectives in connection with the establishment and functioning of the internal market in the field concerned'.[32]

[23] Case 25/70 (n 20), para 6; see also Case 30/70, *Otto Scheer*, EU:C:1970:117, para 15.

[24] AG Poiares Maduro has reminded us, if need be, that 'the legislative procedures laid down by the Treaties establish the extent to which each institution is to be associated with the taking of decisions and thus establish an institutional balance' (Opinion in Case C-133/06 *Parliament v Council*, EU:C:2007:551, point 31).

[25] Case 25/70 *Köster* (n 20), para 6; see also Case 30/70 *Otto Scheer* (n 23), para 15.

[26] See in particular Case 230/78 *Eridania*, EU:C:1979:216, para 7; Case 46/86 *Romkes*, EU:C:1987:287, para 17; Case C-63/90 *Portugal and Spain v Council*, EU:C:1992:381, para 14.

[27] Case C-240/90 *Germany v Council*, EU:C:1992:408, para 36; Case C-355/10 *Parliament v Council*, EU:C:2012:516, para 64.

[28] Case C-156/93 *Parliament v Commission*, EU:C:1995:238, para 18; Case C-303/94 *Parliament v Council*, EU:C:1996:238, para 23.

[29] Case C-48/98 *Söhl & Söhlke*, EU:C:1999:548, para 34.

[30] Case C-356/97 *Molkereigenossenschaft Wiedergeltingen*, EU:C:2000:364, para 21.

[31] Case 66/04 *United Kingdom v Parliament and Council*, EU:C:2005:743, para 48.

[32] Ibid, para 50.

Whatever the changes in the formulas used, the meaning remained always the same. Whereas the provisions that are essential for the matter to be regulated must be reserved to the basic instrument because they were considered to be of a legislative nature, all the remaining provisions were presented as 'being merely of an implementing nature'[33] and could, therefore, be the subject of a delegation of 'implementing' powers.[34]

Since the concept of 'implementation' stemming from the *Köster* case law encompassed all the legal acts that did not found their legal basis directly in the Treaties but rather in secondary law, the delegation of implementing powers in the pre-Lisbon world covered both what are now termed respectively delegated acts (Article 290 TFEU) and implementing acts (Article 291 TFEU).[35] Indeed, the delegation of a legislative power was not legally possible under the pre-Lisbon Treaties.[36] So, it was under cover of implementation[37] that the Commission was often authorized to amend or supplement the legislative text itself.[38] Amending and supplementing measures as well as measures barely implementing the enabling legislative act were conflated in the comitology regime.[39]

[33] Case C-240/90 (n 27), para 36; Case C-356/97 (n 30), para 21; see also Opinion of AG J Kokott in Case C-66/04 (n 31), para 50.

[34] Case C-240/90 (n 27), para 35; Case C-356/97 (n 30), para 20; Case C-48/98 (n 29), para 34.

[35] The Court of Justice explicitly acknowledged this very recently. See Case C-427/12 *Commission v Parliament and Council*, EU:C:2014:170, para 36: 'Before the entry into force of the Lisbon Treaty, the expression "implementing powers" in the third indent of Article 202 EC covered the power to implement, at EU level, an EU legislative act or certain EU provisions and also, in certain circumstances, the power to adopt normative acts which supplement or amend certain non-essential elements of a legislative act. The European Convention proposed making a distinction between those two types of power, which is found in Articles I-35 and I-36 of the Draft Treaty establishing a Constitution for Europe. That amendment was ultimately incorporated in the Lisbon Treaty in Articles 290 TFEU and 291 TFEU'. See also Opinion of AG Cruz Villalón in Case C-65/13 *Parliament v Council (EURES)*, EU:C:2014:2071, paras 22–3; Opinion of AG Jääskinen in Joined Cases C-404/12 and 405/12 P *Council v Stichting natuur en Milieu*, EU:C:2014:309, para 49.

[36] Case C-133/06 *Parliament v Council*, EU:C:2008:257.

[37] As the Working Group on the simplification of the Union's legal instruments, set up by the Convention on the Future of the European Union which drafted the Treaty establishing a Constitution for Europe, deplored it, 'at present there is no mechanism which enables the legislator to delegate the technical aspects or details of legislation…As things stand, the legislator is obliged… to entrust to the Commission the more technical or detailed aspects of the legislation as if they were implementing measures, subject to the control of the Member States, in accordance with the provisions of Article 202 EC'. See Final Report of Working Group IX on Simplification, CONV 424/02, at p 8. See also Case C-133/06 (n 36), paras 43–51, where the Court of Justice indicated that the challenged provisions (granting the power to adopt and amend the lists of safe countries) were illegal only because the Council presented them as a delegation of a secondary legislative power and not as a conferral of implementing powers.

[38] For example Case 230/78 *Eridania* EU:C:1979:216, para 8; Case C-417/93 *Parliament v Council*, EU:C:1995:32, paras 28–33; and Joined Cases C-154/04 and C-155/04 *Alliance for National Health*, EU:C:2005:449, paras 90–2.

[39] Indeed, the (second) 1999 Comitology Decision provided that 'where a basic instrument stipulates that certain non-essential provisions of the instrument may be adapted or updated by way of implementing procedures, such measures should be adopted by use of the regulatory procedure' (Article 2(b) of Decision (EC) 1999/468, OJ 1999 L 184/23). Further, the second Comitology Decision was amended later on in order to introduce a new comitology procedure, the regulatory procedure with scrutiny for the enactment of implementing measures of a general scope designed to amend non-essential elements of a basic instrument adopted in accordance with the

The Lisbon Treaty has split the single delegation regime into two halves and made for the first time a distinction between 'legislative delegation and executive delegation'.[40] Now it emerges from Article 290 TFEU that, once 'the essential elements of an area' have been specified by the EU legislature, a legislative power may be delegated to the Commission 'to supplement or amend certain non-essential elements of the legislative act'. It stems also from Article 291 TFEU that, under certain conditions, the Commission may be enabled to pass implementing acts of Union's legislative acts. Only the latter shall still be subjected to the comitology regime,[41] whereas delegated acts shall fall under the control of the legislator itself set forth in Article 290 TFEU.[42]

To determine whether these treaty amendments change anything as regards the notion of 'essential elements of an area', the function and scope of the latter must now be studied.

7.3 Function: Defining the Legislature's Domain and Opening a Wide Scope for Delegation

By fixing the boundaries between what may be delegated and what may not be delegated and, accordingly, by defining a domain reserved for the legislature, the national constitution makers aim at guaranteeing democracy and separation of powers. The legislature, drawing from its election by the people a democratic legitimacy, must discuss and itself adopt the rules which are essential for the community and the citizen and be accountable for them to the people. At the same time, the objective of legitimate legislative rulemaking is to be balanced against the quest for efficient legislative rulemaking.

In EU law, it can hardly be argued that the same rationale has underpinned the emergence of the domain reserved for the EU legislature since it was not, originally at least, directly appointed by the people. The function of the legislature's domain was, nevertheless, to safeguard, as regards the most important rules, the institutional balance established by the legislative procedures laid down by the founding treaties and, thereby, to ensure that the most important rules would enjoy the different types of legitimacy, be it a democratic, state, or integrative one, represented by the different institutions that the legislative procedures associate with

co-decision procedure, by deleting some of those elements or by supplementing the instrument by the addition of new non-essential elements (see Council Decision (EC) 2006/512 of 17 July 2006, OJ 2006 L 200/11).

[40] P Ponzano, 'Executive and delegated acts: the situation after the Lisbon Treaty', in S Griller and J Ziller (eds), *The Lisbon Treaty—EU Constitutionalism without Constitutional Treaty* (Springer 2008), at p 135.

[41] Regulation (EU) 2011/182 of the European Parliament and of the Council of 16 February 2011 laying down the rules and general principles concerning mechanisms for control by Member States of the Commission's exercise of implementing powers, OJ 2011 L 55/13.

[42] For a more qualified assessment in the light of the changes that occurred within the operation of the Lisbon Treaty, see Chapter 9 by Paul Craig in this volume.

the lawmaking process (Commission, Council, Parliament).[43] Nowadays, since the European Parliament is elected by direct and universal franchise and has been entrusted with a power of legislative co-decision, the concern to grant the most important rules a democratic legitimacy has become more relevant as a justification for the notion of essential elements of an area.[44] More exactly, legislative acts being defined henceforth as acts adopted by legislative procedure, that is, procedure associating on an equal or, at least, unequal footing the Parliament and the Council,[45] the legislature's domain is now designed to give the most important rules the double legitimacy on which the European Union as an union of States and citizens is founded: the European Parliament accounts for the voice of the EU citizens, whereas the Council represents the interests of the Member States.[46]

However, this is not the sole objective of the definition of a realm reserved for the legislature. Since the domain reserved for the legislature proves to be a rather small one, comprising only the essential elements of an area,[47] it is also intended, perhaps most importantly, to determine, as a corollary, the realm open to a delegation to the Commission, whether a legislative delegation or a conferral of implementing powers or, in duly justified specific cases, to a reservation of implementing powers to the Council. To put it succinctly, the aim to be achieved is to open a large space to secondary legislative powers or implementing powers. This goal sounds at odds with the concern of guaranteeing the enactment of legislation whose legitimacy is beyond dispute. But to clutter up EU legislation with excessive details runs counter to the very essence of legislation and the legislature of the EU is unable to cope with changing market circumstances with sufficient speed.

There is a need for delegating the establishment of the more technical or detailed aspects. That is why, as the Court of Justice held in *Köster*, once the legislature has determined the basic elements of the matter to be dealt with in accordance with the procedure provided for in the Treaty, 'an implementing power of appreciable scope'[48] may be conferred on the Commission. Indeed, the Court of Justice inferred from 'the context of the Treaty' and also from 'practical requirements' that the concept of implementation must, as a rule,[49] be given a 'wide interpretation'; the legislature may vest in the Commission 'wide powers of discretion and action', especially in the fields of agriculture and foreign trade, since only the Commission

[43] See, in particular, Chapter 4 by Kieran Bradley in this volume.

[44] Opinion of AG Jääskinen in Case C-270/12 *United Kingdom v Europeam Parliament and Council*, EU:C:2013:562, para 83: 'The main constitutional concern relating to Article 290 TFEU delegated acts appertains to democratic accountability. In other words, how much legislative power can be delegated and how can the exercise of such delegated powers be controlled by the legislature?'. See also, Opinion of AG J Kokott in Case C-66/04, *United Kingdom/Parliament and Council*, EU:C:2005:520, para 56.

[45] Article 289 TFEU.

[46] Final Report of European Convention Working Group IX (n 37), at p 2.

[47] All the more that the concept of 'essential elements of an area' is interpreted 'very strictly' (Opinion of AG Kokott in Case C-66/04 (n 44), para 52), as will be highlighted below when examining the content of the notion.

[48] Case 25/70 (n 20), para 9; see also Case 30/70 (n 23), para 18.

[49] See, however, Case 22/88 *Vreugdenhil and van der Kolk*, EU:C:1989:277, para 17.

is in a position to follow constantly and attentively the trends on the agricultural or international markets and to act with the swiftness called for by the situation.[50] The Commission may be assigned to draw up general rules and the application of rules to specific cases by means of acts of individual application.[51] It may even be authorized to adopt penalties[52] or derogations or amendments[53] from the provisions of the legislative act.

To be sure, the action of the legislature is not limited to specifying the 'essential elements of an area'. In the exercise of its power, the legislature can go beyond the boundaries of its reserved field and regulate all the points it wants, leaving no room for legislative delegation or implementing powers' conferral. There is no sphere of action reserved to the executive power. But there are obvious 'practical requirements' that explain the need to leave it to the executive power, acting by means of implementing or delegated acts, to determine a great deal of the matter envisaged. As everyone knows, it is hardly possible to regulate a whole matter in compliance with the heavy legislative procedures set out in the Treaty.

As a consequence of this broad understanding of the sphere open to delegation, the limits of the powers accorded must be judged in the light of the general objectives of the relevant legislation rather than of the literal meaning of the enabling provision, so that the Commission must be deemed enabled to take all the measures which are necessary or appropriate for the implementation of the basic legislation, provided that they are not contrary to such legislation.[54]

In accordance with that broad understanding, the Court of Justice tended also to require only very little as to the degree of definiteness of a delegation of powers to the Commission. Although the first Comitology Decision compelled the Council to specify the 'essential elements' of the powers conferred on the Commission,[55]

[50] See, on agricultural markets, Case 23/75 *Rey Soda*, EU:C:1975:142, paras 10–11; Joined cases 279, 280, 285 and 286/84 *Rau v Commission*, EU:C:1987:119, para 14; Case 167/88 *Association générale des producteurs de blé*, EU:C:1989:234, para 15; Case C-478/93 *Netherlands v Commission*, EU:C:1995:324, para 30; Case C-285/94 *Italy v Commission*, EU:C:1997:313, para 22; Case C-241/95 *Accrington Beef*, EU:C:1996:496, para 20; on foreign trade, Case C-159/96 *Portugal v Commission*, EU:C:1998:550, paras 40–1.

[51] Case 41/69 *ACF Chemiefarma*, EU:C:1970:71, paras 60–2; Case 16/88 *Commission v Council*, EU:C:1989:397, para 11; Case C-122/04 *Commission v Parliament and Council*, EU:C:2006:134, para 37; Case C-443/05 P *Common Market Fertilizers*, EU:C:2007:511, para 115.

[52] Case C-240/90 (n 27), EU:C:1992:408, para 37.

[53] Provided that they relate to the general system of the legislative act and do not jeopardize the essential elements embodied in it (Case 230/78 *Eridania* (n 26), para 8; Case C-417/93 *Parliament v Council*, EU:C:1995:32, paras 28–33). See also Joined Cases C-9/95, C-23/95 and C-156/95 *Belgium and Germany v Commission*, EU:C:1997:50, paras 26–34. See the analysis of C F Bergström, *Comitology—Delegation of Powers in the European Union and the Committee System* (Oxford University Press 2005), at pp 233–40.

[54] Case 23/75 *Rey Soda*, para 14; Case 121/83 *Zuckerfabrik Franken*, EU:C:1984:175, para 13; Case C-478/93 *Netherlands v Commission*, EU:C:1995:324, para 31; Case C-285/94 *Italy v Commission*, EU:C:1997:313, para 22; Joined Cases C-9/95, C-23/95 and C-156/95 *Belgium and Germany v Commission*, EU:C:1997:50, para 36–7; Case C-159/96 *Portugal v Commission*, EU:C:1998:550, para 41; Case C-48/98 *Söhl & Söhlke*, EU:C:1999:548, para 36; Joined Cases C-37 and 38/02 *Di Leonardo Adriano Srl*, EU:C:2004:443, para 56; Case C-403/05 *Parliament/Commission*, EU:C:2007:624, para 51; Joined Cases C-14 and 295/06 *Parliament and Denmark v Commission*, EU:C:2008:176, para 52.

[55] Council Decision (EEC) 1987/373 of 13 July 1987, OJ 1987 L 197/33.

the Court of Justice held that, 'since the Council has laid down in its basic regulation the essential rules governing the matter in question, it may delegate to the Commission general implementing power without having to specify the essential components of the delegated power; for that purpose, a provision drafted in general terms provides a sufficient basis for the authority to act'.[56] However, since then,[57] the second Comitology Decision restated the requirement of stipulating the essential elements of the powers conferred in the enabling provisions[58] and the Court of Justice has judged that, since the third indent of Article 202 EC, on the basis of which the second Comitology Decision was adopted, empowered the Council to lay down principles and rules with which the manner of exercising the implementing powers conferred on the Commission must comply, those principles and those rules were to be observed when measures conferring implementing powers on the Commission were adopted.[59] And, as regards the enactment of delegated acts, Article 290 TFEU now provides that 'the objectives, content, scope and duration of the delegation of powers shall be explicitly defined' in the legislative enabling act.

7.4 Scope: a Limit to Legislative Delegation Only?

The drawing up of the essential elements of an area rests with the exclusive competence of the EU legislature. Two consequences follow.

First, a limit is put on the EU legislature's power to delegate. As recalled in Article 290 TFEU, the essential elements of an area 'shall not be the subject of a delegation of power'. It follows from this non-delegation clause that the legislature must exhaust its exclusive jurisdiction and define the essential elements of an area itself. If not, the legislature would violate the principle according to which the legislative power is not available to the legislature.[60] When invited to do so, the Court of Justice reviews whether the EU legislature has laid down the essential elements of the matter and has not unlawfully delegated them.[61] And when

[56] Case C-240/90 *Germany v Council*, EU:C:1992:408, para 41. See also Case C-48/98 *Söhl & Söhlke*, EU:C:1999:548, para 34.

[57] See Case 291/86 *Central Import Münster*, EU:C:1988:361, para 13, where the Court of Justice stated that, for the enabling provision to be valid, 'it must be sufficiently specific, that is to say, the Council must clearly specify the bounds of the power conferred on the Commission'. And the Court went on, judging that the provision at issue enabling the Commission to take protective measures applicable to imports of dried grapes met this requirement, since it determined 'the situations in which protective measures may be taken, the criteria for assessing whether such a situation exists, the kind of measures to be adopted and the period of their validity' (para 15).

[58] Article 1 of Council Decision (EC) 1999/468 of 28 June 1999, OJ 1999 L 184/23.

[59] See Case C-378/00 *Commission v Parliament and Council*, EU:C:2003:42, para 40. See also Case C-66/04 *United Kingdom v Parliament and Council*, EU:C:2005:743, para 49.

[60] Cf. French *principe d'indisponibilité de la compétence législative*.

[61] Case C-240/90 *Germany v Council*, EU:C:1992:408, paras 30–9; Case C-417/93 *Parliament v Council*, EU:C:1995:32, paras 28–33; Case C-104/97 P *Atlanta AG*, EU:C:1999:498, paras 70–7; Joined Cases C-154/04 and C-155/04 *Alliance for National Health*, EU:C:2005:449,

performing this task, it does not limit its control to manifest errors of assessment, although the indeterminacy of the notion of essential elements of an area might have prompted to leave it to the legislature's discretion to define its content.[62] As the Court of Justice emphasized it, 'ascertaining which elements of a matter must be categorised as essential is not... for the assessment of the European Union legislature alone, but must be based on objective factors amenable to judicial review'.[63] This jurisprudential attitude deserves full support considering the constitutional importance of the issue and stands in striking contrast with the solution adopted regarding the equally constitutionally important divide between delegated and implementing acts.[64]

Second, a limit is also put on the delegate's power. However wide the powers accorded to a delegate may be, it is never allowed to set essential elements or alter the essential elements laid down in the legislative act.[65] As Article 290 TFEU reminds us, the delegate may only be enabled, where appropriate, to amend non-essential elements of the legislative act. And the Court of Justice exerts a strict scrutiny both on the respect by secondary acts of the essential elements of an area specified in the legislative act[66] and on the point as to whether the secondary act has unduly laid down an essential element.[67]

That being said, what must now be dealt with further is the issue as to whether the two limits recalled above apply whatever the delegator/delegating act and the delegate/delegated or implementing act concerned. Indeed, as pointed above, the notion of essential elements of the matter had been designed to draw the border between what should be specified by basic acts and what may fall within the ambit of implementing acts. Now, pursuant to Article 290 TFEU, the notion of 'the essential elements of an area' helps to determine what must be drawn up by legislative acts and cannot be the subject of delegated acts, that is acts of general application aimed at amending or supplementing certain non-essential elements of the legislative act. Does that mean that, since the entry into force of the Lisbon Treaty, this notion confines only the EU legislature's power to delegate its power and the power of the Commission to adopt delegated acts?

paras 90–2; Case C-66/04 *United Kingdom v Parliament and Council*, EU:C:2005:743, paras 47–8 and 53–8.

62 See Final Report of European Convention Working Group IX (n 37), at 10; Opinion of AG Cruz Villalón in Case C-427/12 *Commission v Parliament and Council*, EU:C:2013:871, para 71; and also K Lenaerts and M Desomer, 'Towards a Hierarchy of Legal Acts in the European Union? Simplification of Legal Instruments and Procedures' (2005) ELJ 744, at p 755, n 52.

63 Case C-355/10 *Parliament v Council*, EU:C:2012:516, para 67.

64 Case C-427/12 *Commission v Parliament and Council*, EU:C:2014:170.

65 Case 46/86 *Romkes*, EU:C:1987:287, para 16; Case 230/78, *Eridania*, EU:C:1979:216, para 8; Case C-156/93 *Parliament v Commission*, EU:C:1995:238, para 18; Case C-355/10 *Parliament v Council*, EU:C:2012:516, para 66.

66 Case C-303/94 *European Parliament v Council*, EU:C:1996:238, paras 23–31.

67 Joined Cases C-296/93 and C-307/93 *France and Ireland v Commission*, EU:C:1996:65, paras 17–18; Case C-355/10 *Parliament v Council*, EU:C:2012:516.

7.4.1 The legislature's domain and acts implementing legislative acts

Article 291 TFEU, which still provides for the possibility of a conferral of implementing powers, does not expressly exclude from it the adoption of provisions relating to the essential elements of an area, even though the act conferring implementing powers[68] may also be a legislative act. Does that mean that the legislature's domain does not constitute a limit to the scope of implementing acts anymore? Most certainly not.[69] Several reasons support a negative answer. Firstly, were it the opposite, this would mean that the *Köster* jurisprudence has been partially overridden. If the authors of the Treaties had wanted this, they would have stated it, and even would have had to state it, explicitly.

Above all, from a teleological point of view, the reserved legislative field shall also apply to the implementing acts in the sense of Article 291 TFEU.[70] The reasons underlying the non-delegation clause, namely to safeguard the institutional balance set by the Treaties and to endow with sufficient legitimacy the EU essential rules, hold as much where a conferral of implementing powers is concerned.[71] I would even say that they hold all the more since the exercise of implementing powers by the Commission is subject only to a political control of the Member States within the comitology regime,[72] whereas the political oversight exerted by the legislature over the exercise of secondary legislative powers enables the Parliament and the Council to be placed on an equal footing to defend their legislative prerogatives.

Moreover, the Court of Justice has granted the EU legislature discretion as to whether to choose between delegated and implementing acts, subject only to a judicial review limited to manifest errors of assessment.[73] As a result, if the sphere reserved to the legislature did not constitute also a limit to the conferral of implementing powers, the legislature could easily free itself from the non-delegation clause by having recourse to Article 291 TFEU instead of Article 290 TFEU.[74]

[68] Which can be any 'legally binding Union act' by virtue of Article 291(2) TFEU.

[69] Opinion of AG Jääskinen in Case C-270/12 *United Kingdom v Parliament and Council*, EU:C:2013:1175, para 89; S Peers and M Costa, 'Accountability for Delegated and Implementing Acts after the Lisbon Treaty' (2012) 18 ELJ 427, at pp 445–6.

[70] See also H Hofmann, 'Legislation, Delegation and Implementation under the Lisbon Treaty: Typology Meets Reality' (2009) 15 ELJ 482, at p 488. For an opposite point of view, see R Schütze, *European constitutional law* (Cambridge University Press 2012), at pp 240–1.

[71] D Ritleng and E David, 'Les actes de l'Union', in V Constantinesco, Y Gautier, and V Michel (eds), *Le Traité établissant une Constitution pour l'Europe, analyses et commentaires* (Presses Universitaires de Strasbourg 2005), at p 203.

[72] See, however, Article 11 of Regulation (EU) 2011/182 of the European Parliament and of the Council of 16 February 2011 laying down the rules and general principles concerning mechanisms for control by Member States of the Commission's exercise of implementing powers, OJ 2011 L 55/13.

[73] Case C-427/12 *Commission v Parliament and Council*, EU:C:2014:170. For an extensive comment see D Ritleng, 'The dividing line between delegated and implementing acts: the Court of Justice sidesteps the difficulty in *Commission* v. *Parliament and Council (Biocides)*' (2015) 52 CMLRev 243. For an additional assessment see also the chapters in this volume by Paolo Ponzano (Section 3.7), Kieran Bradley (Section 4.5.3), Jürgen Bast (Section 8.3.1) and Paul Craig (Section 9.3.1).

[74] Another thing of course is whether the EU legislator would be willing to take this route. It could be argued that it might sometimes be in the interest of the Council acting in accordance with a special

Thus, the absence of any mention in Article 291 TFEU of substantive limits to the conferral of implementing powers can only reasonably have two explanations. Either the treaty drafters believed that it went without saying that the non-delegation doctrine would continue to apply to implementing acts and that they had only to specify it as regards the new category of delegated acts; or they assumed that acts which execute legislative acts without amendment or supplementation could not alter their essential elements or set other essential elements, so that there was no need to lay down a non-delegation clause.[75] But, as we know, even implementing acts add something to legislative acts[76] and, hence, may impinge on the province of the legislature.

7.4.2 The legislature's domain and non-legislative primary acts

In the pre-Lisbon world, the non-delegation doctrine endorsed by the *Köster* case law applied to every delegating primary act. Now, the wording of Article 290 TFEU subjects solely the 'legislative act' to the legislature's domain. Needless to say, the category of legislative acts is narrower than the category of primary acts, for the latter encompasses also, among others, acts passed by the Council without any participation of the Parliament.[77] That it ensues a narrowing of the non-delegation doctrine might sound logical, all the more that Article 290 TFEU from now on limits to legislative acts the possibility to provide for legislative delegations. Yet, pursuant to Article 291 TFEU, any 'legally binding Union act' may confer implementing powers on the Commission and, as seen above, the reserved legislative field shall also still confine the conferral of implementing powers by means of a legislative act. Should it be considered, then, that only basic acts of legislative character conferring implementing powers are bound as well by the non-delegation doctrine in the post-Lisbon world but not, any longer, non-legislative basic acts conferring implementing powers?

Several arguments might give force to such an interpretation. Firstly, if one of the reasons mentioned above for subjecting legislative acts conferring implementing powers to the non-delegation doctrine is to prevent the legislature from using the blurred divide between delegated and implementing acts to escape the constraints of its reserved domain, then it should logically imply that the latter applies also only to conferral of implementing powers by means of legislative acts. Secondly, such an interpretation would draw all the conclusions of the advent of an organic criterion of the EU legislature and of a formal definition of EU legislation.

legislative procedure which requests only the consultation of the Parliament but not in the interest of the EU legislator acting according to the ordinary legislative procedure.

[75] C Blumann, 'Un Nouveau Départ Pour la Comitologie. Le Règlement No 2011/182 du 16 Février 2011' (2011) Cahiers de Droit Européen 23, at p 27.

[76] P Craig, 'Delegated Acts, Implementing Acts and the New Comitology Regulation' (2011) 36 ELRev 671, at p 673. See also Chapter 9 by P Craig in this volume.

[77] See, e.g. before the Lisbon Treaty, Case C-159/96 *Portugal v Commission*, EU:C:1998:550: the basic act was a regulation adopted on the then Article 113 EEC, which did not provide for consultation of the Parliament; see, e.g. under the Lisbon Treaty, Articles 31, 43(3) TFEU.

Article 289 TFEU indeed defines legislative acts as 'legal acts adopted by legislative procedure', that is, either by the 'ordinary legislative procedure' which associates the Parliament and the Council with the decision-making process on an equal footing,[78] or by a 'special legislative procedure' which gives the power to decide, as the case may be, to the Parliament with the participation of the Council or to the Council with the participation of the Parliament.[79] It, then, might be argued that primary acts which are not adopted by legislative procedure shall now be deemed to be the work of the executive power, acting as a regulatory autonomous power,[80] as are secondary acts, be they delegated or implementing acts. Accordingly, the legislative domain, which tends in a separation of powers-based institutional system to protect the prerogatives of the legislature from encroachments of the executive, shall henceforth only limit delegations, of legislative power or implementing powers, accorded by legislative acts.

However appealing this analysis may seem, it falls short. The main reason for this lies in the fact, pointed out by many commentators,[81] that the attempt of the Lisbon Treaty, inspired by separation of powers considerations, to define what legislation is as opposed to executive action is not entirely successful. There are, indeed, procedures laid down in the Treaties that do not constitute special legislative procedures although, like the latter, they associate the Council and the Parliament on an unequal footing with the passage of primary acts. A careful reading of Article 289(2) TFEU reveals that not every procedure which provides for the adoption of a legal act 'by the European Parliament with the participation of the Council, or by the latter with the participation of the European Parliament, shall constitute a special legislative procedure'; it is so only 'in the specific cases provided for by the Treaties'.

In other words, if a treaty provision that provides for the participation of the Parliament and the Council on an unequal footing in the adoption of a legal act does not term this procedure a special legislative procedure, it is not such a procedure, and, accordingly, pursuant to Article 289(3) TFEU, the legal act passed on this basis does not constitute a legislative act. Numerous such instances can be found in the Treaties. To mention but one example,[82] Article 103 TFEU provides

[78] The ordinary legislative procedure is defined in Article 294 TFEU.

[79] In most instances the special legislative procedure consists of the adoption of the legal act by the Council acting unanimously after consent (see especially Articles 13(1), 25, and 352 TFEU) or consultation of the Parliament (see, e.g. Articles 23, 64(3), 81(3) TFEU). In a few instances, the special legislative procedure requires the legal act to be adopted by the Parliament after consent of the Council (see Articles 223(2), 226, and 228(4) TFEU).

[80] So called as a reference to the French concept of *pouvoir réglementaire autonome*. See J Ziller, 'National Constitutional Concepts in the New Constitution for Europe' (2005) 2 ECLR 452, at p 469.

[81] See especially P Craig, *The Lisbon Treaty. Law, Politics and Treaty Reform* (Oxford University Press 2010), at pp 256–60; B De Witte, 'Legal Instruments and Law-Making in the Lisbon Treaty', in S Griller and J Ziller (eds), *The Lisbon Treaty—EU Constitutionalism without Constitutional Treaty* (Springer 2008), at pp 100–1; K Lenaerts and M Desomer (n 62), at pp 753–4 and 764; and J Bast, 'New Categories of Acts after the Lisbon Reform: Dynamics of Parliamentarization in EU Law' (2012) 49 CMLRev 885, at pp 895–8.

[82] See also especially, Articles 95 (3) and 109 TFEU.

for the enactment of regulations or directives to give effect to the principles of competition policy set out in Articles 101 and 102 TFEU. Article 103 TFEU states that such regulations or directives are to be passed by the Council on a proposal from the Commission after consulting the Parliament but without signifying as elsewhere in the Treaty that the Council shall act 'in accordance with a special legislative procedure'.

One is bound to conclude that there need not be any procedural difference between a legislative and a non-legislative act; the definition of legislation is not strictly procedure-based. As a consequence, it might hardly reasonably be argued that the non-delegation doctrine shall apply only where the enabling act is termed a 'legislative act' by the Treaties. Too much importance would be given to legal nominalism and it would run counter to the rationale of the legislature's domain. Non-legislative procedures providing for the participation of the Parliament and the Council in the adoption of non-legislative primary acts set the same institutional balance as corresponding special legislative procedures do. They provide the same legitimacy to non-legislative primary acts as special legislative procedures do to legislative acts. Non-legislative primary acts passed pursuant to these non-legislative procedures are intended to lay down rules which are as essential, that is, of substantive legislative nature, as are the rules designed to be set by legislative acts. For instance, that was clearly so in the case of Council Regulation 2003/1[83] adopted on the basis of Article 83 EC (now Article 103 TFEU), which reformed profoundly the enforcement system of EC competition law, as the Court of Justice implicitly acknowledged by controlling the respect of the legislature's domain by Council Regulation 1962/17 (which has been replaced since then by Council Regulation 2003/1).[84]

Thus there are compelling reasons to continue applying the legislature's domain to non-legislative primary acts that contain a conferral of implementing powers. That said, the application of the non-delegation doctrine to non-legislative primary acts may not be based on Article 290 TFEU for this provision regulates merely legislative delegation made by a legislative act in the sense of Article 289(3) TFEU. Only recourse to the *Köster* jurisprudence, which should not be presumed to have been overridden in the absence of any express treaty provision in that sense, may provide for the legal basis of such a solution. Moreover, it might be argued that the division of the old delegation regime into two halves made by the Lisbon Treaty concerns only legislative acts delegating legislative or implementing powers. Delegation of powers contained in non-legislative primary acts would still be ruled by the old single delegation regime framed by the *Köster* jurisprudence. Accordingly, powers delegated by non-legislative primary acts should still be regarded as implementing powers in the wide pre-Lisbon meaning of the term, enabling the delegate, where appropriate, even to amend the delegating act,

[83] Council Regulation (EC) 2003/1 of 16 December 2002 on the implementation of the rules on competition laid down in Articles 81 and 82 of the Treaty, OJ 2003 L 1/1.

[84] Case 41/69 *ACF Chemiefarma*, EU:C:1970:71, paras 59–70.

provided that it does not alter the essential elements of the area that is to be regulated by the delegating primary act.[85]

7.4.3 The legislature's domain and conferral of powers on EU agencies

In its ruling in *ESMA*, the Court of Justice acknowledged that Articles 290 and 291 TFEU were not intended 'to establish... a single legal framework under which certain delegated and executive powers may be attributed solely to the Commission' and that 'other systems for the delegation of such powers to Union bodies, offices or agencies may be contemplated by the Union legislature'.[86] In other words, decision-making powers that can be accorded to EU agencies are not subject to the limits set by Articles 290 and 291 TFEU.

Is it to be concluded that the conferral of powers to pass legally-binding measures on EU agencies is not confined by the legislature's domain? Here as well, the answer ought to be negative. The very same teleological reasons that support subjecting Article 291 implementing acts to the respect of the reserved legislative sphere militate in favour of forbidding the conferral of the power to regulate the essential elements of an area on European agencies.[87] In any event, the conferral of powers, according to the Court of Justice in *ESMA*, is bound by the *Meroni*[88] principle, which limits the discretion that can be given to agencies: an agency cannot be vested with a power whose use would make possible the exercise of actual economic policy and replace the choices of the delegator by the choices of the delegate, thereby bringing about an actual transfer of responsibility.[89] In short, an agency cannot be given the power to make decisions of policy-making. It is therefore most unlikely that powers conferred on an agency would ever be of such an extent as to encroach on the reserved legislative domain given that, as will be seen below, the essential elements of an area are confined to the drawing up of the fundamental guidelines of the EU policy, to the political choices falling within the responsibilities of the EU legislature. In reality, the sole issue ever discussed[90] was whether the *Meroni* non-delegation doctrine could be limited to a ban from assigning to an agency the setting of the essentials elements of a matter[91] or whether it should be read more expansively.

[85] For other possible interpretations, see P Craig (n 81), at pp 259–60.

[86] Case C-270/12 *United Kingdom v Parliament and Council*, EU:C:2014:18, paras 78–83. For an extensive comment, see C F Bergström, 'Shaping the New System for Delegation of Powers to EU Agencies' (2015) 52 CMLRev 219.

[87] Opinion of AG Jääskinen in Case C-270/12 *United Kingdom v Parliament and Council*, EU:C:2013:562, para 93.

[88] Case 9/56 *Meroni v High Authority*, EU:C:1958:7.

[89] Ibid, paras 41–2.

[90] See in particular, S Griller and A Orator, 'Everything under Control? The "Way Forward" for European Agencies in the Footsteps of the Meroni Doctrine' (2010) 35 ELR 3; R Schütze, *European Constitutional Law* (Cambridge University Press 2012), at p 235.

[91] Some judgments show that the Court of Justice is willing to mix up the *Meroni* non-delegation doctrine and the *Köster* non-delegation doctrine (see especially Joined Cases C-154/04 and C-155/04 *Alliance for National Health*, EU:C:2005:449, paras 90–2).

7.5 Content: To Be or Not To Be Essential, That Is a Tricky Question

If it is easy to determine what the essential elements of an area are not, the same cannot be said about what they are.

7.5.1 What the essential elements of an area are not

Three observations are worth being made from the outset.

Firstly, the determination of the legislative field does not refer to matters which should be reserved to the legislature. The legislative field is defined according to the importance, in each matter, of the rules to be adopted. Only the rules which constitute the essential elements of a matter must be the work of the legislature. In this, EU law refers more to the German *Gesetzesvorbehalt* than to the solution adopted by the French Constitution of 4 October 1958.[92]

Secondly, it emerges both from settled case law[93] and from the wording of Article 290 TFEU that it cannot be for a secondary legislative power or an implementing power to determine 'the essential elements of an area' nor to supplement or amend essential elements of the legislative act. Is it the same restriction? One might a priori contend that essential elements of a legislative act do not necessarily relate to the essential elements of an area. However, in its 2012 ruling *Parliament v Council*, the Court of Justice, after having recalled that 'the essential rules governing the matter in question must be laid down in the basic legislation and may not be delegated' inferred from it 'that implementing measures cannot amend essential elements of basic legislation or supplement it by new essential elements'.[94] Rightly so: once essentials elements of an area have been drawn up by the legislator, they become *ipso facto* essential elements of the legislative act, and since essential elements of an area fall within the exclusive remit of the legislature, essential elements of a legislative act cannot be lawfully modified by implementing or delegated acts. However, the notion of essential elements of an area is broader than the notion of essential elements of the legislative act. Indeed, the legislature may fail to exhaust its exclusive competence and lay down only some essential elements of an area; as a consequence, an implementing or delegated act may encroach on the reserved legislative domain by specifying other essential elements of an area without at the same time altering an essential element of the legislative act.[95]

Thirdly, the essential elements of an area should not be confused with 'the objectives, content, scope and duration' of a delegation of legislative power, although

[92] Article 34 of the French Constitution of 4 October 1958. See also Articles 164 and 165 of the Portuguese Constitution of 25 April 1976.

[93] Case C-355/10 *Parliament v Council*, EU:C:2012:516, 64 and 66.

[94] Ibid.

[95] For an example, see Joined Cases C-296/93 and C-307/93 *France and Ireland v Commission*, EU:C:1996:65, 17–18.

both of them are parts of the minimum content of the legislative delegating act.[96] The two sentences of Article 290 TFEU would otherwise be redundant. Moreover, the settled case law clearly distinguishes the two requirements.[97]

7.5.2 What the essential elements of an area are

The 'essential elements of an area' is a vague legal notion which one is hard pushed to say what it covers. The case law does not offer precise guidance on the dividing line between essential and non-essential elements. To be sure, the Court of Justice has given criteria of the essential elements but they largely fail to bring clarity. The assessment of what is to be deemed an essential element can thus only be made on a case-by-case basis.

(a) The criteria of an 'essential element'

The Treaties do not specify what is to be deemed an 'essential element'. An interesting attempt was made by the 'Penelope' Contribution to a preliminary draft Constitution of the European Union[98] but it did not have any follow-up. So, it is necessary to rely on the case law.

More than twenty years passed after the inauguration of the non-delegation doctrine in *Köster* before the Court of Justice made a first attempt to define the notion of 'essential elements' in its 1992 *Germany v Council* ruling. The German government contested the legality of a system of penalties to be applied in connection with an aid scheme introduced by the Commission under a power delegated by the Council. It contended in particular that those penalties should be considered essential features of the legislation governing the sphere at issue since they affected the fundamental rights of individuals. The Court replied that the classification 'essential' should be 'reserved for provisions which are intended to give concrete shape to the fundamental guidelines of Community policy' and that penalties, such as exclusions or surcharges, which are designed to ensure implementation of those fundamental guidelines did not deserve such a classification.[99] To back the latter assertion, the Court of Justice recalled that the inclusion of the power to impose penalties in the implementing powers was already recognized in the *Köster* judgment, wherein it was held that provisions which made the issue of an export licence conditional upon the provision of security and which provided for the

[96] For another, albeit not convincing, point of view, see H Hofmann (n 70), at pp 488–9.

[97] Case C-240/90 *Germany v Council*, EU:C:1992:408, para 41. See also Case C-48/98 *Söhl & Söhlke*, EU:C:1999:548, para 34.

[98] Article 77(2) of Commission President Romano Prodi's Feasibility Study 'Penelope' of 4 December 2002: EU legislative acts 'shall determine the fundamental principles, general orientation and essential aspects of the measures to be taken to that end; They shall determine the rights and obligations of persons and undertakings and the nature of the guarantees which they are to enjoy in all Member States'.

[99] Case C-240/90 *Germany v Council*, EU:C:1992:408, para 37; see also Case C-356/97 *Molkereigenossenschaft Wiedergeltingen*, EU:C:2000:364, 21–2.

forfeiture of that security when the obligation to export was not fulfilled within the requisite time-limits came within the Commission's implementing powers.[100]

The recent judgment of the Court of Justice in the *Schengen Borders Code* case constitutes another praiseworthy effort to sharpen the notion of an essential element.[101] In this ruling, which concerns the adoption of an implementing decision under European Parliament and Council Regulation 2006/562 (the so-called 'Schengen Borders Code Regulation')[102] the Court endeavoured to supply the EU legislature with a more detailed indication on how to assess whether an element is essential or not. To be sure, the case related to the pre-Lisbon comitology regime, but the Court had obviously in mind the current legal context and strove accordingly to develop an interpretation of the notion of essential elements which was of general relevance. The European Parliament had sought the annulment of the implementing decision adopted (by the Council) under the regulatory procedure with scrutiny and submitted that the decision—which established rules and guidelines for Frontex maritime operations—altered essential elements of the basic enabling act and introduced new essential elements.

In its findings, the Court of Justice began by specifying that 'provisions which, in order to be adopted, require political choices falling within the responsibilities of the European Union legislature' must be regarded as the essential rules governing the matter in question and cannot, therefore, be delegated.[103] The Court then held that deciding which enforcement powers should be exercised by border guards entails political choices falling within the responsibilities of the EU legislature, in that it requires conflicting interests to be weighed up on the basis of a number of assessments. Depending on the political choices made, the powers of the border guards may vary significantly, and the exercise of those powers may require authorization, be an obligation, or be prohibited, for example, in relation to applying enforcement measures, using force, or conducting the persons apprehended to a specific location. In addition, where those powers concern the taking of measures against ships, their exercise is liable, depending on the scope of the powers, to interfere with the sovereign rights of third countries according to the flag flown by the ships concerned.[104] That is why, according to the Court of Justice, the adoption of such measures was a matter for the EU legislature.[105]

One should of course praise the effort made by the judge to define the elusive notion of the essential elements of an area. A criterion is given in the judgment on the implementation of the SBC: an element is essential when it entails policy choices.[106] This criterion refers to the one already given in the ruling in *Germany*

[100] *Germany v Council*, ibid, para 38.

[101] Case C-355/10 *Parliament v Council*, EU:C:2012:516.

[102] See Article 12(5) of Regulation (EC) 2006/562 of the European Parliament and of the Council of 15 March 2006 establishing a Community Code on the rules governing the movement of persons across borders (Schengen Borders Code), OJ 2006 L 105/1.

[103] Ibid, 64–5. [104] Ibid, para 76. [105] Ibid, para 78.

[106] Opinion of AG Jääskinen in Case C-270/12 *United Kingdom v Parliament and Council*, EU:C:2013:562, para 93.

v Council: giving concrete shape to the fundamental guidelines of EU policy amounts to making political choices.

One might however cast doubt on the usefulness of such a criterion.[107] How, indeed, to reconcile this criterion with the solution following from settled case law that the Commission may be delegated wide discretionary powers? As the Court of Justice frequently recalls, the discretionary powers conferred on the Commission by a delegation 'correspond to the political responsibilities of the European Union legislature'[108] and hence their exercise is merely subject to a legality review limited to the search of manifest errors. The reference to 'political choices' is also at odds with solutions indicating, within the course of the assessment of the condition of a sufficiently serious breach of a rule of law intended to confer rights on individuals under which the Union may incur non-contractual liability, that the damaging implementing measure 'involves choices of economic policy'.[109] Arguably, the distinction between the discretion that the drawing up of the essential elements of an area supposes and the discretion that may be granted to the Commission lies in the extent of the margin of discretion. However, one has to admit that the indeterminacy remains for the most part.

Unlike the link made between essential elements and those entailing policy choices, another criterion emerging from the judgment regarding the implementation of the Schengen Borders Code might prove more helpful.[110] The contested implementing decision of the Council has been also regarded as containing essential elements, on the ground that 'conferring powers of public authority on border guards..., which include stopping persons apprehended, seizing vessels and conducting persons apprehended to a specific location—means that the fundamental rights of the persons concerned may be interfered with to such an extent that the involvement of the European Union legislature is required'.[111] This criterion of interference with fundamental rights is not entirely new. In its 1970 ruling *ACF Chemiefarma* the Court of Justice had already hinted that the granting of a fundamental right forms part of the essential elements of an area. In *Chiemefarma* the applicant had challenged a Commission implementing regulation, on the ground that the power delegated to the Commission to draft provisions determining the procedure to be followed as regards the hearing of the persons concerned and of third parties concerned a legislative activity. The Court of Justice found instead that the power conferred on the Commission remained of implementing nature,

[107] See also M Chamon, 'How the Concept of Essential Elements of a Legislative Act Continues to Elude the Court' (2013) 50 CMLRev 849, at pp 859–60.

[108] Case C-221/09 *AJD Tuna Ltd*, EU:C:2011:153, para 80; Case T-367/10 *Bloufin Touna Ellas Naftiki Etaireia*, EU:T:2013:97, para 64; Case 265/87 *Schräder*, EU:C:1989:303, para 22; Joined Cases C-254, 255, and 269/94 *Fattoria Autonoma Tabacchi*, EU:C:1996:320, para 56; Case C-171/03 *Toeters et Verbek*, EU:C:2004:714, para 52.

[109] For examples where the measure in question was of implementing nature, see Case 59/83 *Biovilac*, EU:C:1984:380, para 10; Case T-390/94 *Schröder*, EU:T:1997:51, 59–64; Case T-429/05 *Artedogan*, EU:T:2010:60, 52 and 55.

[110] Albeit explicitly linked to the political choices criterion: see Case C-355/10 *Parliament v Council*, EU:C:2012:516l, para 78.

[111] Ibid, para 77.

since the principle that the persons concerned should be given the opportunity of being heard by the Commission had been adopted by the legislature.[112]

This criterion pertaining to the effects on fundamental rights leads to two remarks.

Firstly, the linkage between the interference with fundamental rights and the province of the legislature seems to be imposed also by the EU Charter of fundamental rights. By virtue of its Article 52(1), any limitation on the exercise of rights and freedoms recognized by the Charter must be 'provided for by law'. It might be argued that the term 'law' refers to the 'legislative act' as defined in Article 289(3) TFEU.[113] But according to the case law of the Strasbourg Court,[114] the same terms enshrined in the European Convention of Human Rights do not mandate the intervention of an act of legislation in the formal sense of the term. And it is to be recalled that Article 52(3) of the EU Charter of Fundamental Rights imposes an obligation of consistent interpretation with the corresponding provisions of the ECHR,[115] and hence the requirement of being 'provided for by law' should not exclude secondary legal bases, be they delegated or implementing acts. And such is the current positioning of the EU's case law. If the Court of Justice has interpreted the terms 'provided for by law' of Article 52(1) of the Charter as meaning that, in the absence of a specific legal basis, a EU act of individual application may not by itself limit a fundamental right recognized by the Charter,[116] it has ruled also that this requirement is met by an implementing regulation.[117] It is thus to be concluded that the inclusion of interference with fundamental rights into the legislature's domain does not stem from the requirement of being 'provided by law' laid down in Article 52(1) of the Charter[118] but only from the understanding of the 'essential elements of an area' developed by the Court of Justice.

Secondly, regarding interference with fundamental rights as an essential element seems in conflict with the *Germany v Council* judgment, where the Court of Justice ruled that the definition of penalties which fraudulent farmers incurred did not constitute an essential element of the area concerned. Yet, the imposition of penalties would affect fundamental rights. But a careful reading of the ruling on the implementation of the Schengen Borders Code might help to reconcile both

[112] Case 41/69 *ACF Chemiefarma*, EU:C:1970:71, paras 59–65.

[113] For such an argument put forward in the context of the Constitutional Treaty where legislative acts were named 'laws', see HCH Hofmann, 'A Critical Analysis of the New Typology of Acts in the Draft Treaty Establishing a Constitution for Europe' (2003) 7 European Integration Online Papers (EIoP) No 9, at pp 10–11; see also in the context of the Lisbon Treaty, J Ziller, 'La constitutionnalisation de la Charte des droits fondamentaux et les traditions constitutionnelles communes aux Etats membres', in N De Grove-Valdeyron and M Blanquet (eds), *Liber amicorum – Mélanges en l'honneur du professeur Joël Molinier* (LGDJ 2012) 665, at pp 669–70.

[114] See for instance ECtHR, Judgment of 26 April 1979, *Sunday Times*, Appl. No 6538/74, para 47; ECtHR, Judgment of 16 April 2002, *Société Colas Est*, Appl. No 37971/97, para 43.

[115] Opinion of AG Cruz Villalón in Case C-70/10 *Scarlet Extended SA*, EU:C:2011:255, para 10; Opinion of AG Cruz Villalón in Case C-293/12 *Digital Rights Ireland*, EU:C:2013:845, para 109.

[116] Case 407/08 P *Knauf Gips*, EU:C:2010:389, 87–91.

[117] Joined Cases C-92/09 and C-93/09 *Volker and Markus Schecke*, EU:C:2010:662, para 66.

[118] For a similar point of view, see J Bast, 'Legal Instruments and Judicial Protection', in A Von Bogdandy and J Bast (eds), *Principles of European Constitutional Law*, 2nd edn (Hart Publishing 2011), at pp 391–2.

solutions. The Court of Justice noted that the fundamental rights 'may be interfered with *to such an extent* that the involvement of the European Union legislature is required' (emphasis added). So, not every interference with fundamental rights calls for the passing of a legislative act; measures which impinge only marginally on fundamental rights may be taken by way of delegated or implementing acts.[119] The threshold beyond which the interference with fundamental rights will be a matter for the legislature may only be determined on a case-by-case basis.

(b) A case-by-case assessment

As seen above, the criteria of an 'essential element' provided by the case law diminish the indeterminacy which affects the content of the notion but do not remove it all. The dividing line between essential and non-essential elements can thus only be drawn on a case-by-case basis. As the Court of Justice held, determining which elements are essential and which are not requires to 'take account of the characteristics and particularities of the domain concerned'.[120] The type of political choices which are the legislature's preserve will depend on the legal basis of the act concerned.[121]

For instance, the Court of Justice ruled that an essential element of a basic directive designed to set uniform rules for authorization of plant protection products was the requirement of respect of groundwater as an essential precondition for the authorization of such products.[122] In the *Atlanta* case, the Court of Justice seems to have acknowledged that the definition of the concept of operator is one of the essential elements of the common organization of a market and must, therefore, be a matter reserved for the legislature.[123] Likewise, the principle of awarding service contracts by restricted invitations to tender and by private treaty was regarded as essential for the Technical Assistance to the Commonwealth of Independent States (TACIS) programme, in contrast to the threshold beyond which the use of that method of awarding the contracts in question was no longer possible.[124] It was also held that a measure limiting the weight of carcases eligible for intervention cannot be deemed an essential element of the common organization of the market for beef and veal, although it may lead to a reorientation of beef and veal production, for its aim is to implement in the most appropriate way the intervention mechanism laid down by the legislator in order to deal with the structural imbalance, which exists between supply and demand on the market for beef and veal.[125] The criteria to be applied when the Commission seeks to modify the lists of food supplements

[119] For a similar observation, see M de Heijer and E Tauschinsky, 'Where Human Rights Meet Administrative Law: Essential Elements and Limits to Delegation' (2013) 9 EuConst 513, at pp 527.

[120] Case C-355/10 *European Parliament v Council*, EU:C:2012:516, para 68.

[121] As Kieran Bradley rightly points out at in his chapter in this volume (Section 4.2.2).

[122] Case C-303/94 *Parliament v Council*, EU:C:1996:238, 28 and 31.

[123] Case C-104/97 P *Atlanta AG*, EU:C:1999:498, para 76.

[124] Case C-417/93 *Parliament/Council*, EU:C:1995:32, para 32.

[125] Joined Cases C-296/93 and C-307/93 *France and Ireland/Commission*, EU:C:1996:65, para 18.

included in the basic directive were considered essential elements.[126] Lastly, in the *Smoke Flavours* case, it was judged that a basic regulation contained the essential elements typifying a measure intended to approximate the national laws that regulate the characteristics of smoke flavourings used or intended for use in or on foods in the light of the following considerations: the contested regulation defined the parameters for the evaluation and authorization of primary smoke condensates and primary tar fractions used or intended for use as such in or on foods or in the production of derived smoke flavourings used or intended for use in or on foods; it set out the two fundamental safety rules that must be observed before smoke flavourings can be the subject of an authorization valid throughout the Community; it laid down the conditions which must be satisfied by the wood used for the production of the primary products and the conditions for the production of primary products; it set out the rules concerning the effects of authorizations granted, the consequent rights and obligations, the identification and traceability of primary products, as well as public access, the confidentiality of certain information, and data protection.[127]

Like the legislative domains known in many Member States' constitutional laws and in contrast to the American non-delegation doctrine,[128] the legislative domain is, under European law, not moribund. Its respect is subject to a strict judicial review and its formal recognition by the Lisbon Treaty raises new issues, given the new typology of acts within which it is henceforth to be applied.

[126] Joined Cases C-154/04 and C-155/04 *Alliance for National Health*, EU:C:2005:449, 90–2.

[127] Case C-66/04 *United Kingdom v Parliament and Council*, EU:C:2005:743, 53–8.

[128] As regards the latter, see the analysis by H Pünder (n 3), at pp 358–60; R Schütze (n 5), at pp 664–6.

8

Is There a Hierarchy of Legislative, Delegated, and Implementing Acts?

*Jürgen Bast**

8.1 Introduction

Most doctrines of legal instruments translate the concerns of the separation of powers into formal categories of legal norms and put these categories into a hierarchical order.[1] In EU law, however, the system of legal instruments traditionally was not based on the *trias politica*. Among the criteria for determining the legal effects of acts adopted by an EU institution, the functions and composition of that institution and the relevant decision-making procedure were least relevant, if at all.[2] This essentially non-hierarchical structure was increasingly seen as an anomaly in view of the progressive parliamentarization of the EU's political system.[3] The increasing legitimacy and powers of the European Parliament gave rise to various proposals for a hierarchy of norms which aimed to reflect the degree of parliamentary involvement in the making of a legal act. In line with this thinking, the European Convention's proposal for a Constitutional Treaty suggested the creation of 'European laws' and 'European framework laws' as new standard instruments for the EU legislature. However, when the political decision was made to save the substance of the Constitution by withdrawing the language of constitutionalism, the concept of 'laws' almost naturally fell foul of the semantic demobilization. All binding instruments of Article 288 TFEU can now constitute 'legislative acts' or 'non-legislative acts', as the case may be. According to Article 289(3) TFEU, any acts supported by a legal basis that prescribes the application of one of the designated legislative procedures shall constitute 'legislative acts' (cf. French *actes*

* The present contribution develops an argument first presented in 'New Categories of Acts after the Lisbon Reform: Dynamics of Parliamentarization in EU Law' (2012) 49 CMLRev 885. The author would like to thank Jelena von Achenbach for valuable comments.

[1] See C Möllers, *Gewaltengliederung* (Mohr Siebeck 2005), at pp 86 *et seq*.

[2] For details, see J Bast, 'Legal Instruments and Judicial Protection', in A von Bogdandy and J Bast (eds), *Principles of European Constitutional Law* (Hart 2010), at pp 345, 377–82.

[3] See, e.g. K Lenaerts and D Gerard, 'The structure of the Union according to the Constitution for Europe: The Emperor is getting dressed' (2004) 29 ELRev 289, at p 309.

législatifs, and German *Gesetzgebungsakte*). By implication, all the others are 'non-legislative acts' (the term appears in Articles 290(1) and 297(2) TFEU; cf. French *actes non législatifs*, and German *Rechtsakte ohne Gesetzescharakter*).

Dividing the totality of acts adopted under the reformed EU Treaties into those two categories entails different sets of operative functions. The first set concerns certain legal capacities that are reserved for legislative acts. The most visible is the rule according to which only a legislative act has the capacity to include a delegation pursuant to Article 290 TFEU.[4] The second and perhaps more defining set is formed by certain procedural rules that are applicable solely to legislative action. They concern the openness and deliberative quality of EU lawmaking (see, e.g. Article 15(2) TFEU and Articles 2, 6, and 7 of Protocol No 2). Third, an act's legislative character has implications for the system of judicial protection. The Lisbon Treaty has led to a modest expansion of private applicants' standing before the Court of Justice. Under certain conditions, the applicant can directly challenge 'a regulatory act' (cf. French *les actes réglementaires*, and German *Rechtsakte mit Verordnungscharakter*).[5] Some scholars argued against a restrictive interpretation of the term, advocating that any act of general application could constitute a 'regulatory act'.[6] However, the Court of Justice held that a legislative act is precluded from being 'a regulatory act' for the purposes of an action for annulment.[7] Thus, the parliamentarization of the Union has provoked an—arguably dysfunctional—spillover into EU procedural law.[8]

The remainder of the present chapter treats the internal differentiations within the so-defined class of non-legislative acts. Under the present EU Treaties, three subtypes of non-legislative acts exist: one composed of non-legislative acts directly based on the Treaty and two composed of acts based on a delegation. While the first subtype has no name and tends to be overlooked by legal commentators,[9] the latter figure prominently in Articles 290 and 291 TFEU and are called 'delegated' and 'implementing' acts. According to a widespread assumption, the Lisbon Treaty has established a three-tiered hierarchy between legislative, delegated, and implementing acts. This contribution challenges this view. It argues that only incomplete and partial hierarchies between different categories of acts adopted by the EU institutions do exist. In particular, the distinction between delegated and implementing acts constitutes a horizontal divide, rather than a vertical one, at the same level of the hierarchy of norms within EU law.

[4] For a further example, see Article 3(2) TFEU. [5] Article 263(4) TFEU.

[6] M Kottmann, 'Plaumanns Ende: Ein Vorschlag zu Article 263 Abs. 4 AEUV' (2010) 70 Zeitschrift für ausländisches öffentliches Recht und Völkerrecht 547, at pp 559–62; S Balthasar, '*Locus standi* rules for challenges to regulatory acts by private applicants' (2010) 35 ELRev 542; J Bast (n 2), at pp 395–7.

[7] Case T-18/10 *Inuit Tapiriit Kanatami* et al *v Parliament and Council* EU:T:2011:419; confirmed in Case C-583/11 P *Inuit Tapiriit Kanatami and Others v Parliament and Council*, EU:C:2013:625.

[8] See J Bast, 'New Categories of Acts after the Lisbon Reform' (2012) 49 CMLRev 885, 898–907. See also Chapter 10 by Maria Bergström.

[9] The challenges raised by lawmaking powers of the Council that deny their legislative character are discussed in J Bast (n 8) at pp 894–8.

8.2 The Commission's Delegated and Implementing Powers: two Distinctive Regimes of Control

As a first step, the legal regimes for controlling the exercise of delegated and implementing powers will be elaborated. The reformed Treaty clearly distinguishes the applicable regimes of control.

8.2.1 The pre-Lisbon regime in a nutshell: a broad concept of implementing powers

All constitutional states are familiar with rulemaking by executive bodies, in particular by the national government. The relevant authorities are typically vested with their own standard instruments named and framed differently from acts of parliament. By contrast, the Court of Justice had consistently rejected any attempts to distinguish the legal effects of a Community instrument according to the acting institution.[10] However, EU law has developed the concept of implementing acts, that is, acts that do not find their legal basis directly in the Treaties but rather in an act of the institutions that has delegated the power to adopt implementing measures. The Court has declared such interinstitutional conferral of powers prima facie permissible as long as the basic elements of the matter have been stipulated in accordance with the procedure laid down in the Treaty.[11] The Court employed a broad reading of the term 'implementation' embodied in Article 202 EC, which accordingly ranges from individual administrative decisions to supplementary legislation, including amendments of the provisions of the basic act.[12] An implementing act must in any case be consistent with the procedural as well as the substantive requirements set forth in the basic act.[13]

Moreover, institutional practice has developed a system of committees composed of Member State officials who assist and control the Commission, the famous comitology committees.[14] The history of the interinstitutional battle over comitology has often been told,[15] and we are certainly not yet at the end

[10] Case 41/69 *ACF Chemiefarma v Commission*, EU:C:1970:71, paras 60–2; Cases 188/80–190/80 *France* et al *v Commission*, EU:C:1982:257, para 6.

[11] Case 25/70 *Köster*, EU:C:1970:115, para 6; see H Eberhard, 'Das Legalitätsprinzip im Spannungsfeld von Gemeinschaftsrecht und nationalem Recht' (2008) 63 Zeitschrift für Öffentliches Recht 49, at pp 64–5, 84–8; R Schütze, 'Constitutional Limits to Delegated Powers', in Antonis Antoniadis et al (eds), *The European Union and Global Emergencies* (Hart, 2011) pp 49, 51–8.

[12] For example Case 16/88 *Commission v Council*, EU:C:1989:397, para 11, and Case C-417/93 *Parliament v Council*, EU:C:1995:127, para 30. In retrospect, see Case C-427/12 *Commission v Parliament and Council*, EU:C:2014:170, para 36.

[13] Case 46/86 *Romkes* EU:C:1987:287, para 16; Case C-133/06 *Parliament v Council*, EU:C:2008:257, para 54 *et seq*.

[14] See, C F Bergström, *Comitology: Delegation of Powers in the European Union and the Committee System* (Oxford University Press 2005) and M Savino, *I comitati dell'Unione europea: La collegialità amministrativa negli ordinamenti composite* (Giuffrè 2005).

[15] See, e.g. G Haibach, 'The History of Comitology', in M Andenas, and A Türk (eds), *Delegated Legislation and the Role of Committees in the EC* (Kluwer 2000), at pp 185–215

of it.[16] A major factor determining each institution's relative political weight in the process of adopting implementing rules was the choice of the type of committee in the basic act. However, the different types of comitology procedures were not related to particular types of acts. In other words, the means of control of the exercise of rulemaking powers did not translate into the system of legal instruments. Here, the Lisbon Treaty has taken new paths.

8.2.2 The legal regime of Article 291: controlling Commission rulemaking by means of committees

It seems appropriate to start with Article 291 TFEU, which uses the familiar concept of implementation. Article 291(1) TFEU confirms the responsibility of a Member State to take all measures necessary to implement binding Union acts, that is, the well-known principle of indirect implementation of EU law. Article 291(2) TFEU clarifies why this principle of European administration is of relevance for defining the nature of implementing Union acts. It establishes the conditions for an implementing power to be conferred on the Commission or, in exceptional circumstances, on the Council. The test for such a conferral is a need of 'uniform conditions' for implementing a Union act, that is, the task mentioned in the first paragraph. Article 291(3) TFEU provides a legal basis for a piece of EU legislation that lays down 'the rules and general principles concerning mechanisms for control' of the Commission's implementing powers. According to this paragraph, the controlling principal are the Member States, the agent subjected to the control is the Commission. The fourth and final paragraph determines the obligatory denomination of the acts made in the framework of Article 291 TFEU.

The institutions took this to mean that operation of the new legal regime for the Commission's implementing acts is applicable only after the regulation foreseen in Article 291(3) TFEU has entered into force. In February 2011 the European Parliament and the Council adopted the so-called Comitology Regulation.[17] It replaced the Comitology Decision adopted under Article 202 EC.[18] The Comitology Regulation took effect on 1 March 2011. Any references in existing basic acts to a control procedure defined in the Comitology Decision were automatically aligned to successor procedures under the Comitology Regulation. The new standard comitology procedure is called examination procedure. It combines elements of the former management and regulatory committees.

[16] See G J Brandsma and J Blom-Hansen, 'Negotiating the Post-Lisbon Comitology System: Institutional Battles over Delegated Decision-Making' (2012) 50 JCMS 939–57; T Christiansen and M Dobbels, 'Non-Legislative Rule Making after the Lisbon Treaty: Implementing the New System of Comitology and Delegated Acts' (2013) 19 ELJ 42. See also the various chapters in this volume.

[17] Regulation (EU) 182/2011; cf. T Kröll, 'Delegierte Rechtsakte und Durchführungsrechtsakte und das institutionelle Gleichgewicht der Europäischen Union' (2011) 66 Zeitschrift für Öffentliches Recht 253, at pp 291–6.

[18] Council Decision 1999/468/EC, OJ 1999 L 184/23, as last amended by Council Decision 2006/512/EC of 17 July 2006, OJ 2006 L 200/11.

The Commission swiftly adapted its day-to-day rulemaking practice. Ever since it has routinely issued acts titled 'Commission Implementing Regulation', 'Commission Implementing Decision' or, though less often, 'Commission Implementing Directive'. Judging from a selection of acts, there is no visible trace of a new area in the Commission's exercise of implementing powers apart from the new headings of the acts that follow the rule of Article 291(4) TFEU. In terms of the Commission's implementing powers, everything is just business as usual.

Such stunning continuity provokes a closer look at the definition of implementing acts provided in Article 291 TFEU. Both the application of Union acts at the Member State level and the adoption of certain Union acts are referred to as 'implementing' measures, the latter being defined as a means to ensure a sufficient level of uniformity in the former. Although such 'vertical' perspective on implementing powers deviates from the 'horizontal', that is, inter-institutional logic of Article 202 EC, the new functional definition is broad enough to cover the whole range of implementing acts adopted under the previous regime. Establishing uniform conditions for applying Union law may in some cases require regulations of a rather technical nature, such as designing a form to be applied by the competent authorities, specifying data to be reported to the Commission, keeping a register of certified laboratories, and so forth. In other cases, ensuring uniformity may require making substantive determinations, either in the form of individual decisions addressed to a Member State or through acts of general application. In some cases, ensuring uniform implementation of a binding Union act may even require conferral on the Commission of the power to adopt individual measures addressed to private parties, thus replacing the Member States' implementing authorities (so-called direct implementation of EU law). However, there is nothing in Article 291 TFEU that limits the procedural or substantive regulations made by the Commission (or exceptionally, the Council) to matters of a mere technical character. *Any* regulations that complement the provisions of the basic act will, by definition, further constrain the scope of implementing action left to the Member States and therefore contribute to enhancing uniformity in the application of the basic act. As a result, the scope of application of Article 291 TFEU does not fall short of what Article 202 EC had termed 'implementation of rules'.[19] Consequently, there was no need for reviewing the existing basic acts on a case-by-case basis before adopting the Comitology Regulation.[20]

Rather than limiting the scope of implementing powers, the aim of Article 291 TFEU is to provide a narrative on the nature of these powers. The members of the Convention who delivered the blueprint for the current text deliberately departed from the de-contextualized use of the term 'implementation of rules' in Article 202 EC. The new context was to be the *trias politica* of the separation-of-powers doctrine. The adoption of implementing acts by the Commission is now construed as

[19] Revealingly, the Court of Justice refers to its settled case law to clarify the concept of implementation, see Case 65/13 *Parliament v Commission*, EU:C:2014:2289, para 44.

[20] For a different opinion, see S Peers and M Costa, 'Accountability for Delegated and Implementing Acts after the Treaty of Lisbon' (2012) 18 ELJ 427, at p 443 ('surely illegal').

the exercise of *executive powers* that complement the homologous Member States' powers.[21] In the multilevel system of European government, both levels combined form the composite executive branch of EU law.[22] Hence, Article 291 TFEU provides the Commission's role within these administrative networks with a theoretical foundation in constitutional theory: shared exercise of executive powers.

Overall, the new language of the Lisbon Treaty effects no substantial change regarding implementing acts. The central means of control is the plethora of committees that the Commission has to consult before adopting such acts. Comitology procedures serve as a 'fire alarm' system enabling deliberation on a contested issue once a failure of the Commission to ensure support for its proposal indicates that the matter is not of a purely technical nature. This continuity gives reason to heave a sigh of relief for all those who consider comitology a congenial historical finding to facilitate risk regulation in the internal market and to tie transnational networks of administrations.[23] Yet for those who regard its lack of transparency and of parliamentary supervision as part of the Union's accountability deficit, there is no reason to sound the all-clear.[24]

8.2.3 The legal regime of Article 290: Commission rulemaking in the shadow of a political veto

The structure of Article 290 TFEU is similar to that of Article 291 TFEU, however, with notable differences. The first subparagraph of Article 290(1) TFEU provides a definition of delegated acts. They are 'acts of general application' adopted by the Commission 'to supplement or amend' the delegating legislative act. Note that no mention is made of the Council. The second subparagraph lays down certain requirements concerning the necessary specification of the delegation and rules out the delegation of 'essential elements' of an area regulated by legislative acts. Article 290(2) TFEU provides for two control mechanisms from which the legislature can chose one or two to be included in a basic act. A delegation may be revoked by the European Parliament and the Council (*lit.* a), or Parliament and Council may object to a particular delegated act adopted by the Commission, thus precluding it from taking effect (*lit.* b). Each institution can exercise both control

[21] E Vírgala Foruria, 'Los actos no legislativos en la Constitución europea' (2006) 6 Revista de Derecho Constitucional Europeo 279, at p 316. The Court seems to use the English terms 'executive powers' and 'implementing powers' interchangeably, see C F Bergström, 'Shaping the New System for Delegation of Powers to EU Agencies: *United Kingdom* v. *Parliament and Council (Short selling)*' (2015) 52 CMLRev 219, 238, referring to Case C-270/12, EU:C:2014:18, para 78.

[22] On the multilayered structure of European administration, see G della Cananea, 'The European Union's Mixed Administrative Proceedings' (2004) 68 Law and Contemporary Problems 197, and H Hofmann and A Türk, 'The Development of Integrated Administration in the EU and its Consequences' (2007) 13 ELJ 253.

[23] See, e.g. E Vos, 'The Fall of Committees?', in J W de Zwaan et al (eds), *The European Union: An Ongoing Process of Integration* (TMC Asser Press 2004), at pp 111, 117–19.

[24] See, e.g. S Peers and M Costa (n 20), at pp 459–60; J Mendes, 'Delegated and Implementing Rule Making: Proceduralisation and Constitutional Design' (2013) 19 ELJ 22.

options independently. The third paragraph of Article 290 TFEU prescribes the act's title to include the adjective 'delegated'.

In contrast to Article 291, Article 290 TFEU does not provide a legal basis for a general act laying down in advance the rules and principles concerning mechanisms for control of the Commission's exercise of delegated powers. As a functional equivalent, the European Parliament, the Council, and the Commission have negotiated standard clauses for future basic acts and agreed on further practical arrangements regarding their cooperation. The understanding eventually took the form of an interinstitutional agreement called 'Common Understanding on Delegated Acts' concluded in March 2011 (at the time of writing negotiations on its revision are pending).[25]

The development of legislative practice was slowed down by the fact that no automatic changeover from existing delegations has taken place. Hence, the Commission cannot adopt delegated acts in a particular field until a new legislative act has introduced a delegation or an existing basic act was amended to that effect. The process of reviewing the *acquis* of existing legislation started seriously only after the institutions had reached agreement on the related issue of comitology in late 2010. Regarding the duration of the delegation, the usual practice is to empower the Commission to adopt delegated acts for a determined period. The period however extends automatically for periods of an identical duration unless the European Parliament or the Council opposes the extension.[26]

The political explanation for the slow pace on the part of the institutions is to be found in a transitional arrangement in the Comitology Regulation, which has prolonged the validity of one single provision of the old Comitology Decision. The so-called 'regulatory procedure with scrutiny' pursuant to Article 5a of the Decision remains applicable as long as references to this procedure in basic acts adopted before the Lisbon Treaty do exist. The 'regulatory procedure with scrutiny' was invented in 2006 in order to meet the European Parliament's demands for reform while the Constitutional Treaty was still pending and its entry into force uncertain.[27] Although some differences remained, the 2006 reform was largely guided by Article 290 TFEU since it gave the Parliament de facto a right to veto a draft implementing act, provided that the basic act has been subject to parliamentary co-decision. With the bulk of co-decision acts just recently adapted to the requirements of the 2006 reform, the institutions did not feel much pressure for a semi-automatic, *en bloc* alignment to the similar regime of Article 290 TFEU.

The institutions obviously regard the type of acts framed in Article 290 TFEU to be the successor of a particular group of implementing acts adopted under the old regime. Reading the plain text of the Treaty, the difference between implementing and delegated acts seems more marked. While both types of acts are defined as being non-legislative for the purposes of the Treaties, only the latter

[25] Common Understanding on Delegated Acts, Council Doc 8753/1/11 of 14 April 2011.

[26] Ibid, points 8 and 9.

[27] G Schusterschitz and S Kotz, 'The Comitology Reform of 2006: Increasing the Powers of the European Parliament Without Changing the Treaties' (2007) 3 EuConst 68.

is characterized by its close association with a basic act adopted in the exercise of a legislative function. Again, the theoretical narrative is that of the separation of powers. Adopting delegated acts is tantamount to acting within the domain of the legislature (in French *domaine de la loi*, in German *Gesetzesvorbehalt*), that is, matters that are reserved for parliamentary legislation save for an express delegation to the contrary.[28] Some commentators employ the term 'quasi-legislative' to distinguish such acts.[29]

In the given context, highlighting the connexion between the delegating legislative act and the delegated non-legislative act is meant to justify a particular method of controlling the Commission's rulemaking practice. In contrast to Article 291 TFEU, the control mechanisms laid down in Article 290(2) TFEU have been designed with a view to guard the *horizontal* balance of powers. They serve as a means of control by the EU legislature (principal) over the Commission (agent). The right to unilaterally withdraw an existing delegation by a 'revocation decision' of merely one legislative institution is noteworthy from a theoretical point of view since it implies a procedure for amending an act that is different from adopting it, that is, a deviation from the principle of *parallélisme des formes*. However, revoking the delegation would not have an effect on the validity of delegated acts already in force. Hence, the right to veto a delegated act within a period set by the basic act is probably more important from a practical perspective. The Commission must refrain from publishing a delegated act immediately, thus delaying its entry into force to enable the European Parliament and the Council to scrutinize the act's content (see Article 297(2) TFEU, 2nd subparagraph). The institutions have agreed in the Common Understanding that the period for objection should in principle be two months starting from the act's simultaneous notification to the legislative institutions (No 10 and 11).

Rather than the delegated acts themselves, these control mechanisms are the innovative element of this new category.[30] The legal framework set by Article 290 TFEU exposes the exercise of delegated authority to the 'unfiltered' political supervision by the institutions that have created it. Both the Council and the European Parliament possess the legal means to prevail in case of political disagreement with the Commission. There is no need for constructing the argument in juridical terms claiming that the Commission is overstepping its powers.[31] This is a remarkable advance for the European Parliament and the democratic legitimacy of the EU at large.[32] It enables the political contestation of value judgments taken in the guise of administrative decision-making. Although we are not likely to witness

[28] Cf. H Rieckhoff, *Der Vorbehalt des Gesetzes im Europarecht* (Mohr Siebeck 2007), at pp 175–96.

[29] See, e.g. D Curtin, *Executive Power of the European Union* (Oxford University Press 2009), at p 122.

[30] CF Bergström (n 14), at pp 354–5.

[31] G Garzón Clariana, 'Los actos delegados en el sistema de fuentes de derecho de la Unión Europea' (2010) 37 Revista de Derecho Communitario Europeo 721, at p 756.

[32] Cf. C Möllers and J von Achenbach, 'Die Mitwirkung des Europäischen Parlaments an der abgeleiteten Rechtsetzung der Europäischen Kommission nach dem Lissabonner Vertrag' (2011) 46 Europarecht 39, at pp 42–3.

a frequent use of that power, delegated rulemaking by the Commission is taking place in the shadow of a parliamentary veto.

Also the Commission has much to gain from the new control mechanisms. It is no more subject to a comitology procedure at any stage during the process of drafting and adopting a delegated act. The absence of a formal role of a committee composed of Member States representatives marks a striking difference even to the 'regulatory procedure with scrutiny' that anticipated Article 290 TFEU. In the light of the heated political battles over comitology that have lasted for decades, a silent revolution has occurred with the introduction of Article 290 TFEU. In the most crucial sectors of its rulemaking powers, the Commission has freed itself from the oversight of Member State officials. By way of compensation, however, Member States have gained the political assurance from the Commission to carry out 'adequate consultations' with Member States' experts when preparing and drawing up delegated acts. The pledge has become part of the Common Understanding (No 4). Of course, even the Commission does not want to tear up the networks of administrative cooperation that provide it with expert knowledge and other resources, which its own narrow administrative basis cannot generate.[33] Nonetheless, holding consultations in an advisory committee is something completely different from pacifying the dilatory veto power of a 'real' comitology committee.[34] Article 290 TFEU implies a substantial shift in the institutional power game in favour of the Commission.[35]

8.3 The Relationship between Delegated and Implementing Acts: neither Exclusivity nor Subordination

As a next step, it will be demonstrated that the scope of application of delegated and implementing acts, as respectively defined by the Treaties, is not mutually exclusive (Section 8.3.1). This finding reinforces the argument that the Treaty drafters did not intend to establish a subordination relation between the two types of acts (Section 8.3.2).

8.3.1 The scopes of application: a large overlap area

Comparing the two functional definitions in Articles 290(1) and 291(2) TFEU, they prima facie do not provide for a selective divide. They define the respective type of act from a different angle: a horizontal, inter-institutional perspective in the first case, a vertical, inter-organizational perspective in the second case. While

[33] S Peers and M Costa (n 20), at p 453.

[34] On the potential effects of the revision of the Common Understanding as proposed by the Council (Council Doc 6774/14 of 21 February 2014), see for example Chapter 9 by Paul Craig, Section 9.4.1.

[35] For a defence of that development, see G Garzón Clariana, 'Les actes délégués dans le système des sources du droit de l'Union Européenne' (2011) 12 ERA Forum 105–34.

these functions do not necessarily coincide, there is no inherent tension between them, either. Why should an act supplementing or amending a basic act not at the same time serve to foster uniform implementation at the Member State level, and vice versa?

There are two uncontested differences in the scope of the categories. First, the delegating act under Article 290 TFEU necessarily is a legislative act according to the nomenclature of the Treaties. It follows that non-legislative acts, including acts based on the Treaty itself, cannot provide a delegation in the sense of Article 290 TFEU. Second, a delegated act has to be an act of general application whereas Article 291 TFEU also includes individual acts. The latter requirement of delegated acts was inserted in the course of the Intergovernmental Conference of 2007 in order to make sure that individual administrative decisions are subject to a comitology procedure rather than a parliamentary veto.[36] These two elements do establish an exclusive field of application for some implementing acts (viz., individual acts and acts based on a non-legislative basic act), yet the remaining overlap area is still large.

A possible argument establishing a distinguishing feature concerns the expression 'to supplement' (cf. French *qui complètent*, and German *zur Ergänzung*). Some hold it to imply that a delegated act substantially changes the legal framework of the basic act in adding new rules of the same kind.[37] Any less substantial conferral could thus only take the form of an implementing power pursuant to Article 291 TFEU. At the same time, any substantial supplementation should not present itself as mere implementation. Legislation, supplementation, and implementation would thus constitute a scale (and, by implication, a hierarchy) of highly, medium, and less essential rules.

Yet, such essentialist understanding seems rather naïve in view of the complexities of a modern legal system. Attempts at deriving a formal hierarchy of norms from the substantive contents of the law are as old as the doctrine of the separation of powers itself. For example, the German constitutional lawyer Paul Laband invented in the 1870s the distinction between executive laws in the substantive sense and mere implementation of laws in order to justify the Prussian King's power to make autonomous regulations. However, the theoretical basis and empirical validity of the distinction between substantial *Ergänzung* (supplementation of laws) and mere *Ausführung* (implementation of laws) have repeatedly been demystified and deconstructed.[38] Even a norm that intends only to provide further detail or give effect to existing norms adds to the present normative framework. The extent to which the latter is changed is a matter of degree rather than

[36] G Schusterschitz, 'Komitologie und Binnenmarkt: Von der Komitologiereform 2006 zum Vertrag von Lissabon', in W Schroeder (ed), *Europarecht als Mehrebenensystem* (Facultas WUV 2008), at pp 123, 137.

[37] E.g. R Schütze, 'Delegated Legislation in the (New) European Union' (2011) 74 MLR 661, at p 684.

[38] For a forceful critique, see A Ross, *Theorie der Rechtsquellen* (Scientia 1929, repr. 1989), at pp 371–422.

of categorical distinction. Hence, a loaded concept of supplementation does not provide a solid ground for distinguishing delegated and implementing acts, with the effect of preventing the EU legislature from making political judgements, on a case-by-case basis, as to which control regime it considers proper for the conferred power at hand.

One should therefore be ready to accept that a substantial overlap of the two definitions provided by the Treaty does exist.[39] This finding contradicts the premise of those who suppose that a clear-cut distinction is necessary in order to preserve the integrity of the control mechanisms and to do justice to the drafters' intentions.[40] To address these concerns, it is essential to understand whose political discretion is concerned. In the view of the present author, a freedom of choice on the part of the Commission would indeed be problematic since this would enable the Commission to navigate between different control regimes as it pleases. It is also true that one particular act cannot be at the same time a delegated act and an implementing act. Yet there is no convincing teleological argument to eliminate the freedom of choice on the part of the legislative institutions to opt for a particular regime of controlling the Commission. This is particularly true from the perspective of the European Parliament. As with any other parliamentary assembly, the European Parliament's capacity to exercise its formal powers is de facto constrained by its limited resources, the scarcest of which is time. Arguably, the 'unfiltered' control mechanism of Article 290 TFEU can hardly be applied to a large numbers of cases effectively.[41] Eliminating the overlap area between delegated and implementing acts would thus deprive the EU legislature (and thus, the European Parliament) of its command over its own resources.

In its first judgment on the matter, in *Biocides*, the Court of Justice has only implicitly addressed the issue of a potential overlap between the respective scopes.[42] In the given case, the Commission claimed that the EU legislature incorrectly conferred on it an implementing power pursuant to Article 291 TFEU. It submitted that the relevant power (the setting of fees) should have taken the form of a delegation pursuant to Article 290 TFEU. In its findings, the Court sent a somewhat ambiguous message. On the one hand, it tried to give an interpretation of the treaty provisions that highlights the differences between the two types of rulemaking powers. The conferral of implementing powers calls upon the Commission 'to provide further detail' in relation to the content of a legislative act (cf. French *preciser*,

[39] W Weiß, *Der Europäische Verwaltungsverbund* (Duncker & Humblot 2010), at pp 59–60; U Stelkens, 'Art. 291 AEUV, das Unionsverwaltungsrecht und die Verwaltungsautonomie der Mitgliedstaaten' (2012) 47 Europarecht 511, at p 543; CF Bergström (n 14), at pp 356–7.

[40] E.g. P Craig, *The Lisbon Treaty* (Oxford University Press 2010), at pp 279–80, and Section 9.3.1 in this volume; S Peers and M Costa (n 20), at pp 441–2; D Ritleng, 'The Dividing Line between Delegated And Implementing Acts: The Court of Justice Sidesteps the Difficulty in *Commission* v. *Parliament and Council (Biocides)*' (2015) 52 CMLRev 243, at p 251.

[41] Z Xhaferri, 'Delegated acts, Implementing Acts and Institutional Balance Implications Post-Lisbon' 2013 (20) Maastricht Journal of European and Comparative Law 557, at pp 573–4, and Chapter 11 by Joana Mendes, Section 11.2.1.

[42] Case C-427/12 *Commission v Parliament and Council*, EU:C:2014:170.

and German *präzisieren*),[43] whereas delegated powers aim at the adoption of rules 'coming within the regulatory framework' as defined by the basic legislative act (cf. French *s'insèrent dans le cadre réglementaire*, and German *sich in den rechtlichen Rahmen einfügen*).[44]

On the other hand, the Court only seemingly treated the issue as a purely legal matter that could be solved by hermeneutical operations. Contrary to what the Commission demanded,[45] the Court did not borrow from its jurisprudence on the choice of the legal basis. It is settled case law that the choice of the appropriate legal basis for a EU measure must be based on 'objective factors which are amenable to judicial review'.[46] The Court was well aware of the fact that even its new definitions, which focus on the relationship with the basic act, are inadequate for the task. It therefore held that the EU legislature has discretion when it decides to confer a delegated power on the Commission pursuant to Article 290(1) TFEU or an implementing power pursuant to Article 291(2) TFEU. Consequently, judicial review of that choice is limited to manifest errors of assessment.[47]

Hence, without explicitly recognizing that the two categories are not mutually exclusive, the Court accepted the political nature of the choice made by the EU legislature between the available types of rulemaking powers. From a constitutional point of view, this rationale would be unacceptable with regard to the choice of the legal basis, given that this choice affects the standards of testing the legality of the measure taken by the EU legislature. This is not the case, however, regarding the choice between conferring delegated or implementing powers.[48] The Court's approach rather shows similarities with the marginal judicial review exercised with regard to the choice of the appropriate legal instrument where the Treaties do not specify the type of act to be adopted (see Article 296(1) TFEU). The Court has always accepted that the discretion as to the choice of legal instrument is, as a rule, very broad and hardly amenable to judicial review.[49] Following this jurisprudence, the Court is also willing to accept that the EU legislature may choose whichever category of non-legislative acts and, by implication, which means of control seem best suited to the case in hand.

8.3.2 The derogatory force: on the same level of the hierarchy of norms

This leads us to the question of whether and to what extent Articles 290 and 291 TFEU have established a hierarchy of norms. In legal discourses, the concept of hierarchy does not have a uniform meaning. For the present purposes, it suffices

[43] Ibid, para 39. This defining element was confirmed in Case C-65/13 *Parliament v Commission (EURES)*, EU:C:2014:2289, para 43.

[44] Case C-427/12 (n 42), para 38.

[45] Case C-427/12 (n 42), para 23.

[46] Case 45/86 *Commission v Council*, EU:C:1987:163, para 11.

[47] Case C-427/12 (n 42), para 40.

[48] For a different view, see D Ritleng (n 40), at pp 243, 253.

[49] Case 5/73 *Balkan-Import-Export*, EU:C:1973:109, para 18; Case C-163/99 *Portugal v Commission*, EU:C:2001:189, para 20.

to define a hierarchy of norms as the layered structure of a particular legal order resulting from the varying derogatory force of its legal acts. While acts sharing the same rank within the 'pyramid of law' are in principle able to mutually derogate, an act placed on a lower level cannot derogate from a higher-ranking act. Such a relation usually follows from the fact that the lower act was derived from the higher (cf. German *Stufenbau nach der rechtlichen Bedingtheit*), unless the legal order establishes specific rules on derogatory force based on other criteria (cf. German *Stufenbau nach der derogatorischen Kraft*).[50]

Asking for the position of delegated and implementing acts in the hierarchy of norms, two different issues arise. The first question concerns the ability of delegating or implementing acts to derogate from their respective basic act. Looking merely at the constitutive conditions, one arrives at clear-cut priority of the basic act since it, by definition, provides the legal basis for the delegated or implementing act. The wording of Article 290(1) TFEU would offer a starting point for a slightly different perspective on EU law's specific hierarchy according to the derogatory force. The fact that a delegated act may amend certain elements of its basic act seems to place both acts on the same level in the hierarchy of norms. However, in view of the requirement under Article 290(1) TFEU to specify the content and scope of the delegation such derogatory force vis-à-vis the basic act must in any case be explicitly defined in the basic act itself. The ability to derogate from the basic act is thus contingent on a permission granted in the basic act rather than an inherent quality of delegated acts. Hence, Article 290 TFEU does establish a hierarchical distinction between the basic legislative act and the delegated act.[51] We do not need to enter here in any depth into the complex question of the precise legal nature of this hierarchy. Arguably, the priority of legislative acts is only relative to the basic act and does not imply a general hierarchy with respect to other legislative acts, but merely constitutes a partial hierarchy.[52]

How does the silence of Article 291 TFEU on the derogatory force of implementing acts fit into the picture? On the one hand, the general permission to amend the basic act granted in Article 290 TFEU provokes a systematic argument *e contrario* to the effect that implementing acts must not amend their basic act. This stance has been indeed taken.[53] On the other hand, the wording of Article 291 TFEU is generally less concerned with the relationship between the basic act and the implementing act. From a systematic point of view, it would be difficult to argue that any requirement explicitly mentioned in Article 290 TFEU (such as the prohibition to delegate the essential elements of an area) is non-operative under

[50] Cf. A Jakab, 'Probleme der Stufenbaulehre' (2005) 91 Archiv für Rechts- und Sozialphilosophie 333.

[51] R Schütze (n 37), at p 683.

[52] On the concept of partial hierarchies, see J Bast, *Grundbegriffe der Handlungsformen der EU* (Springer 2006), at pp 297 *et seq*; on the partial hierarchy effected by Article 202 of the EC Treaty, see Case C-378/00 *Commission v Parliament and Council*, EU:C:2003:42, paras 39–40.

[53] B Driessen, 'Delegated legislation after the Treaty of Lisbon' (2010) 35 ELRev 837, at p 845. Also the CJEU draws a legal argument from Article 290(1) TFEU, see Case 65/13, para 45 (n 19). However, the critical case of an express authorization to amend the basic act is still uncertain.

Article 291 TFEU.[54] This speaks in favour of a capacity of implementing acts to amend the basic act if the latter expressly so provides.

The legislative institutions seem to share the view that amending a basic act is not exclusive for delegated acts, at least for a transitional period.[55] Under the old Comitology Decision, various implementing powers enabled the Commission to amend the respective basic act. Due to the automatic alignment to the Comitology Regulation, these empowering provisions are still operative under the new regime. Yet, some implementing powers of that type fail to meet the requirements of Article 290 TFEU and therefore will remain permanently within the ambit of Article 291 TFEU. For example, the fact that delegated acts can only be adopted under a legislative act excludes the bulk of basic acts in the agriculture sector, where parliamentary co-decision was introduced only recently.[56] Amending the technical annexes to such basic acts adopted by the Council has to take the form of a Commission implementing act.[57] There is no principled argument why the Commission should cease to use such powers that perfectly match the definition of Article 291(2) TFEU. Hence, the concept of 'implementation' of Article 291 TFEU does include amendments to certain non-essential provisions of the basic act.

The second question concerns a possible hierarchy of norms established between delegated acts and implementing acts. While the Treaty is remarkably silent on this issue, legal discourse is full of references to the notion of a three-tiered hierarchy between legislative, delegated, and implementing acts.[58] But it frequently remains unclear whether the notion implies a hierarchy in its legal-technical sense, namely, the relative derogatory force of an act, or merely a semantic distinction in terms of public visibility, sources of legitimacy or political significance. Absent a rule of positive law to this effect, such material distinctions do not automatically translate into a hierarchy of norms properly so-called.

The issue of a presumed hierarchy of delegated and implementing acts can be approached by starting from the safe assumption that a hierarchy has been established according to the constitutive conditions if a delegated act provides the legal basis for an implementing act. The wording of Article 291 TFEU would cover such a sub-delegation. In legislative practice, this option has yet remained hypothetical. One may even doubt if it would be lawful at all in view of the requirement

[54] On the non-delegation doctrine applicable under Article 291 TFEU, see Chapter 7 by Dominique Ritleng.

[55] For a recent example, see Commission Regulation (EU) 2014/1368 of 17 December 2014 amending Regulation (EC) 987/2009 of the Parliament and of the Council laying down the procedure for implementing Regulation (EC) 883/2004 on the coordination of social security systems, OJ 2014 L 366/15.

[56] See C Roederer-Rynning and F Schimmelfennig, 'Bringing Codecision to Agriculture: a Hard Case of Parliamentarization' (2012) 19 JEPP 951.

[57] See, e.g. Commission Implementing Decision 2012/766/EU of 7 December 2012 amending Part A of Annex XI to Council Directive 2003/85/EC as regards the list of national laboratories authorised to handle live foot-and-mouth disease virus, OJ 2012 L 337/5.

[58] See, e.g. P Craig (n 40), at pp 252–5 and pp 260–82; see also Section 9.2 in this volume.

to preserve the integrity of the control mechanisms of Article 290(2) TFEU, and, hence, the institutional balance.[59]

In the normal course of events the constitutive conditions of both acts will be determined in acts directly based on the Treaty, perhaps even in different provisions of the very same legislative act. In this case, the constitutive conditions do not establish a hierarchy between delegated and implementing acts. A specific rule of EU law positively establishing a hierarchy would thus be required to rebut the assumption of mutual derogatory force. Such a rule is nowhere in sight.[60] Quite the contrary, as previously argued, the delineation between the two categories is not clear-cut and their respective scopes are not mutually exclusive. It would place an unduly heavy burden upon the legislative institutions—and in turn, on the Court of Justice reviewing their action—to require them to take into account the far-reaching legal consequences of a general rule of priority whenever they make the choice of the type of rulemaking powers.

In sum, the Treaty does not provide for a hierarchical distinction between delegated and implementing acts. They are *Verordnungen im rechtstheoretischen Sinne*, that is, two kinds of regulations—as opposed to laws—in the legal-theoretical sense.[61]

8.4 Conclusion

The Treaty provides for a substantial overlap of two functional definitions as regards the scope of application of delegated and implementing acts, respectively. While implementing acts serve to ensure uniform conditions for the implementation of Union law, the function of a delegated act is to supplement or amend the delegating legislative act. These functions are not mutually exclusive. In fact, most implementing acts of general application adopted by the Commission under the pre-Lisbon regime would qualify for both definitions. Thus, in cases where a particular power to be conferred on the Commission would satisfy the requirements of both provisions, it is incumbent upon the EU legislature to choose the category of acts it deems appropriate. This view is shared by the Court of Justice, albeit somewhat reluctantly, as was apparent when it declined to subject the choice of the type of rulemaking powers to strict judicial scrutiny.

Accordingly, contrary to a widespread opinion it is concluded that the Lisbon Treaty did not establish a three-tiered hierarchy between legislative, delegated, and implementing acts. The latter two categories—each one of them uniquely linked to characteristic means of control of the Commission's rulemaking powers—constitute a horizontal divide at the same level of the system of EU law. Absent a rule of positive law to this effect, the degree of parliamentary supervision does not translate into a hierarchy of norms.

[59] J von Achenbach, *Demokratische Gesetzgebung in der Europäischen Union* (Springer 2014), at p 48.

[60] But see Section 4.3 by Kieran Bradley.

[61] A Ross (n 38), at p 393.

9

Comitology, Rulemaking, and the Lisbon Settlement

Tensions and Strains

Paul Craig

9.1 Introduction

The Lisbon Treaty created the dichotomy between delegated and implementing acts in Articles 290 and 291 TFEU, having taken over the core assumptions in this regard from the Constitutional Treaty.[1] The chapter begins by considering the core assumptions underlying the Lisbon model and the rationale for the division between the two species of secondary acts. The subsequent analysis then addresses the tensions and strains in the application of this divide in the years since the Lisbon Treaty was ratified.

There is discussion of the 'analytical and temporal' tension that lies at the heart of the distinction between delegated and implementing acts. It includes analysis of the relative use of the two types of measure, the factors that have driven legislative assignation of secondary measures to the two categories, and judicial attempts to clarify the distinction between the two. The focus then shifts to the 'constitutional' dimension, signifying in this respect the ways in which key constitutional assumptions underlying the Lisbon schema have been undermined by political change in the form of, for example, the Common Understanding, and the impact

[1] P Craig, 'Delegated Acts, Implementing Acts and the New Comitology Regulation' (2011) 36 ELRev 671; R Schütze, '"Delegated Legislation" in the (New) European Union: A Constitutional Analysis' (2011) 74 MLR 661; S Peers and M Costa, 'Accountability for Delegated and Implementing Acts after the Lisbon Treaty' (2012) 18 ELJ 427; J Bast, 'New Categories of Acts after the Lisbon Reform: Dynamics of Parliamentarization in EU law' (2012) 49 CMLRev 885; J Mendes, 'Delegated and Implementing Rule Making: Proceduralisation and Constitutional Design' (2013) 19 ELJ 22; T Christiansen and M Dobbels, 'Non-Legislative Rule Making after the Lisbon treaty: Implementing the New System of Comitology and Delegated Acts' (2013) 19 ELJ 42; A Alemanno and A Meuwese, 'Impact Assessment of EU Non-Legislative Rulemaking: The Missing Link in "New Comitology"' (2013) 19 ELJ 76; M Kaeding and A Hardacre, 'The European Parliament and the Future of Comitology after Lisbon' (2013) 19 ELJ 382.

that this has had on the relative power of the Council, European Parliament, and Commission.

This is followed by a discussion of the 'institutional' tension, which connotes for these purposes the way in which institutional change such as establishment of the new European Supervisory Authorities in the financial area has impacted on the regime for delegated and implementing acts in the Lisbon Treaty. The penultimate tension is 'legal form' and the way in which the relative use of soft law and hard law can affect application of the normative assumptions underlying Article 290 and Article 291 TFEU. The discussion concludes with the 'conceptual' dimension, which signifies the ways in which administrative choice as to whether to develop policy through rulemaking or adjudication can affect the Lisbon dichotomy between the two kinds of act.

9.2 The Lisbon Model: Core Assumptions

The Lisbon model is predicated on certain conceptual assumptions as to the categories of EU legal norms, this being most visible in the divide between legislative, delegated, and implementing acts contained in Articles 288–94 TFEU. This schema concerning the hierarchy of norms was taken over, like much else, from the Constitutional Treaty.[2]

Prior to the Lisbon Treaty there was no divide between what are now termed delegated and implementing acts. The standard pattern was for there to be a 'primary' regulation or directive that governed a particular policy area. This was complemented by 'secondary' legal measures that 'implemented' the primary rules in accord with Article 202 EC. This admixture of primary and secondary rules is common in legal systems.

The Council recognized from the outset of the EEC that not everything could be done by primary regulation and that it would need to delegate power to the Commission to make secondary norms. The Council was however unwilling to accord the Commission a blank cheque, because it realized that regulatory choices and contentious issues could be resolved through such measures, the devil being in the detail. This was the rationale for the birth of what became known as 'comitology', whereby national technocrats would sit with the Commission when it made

[2] A von Bogdandy, J Bast, and F Arndt, 'Legal Instruments in European Union Law and their Reform: A Systematic Approach on an Empirical Basis' (2004) 23 YBEL 91; K Lenaerts and M Desomer, 'Towards a Hierarchy of Legal Acts in the European Union? Simplification of Legal Instruments and Procedures' (2005) 11 ELJ 744; J Liisberg, 'The EU Constitutional Treaty and its Distinction between Legislative and Non-Legislative Acts', in B Olsen and K Sorensen (eds), *Regulation in the EU* (Thomson 2006), at pp 133–68; B de Witte, 'Legal Instruments and Law-Making in the Lisbon Treaty', in S Griller and J Ziller (eds), *The Lisbon Treaty, EU Constitutionalism without a Constitutional Treaty* (Springer 2008), at pp 79–108; H Hofmann, 'Legislation, Delegation and Implementation under the Lisbon Treaty: Typology Meets Reality' (2009) 15 ELJ 482; B Driessen, 'Delegated Legislation after the Lisbon Treaty: An Analysis of Article 290 TFEU' (2010) ELRev 837; P Craig, *The Lisbon Treaty, Law, Politics and Treaty Reform* (Oxford University Press 2010), chaps 2, 7.

these secondary measures, with the possibility of sending them to the Council in accord with the management and regulatory committee procedures if the national technocrats disagreed with the Commission proposal.[3]

The European Parliament was not happy with this regime, because although it had some role in the comitology process, it was very much dominated by Council and Member State interests. The Commission for its part always chafed at what it regarded as unwarranted comitology constraints on its executive autonomy. The front line Directorates-General might have been content working with national technocrats, but the higher levels within the Commission were never happy with management and regulatory committees. The Commission strategy was to devise some method whereby it could be freed from these limitations.[4] It advocated a regime of *ex ante* and *ex post* constraints on non-legislative acts of the kind that are now contained in Article 290 TFEU.

The Commission strategy was fulfilled in part through the Constitutional Treaty, which distinguished between secondary measures that were 'legislative'[5] or 'quasi-legislative' in nature, delegated acts, and those that could be regarded as more purely 'executive', implementing acts. This distinction was then embodied in the Lisbon Treaty, which is predicated on certain assumptions as to the way in which these norms are made. This is indeed a defining feature of the Lisbon model.

Thus in relation to legislative acts it is central to the Lisbon schema in Article 289 TFEU that the ordinary legislative procedure,[6] the successor to co-decision, should truly be regarded the default method for the enactment of legislative acts, subject to limited instances where a special legislative procedure was mandated. This message was further reinforced by Article 14(1) and Article 16(1) TEU, which provide that the European Parliament and the Council jointly exercise legislative authority in the EU.

In relation to delegated acts, Article 290 TFEU states that a legislative act may delegate to the Commission the power to adopt non-legislative acts of general application to supplement or amend certain non-essential elements of the legislative act. A defining feature of the new Lisbon order was the formal exclusion of old style comitology committees, to be replaced by the *ex ante* and *ex post* controls

[3] C F Bergstrom, *Comitology—Delegation of Powers in the European Union and the Committee System* (Oxford University Press 2005).

[4] Commission Communication of 25 July 2001, European governance—A white paper, COM(2001) 428 final, [20]–[29]; Institutional Architecture, COM(2002) 728 final, [1.2], [1.3.4]; Proposal for a Council decision amending Decision (EC) 1999/468 Laying Down the Procedures for the Exercise of Implementing Powers Conferred on the Commission, COM(2002) 719 final, at p 2; Final Report of Working Group IX on Simplification of 29 November 2002, CONV 424/02 (at http://european-convention.europa.eu), at p 12.

[5] Article 290 TFEU states that delegated acts are non-legislative, but this simply reflects the formal position that under the Treaty legislative acts are those made in accordance with a legislative procedure, Article 289 TFEU. The appellation non-legislative applied to delegated acts should not therefore mask the fact that they are commonly legislative or quasi-legislative in nature, in the sense that they are acts of general application that establish secondary rules, which specify in greater detail the meaning or application of articles within the legislative act itself.

[6] The details of the procedure are set out in Article 294 TFEU.

specified in Article 290 TFEU. The *ex ante* control requires that the legislative act should specify the essential elements of the area, and that the objectives, content, scope, and duration of the delegation of power must be explicitly defined in the legislative acts. The *ex post* control consists either of the nuclear option, which is to revoke the delegation, or the less extreme response, whereby it is open to the Council or the European Parliament to veto the particular delegated act. The conceptual premise underlying this schema is that subject to these controls the Commission has regulatory authority and autonomy over delegated acts. There are, however, some advisory committees, which operate in an informal world structured by a Common Understanding between the major institutional players.[7] The very fact that some looser form of advisory committees continues to exist in the post-Lisbon world should not mask the change that has occurred. The Commission went to considerable lengths to devise a scheme for delegated acts with the express intent that it would lead to the demise of a regime that it had resisted for many years.

In relation to implementing acts, Article 291(2) TFEU provides that where uniform conditions for implementing legally binding Union acts are needed, those acts shall confer implementing powers on the Commission, or in limited instances on the Council. Article 291(3) TFEU stipulates that provision should be made for control of the implementing powers by the Member States, which thereby ensured the survival of comitology in relation to implementing acts, as regulated by the new Comitology Regulation.[8] The conceptual assumptions in this area are that these committees are representatives directly of the Member States, with the consequence that there is no formal recourse to the Council in the event that the committee disagrees with the Commission proposal; there is a very limited role for the Council and European Parliament in formal terms; and the emphasis is squarely on national technocrats as representatives of the Member States.[9]

The constitutional implications of the different regimes for delegated and implementing acts were noted by Advocate General Jääskinen.[10] He stated that the TFEU had introduced a 'sharp conceptual distinction between delegated acts and implementing acts'.[11] Article 290 TFEU delegated acts were non-legislative (regulatory) acts of general application adopted by the Commission to amend or supplement non-essential elements of a legislative act. Article 291 TFEU implementing acts could be either regulatory acts or individual administrative decisions, and were adopted by the Commission or the Council to secure uniform implementation of legally binding EU measures. The principal concern in relation to delegated acts pertained, said the Advocate General, to democratic accountability,

[7] Common Understanding on Delegated Acts, Council Doc 8753/1/11 of 14 April 2011.

[8] Regulation (EU) 2011/182 of the European Parliament and of the Council of 16 February 2011 laying down the rules and general principles concerning mechanisms for control by Member States of the Commission's exercise of implementing powers, OJ 2011 L 55/13.

[9] P Craig (n 1).

[10] Case C-270/12 *United Kingdom v Council and Parliament*, EU:C:2013:562.

[11] Ibid [81].

namely, how much legislative power could be delegated and how could the exercise of such power be controlled by the legislature.[12] By way of contrast, the main constitutional focus in relation to implementing acts related to 'respect for the primary competence of the Member States with respect to implementation of EU law, and the institutional balance between the Council and the Commission when they assume implementing roles'.[13]

There are, however, a number of reasons why the assumptions underlying the Lisbon model have been called into question in the years since the Lisbon Treaty was ratified. The remainder of this chapter explores tensions in the Lisbon schema.

9.3 Analytical and Temporal: the Fragile Divide between Articles 290 and 291

9.3.1 The analytical and temporal problem

The creation of two types of measure below legislative acts necessarily demands a criterion to distinguish between them. The European Parliament attested to the difficulty of drawing the divide, and the contestation that it provoked in the consideration of legislative dossiers.[14] The nature of the criterion is clear from Article 290 TFEU, which stipulates that an act that amends or supplements a legislative act must be a delegated act. It is the application of this criterion that has proven problematic from the outset, more especially that part concerning supplementation of a legislative act, since it is very difficult to conceive of any act made pursuant to a legislative act that does not in some manner supplement that legislative act. If a secondary measure does so it must be a delegated act. If it does not, then it can be an implementing act.

All secondary measures however involve some addition to the basic or primary act. Many thousands of secondary measures have been enacted since the inception of the EEC. In the paradigm case they are of general application and bring greater exactitude to the meaning of an article of the primary act. Thus, for example, there might be a complex primary act dealing with agriculture, and a secondary measure specifies in greater detail one part of the primary act relating to, for example, the requirements for the independence of agencies that pay money pursuant to the primary regulation. Such measures clearly 'add something' to the primary act. This will be equally true for any measure classified as an implementing act in the post-Lisbon world, since the very specification of uniform conditions of implementation will be 'adding something' to the enabling provision in the legislative act. The Lisbon schema therefore demands the drawing of the following difficult distinction.[15]

[12] Ibid [83]. [13] Ibid [83].

[14] Report of 4 December 2013 drawn up on behalf of the Committee on Legal Affairs Institutional Affairs on follow up on delegation of legislative powers and control by Member States of the Commission's exercise of implementing powers (rapporteur: J Szajer), EP Doc A7-435/2013.

[15] P Craig (n 1).

It might be considered that the article in the legislative act sufficiently resolved the relevant issues, the conclusion being that the secondary measure, while obviously imbuing the article of the legislative act with greater detail, and hence 'adding something', did not supplement it by adding any 'new' non-essential element so as to trigger recourse to Article 290 TFEU, and therefore Article 291 TFEU could be used.

It might in other instances be considered that the relevant article in the legislative act is less definitive, the conclusion being that while the legislative act provided sufficient guide as to essential principles so as to be lawful under Article 290 TFEU, the secondary measure nonetheless 'supplemented' it by the addition of 'new' non-essential elements, and therefore Article 290 TFEU had to be used.

Advocate General Jääskinen acknowledged that the borderline between 'supplementing a legislative act with non-essential elements and providing more detailed implementing rules is not always easy to draw',[16] but contended that the existence of such borderline cases did not imply the absence of clear cases on either side of the line. There is truth in this. The salient issue is, however, the relative ease or difficulty of identifying the clear cases, and by way of corollary the breadth of the grey area. The reality is in many instances that plausible arguments could be made either way for classification of an act as delegated or implementing.

The argument advanced by Advocate General Jääskinen that implementing acts are 'quite different' from delegated acts because the former enable 'the promulgation of the normative content of the act that is being implemented, in a more detailed manner, in order to facilitate its application', while the latter obviate the EU legislature from the need to amend or supplement non-essential elements of a legal act, does not with respect withstand examination.[17]

The reality is that both delegated and implementing acts imbue the normative content of the relevant measure with greater specificity. This is indeed exemplified by the instant case. The UK challenged Article 28 of European Parliament and Council Regulation 2012/236,[18] which was a legislative act empowering ESMA to act where there was a 'threat to the orderly functioning and integrity of financial markets or to the stability of the whole or part of the financial system in the Union'. This was then supplemented by Commission Delegated Regulation 2012/918, Article 24 of which defined in greater detail the meaning of the criterion in the legislative act.[19] It supplemented the legislative act by imbuing Article 28 with greater normative specificity.

[16] Case 270/12 (n 10) [78], AG Jääskinen.

[17] Ibid [77]. The Court of Justice did not advert to this particular issue when giving judgment, Case C-270/12 *United Kingdom v Council and Parliament*, EU:C:2014:18.

[18] Regulation (EU) 2012/236 of the European Parliament and of the Council of 14 March 2012 on short selling and certain aspects of credit default swaps, OJ 2012 L 86/1.

[19] Commission Delegated Regulation (EU) 2012/918 of 5 July 2012 supplementing Regulation (EU) 2012/236 with regard to definitions, the calculation of net short positions, covered sovereign credit default swaps, notification thresholds, liquidity thresholds for suspending restrictions, significant falls in the value of financial instruments, and adverse events, OJ 2012 L274/1.

The distinguishing feature as laid down in Article 290 TFEU is that delegated acts must be used when this occurs through amendment or supplementation of the non-essential elements of a legislative act. Given that all secondary measures entail some supplementation of the earlier measure this then necessitates inquiry as to when this supplementation must be achieved through a delegated act and when it can occur through an implementing act. And the answer to that inquiry requires the drawing of the very difficult line set out above.

The leading decision from the Court of Justice on the divide between delegated and implementing acts thus far is *Biocides*.[20] A legislative act had been enacted concerning biocidal products and empowered the Commission to make implementing regulations pursuant to Article 291 TFEU. The Commission contended that Article 290 TFEU should rather be used, because the regulation supplemented the legislative act and thus should be regarded as a delegated act.

The Commission argued that the power conferred by Article 291 TFEU was purely implementing in nature, whereas that contained in Article 290 TFEU was a quasi-legislative power. It contended that the choice as between a delegated and an implementing act should be based on objective and clear factors that were amenable to judicial review, a view supported by the European Parliament.[21] The respective scopes of Articles 290 and 291 TFEU were mutually exclusive and implementing acts could not affect the content of the legislative act. If the purpose was to adopt non-essential rules of general application, which completed the normative framework of the legislative act, then those rules supplemented the legislative act and had to be made via TFEU 290. If however the purpose was merely to give effect to the rules already laid down in the basic act while ensuring uniform conditions of application within the EU then Article 291 TFEU could be used.[22]

Advocate General Cruz Villalón examined the distinction between delegated and implementing acts at some length, noting the different purposes of the respective provisions, the former being to accord the Commission with some regulatory power to amend or supplement the legislative act, subject to the conditions in Article 290 TFEU, the latter being to give the Commission implementing powers normally reserved to Member States where this was necessary to ensure uniform conditions for implementation. For the Advocate General, the key difference between the two was the 'fact that delegation allows a measure of discretion which is not mirrored in the case of implementation' in the sense that 'the legislature delegates to the Commission the ability to decide issues that, in principle, it should itself have decided, whereas implementation under Article 291 TFEU operates in relation to provisions the content of which has, as regards the substance, been defined by the legislature'.[23]

[20] Case C-427/12 *Commission v Parliament and Council*, EU:C:2014:170.

[21] Committee on Legal Affairs (n 14).

[22] Ibid [22]–[23].

[23] Case C-427/12 *Commission v Parliament and Council*, EU:C:2013:871, [62].

This may well be so, but the criterion used by the Advocate General restates the analytical problem. It does not, with respect, resolve it. Given that all delegated and implementing acts 'add something' to the legislative act, it still must be determined when that should be regarded as supplementing the legislative act so as to trigger Article 290 TFEU, and when it should not be so regarded so as to justify recourse to Article 291 TFEU. The answer to that inquiry demands application of the criterion set out above or something analogous thereto.

In its judgment, the Court of Justice acknowledged that prior to the Lisbon Treaty the term 'implementing powers' in Article 202 EC covered the entire terrain now divided between delegated and implementing acts. The Court however provided little by way of guidance as to the divide between the two species of act, saying merely that delegated acts supplemented or amended non-essential elements of the legislative act, whereas implementing acts enabled the Commission to provide further detail in relation to the content of a legislative act, in order to ensure that it was implemented under uniform conditions in all Member States.[24] The Court did not therefore sharpen the nature of the analytical divide, but chose rather to leave considerable choice to the EU legislature, as is readily apparent from the following extract:[25]

> It must be noted that the EU legislature has discretion when it decides to confer a delegated power on the Commission pursuant to Article 290(1) TFEU or an implementing power pursuant to Article 291(2) TFEU. Consequently, judicial review is limited to manifest errors of assessment as to whether the EU legislature could reasonably have taken the view, first, that, in order to be implemented, the legal framework which it laid down regarding the system of fees referred to in Article 80(1) of Regulation No 528/2012 needs only the addition of further detail, without its non-essential elements having to be amended or supplemented and, secondly, that the provisions of Regulation No 528/2012 relating to that system require uniform conditions for implementation.

This approach obviated the need for the Court to give clear guidance on the nature of the dichotomy between delegated and implementing acts. Some may approve this type of approach,[26] but it is problematic. The difficulty resides in the very premise in the extract, namely, that the EU legislature has discretion as to whether to confer a delegated or an implementing power on the Commission. This proposition elides two distinct issues, these being the legislature's power to use both delegated and implementing acts, and whether the conditions for the application of the respective types of act have been met.

Thus it is true that the legislature has 'discretion' as to the former issue, but only in the reductionist sense that the Lisbon Treaty makes provision for both delegated and implementing acts, with the consequence that it is open to the EU legislature in the legislative act to choose whether further rules should be made pursuant to Article 290 TFEU or Article 291 TFEU.

[24] Case C-427/12 *Commission v Parliament and Council*, EU:C:2014:170, [37]–[39].

[25] Ibid [40].

[26] J Bast (n 1).

This provides however no foundation for the conclusion that the EU legislature has 'discretion' as to the latter issue, which is whether the conditions for the application of Article 290 TFEU or Article 291 TFEU have been met in any particular instance. Thus the fact that the EU legislature may take the view that, for example, an implementing act will suffice for rules made pursuant to a particular article of the legislative act because they only add some further detail that does not thereby amend or supplement its non-essential elements does not 'make it so'. This is more especially so given that the analytical problem is compounded by a temporal one. The EU legislature will stipulate the type of secondary act to be used pursuant to different articles of the legislative act. However the particular delegated or implementing act has by definition not been made at this point. It is only when it is made that it can be determined whether it does in reality conform to the definition of a delegated or implementing act provided in the Treaty. This problem is compounded by the fact that different procedures are used for the two kinds of act, with the consequence being that once an act is prima facie regarded as being a delegated rather than an implementing act, or vice versa, the institutions will be reluctant to accept that it should be reclassified since it would render the procedure for its enactment *ultra vires*.

It was decided in the Lisbon Treaty to differentiate delegated and implementing acts, and to establish different regimes of control to reflect the differences between the two types of measure. These differences were felt to be of constitutional significance. It can be accepted that when reviewing the choice made by the legislature the Court should consider the reasons why it chose to proceed via a delegated act rather than an implementing act, or vice versa. This is however to say no more than that when exercising judicial review a Court should be properly informed as to the reasoning that underpinned the decision of the body being reviewed. It provides no foundation for the conclusion that the body subject to review has 'discretion' as to whether the conditions for the application of delegated or implementing acts are met, with the consequence that the Court uses only light touch review for manifest error. The EU legislature must perforce exercise interpretive judgment as to the application Articles 290–91 TFEU, but if the exercise of such judgment by an EU institution in relation to a treaty provision is to be equated with discretion justifying only light touch review this would have major ramifications across the entirety of EU law.

The real lesson from this case is that the analytical divide between delegated and implementing acts is fragile and difficult. The Court of Justice was faced with a choice. It could choose to give guidance as to the nature of this divide, but this would lead to the analytical criterion set out above, or something analogous thereto as suggested by the Commission in argument in the instant case. This would then invite frequent challenges as to whether an act fell on the right or wrong side of this analytical divide, a scenario that the Court would not welcome. The Court therefore chose the alternative route, which was to avoid close analytical scrutiny of the dichotomy between the two types of act through recourse to the intensity of review, manifest error being said to be warranted because of the 'discretion' possessed by the legislature. This will discourage claimants from challenging the correctness of the use of delegated or implementing acts in any particular instance, because of the difficulty of proving manifest error.

This cannot however conceal the paradox that besets this area. The distinction between delegated and implementing acts was adopted because it was felt to be important constitutionally and pragmatically. The paradox is that it is the very problematic nature of this divide which led the Court to back away from addressing the substantive distinction between the two types of act, and to sidestep the issue by assigning 'discretion' as to its application to the EU legislature, to be policed only through light touch review for manifest error.

9.3.2 The relative use of Articles 290 and 291: current practice

We can now focus on what light post-Lisbon experience sheds on the way in which this analytical divide is applied. It is important to be clear about four fundamentals when considering how delegated and implementing acts are used in the post-Lisbon world.

Firstly, the standard practice is for the primary legislative act to make provision for the passage of both delegated and implementing acts. It will specify the articles in relation to which the respective secondary measures must be used and will often specify the period for which any delegation of power is to run. Thus, to take an example, Directive 2013/34[27] deals with the making of annual financial statements and provides in Article 49 that delegated acts must be used when enacting measures pursuant to Article 1(2), Article 3(13), and Article 46(2) of the Directive. Article 49(2) states that the delegation shall be for an indeterminate time, subject to the recognition in Article 49(3) that the Council or European Parliament may, in accord with Article 290 TFEU, revoke the delegation of power at any time. In a similar vein, Article 33 of European Parliament and Council Regulation 2013/610 on the Schengen Borders Code states that delegated acts should be used for measures made pursuant to Article 12(5) and Article 32.[28] The delegation is once again said to be for an indeterminate period, subject to the proviso that it can be revoked at any time by the European Parliament or the Council.

Secondly, there are relatively rare instances in which the legislative act makes no provision for the enactment of implementing acts, stipulating that every secondary measure must take the form of a delegated act. This is exemplified by European Parliament and Council Regulation 2012/966, which is the general financial regulation for the EU, replacing that enacted in 2002.[29] All secondary measures must

[27] Directive (EU) 2013/34 of the European Parliament and of the Council of 26 June 2013 on the annual financial statements, consolidated financial statements and related reports of certain types of undertakings, amending Directive (EC) 2006/43/EC of the European Parliament and of the Council, OJ 2013 L 182/19.

[28] Regulation (EU) 2013/610 of the European Parliament and of the Council of 26 June 2013 amending Regulation (EC) 2006/562 of the European Parliament and of the Council establishing a Community Code on the rules governing the movement of persons across borders (Schengen Borders Code), OJ 2013 L 182/1.

[29] Regulation (EU, Euratom) 2012/966 of the European Parliament and of the Council of 25 October 2012 on the financial rules applicable to the general budget of the Union and repealing Council Regulation (EC, Euratom) 1605/2002, OJ 2012 L 298/1.

take the form of delegated acts, and the Regulation accords this power to the Commission in relation to measures made in furtherance of 115 articles of the legislative act. The delegation is conferred on the Commission to the end of the first post-2013 multiannual financial framework referred to in Article 312 TFEU.[30]

Thirdly, by way of contrast to the preceding point, there are numerous instances in which an implementing regulation is used to amend an earlier implementing regulation. This may seem strange, but it is in fact lawful within the Lisbon schema. This is because Article 290 TFEU only mandates use of a delegated act where a legislative act is amended or supplemented. Thus where the relevant act supplements or amends an implementing act this can be done by a later implementing act.[31]

Fourthly, implementing acts constitute the principal instrument used for the enactment of secondary measures. At the end of 2014 there were, published in the EU Official Journal, 3,426 implementing regulations (220 adopted by the Council), 44 implementing directives (0 adopted by the Council), and 1,055 implementing decisions (180 adopted by the Council). There were by way of contrast 173 delegated regulations, 28 delegated directives, and 4 delegated decisions. It is clear therefore that implementing measures, judged in quantitative terms at least, predominate. This does not tell one anything about the relative importance of the respective measures. It does nonetheless furnish some perspective on the relative use of the respective measures and provides also important empirical information against which to judge the significance of the accountability regimes that operate in the context of Article 290 and Article 291 TFEU, an issue that will be considered in more detail below. The preceding figures should however be read in the light of the discussion on transitional issues, since this will increase the number of acts officially recorded as 'delegated acts'.

9.3.3 The choice between Article 290 and Article 291: limited legislative guidance

The very difficulty with the criterion for the divide between delegated and implementing acts poses an interesting academic conundrum, which is how precisely to assess the way in which the division has been used in the post-Lisbon world. Given that the criterion for the distinction is inherently problematic this in turn renders it difficult to determine how far it has been correctly or incorrectly used in subsequent practice. Subject to this caveat, there are nonetheless a number of points relevant to the way in which the analytical divide between delegated and

[30] Ibid Article 210.

[31] See, e.g. Commission Implementing Regulation (EU) 2003/17 of 14 January 2013 approving the active substance Trichoderma atroviride strain I-1237, in accordance with Regulation (EC) 2009/1107 of the European Parliament and of the Council concerning the placing of plant protection products on the market, and amending the Annex to Implementing Regulation (EU) 2011/540, OJ 2013 L 9/5; Commission Implementing Regulation (EU) 2013/22 of 15 January 2013 approving the active substance cyflumetofen, in accordance with Regulation (EC) 2009/1107 of the European Parliament and of the Council concerning the placing of plant protection products on the market, and amending the Annex to Commission Implementing Regulation (EU) 2011/540, OJ 2013 L11/8.

implementing acts is unfolding in the post Lisbon world. We begin with the extent to which the legislative act provides guidance as to choice between the two forms of secondary measure.

It is common for the preamble to the legislative act to provide some information as to why delegated acts have been chosen for changes to certain articles of the legislative act, while in other instances the secondary measure of choice is an implementing act. How much information is provided however varies significantly. There is also considerable variance as to the extent to which the information in the preamble provides adequate explanation as to why change to a certain article of the legislative act is felt to amend or supplement it, thus requiring a delegated act, while in other instances it is felt that the secondary measure can take the form of an implementing act, which is predicated on the assumption that the secondary measure does not amend or supplement the legislative act so as to demand a delegated act. The reality is that in most instances the preamble will simply state that a delegated act is needed or not as the case may be, without providing any indication as to why this should be so.[32]

This does not mean that the drafters of the legislative act were necessarily wrong in this respect. What it does mean is that the way in which the divide between delegated and implementing acts is applied does not immediately strike one as principled. What it also means is that it is very difficult to test the soundness of that divide, given the fragility of the definitional distinction between the two species of act, and given also that it would take a lifetime to test that fragile divide in the many circumstances in which it has been applied.

9.3.4 The choice between Article 290 and Article 291: particular regulatory schemes

Following from the above, it is clear that when one looks more closely at the choice made between delegated and implementing acts in a particular context it is not self-evident that the choice is correct. Put more directly, what this means is that just because an implementing act is chosen on the assumption that it does not supplement the legislative act does not mean that the assumption is sustainable or correct. The fact that the legislative act says that it is so, does not make it so.

This can be exemplified by consideration of rules drawn from air navigation. European Parliament and Council Regulation 2009/1070 was a primary regulation concerning the performance of the European Aviation System.[33] To attain this

[32] See, e.g. Directive (EU) 2013/34 (n 27) preamble paras 50, 54; Regulation (EU) 2012/648 of the European Parliament and of the Council of 4 July 2012 on OTC derivatives, central counterparties and trade repositories Text with EEA relevance, OJ 2012 L 201/1, preamble para 91; Regulation (EU) 2012/236 of the European Parliament and of the Council of 14 March 2012 on short selling and certain aspects of credit default swaps, OJ 2012 L 86/1, preamble paras 43, 46.

[33] Regulation (EC) 2009/1070 of the European Parliament and of the Council of 21 October 2009 amending Regulations (EC) 2004/549, (EC) 2004/550, (EC) 2004/551 and (EC) 2004/552 in order to improve the performance and sustainability of the European aviation system, OJ 2009 L 300/34.

end, Article 11 contained rules concerning EU-wide targets on key performance areas of safety, the environment, capacity, and cost-efficiency; national plans for airspace blocks; and periodic review, monitoring, and benchmarking of the performance of air navigation services. These targets were to be adopted using the old-style regulatory procedure, and provision could be made for the establishment of a body that would assist the Commission in assessment. Compliance was to be assessed through, inter alia, validation, examination, evaluation, and dissemination of relevant data related to the performance of air navigation services and network functions from all relevant parties. The list of factors relevant to compliance could be augmented through use of the old-style regulatory procedure with scrutiny, but the detailed rules concerning the workings of the scheme were to be laid down by implementing rules adopted by the Commission under the old-style regulatory procedure, which in the post-Lisbon world translated into implementing acts enacted pursuant to the new Comitology Regulation.[34]

The Commission duly enacted Implementing Regulation 2013/390.[35] It is a long regulation, which specifies in great detail issues that were left at a higher level of abstraction by the earlier primary regulation, including: the powers of the body to assist the Commission with its performance reviews; the duties of national supervisory authorities; the role of the network manager; the meaning of performance indicators; the preparation and adoption of performance plans; monitoring of performance targets; the collection and validation of data relating to performance reviews; and the template for the network strategy plan.

Regulation 2013/390 clearly supplements the earlier primary regulation. It imbues it with very much greater detail on the preceding issues. Nor should use of the word 'detail' be equated with 'unimportant'. The regulatory specificity brought to the performance schema by Regulation 2013/390 covers a plethora of important issues that are central to the efficacy of the overall legislative objective. Regulation 2013/390 can therefore only be a valid implementing regulation on the assumption that although it supplemented the earlier legislative norm it did not add any 'new' non-essential element so as to trigger the need for a delegated act. This in turn depends on the level of abstraction with which one poses the inquiry.

It might be argued that the issues dealt with by Regulation 2013/390 can all be related to terms mentioned in the primary regulation. It might then be contended that there is no new non-essential element such as to warrant recourse to a delegated regulation. This is, however, a dangerously reductionist conclusion. It would mean that provided one could locate some textual touchstone in the legislative act then pretty much anything done pursuant thereto could be regarded as an implementing act, irrespective of the fact that the very detailed regulatory specificity embodied in the latter was not predetermined by anything in the legislative act.

[34] Regulation (EU) 2011/182 of the European Parliament and of the Council of 16 February 2011 laying down the rules and general principles concerning mechanisms for control by Member States of the Commission's exercise of implementing powers, OJ 2011 L 55/13.

[35] Commission Implementing Regulation (EU) 2013/390 of 3 May 2013 laying down a performance scheme for air navigation services and network functions, OJ 2013 L 300/34.

The reality is that this example drawn from air navigation simply exemplifies the difficulty in applying the delegated/implementing divide in a principled manner.

9.3.5 The choice between Article 290 and Article 291: transitional issues

It is also important when navigating this area to be aware of transitional issues that affect the assignment of acts to the categories of delegated and implementing. A bare reading of some secondary measures reveals acts that are not labelled delegated or implementing, and it can moreover be confusing as to which category they should be assigned to, adjudged by their substance.

The explanation is that such measures were made post-Lisbon under primary regulations made pre-Lisbon. The typical scenario is that the primary regulation specifies that the secondary measure should be made through the old-style regulatory procedure with scrutiny.[36] The revised Comitology Regulation repealed the previous Comitology Decision, but preserved the regulatory procedure with scrutiny for basic acts that made reference thereto.[37] The rationale for this exception was that acts made under the old regulatory procedure with scrutiny were akin to delegated acts and should not therefore fall within the scope of the new Comitology Regulation that only dealt with implementing acts.

The Commission made a commitment that it would adapt such provisions to the schema for delegated acts under Article 290 TFEU. There were 288 such provisions existing at the end of 2012. To this end, the Commission proposed three framework regulations, which provided that where an instrument made reference to the regulatory procedure with scrutiny the Commission was empowered to adopt a delegated act.[38] The proposals were however subject to significant amendment by the European Parliament, and were not approved by the Council. The reason for Council reluctance in this respect is interesting and reflective of the tensions that underlie the Lisbon schema. It appears that the Council withheld consent because it sought in general terms greater control by national experts over delegated acts than that provided for by Article 290 TFEU. It preferred therefore to retain old-style regulatory procedure with scrutiny, because old-style comitology committees continued to exist in this area. We shall return to this issue below, but suffice it to say for the present that while the Lisbon schema formally excluded a comitology-type regime from the sphere of delegated acts, the Council has sought to reverse this de facto. Council opposition led the Commission to withdraw the proposals in March 2015.

[36] Council Decision (EC) 1999/468 laying down the procedures for the exercise of implementing powers conferred on the Commission, OJ 1999 L 184/23, Article 5a.

[37] Regulation (EU) 2011/182 (n 8) Article 12.

[38] Proposal for a Regulation of the European Parliament and of the Council adapting to Article 290 and 291 of the Treaty on the Functioning of the European Union a number of legal acts providing for the use of the regulatory procedure with scrutiny, COM(2013) 451 final, COM(2013) 452 final and COM(2013) 751 final.

9.4 Constitutional: Politics and Constitutional Architecture

The discussion thus far has considered the analytical difficulties with the divide between delegated and implementing acts. The focus now shifts to the ways in which practical politics in the post-Lisbon world have impacted on the constitutional architecture in this part of the Lisbon Treaty.

9.4.1 Constitutional 'modification': decision-making under Article 290

A significant development in relation to the way in which Article 290 TFEU operates was the reintroduction by the backdoor of what had been excluded from the front, as manifest in the role played by national experts in Council and European Parliament deliberations.[39] The Commission's Communication to the Council concerning Articles 290 and 291 TFEU in December 2009 was premised on the demise of management and regulatory committees in relation to Article 290 TFEU.[40] The Commission, without mentioning the previous committee regime, accepted that it would consult with national experts in the making of delegated acts, but stressed that the experts would have a 'consultative rather institutional role in the decision-making procedure'.[41] When the consultations were concluded the experts would merely be informed of the Commission's conclusions and how it intended to proceed.[42] The Council for its part suddenly woke up to the imminent demise of the old comitology regime and responded to the Commission document by stressing the importance it attached to consultation with national experts,[43] which should be undertaken in time to allow for meaningful input by such experts.

The rationale for this was not difficult to divine. The *ex ante* control in Article 290(1) TFEU to the effect that the legislative act must define the 'objectives, content, scope and duration of the delegation of power' is not easy to monitor and enforce, since it will often be difficult for the Council and the European Parliament in the legislative act to specify with exactitude the criteria that should guide the exercise of delegated power by the Commission. They may lack the knowledge and time to delineate in the legislative act precise parameters for the exercise of regulatory choices. The *ex post* controls in Article 290(2) TFEU also have limitations. Revocation of the entire delegation is a nuclear strike option, but inherently ill-suited to more subtle control over particular delegated acts. The ability to veto

[39] The Lisbon Treaty, Declaration 39 spoke of continued consultation national experts in the financial area, when making delegated acts under Article 290 TFEU. Its significance is considered in Section 9.5.3.

[40] Implementation of Article 290 of the Treaty on the Functioning of the European Union, COM(2009) 673 final.

[41] Ibid [4.2]. [42] Ibid [4.2].

[43] Council Doc 17477/09, Implementation of the Lisbon Treaty, Article 290, Article 291, Brussels, 11 December 2009.

the particular delegated act is more promising in this respect, but there is no formal power to amend the proposed measure, and more importantly exercise of the veto is crucially dependent on understanding the relevant measure. Neither the Council nor the European Parliament can decide whether to object to the measure unless they understand it. The Member State representatives on the Council clearly have neither the time nor expertise to perform this task unaided. The European Parliament committees might develop such expertise, but it would be difficult.

This then was the rationale for the 2011 Common Understanding,[44] the result of tough negotiations between the major institutional players. It dealt with a range of issues. Thus a delegation to the Commission that is temporally limited can be tacitly extended by the same period of time as the initial delegation.[45] There are provisions dealing with the period within which objections by the European Parliament and Council should be raised.[46] It is however the provisions on consultation that are most important. The Commission is charged when preparing delegated acts with ensuring 'a simultaneous, timely and appropriate transmission of relevant documents to the European Parliament and the Council and carry out appropriate and transparent consultations well in advance, including at expert level'.[47] The significance of this provision is attested by the fact that the Common Understanding includes an annex containing a standard clause to be included in the recital to legislative acts that delegate power to the Commission, in which the substance of the obligation to transmit documents in a timely fashion and consult the European Parliament and Council, including at expert level, is iterated. This now occurs as a matter of course, and such a clause is included routinely in all legislative acts that delegate power to the Commission.[48]

In 2014 the Council sought to revise the Common Understanding and strengthen the role of experts.[49] Whether this will be successful remains to be seen, since the European Parliament has to express its view. The Commission not surprisingly wishes to concede as little ground as possible on this issue. This is readily apparent in a letter from Maroš Šefčovič, Vice President of the Commission, in response to Council initiatives to revise the Common Understanding.[50] The Commission was, he said, mindful of the need to consult national experts in the manner specified by the 2011 Common Understanding and would seek ways to

[44] Common Understanding on Delegated Acts, Council Doc 8753/1/11 of 14 April 2011.

[45] Ibid [7]–[8]. [46] Ibid [10]–[11]. [47] Ibid [4].

[48] See, e.g. Directive (EU) 2013/34 (n 27) recital (54), 'In order to take account of future changes to the laws of the Member States and to Union legislation concerning company types, the Commission should be empowered to adopt delegated acts in accordance with Article 290 of the TFEU in order to update the lists of undertakings contained in Annexes I and II. The use of delegated acts is also necessary in order to adapt the undertaking size criteria, as with the passage of time inflation will erode their real value. It is of particular importance that the Commission carries out appropriate consultations during its preparatory work, including at expert level. The Commission, when preparing and drawing up delegated acts, should ensure a simultaneous, timely and appropriate transmission of relevant documents to the European Parliament and to the Council'.

[49] Initiative to complement the Common Understanding on Delegated Acts as regards the consultation of experts, Council Doc 6774/14 of 21 February 2014.

[50] Council Doc 7792/14 of 17 March 2014.

ensure that this worked better in the future. The Vice President nonetheless drew the line at suggestions that there should be a mandatory consultation procedure under Article 290 TFEU, which was akin to the advisory committee procedure under Article 291 TFEU, saying that this would not be compatible with the Treaty.

It is nonetheless worth considering the draft revisions since they shed light on Council thinking. The proposed revisions reinforce the earlier version by providing that the consultation in relation to delegated acts must be 'systematically' undertaken, 'with groups composed of experts designated by all the Member States'.[51] The Commission can 'rely on existing expert groups, or if necessary, create new ones'. The Commission is moreover obliged, if so requested by the European Parliament or the Council, to invite observers from the European Parliament and/or Council to attend the meetings of the expert groups. The 2014 version also states that preparation of delegated acts may include consultation with stakeholders, which should take place before consultation with expert groups.

These changes are reflected in the annex, which contains standard clauses to be included in legislative acts that empower the Commission to make delegated acts. Thus the standard recital clause would provide that the Commission should endeavour to find solutions that command the widest possible support within the expert group, and should inform the expert group of the manner in which its suggestions for amendment should be taken into account. Even more important are the proposed revisions that would be made to the standard article included in legislative acts specifying how the delegation should be exercised. There is a new formal obligation on the Commission to consult the experts before the delegated act is adopted, and the expert group must in addition be given the opportunity to comment on all major changes to the draft delegated act before it is adopted. The Commission is charged to 'take the utmost account' of the opinion of the expert group, and must give reasons where it does not act in accordance with the opinion of that group.

The 2011 Common Understanding was given formal imprimatur by its repeated inclusion in the recitals to legislation. It reinvented the wheel insofar as it brought back some advisory committees to provide the informational resource that is especially useful in deciding whether to exercise a veto power. These committees do not have the formal powers of their management and regulatory comitology predecessors, although whether their input into Council decision-making is markedly different in substance is difficult to determine. The proposed 2014 version of the Common Understanding would strengthen the position of expert groups, and open the possibility that existing comitology expert committees used under Article 291 TFEU could be used here in relation to Article 290 TFEU.

The paradox is that the Lisbon reforms were intended to simplify the decision-making process, including the role of committees therein. The political reality is that in the immediate aftermath of the Lisbon Treaty, we had the new comitology regime within Article 291 TFEU, where the committees are at least relatively

[51] Council Doc 6774/14, (n 49), [4].

transparent, coupled with the more shadowy world of advisory committees created pursuant to the 2011 Common Understanding operating within Article 290 TFEU, the membership and proceedings of which were not readily available. The proposed 2014 Common Understanding would improve matters in this respect by mandating the Commission to keep a list of expert groups used under Article 290 TFEU, including the agendas of their meetings, their opinions, and summaries of the consultations.[52]

There is then the further paradox that the greater the formality introduced for the Article 290 committees by the proposed 2014 Common Understanding, the smaller the difference de facto between the decision-making process for delegated and implementing acts, more especially if the ability to use 'existing expert groups' leads to Article 291 comitology committees fulfilling the role of expert advisors within Article 290.

9.4.2 Constitutional 'modification': the new schema and the Parliament

The constitutional architecture in Articles 289–91 TFEU, and in particular the format of Article 290 TFEU, was the result of pressure from the European Parliament as well as the Commission. The European Parliament had always felt that the old-style comitology regime was weighted in favour of the Council, as indeed it was even after the changes introduced in 1999[53] and 2006.[54] It therefore favoured reform that would afford it parity with the Council in relation to the controls over delegated acts. The battles waged in the 1990s have been related admirably by Carl Fredrik Bergström.[55] The European Parliament was not aided in this respect by the Council, which felt that its dominance over secondary measures was warranted, nor by the Commission, which was opposed to comitology constraints and had no appetite for according analogous controls to the European Parliament.

Truth to tell the Commission position was more complex than this, reflective of the fact that the Commission is not a monolithic institution. The reality was that leaders within the Commission disliked comitology and the constraints that it imposed on what the Commission believed should be its executive autonomy over measures other than primary legislative-type norms. There was nonetheless an element within the Commission that took the line that the European Parliament should be given 'everything' relating to secondary measures, the assumption being

[52] Council Doc 6774/14, (n 49), [15a].

[53] Council Decision (EC) 1999/468 (n 36); K Lenaerts and A Verhoeven, 'Towards a Legal Framework for Executive Rulemaking in the EU? The Contribution of the New Comitology Decision' (2000) 37 CMLRev 645.

[54] Council Decision (EC) 2006/512 of 17 July 2006 amending Decision (EC) 1999/468 laying down the procedures for the exercise of implementing powers by the Commission, OJ 2006 L 200/11.

[55] C F Bergstrom, *Comitology, Delegation of Powers in the European Union and the Committee System* (Oxford University Press 2005).

that it simply would not be able to cope with the truckloads of documentation. The front line of the Commission working within particular Directorates-General were, by way of contrast, reasonably content with the committee system, since it was the mechanism through which they could liaise with national experts.

Be that as it may, the European Parliament largely achieved its desired parity in Article 290 TFEU. The *ex ante* controls in Article 290(1) TFEU pertain to the European Parliament as well as the Council, while the *ex post* controls in Article 290(2) TFEU relating to revocation of the delegation and veto of the particular delegated act can be exercised by either the Council or the European Parliament. This parity was reinforced by the argument put forcefully by the European Parliament that old style comitology committees could not operate within the confines of Article 290 TFEU.[56] There are, however, two aspects of the post-Lisbon schema that have undermined this parity.

There is, on the one hand, the fact that national experts have been reintroduced de facto by the 2011 Common Understanding. The fact that such consultation is equally applicable to the European Parliament and Council, and the fact that the Committee on Legal Affairs placed emphasis on the flow of information from the Commission to the relevant committees of the European Parliament, including information about successive drafts of delegated acts,[57] does not alter the fact that reintroduction of consultation with expert committees benefited the Council more than the European Parliament, and hence upset the hard-won parity achieved though Article 290 TFEU in the Lisbon Treaty. This imbalance would be exacerbated if the proposed 2014 Common Understanding becomes a reality, since the operative language is that there should be systematic consultation on delegated acts with 'groups composed of experts designated by all Member States', albeit subject to the possibility that the European Parliament or Council can send observers to attend the meeting of the expert group.

There is, on the other hand, the fact noted above that quantitatively so much more is done by implementing acts than by delegated acts, and that is so even taking account of the fact the number of delegated acts will rise somewhat as a result of the transitional measures. To be sure this figure provides little by way of information as to the relative importance of the measures. It can be accepted that numerous implementing acts are minor changes to, for example, annexes listing regulated substances. This does not alter the fact that the borderline between delegated and implementing acts remains fragile and that many people would be hard pressed to discern which category an act fell within if the labels were removed. The upshot is that the parity achieved by the European Parliament under Article 290 TFEU is undermined by the very fact that so much is done under Article 291 TFEU, where it has considerably less input into the new comitology procedure than it did under the old.

[56] Committee on Legal Affairs, (n 14) (Szajer), at pp 11–12.

[57] Committee on Legal Affairs, Report of 29 March 2010 on the power of legislative delegation, A-7 0110/2010, 10.

It might be argued that the same is true in relation to the Council, and indeed the Commission asseverated that neither the European Parliament nor the Council had formal controls over implementing acts.[58] It is moreover true that the new Comitology Regulation formally disaggregates the representatives of Member States that serve on the committees from those on the Council.

The fact nonetheless remains that the members of comitology committees are national representatives, and ministers that represent the Member States on the Council may well take a keen interest in the appointees from their respective states that serve on these committees. There is likely to be exchange of views between the two sets of personnel. The Commission's desire to preserve the distinction between input into implementation via Member State representatives on comitology committees, and Member State interests as vocalized in the Council, may therefore be hard to sustain, more especially because the committee voting rules mirror those of the Council itself. Channels of communication are likely to emerge, which may well be used to effectuate Council objectives indirectly even if this cannot be done through more direct means.

The European Parliament has nothing analogous to draw on when a matter is dealt with through Article 291 TFEU. There are only the limited formal powers accorded to it and the Council under the Comitology Regulation.[59] The European Parliament and Council can access information about committee proceedings leading to implementing acts,[60] and they can indicate to the Commission that they consider a draft implementing act to exceed the implementing powers provided for in the basic act. This only applies where the basic act is made under the ordinary legislative procedure,[61] and hence does not apply in relation to implementing acts made pursuant to delegated acts. The Commission has a duty to review the draft act, taking into account the views of the European Parliament and Council, but is not obliged to withdraw the act. It must rather inform these institutions whether it intends to maintain, amend, or withdraw the draft implementing act.

9.4.3 Constitutional 'Modification': Commission and the 'new' status quo

There is also evidence of modification when one considers the position of the Commission in relation to the *modus operandi* of the constitutional architecture post-Lisbon.

In relation to the overall constitutional architecture, the Commission succeeded in excising old-style comitology from the realm of delegated acts, replacing it with the *ex ante* and *ex post* controls found in Article 290 TFEU. It thereby secured its aim of establishing regulatory autonomy over the content of delegated

[58] Proposal for a Regulation of the European Parliament and of the Council laying down the rules and general principles concerning mechanisms for control by Member States of the Commission's exercise of implementing powers, COM(2010) 83 final p 3.

[59] Regulation (EU) 2011/182 (n 8).

[60] Ibid Article 10.

[61] Ibid Article 11.

acts, subject to the controls in Article 290 TFEU. This has, however, been qualified by the return of advisory committees through the Common Understanding, and through the role of agencies discussed in Section 9.5. The Commission succeeded also in formally excluding the European Parliament and Council from the world of implementing acts, insisting that the new committees were representatives of the Member States, and that there should be no formal recourse to the Council in the event that the committee disagreed with the Commission proposal. The reality is nonetheless that the committees are composed of national representatives, they vote in accord with the criteria for voting in the Council, and there will inevitably be close linkages between the national view as expressed in the Council and Coreper, and the national view expressed through the new comitology committees. The Commission was, moreover, forced to accept an appeal committee within the comitology regime, which had been absent from the original Commission proposal.[62] There were hard fought battles about the precise role to be played by such a committee within the new comitology regime, and it is accorded a prominent place in the new schema, in particular in relation to the examination procedure.[63]

Constitutional modification is also apparent in relation to the new comitology regime for implementing acts, and the role of the Commission therein. The new Comitology Regulation was sold on the basis that it would simplify the status quo ante, through reduction to only the advisory and the examination procedures. The legal and political reality is however that there are four procedures operating in the Comitology Regulation. Thus in addition to the advisory and examination procedures there is also provision for immediately applicable implementing acts that constitute a third kind of comitology procedure.[64] Less obvious, but of more practical significance, is the fact that within the complex rules relating to the examination procedure there are different regimes that apply depending on whether the committee votes against the measure, or fails to vote in favour of it. Where the committee delivers a negative opinion the default position is that the Commission shall not adopt the draft implementing act, but this is then qualified in four ways.[65] Where the committee delivers no opinion the default position is that the Commission can adopt the draft implementing act, or submit an amended version to the committee, albeit subject to five qualifications.[66] There is therefore much here that replicates the pre-existing divide between the management and regulatory procedure, which is further reinforced by differential provisions that apply within the appeal procedure, depending on whether the Appeal Committee votes in favour of the measure, against it, or delivers no opinion.[67]

[62] COM(2010) 83 final.

[63] Committee on Legal Affairs, 26 November 2010, 2010/0051, Rapporteur József Szájer. See also, Council, 30 November 2010, Doc 16976/10.

[64] Regulation (EU) 2011/182 (n 8), Article 8.

[65] Ibid Article 5(3).

[66] Ibid Article 5(4).

[67] Ibid Article 6(3).

9.5 Institutional: Agencies, Conferral, Delegated Acts, and Implementing Acts

The constitutional regime embodied in Articles 290 and 291 TFEU has also been affected by institutional change, most markedly through the creation of the new breed of European Supervisory Authorities (ESAs).

9.5.1 Agencies: conferral and delegation

It is clear from *ESMA*[68] that power can be conferred directly on an EU agency independent of the confines of Articles 290 and 291 TFEU. The European Security Markets Authority (ESMA) had been given power by a legislative act to take action in relation to short selling on stock in certain defined circumstances.[69] The UK argued that this was unlawful on a number of grounds, inter alia, that Articles 290 and 291 TFEU circumscribed the circumstances in which powers could be given to the Commission, and that the Council and European Parliament had no authority under the Treaties to delegate powers such as those in the instant case to an EU agency.

The Court of Justice acknowledged that the contested provision, Article 28 of European Parliament and Council Regulation 2012/236, delegated power not to the Commission but to an EU agency. This required the Court to decide whether Articles 290 and 291 TFEU were intended to establish 'a single legal framework under which certain delegated and executive powers may be attributed solely to the Commission or whether other systems for the delegation of such powers to Union bodies, offices or agencies may be contemplated by the Union legislature'.[70]

The Court noted that while the Treaties contained no express provision allowing this, certain treaty provisions presumed that such a possibility existed. Agencies were subject to judicial review via Articles 263, 265, and 267 TFEU, which was applicable to EU bodies, offices, and agencies that were given powers to adopt legally binding measures on natural or legal persons.[71]

The power accorded to ESMA in the present case must, said the Court, be seen in the context of the overall purpose of the regulatory scheme to deal with integration of financial markets and prevent the risk of financial contagion. This required that ESMA have power to impose temporary restrictions on the short selling of certain stocks, in order to prevent an uncontrolled fall in the price of those instruments.[72] This 'conferral of powers'[73] did not therefore correspond to the situations in Articles 290 and 291 TFEU, nor did it undermine them.

[68] Case C-270/12 *United Kingdom v Council and Parliament*, EU:C:2014:18.

[69] Regulation (EU) 2012/236 (n 18), Article 28.

[70] Case C-270/12 (n 68) [78].

[71] Ibid [80]–[81]. The Court cited by way of example the European Chemicals Agency, the European Medicines Agency, the Office for Harmonization in the Internal Market, the Community Plant Variety Office and the European Aviation Safety Agency.

[72] Case C-270/12 (n 68) [84]–[85].

[73] Ibid [83].

There is force in this reasoning. The legal reality was that the European Parliament and the Council had directly conferred power on ESMA via Article 28 of the legislative act to take action against short selling of stock in certain defined circumstances. That power was then further refined through a delegated act made pursuant to Article 290 TFEU, which was expressly authorized by the legislative act.[74] There was then force in the Court's conclusion that the conferral of power did not correspond to the situations contemplated by Articles 290 and 291 TFEU, nor did it undermine them.

It might be argued, as the UK did, that the direct conferral of power in Article 28 of Regulation 2012/236 infringed the *Meroni* principle,[75] which limits the discretion that can be given to agencies. The Court however rejected this argument, stating that the powers exercised by ESMA pursuant to Article 28 were sufficiently delineated and precise so as not to offend the *Meroni* principle.[76] Its reasoning in this respect, and the broader implications for agency powers, cannot be examined here.

9.5.2 ESAs and delegated acts

The old style-comitology committees may well have gone, but in some areas new 'agencies' have been created and Member States are accorded significant decisional authority on such bodies. This has been the solution adopted for the ESAs, the new financial supervisory authorities: the European Securities and Markets Authority (ESMA);[77] the European Banking Authority (EBA);[78] the European Insurance and Occupational Pensions Authority (EIOPA).[79] The ESAs are technically regarded as Union bodies with legal personality.[80]

They are EU agencies, but Member States dominate their organizational structure. The Board of Supervisors is composed primarily of high-level national representatives, exemplified by the assumption in relation to the EBA that this will be the head of the national central bank of each Member State.[81] It is this Board that adopts the draft regulatory standards and decisions made by the agency.[82] The Board of Supervisors is mandated to act in the interest of the EU, and must not take instructions from national authorities.[83]

[74] Commission Delegated Regulation (EU) 2012/918 (n 19).

[75] Case 9/56 *Meroni v High Authority*, EU:C:1958:7.

[76] Case C-270/12 (n 68) [41]–[55].

[77] Regulation (EU) 2010/1095 of the European Parliament and of the Council of 24 November 2010 establishing a European Supervisory Authority (European Securities and Markets Authority), OJ 2010 L 331/84; http://ec.europa.eu/economy_finance/other/index_en.htm.

[78] Regulation (EU) 2010/1093 of the European Parliament and of the Council of 24 November 2010 establishing a European Supervisory Authority (European Banking Authority), OJ 2010 L 331/12.

[79] Regulation (EU) 2010/1094 of the European Parliament and of the Council of 24 November 2010 establishing a European Supervisory Authority (European Insurance and Occupational Pensions Authority), OJ 2010 L 331/48.

[80] See, e.g. Regulation (EU) 2010/1095 (n 77) Article 5(1).

[81] See, e.g. Regulation (EU) 2010/1093 (n 78) Article 40.

[82] Ibid Article 43.

[83] Ibid Article 42.

Having said this, the legal and political reality is that such agencies are 'institutionally ambivalent'. This is because while the Board of Supervisors is formally required to act in the EU interest, its voting rules on all important issues formally mirror those of the Council.[84] Qualified majority voting in accord with Article 16(4) TEU is the legal norm,[85] thereby embodying the assumption that the rules normally applicable to decision-making by state representatives in the Council should be equally applicable to decisions or recommendations made by Boards of Supervisors on ESAs. The Board of Supervisors can moreover establish panels for attainment of the Board's tasks.[86] The panels are chaired by senior representatives of national supervisory authorities and composed of national experts and agency staff.[87]

The ESAs are empowered to draft regulatory technical standards (RTS), many of which have policy implications,[88] notwithstanding the formal requirement that the standards are meant to be technical and not entail policy choices.[89] The schema is that where the primary regulation delegates power to the Commission to make delegated acts pursuant to Article 290 TFEU, it is the agency that drafts these acts, which are then endorsed by the Commission, subject to the possibility of veto by the Council or the European Parliament in accordance with Article 290 TFEU.[90] The recitals to the Regulation make it clear that the Commission should amend the draft produced by, for example, the EBA only in 'very restricted and extraordinary circumstances', the rationale being that the EBA has the expertise within this area.[91] These sentiments are reflected in the Regulation. The Commission is only able to adopt a draft delegated act itself if the EBA has failed to do so within the time specified in the legislative act.[92] The Commission must also give a reasoned explanation for departure from the EBA draft rule and cannot make any such change without discussion with the EBA.[93] This schema for delegated acts made by ESAs has impacted on the constitutional architecture of Article 290 TFEU in three ways.

Firstly, it has qualified the parity between Council and European Parliament that underlies the Lisbon schema of Article 290 TFEU. Niamh Moloney has, for example, described ESMA as structurally intergovernmental.[94] It is true as seen earlier that national representatives must be independent and represent the EU

[84] Ibid Article 44, provides as a general rule that voting is by simple majority, with each member having one vote, but this is then subject to the exception in the next paragraph, which provides that for all decisions, recommendations or opinions made pursuant to Articles 10–16 a qualified majority determined in accord with Article 16(4) TEU is used.

[85] Ibid Article 44, recital 53.

[86] Ibid Article 41.

[87] N Moloney, 'The European Securities and Markets Authority and Institutional Design for the EU Financial Market—A Tale of Two Competences: Part (1) Rulemaking' (2011) 12 European Business Organization Law Review 41, 63.

[88] Ibid 67–70.

[89] See, e.g. Regulation (EU) 2010/1093 (n 78) Article 10(1).

[90] Ibid Articles 10, 13.

[91] Ibid Rec 23, although the recital also states that a draft RTS can be amended if it is not compatible with EU law, does not respect proportionality, or runs counter to the fundamental principles of the *acquis* of Union financial services legislation.

[92] Ibid Article 10(3).

[93] Ibid Article 10(1).

[94] N Moloney (n 87), at p 82.

rather than national interests. This does not alter the fact that national interests predominate in the formulation of the detailed agency regulatory standards and the decision-making rules in the Board of Supervisors mirror those for Council decision-making. Thus while the European Parliament may have the same powers as the Council when the draft regulatory standard is presented by the Commission, this should not mask the fact that national representatives within the agency play a central role in deciding the content of those standards.[95]

Secondly, the schema for delegated acts made by ESAs has impacted on the constitutional assumptions concerning the role of the Commission in Article 290 TFEU. The premise underlying Article 290 TFEU is that the Commission has regulatory autonomy over delegated acts, subject to the *ex ante* and *ex post* controls contained therein. This was what the Commission fought for in the years preceding the Lisbon Treaty. It has however been undermined *de jure* and de facto by the schema introduced for delegated acts made by ESAs, since the substance of the regulatory power has been taken out of its hands and its input curtailed.

Thirdly, the creation of ESAs reveals more general tensions underlying the Lisbon divide between Article 290 TFEU and Article 291 TFEU. The pre-existing Lamfalussy system[96] was premised on secondary norms that were validated by processes more akin to those used in relation to implementing acts, with a strong role for a special comitology-type regime. It would have been difficult to fit this within Article 290 TFEU given that comitology committees are not permitted in relation to delegated acts. However it would also have been difficult to regard the Lamfalussy system as coming within Article 291 TFEU, since many measures passed pursuant to Lamfalussy 2 or 3 could not be regarded as merely implementing acts in the Article 291 TFEU sense, given that they supplemented or amended the legislative act, and would therefore have to be enacted via Article 290 TFEU in the post-Lisbon world. The system was therefore caught between a rock and a hard place: comitology-style committees could not be created pursuant to Article 290 TFEU because such committees were not legitimate post-Lisbon, but detailed national input into the regulatory process was central to this area, and while such committees continued to have a role in Article 291 TFEU, not all such secondary measures could be regarded as merely implementing in the Article 291 TFEU sense. This tension serves to explain the inclusion of Declaration 39 in the Lisbon Treaty which states the 'Conference takes note of the Commission's intention to continue to consult experts appointed by the

[95] See however N Moloney (n 87), at p 77, noting close relations between ESMA and the EP.

[96] http://ec.europa.eu/internal_market/securities/lamfalussy/report/index_en.htm. Level 1 consisted of framework Directives or Regulations; Level 2, regulatory Committees assisted the Commission in adopting implementing measures, to ensure that technical provisions were up to date with market developments; Level 3, committees of national supervisors responsible for measures to improve implementation of Level 1 and 2 acts in the Member States; Level 4, Commission strengthening the enforcement of EU law.

Member States in the preparation of draft delegated acts in the financial services area, in accordance with its established practice'.

The 'genius' solution was to create the new breed of ESAs. These were agencies, which 'by definition' were not comitology committees. They could be heralded as fulfilling the imperative advocated by the de Larosiere report[97] for more effective regulatory mechanisms in the wake of the financial crisis. They could be tolerated under Article 290 TFEU, because they were not comitology committees. The reality nonetheless is that high-level national representatives make decisions and agree the draft regulatory measures in accord with the rules for Council decision-making under Article 16(4) TEU, albeit with the formal injunction to act in the EU interest.

9.5.3 ESAs and implementing acts

The ambivalent nature of the ESAs and their impact on the constitutional fabric in Articles 290 and 291 TFEU is further evidenced in the context of implementing acts. The constitutional paradigm in the Lisbon Treaty is that where uniform conditions for implementation are required the Commission may enact implementing acts, assisted by comitology committees acting pursuant to the Comitology Regulation.

The regime under the ESA Regulations for implementing acts is subtly different, and echoes that for draft regulatory technical standards. It is the ESA that is charged with developing implementing technical standards, by means of implementing acts pursuant to Article 291 TFEU, in the areas specifically set out in the legislative acts.[98] The implementing technical standards must be technical, and must not imply strategic decisions or policy choices. The Authority submits its draft implementing technical standards to the Commission for endorsement, which decides whether to endorse it within 3 months. Where the Commission decides not to endorse the ESA draft implementing act, or decides to amend it, it must provide a reasoned explanation to the ESA. The Commission cannot change the content of a draft implementing technical standard prepared by the ESA without prior coordination with the Authority.[99] It is only where the ESA does not submit a draft implementing technical standard to the Commission within the relevant time limits that the Commission can adopt an implementing technical standard by means of an implementing act without a draft from the ESA.[100]

The ESA regime for implementing acts entails two notable qualifications to the constitutional orthodoxy in Article 291 TFEU. It places the ESA rather than the Commission in the driving seat in drafting the implementing act. The Commission must formally accept the measure, but its room for manoeuvre is limited in the manner adumbrated above. The other qualification is equally important, albeit less obvious. The legal and political reality is that the role played by comitology

[97] Report of 25 February 2009 from the High Level Group on Financial Supervision in the EU chaired by J de Larosiere, at http://ec.europa.eu/finance/general-policy/docs/de_larosiere_report_en.pdf.

[98] See, e.g. Regulation (EU) 2010/1093 (n 78) Article 15(1).

[99] Ibid Article 15(1).

[100] Ibid Article 15(3).

committees within Article 291 TFEU is played by the national representatives that make up the Board of Supervisors and the Management Board on the ESAs. It is the Supervisory Boards that adopt the drafts that are then sent to the Commission, and they decide once again through using the rules on qualified majority voting in Article 16(4) TEU.[101]

9.6 Legal Form: Hard Law, Soft Law, and Articles 290 and 291

The regime embodied in Articles 290 and 291 TFEU is applicable to delegated and implementing acts that have formal legal force. It does not apply to the making of soft law, which may be used to flesh out the meaning of a delegated act,[102] or be used instead of formal law. This simple proposition has important consequences, more especially because soft law can vary very significantly, from measures that are truly just recommendatory, to those that are imbued with some real force. It follows that if the Commission or an EU agency decides to proceed via soft law, it remains free of the constitutional constraints in Article 290 and 291 TFEU.

There remains the longstop possibility of a legal challenge, the argument being that the institution was seeking to evade the Treaty regime by proceeding in this manner. The claimant would however have an uphill battle in any such case, because the defendant institution could almost always put forward plausible reasons for using soft law, and the Court of Justice would be reluctant to interfere with this choice. Using soft law enhances regulatory autonomy of the creator institution, even if it may entail some net loss of enforceability. The extent of such loss will depend in turn on how 'hard' the soft law actually is.

Consider in this respect an example drawn from the world of ESAs. We have already seen their role in formulating draft technical regulatory and implementing standards. They are also empowered to issue guidelines. The standard formulation is contained in Article 16(1) of the Regulations governing ESAs.[103] It provides that,

> The Authority shall, with a view to establishing consistent, efficient and effective supervisory practices within the ESFS, and to ensuring the common, uniform and consistent application of Union law, issue guidelines and recommendations addressed to competent authorities or financial market participants.

The guidelines are however imbued with some real force. Thus Article 16(3) states that the competent authorities and financial market participants shall make every

[101] Ibid Articles 43, 44.

[102] See, e.g. Guidelines accompanying Commission Delegated Regulation (EU) 2010/244 of 16 January 2012 supplementing Directive (EU) 2010/31 of the European Parliament and of the Council on the energy performance of buildings by establishing a comparative methodology framework for calculating cost-optimal levels of minimum energy performance requirements for buildings and building elements, OJ 2012 C 115/1.

[103] See earlier nn 77, 78, 79.

effort to comply with those guidelines and recommendations. Within two months of the issuance of a guideline or recommendation, each competent authority must confirm whether it complies or intends to comply with that guideline or recommendation. In the event that a competent authority does not comply or does not intend to comply, it must inform the ESA, stating its reasons. The ESA must then publish the fact that a competent authority does not comply, or does not intend to comply, with that guideline or recommendation. The ESA may also decide, on a case-by-case basis, to publish the reasons provided by the competent authority for not complying with that guideline or recommendation. If so required by a guideline or recommendation, financial market participants must moreover report, in a clear and detailed way, whether they comply with it. Article 16(3) is then further reinforced by Article 16(4), which requires the ESA, when making its annual report, to inform the European Parliament, Council, and Commission of the guidelines and recommendations that have been issued, stating which competent authority has not complied with them, and outlining how the ESA intends to ensure that the competent authority concerned follows its recommendations and guidelines in the future.

None of the above changes the fact that ESA guidelines are still soft law. They are however very much at the 'hard end' of soft law, being imbued with force by legal provisions in the ESA Regulations imposing obligations on the national authorities that do not wish to comply.

9.7 Conceptual: Rulemaking and Adjudication

It is axiomatic that administrative authorities can develop policy in their assigned area through rulemaking or adjudication, assuming that they are empowered to do both. They can promulgate secondary rules to effectuate the objectives in the primary legislation, subject to whatever procedural constraints exist for their enactment. They can also develop policy through individualized adjudication, whereby they apply the dictates of the legislation to resolve particular cases. The decision thus made may only apply to the particular party to the case, but it may nonetheless embody a point of principle that is of wider application. This is of course to say no more or less than that adjudication may be de facto constitutive of new policy, even where the adjudicator states that it is *de jure* merely declaratory of what the policy embedded in the legislation always was.

The factors that impact on the choice between rulemaking and adjudication are well known.[104] Rules have the advantage of guiding behaviour for those affected

[104] See e.g. D Shapiro, 'The Choice of Rulemaking or Adjudication in the Development of Administrative Policy' (1965) 78 HarvLRev 921; G Robinson, 'The Making of Administrative Policy: Another Look at Rulemaking and Adjudication and Administrative Procedures Reform' (1970) 118 UPaLRev 485; R Baldwin and K Hawkins, 'Discretionary Justice: Davis Reconsidered' [1984] PL 570.

and for others within the administration, thereby fostering efficiency in terms of not having to think out the answer afresh on each occasion, and justice in terms of treating like cases alike. An administrative authority however may prefer to use adjudication where it does not yet have sufficient experience in the relevant area to promulgate a rule, or where it feels that rulemaking would be inappropriate given the range of variables that would have to be taken into account such that it would be difficult to enact anything that could meaningfully be called a rule.

Procedure broadly conceived will also influence the choice between rulemaking and adjudication. If the Commission uses rulemaking it will have to decide whether the matter can be dealt with via Article 290 TFEU or Article 291 TFEU and then negotiate the respective decision-making processes. If the Commission is uncertain as to whether it will succeed it may choose to use soft law, or it may develop the relevant area through greater use of adjudication, where it is not subject to the controls in Articles 290 and 291 TFEU. The same is true of those EU agencies or authorities, which have power to draft delegated and implementing standards, and also to punish certain types of violation through an individualized decision directed at a particular firm.[105] Such bodies may use rulemaking where there are problems with supervisory power.[106] They may conversely make use of extensive adjudication powers, which in the case of the ESAs allow them, subject to certain conditions, to take enforcement action against a national authority that is not complying with relevant legislative, delegated, or implementing acts, and also in certain circumstances against particular financial institutions.[107]

These are early days, but it will be interesting to see how far, consciously or unconsciously, EU administrative authorities use adjudication to develop the law in their area, thereby freeing themselves from the procedural dictates applicable to both Article 290 TFEU and Article 291 TFEU.

9.8 Conclusion

The divide between delegated and implementing acts is at the heart of the Lisbon settlement. The analytical and temporal difficulties that beset this distinction however remain. They have not been removed through judicial clarification in the years since the Lisbon Treaty came into effect. It is unclear how far the EU legislature gives systematic considered thought as to whether delegated or implementing acts should be used, and insofar as it does so the choice can be affected as much if not more by political considerations as by the analytical nature of the distinction between the two types of act. The effluxion of time has revealed moreover the constitutional, institutional, and conceptual tensions considered above, and the way in which issues of legal form can impact on the normative assumptions underlying the divide between Article 290 TFEU and Article 291 TFEU. It would

[105] See, e.g. OHIM, CPVO, EASA, EBA, ESMA, and EIOPA.
[106] N Moloney (n 87), at p 69.
[107] See, e.g. Regulation (EU) 2010/1093 (n 78) Article 17.

be tempting but mistaken to identify a clear institutional winner from the new schema. The truth is that all institutional players have lost out in some respects.

For the European Parliament, the hope was parity with the Council in relation to Article 290 TFEU, and the excision of comitology committees on which Member State representatives dominated this terrain. The reality is that it has formal parity with the Council under Article 290 TFEU, but the Common Understanding has brought advisory expert committees back into this area on which national representatives are still dominant. There is the additional fact that so much rulemaking now occurs via Article 291 TFEU and the European Parliament has less input into this new comitology regime than it did in relation to the old one.

For the Commission, the ideal was to remove what it felt were unwarranted comitology constraints from Article 290 TFEU, thereby reinforcing its executive autonomy over this area, albeit subject to the controls contained therein. The reality is that some Member State input was retained directly through the Common Understanding 2011, a feature that will be further enhanced if the 2014 version takes effect, and indirectly through the provisions for rulemaking in the new agency regulations. There is the additional fact that the new comitology regime under Article 291 TFEU places as many constraints on the Commission as did the old, and that is so notwithstanding that in formal terms the national representatives on the committees are formally separate from those in the Council.

From the perspective of the Council, the initial loss was the demise of the comitology regime from Article 290 TFEU, although it has since been seeking to recover ground through the Common Understanding and if the revised version does come into effect the committee system under Article 290 TFEU will come ever closer to the formalization that existed prior to the Lisbon Treaty and to that which operates under Article 291 TFEU.

There are inevitably differences of view as to whether the Lisbon schema of distinguishing between legislative, delegated, and implementing acts should be regarded a success or not. It will come as no surprise that I fall into the sceptical camp with regard to the utility of the divide between delegated and implementing acts. What is clear is that any conclusion one way or another in this regard must be based on full assessment of the analytical, constitutional, conceptual, and institutional dimensions that affect the dichotomy between the two types of act. What is clear also is that whatsoever one's conclusion it is very difficult to defend the new status quo on the ground that it has simplified the pre-existing regime.

PART IV

A PARTICIPATORY DIMENSION

10

Judicial Protection for Private Parties in European Commission Rulemaking

Maria Bergström

10.1 Introduction

Against the background of the general developments of judicial protection of private parties within the European Union, this chapter analyses the remaining incoherencies of judicial protection for private parties in European Commission rulemaking. Whereas enhanced judicial control would increase the democratic legitimacy of Commission rulemaking, the Lisbon Treaty introduced some relaxed rules on standing for private parties to challenge non-legislative acts. Although stronger scrutiny of non-legislative acts involving non-majoritarian institutions such as the Commission is welcome, it is still unclear how far the Lisbon changes allow for judicial protection for private parties in Commission rulemaking. The remaining questions concern the coherence of the terminology used in Articles 290 and 291 TFEU on the one hand and in Article 263 TFEU on the other.[1] A narrow interpretation of the Article 263 criteria of regulatory acts, direct concern, and implementing measures might clash with demands put on the EU legal order by the European Convention on Human Rights (ECHR) and the EU Charter of Fundamental Rights (EU Charter). In contrast, a wider interpretation of the key concepts would increase democratic control of Commission rulemaking, enhance judicial protection of private parties, and meet the demands of the ECHR and the EU Charter. In particular, the Court of Justice's approach when interpreting the imprecise term 'regulatory act' (cf. French *les actes réglementaires*, and German *Rechtsakte mit Verordnungscharakter*), will provide 'a measure of the importance it now attributes to the principle of effective judicial protection'.[2]

[1] To avoid confusion as far as possible, throughout the chapter reference is made to the current numbering of the Treaty articles. For an article on the work behind the renumbering and reorganization of the Treaties before the Lisbon Treaty, see B De Witte, 'Simplification and Reorganization of the European Treaties' (2002) 39 CMLRev 1255.

[2] A Arnull, 'The Principle of Effective Judicial Protection in EU law: An Unruly Horse?' (2011) 36 ELRev 51, at p 70.

In order to analyse the remaining incoherencies of judicial protection for private parties in Commission rulemaking, the chapter will discuss the following points: this first section will introduce the wider notion of judicial protection for private parties, and will also provide a brief overview of the main types of acts in EU lawmaking analysed in several of the previous chapters of this volume, thereby focusing upon Commission rulemaking. The next section will then analyse the criteria for judicial protection for private parties in Commission rulemaking, that is, Article 263 TFEU on the one hand, and Articles 290 and 291 TFEU on the other. The chapter concludes with a section stressing the main obstacles met when challenging EU lawmaking in general, and the remaining incoherencies concerning Commission rulemaking in particular, including an analysis of the consequences of a narrow and a wide interpretation respectively and whether any uncertainty remains, before finally pointing towards some possible ways around these identified but remaining obstacles. In other words, this chapter aims at answering the following questions: 1) what are the main obstacles met by private parties when challenging EU lawmaking; 2) more specifically, what are the remaining incoherencies of judicial protection for private parties in Commission rulemaking; and finally, 3) what might the possible ways around these obstacles be?

10.1.1 Judicial protection for private parties

It has been said that '[t]he extent to which non-privileged applicants should enjoy standing to challenge the legality of government action poses one of the great dilemmas of modern administrative law'.[3] It is not easy to balance between ensuring the availability of judicial review to persons genuinely aggrieved while at the same time guarding the Courts from meaningless, vexatious litigation.[4]

Whereas on the one hand, procedural rules which make substantive rules effective are equally as important as the development of substantive rules for the proper functioning and development of a given policy area, on the other hand, procedural rules including rules of *locus standi* arguably need to be constructed in accordance with the current aim of the judicial system, which may well need to change with time in order to reflect reality. Accordingly, if rules on standing reflect an old-fashioned vision of the aim of the judicial system, there is a risk of too limited access to justice.

Today an intermediate approach to rules on standing seems to be the most widespread after *locus standi* has been relaxed both in civil and common law jurisdictions.[5] However, where the proper line should be drawn depends a great deal on the discretion of the Courts, which inevitably will be influenced 'by their views on

[3] A Arnull, 'Private Applicants and the Action for Annulment under Article 173 of the EC Treaty' (1995) 32 CMLRev 7, at p 7.

[4] R Lane, entry on 'Locus Standi', in J Monar et al (eds), *Butterworths Expert Guide to the European Union* (Butterworths 1996), at p 220.

[5] A Arnull, 'Challenging Community Acts—An Introduction', in H-W Micklitz and N Reich (eds), *Public Interest Litigation before European Courts* (Nomos 1996), at p 40.

the proper constitutional relationship between judges, politicians and the citizen'.[6] Although stronger scrutiny of non-legislative acts involving non-majoritarian institutions such as the Commission is welcome, much might also depend on practical concerns, such as the need not to disrupt the process of government or to overload the Courts.

It has been submitted that during the early years of European cooperation, the basic argument for restrictive *locus standi* was the need to prevent the Court of Justice from being flooded with litigation and to ensure that 'Community legislation would not be continually and unnecessarily shrouded in legal uncertainty'.[7] Still, the main distinction made was that between privileged and non-privileged access, where the former reflects international law. Accordingly, surprise has even been expressed about the fact that non-privileged applicants were admitted to the Court at all, taking into account the character of the Treaties at that time.[8] Nevertheless, hand in hand with the increase of directly effective Union legislation, also within new areas, and the more relaxed attitude to standing increasingly taken by many national courts,[9] the pressure for stronger standing rights has developed.[10]

10.1.2 Different models of access

The successful challenge of Union acts by private parties is conditioned by access to the European judicial system, which consists of national courts and the Court of Justice of the EU (CJEU, including the General Court).[11] Access to national courts, including the preliminary reference procedure via national courts to the Court of Justice, differ between the Member States. The current situation within the Member States is too varied to give rise to any generalizations, and will not be discussed further here.[12] Yet, in principle, three different models of access can be perceived. Firstly, a traditional or rather narrow model, legally designed to protect strictly private or legal interests. Such a model often also involves narrowly defined interests confined to property or other tangible interests. Secondly, the complete opposite, even if not going as far as allowing an *actio popularis*, which would be

[6] Ibid.

[7] M Hedemann-Robinson, 'Article 173 EC, General Community Measures and *Locus standi* for Private Persons: Still a Cause for Individual Concern?' (1996) 2 European Public Law 127, at p 128.

[8] E Stein and J Vining, 'Citizen Access to Judicial Review of Administrative Action in a Transnational and Federal Context', in F R Jacobs (ed), *European Law and the Individual* (North Holland 1976), at p 113.

[9] A Arnull, 'Private Applicants and the Action for Annulment since *Codorniu*' (2001) 38 CMLRev 7, at p 7.

[10] See references to academic commentators before and after the Lisbon changes, in n 21.

[11] See Article 19(1) TEU which emphasizes that the Member States shall provide remedies sufficient to ensure effective judicial protection in the fields covered by Union law.

[12] For a general overview see e.g. J Schwarze, *European Administrative Law* (Sweet and Maxwell 1992); and a more recent overview, M Eliantonio, C Backes, CH van Rhee, T Spronken, and A Berlee, *Standing Up for Your Right(s) in Europe, A comparative study on Legal Standing (Locus Standi) before the EU and Member States' Courts* (Intersentia 2013).

tantamount to having no access rules at all. Such a model, sometimes exemplified by reference to the 'American freeway' system,[13] resembles the pluralist political process and allows wide access for persons and groups.[14] Simplified, such a model could be referred to as a public interest model, allowing different persons and groups to appear before courts claiming to defend the public interest.[15] Thirdly, the so-called 'funnel model'.[16] Although allowing rather wide access to courts, this is counterbalanced through narrow grounds for review, and few available remedies. In reality, different models of access, including this third model, can in principle be seen as a mixture between the first and the second model.[17]

On the Union level, action for annulment under Article 263 TFEU provides the principal means of judicial redress before the Union courts when questions of the legality of actions of Union institutions are raised. Whereas the focus of this chapter is mainly on direct action under Article 263 TFEU (action for annulment), judicial review also covers Article 265 TFEU (action for a failure to act), and the indirect action under Article 277 TFEU (the plea of illegality) at the Union level. Indirectly, the legality of Union measures can also be put into question before the Court of Justice under the Article 267 TFEU procedure (references for a preliminary ruling), especially, but not exclusively,[18] when the legality of a national measure based on a Union measure is being challenged. Questions of *locus standi* also appear in other forms of actions such as actions in damages, opinions, and appeals.

Against the background of different models of access, direct access to the General Court for non-privileged applicants is still construed and applied narrowly.[19] In

[13] In Europe, an *actio popularis* is known only in a small number of the legal systems and only in special cases. See further M Eliantonio et al (n 12), Chapter 4, at p 65.

[14] See further C Harlow, 'A Special Relationship? American Influences on Judicial Review in England', in I Loveland (ed), *Lessons From America* (Clarendon Press 1996), at pp 79–97.

[15] Cf. classic articles including: R B Stewart, 'The Reformation of American Administrative Law' (1975) 88 HarvLRev 1668; A Chayes, 'The Role of the Judge in Public Law Litigation' (1976) 89 HarvLRev 1281; D Kennedy, 'Form and Substance in Private Law Adjudication' (1976) 89 HarvLRev 1685.

[16] This term was introduced by Carol Harlow and Richard Rawlings, in relation to access before English and Welsh courts. See C Harlow, and R Rawlings, *Pressure through Law* (Routledge 1992), at pp 310–14.

[17] According to Laurence Gormley (2000) and (2001), (n 21), questions of public interest litigation attracted surprisingly little academic comment in the English language at least, until the major conference devoted to that subject in Berlin in December 1995. The result of this conference, the collected volume *Public Interest Litigation before European Courts* encloses a wide range of specific topics, yet many of which are of less relevance in this context. H-W Micklitz and N Reich (n 5). See also M Bergström, *Advocacy Groups and Multilevel Governance: The Use of EC Law as a Campaigning Tool,* Doctor of Laws Thesis defended at the European University Institute on 13 June 2003; and H-W Micklitz, *The Politics of Judicial Co-operation in the EU: Sunday Trading, Equal Treatment, and Good Faith* (Cambridge University Press 2005).

[18] See, e.g. Case C-491/01 *Q v Secretary of State for Health, ex parte: British American Tobacco (Investments) Ltd and Imperial Tobacco Ltd*, EU:C:2002:741.

[19] Often referred to as private applicants in the literature. For a comprehensive monograph see A Ward, *Judicial Review and the Rights of Private Parties in EU Law* (Oxford University Press 2007); See also A Arnull, *The European Union and its Court of Justice* (Oxford University Press 2006), chap 3; and M Eliantonio et al (n 12).

addition, the dominant position of the Member States 'suggests an old-fashioned and undemocratic equation of government with public interests'.[20]

Much has been written concerning this article and it has often been seen as granting a too limited right of standing.[21] Accordingly, non-privileged applicants have limited *locus standi* under the fourth paragraph of Article 263 TFEU. Taken together, this implies that judicial protection of certain rights and interests protected by EU law is limited. Yet, in order to analyse the level of judicial protection for private parties in Commission rulemaking, it is necessary to focus upon the formal entry points and a legal evaluation of these, including an analysis of which acts are open for review.

10.1.3 Main types of legal acts in EU lawmaking

According to Article 288 TFEU, the institutions shall adopt regulations, directives, decisions, recommendations, and opinions. The political institutions in a large number of cases have a choice whether to enact a regulation, a directive, or a decision. This choice is usually made by the Commission under its power to initiate legislation.[22] Whereas it is explicitly stated that recommendations and opinions have no binding force, all binding legislation, that is, regulations, directives, and decisions, can in principle be reviewed and declared invalid by the CJEU. Acts which could be successfully challenged include those going beyond the powers granted in the Treaties where such powers have been misused, or when essential procedural requirements or judicially developed general principles have been infringed.[23]

After the entry into force of the Lisbon Treaty, a new version of the hierarchy of norms partially based on the changes proposed in the Constitutional Treaty,[24] has

[20] C Harlow, 'Towards a Theory of Access for the European Court of Justice' (1993) 12 YEL 213, at p 245.

[21] See A Arnull (n 3), at pp 7–49; A Arnull (n 5); and A Arnull (n 9); A Biondi, 'Effectiveness Versus Efficiency: Recent Developments on Judicial Protection in EC Law' (2000) 6 European Public Law 311; P Craig, 'Legality, Standing and Substantive Review in Community Law' (1994) 14 Oxford Journal of Legal Studies 507; P Craig, 'Standing, Rights and the Structure of Legal Argument' (2003) 9 European Public Law 493; P Craig (n 34), at p 129; LW Gormley, 'Public Interest Litigation', in D O'Keeffe and A Bavasso (eds), *Judicial Review in European Union Law: Liber Amicorum in Honour of Lord Slynn of Hadley, Vol. I* (Kluwer Law International 2000), at pp 191–201; LW Gormley, 'Public Interest Litigation in Community Law' (2001) 7 European Public Law 51; C Harlow (n 20); M Hedemann-Robinson (n 7); M Nettesheim, 'Article 173 of the EC Treaty and Regulations: Towards the Development of Uniform Standing Requirements', in H-W Micklitz and N Reich (n 5), at pp 225–42. See, however, K Adamantopoulos, 'Access to Justice in the European Courts for Consumers', in H-W Micklitz and N Reich (n 5), at pp 359–84. See also H Rasmussen, 'Why is Article 173 Interpreted against Private Plaintiffs?' (1980) 5 ELRev 112; B Vesterdorf and K Lundgaard Hansen, 'Søgsmålsret ved fællesskabsdomstolene. Et forhindringsløb for sagsøgerne?' *Ugeskrift for Retsvæsen* 1996, at p 275; and R Barents, 'The Court of Justice after the Treaty of Lisbon' (2010) 47 CMLRev 709.

[22] For a recent case curtailing the right of the Commission to withdraw, see Case C-409/12 *Council v Commission* EU:C:2015:217.

[23] Article 263(2) TFEU refers to the following grounds for lack of competence, infringement of an essential procedural requirement, infringement of the Treaties or of any rule of law relating to their application, or misuse of powers.

[24] See further Chapter 1 in this volume.

led to new legal difficulties.[25] According to the new regime, a distinction is made between legislative acts (Article 289(3) TFEU) containing the essential elements and the fundamental policy choices in a certain field,[26] and non-legislative acts of general application.[27] Non-legislative acts are explicitly referred to in Article 290 TFEU on delegated acts, but include also implementing acts regulated in Article 291 TFEU and other non-legislative acts directly based on the treaties. Regulations, directives, and decisions may thereby be any of these, depending on how and in accordance with which Article, conditions, and criteria they have been adopted. Besides difficulties in deciding which provision should be used in each individual case, there might be some uncertainly in distinguishing between categories. As has been stated in Chapter 1 of this volume, no attempt was made to establish any substantial distinction between delegated and implementing acts before the adoption of the Lisbon Treaty. This was left to the EU legislator to decide on a case-by-case basis, effectively leaving the judicial control to the CJEU.

(a) Article 289 TFEU and legislative acts

According to Article 289 TFEU a legislative act is a legal act in the form of a regulation, directive, or decision adopted by a legislative procedure. This could either be the ordinary legislative procedure stipulated in Article 294 TFEU, or any of the special legislative procedures where a regulation, directive, or decision is adopted by the European Parliament with the participation of the Council or by the latter with the participation of the European Parliament in cases provided for by the Treaties. Only regulations, directives, or decisions which are the result of such legislative procedures are legislative acts.[28]

Whereas the use of regulations is specified in the Treaty only in a few cases, the use of directives is required in a number of cases.[29] Still, the Treaty leaves open the choice of the form of legislation on a large number of occasions and Article 296 TFEU stipulates that where the Treaties do not specify the type of act to be adopted, the institutions shall select it on a case-by-case basis, in compliance with the applicable procedures and with the principle of proportionality. Yet, regardless

[25] For a comprehensive discussion, see P Craig (n 34).

[26] See further Section 1.3 in this volume.

[27] See further Opinion of Advocate General Kokott delivered on 17 January 2013 in Case C-583/11 P *Inuit Tapiriit Kanatami and Others v Parliament and Council*, EU:C:2013:21, in particular point 40 discussing the notion of 'regulatory act' with further references to the Constitutional Treaty and the preparatory documents of the European Convention on Article III-270(4) of the Draft Treaty establishing a Constitution for Europe, and later the Constitutional Treaty as Article III-365(4).

[28] Case C-583/11 P *Inuit Tapiriit Kanatami and Others v Parliament and Council*, EU:C:2013:625. This might mean that legal acts adopted under articles such as Articles 103 or 109 TFEU which are neither ordinary nor special legislative procedures are not legislative acts in the formal sense. See further P Craig (n 34), at p 257 ff and p 283 arguing that the hierarchy of legal acts does not capture the totality of the ways in which legal norms are made.

[29] See eg the legal bases related to EU Criminal Law such as Articles 82 and 83 TFEU. See also Article 59 TFEU.

of the above, the most commonly used binding legislation is regulations, and not directives.[30] This forms part of a trend whereby the Commission is responsible for the adoption of a major part of EU lawmaking while the responsibility of the Council, and where applicable the European Parliament, not only is small, but even more noteworthy, decreasing.[31] Without purporting to draw any far-reaching conclusions, this nevertheless seems to contradict, or counterbalance, the increased formal powers of the European Parliament. One explanation for this can be found in the amount of delegated legislation.

(b) European Commission rulemaking

With the entry into force of the Lisbon Treaty and Articles 290 and 291 TFEU, which replaced the old Article 202 EC, there are now two legal bases that regulate delegated and implementing acts. Whereas the application of Article 290 TFEU has been facilitated by a Common Understanding, Article 291 TFEU had to be implemented through negotiations and secondary legislation.[32] Arguably, since comitology applies only in relation to Article 291 TFEU,[33] it may be more appropriate to refer to Commission rulemaking when discussing both Articles 290 and 291 TFEU. Yet, as maintained by Craig, 'the legal status of comitology in relation to delegated acts will ultimately be decided by the Court of Justice'.[34] Although admitting that the likely legal conclusion is that Article 290 TFEU signals the demise of comitology, Craig has argued that it is important to consider Article 290 TFEU 'on alternative scenarios in which comitology continues to exist, and in which it does not'.[35] A possible, although less probable development would therefore be that comitology could continue to operate within Article 290(2)(b) TFEU.[36] Still, a problem for the Council is that without the information provided through the comitology procedure, it will not have the expertise to determine whether or not to exercise its veto powers. In addition, one should certainly not underestimate the difference between 'exercising a control through a veto when a delegated act has been made', and 'participation in the making of the delegated act itself'.[37]

[30] See current figures available on EUR-Lex.
[31] See further Chapters 1 and 9 in this volume.
[32] Regulation (EU) No 182/2011 of the European Parliament and of the Council of 16 February 2011 laying down the rules and general principles concerning mechanisms for control by Member States of the Commission's exercise of implementing powers, [2011] OJ 2011/13. For a brief introductory guide analysing the procedural and political changes brought about by these two articles, see, e.g. A Hardacre and M Kaeding, *Delegated and Implementing Acts: The New Comitology, EIPA Essential Guide*, 5th edn, September 2013.
[33] Argument put forward by A Hardacre and M Kaeding (n 32). See however the alternative analyses by P Craig (n 34), chap 2.
[34] P Craig, *The Lisbon Treaty: Law, Politics, and Treaty Reform* (Oxford University Press 2010), at p 58.
[35] Ibid, p 58. [36] See further, ibid, at pp 264–5.
[37] P Craig, 'Institutions, Power, and Institutional Balance', in P Craig and G De Búrca (eds), *The Evolution of EU Law* (Oxford University Press 2011), at p 78.

(c) Article 290 and delegated acts

According to Article 290 TFEU, a legislative act may delegate to the Commission the power to adopt *non-legislative acts of general application* to supplement or amend certain non-essential elements of the legislative act.[38] In a strict sense, this was also done through comitology beforehand. The adjective 'delegated' shall be inserted in the title of such a delegated act that can take the form of a regulation, a directive, or a decision, but would normally be a regulation.[39]

This new procedure allows the Commission to present its proposed delegated act to the Parliament and the Council at the same time. The basic act must define the objectives, content, scope, and duration of the delegation of power,[40] and stipulate the time within which the legislator(s) will have to object to the proposal or revoke the delegation, but there is also a possibility for the Commission to adopt it faster upon communication of a non-objection. Hence, whereas the *ex ante* controls over the enactments of delegated acts, described in Article 290(3) TFEU, allow the Council and the European Parliament to withdraw delegation and veto delegated acts, this will also lead to adjudication,[41] not least concerning how to distinguish between delegated and implementing acts based on the different conditions, criteria, and controls for these different categories.[42] As discussed above, implementing acts may however also be non-legislative acts of general application.[43]

(d) Article 291 and implementing acts

Like Article 290 TFEU, Article 291 TFEU was introduced by the Lisbon Treaty, following the Constitutional Treaty.[44] According to Article 291(3) TFEU the European Parliament and the Council, acting by means of regulations in accordance with the ordinary legislative procedure, shall lay down in advance the rules and general principles concerning mechanisms for control by Member States of the Commission's exercise of implementing powers. Hence, a new co-decided regulation was required to specify the new comitology procedures. The adopted

[38] Cf. Case 25/70 *Einfuhr- und Vorratsstelle für Getreide und Futtermittel v Köster and Berodt & Co.*, EU:C:1970:115, paras 6 and 9, see also Chapters 1, 4, 7, and 8.

[39] P Craig (n 34), at p 131.

[40] P Craig, 'Institutions, Power, and Institutional Balance', in P Craig, and G De Búrca (eds), *The Evolution of EU Law* (Oxford University Press 2011), at p 77.

[41] P Craig (n 34), at p 265.

[42] The unclear divide between delegated and implementing acts is analysed by P Craig (n 34), chap 7. See e.g. Case C-427/12 *Commission v Parliament and Council*, EU:C:2014:170. This judgment does however not provide a definitive answer about how to distinguish between delegated and implementing acts. See eg A Alemanno, 'The Biocides Judgment: In Search of a New Chemistry of the Principle of EU Institutional Balance', European Law Blog, at: http://europeanlawblog.eu/?p=2336. See also Case C-88/14 *Commission v Parliament and Council*: Action brought on 21 February 2014, OJ 2014 C 135/24.

[43] Besides Article 290(1) TFEU Article 297(2) TFEU also refers to non-legislative acts of general application.

[44] Articles 290 and 291 TFEU draw directly on Articles I-36 and I-37 of the 2004 Treaty on a Constitution for Europe.

Regulation 182/2011 entered into force on 1 March 2011.[45] As a result, comitology implementing acts are regulated in Article 291 TFEU and Regulation 182/2011, which thereby provide for a continuation of implementation of EU law through comitology procedures. The word 'implementing' shall be inserted in the title of implementing acts.

Member States shall adopt all measures of national law necessary to implement legally binding Union acts. Yet, where uniform conditions for implementing legally binding Union acts are needed, those acts shall confer implementing powers on the Commission, or, in duly justified specific cases and in the cases provided for in Articles 24 and 26 TEU, on the Council. Hence, implementing acts are premised on the need for uniform conditions of interpretation,[46] and can take the form of regulations, directives, or decisions.

10.2 A Systematic Analysis of Articles 263, 290, and 291

In order to analyse which the main obstacles are for private parties when challenging EU lawmaking, and what the remaining incoherencies of judicial protection for private parties in European Commission rulemaking might be, the following section will take a closer look at the criteria stipulated in Articles 263, 290, and 291 TFEU.

10.2.1 Introducing the current Article 263 criteria

After the entry into force of the Lisbon Treaty, Article 263 TFEU now reads:

> The Court of Justice of the European Union shall review the legality of legislative acts, of acts of the Council, of the Commission and of the European Central Bank, other than recommendations and opinions, and of acts of the European Parliament and of the European Council intended to produce legal effects vis-à-vis third parties. It shall also review the legality of acts of bodies, offices or agencies of the Union intended to produce legal effects vis-à-vis third parties.
>
> It shall for this purpose have jurisdiction in actions brought by a Member State, the European Parliament, the Council or the Commission on grounds of lack of competence, infringement of an essential procedural requirement, infringement of the Treaties or of any rule of law relating to their application, or misuse of powers.
>
> The Court shall have jurisdiction under the same conditions in actions brought by the Court of Auditors, by the European Central Bank and by the Committee of the Regions for the purpose of protecting their prerogatives.
>
> Any natural or legal person may, under the conditions laid down in the first and second paragraphs, institute proceedings against an act addressed to that person or which is of direct and individual concern to them, and against a regulatory act which is of direct concern to them and does not entail implementing measures.

[45] Regulation (EU) 2011/182 (n 19). [46] P Craig (n 34), at p 283.

Acts setting up bodies, offices and agencies of the Union may lay down specific conditions and arrangements concerning actions brought by natural or legal persons against acts of these bodies, offices or agencies intended to produce legal effects in relation to them.

The proceedings provided for in this Article shall be instituted within two months of the publication of the measure, or of its notification to the plaintiff, or, in the absence thereof, of the day on which it came to the knowledge of the latter, as the case may be.

This means that the Court of Justice shall review the legality of:

1. legislative acts,
2. acts of the Council, of the Commission, and of the European Central Bank, other than recommendations and opinions,
3. acts of the European Parliament and of the European Council intended to produce legal effects vis-à-vis third parties,
4. acts of bodies, offices, or agencies of the Union intended to produce legal effects vis-à-vis third parties.

This further means that private parties may institute proceedings against an *act*:

1. addressed to that person, or
2. which is of direct and individual concern to them,
3. and against a *regulatory act* which is of direct concern to them and *does not entail implementing measures.*

In order to answer the question, which acts are open for review for private parties, we must analyse the meaning of legal acts, including regulatory acts, legislative acts, non-legislative acts, delegated acts, implementing acts, and implementing measures. For all acts not addressed to a private party, that is, acts of general application, direct and individual concern still need to be established, except for regulatory acts that do not entail implementing measures. In the latter case, private parties only need to show direct concern.[47]

10.2.2 Acts open for review

According to the pre-Lisbon case law of the CJEU, the General Court examined all types of acts, thereby considering the substance and not the form of the act.[48] Further, although Article 263 TFEU in its previous wording did not provide for applicants to challenge true regulations and true directives, there has been a gradual

[47] Although not analysed in this context, it should be noted that Article 263(5) TFEU now stipulates that acts setting up bodies, offices, and agencies of the Union may lay down specific conditions and arrangements concerning actions brought by natural or legal persons against acts of these bodies, offices, or agencies intended to produce legal effects in relation to them.

[48] An act that applies to a limited number of specific persons rather than categories of persons viewed objectively, abstractly, and generally ought to be characterized as a decision: Joined Cases 16-17/62 *Confédération nationale des producteurs des fruits et légumes v EEC Council* (*Fruit and Vegetables Cases*), EU:C:1962:47; Case 25/62 *Plaumann v Commission*, EU:C:1963:17; Case 26/86 *Deutz & Geldermann v Commission*, EU:C:1987:102; Case T-480 and 483/93 *Antillean Rice Mills v Commission*, EU:T:1995:162.

relaxation in the case law towards a situation where non-privileged applicants in principle could challenge these types of acts even without showing that the contested act was in substance a decision. This change came about in the widely commented rulings in *Extramet* and *Codorniu*,[49] and has been followed in subsequent cases.

Since Article 263(4) TFEU in its new wording does not specifically mention that an act in the form of a regulation might in reality be a decision that is of direct and individual concern to the applicant, there is no direct invitation in the article to look behind the form of the measure to its substance.[50] As Craig points out, it will probably be easier to argue that the Courts should look to the substance of a measure within a category of legal act, than across the categories of legal act. This is most probably so, since an argument that a delegated act should be classified as a legislative act, or the other way around, would be equal to arguing that the act should be invalid, since it would not have been enacted by the proper procedure.[51] A comparison can be made to the ruling in *France v Commission* in which case the Court of Justice looked at the substance, and not only at the form of an act. In this case the Court held that the contested measure constituted a decision adopted by an authority that had no power to do so. This meant that the application for annulment was declared to be both admissible and well founded.[52] The importance of looking beyond the form of a measure to its substance, may, however, still have bearing upon the Courts' categorization of an act within a particular category of legal act.

Generally, the Lisbon Treaty has made it clear that 'acts', including acts of general application such as regulations and directives, as well as decisions, can be challenged by private parties if they have binding force, or produce legal effects. According to the Court of Justice in the *Inuit* case,[53] guidance can still be found in *IBM v Commission*:[54]

In order to ascertain whether the measures in question are acts within the meaning of Article 173 [263 TFEU] it is necessary, therefore, to look to their *substance*. According to the

A regulation may in truth constitute a decision: Joined Cases 16-17/62 (*Fruit and Vegetables Cases*). Provisions in a directive may in truth be a decision: Case 160/88 *FEDESA v Council*, EU:C:1988:397; Case C-298/89 *Government of Gibraltar v Council*, EU:C:1993:267; Case C-10/95 P *Asocarne v Council*, EU:C:1995:406; Case 408/95 *Eurotunnel and Others v Sea France*, EU:C:1997:532.

[49] Examples of cases where directly and individually affected non-privileged applicants could not challenge measures which were true regulations and directives: Cases 789 and 790/79 *Calpak v Commission*, EU:C:1980:159; Case 307/81 *Alusuisse* v *Council and Commission*, EU:C:1982:337; Case 26/86 *Deutz & Geldermann v Commission*, EU:C:1987:102; Case C-298/89 *Government of Gibraltar v Council*, EU:C:1993:267. This was changed by the Court of Justice in two cases according to which directly and individually affected non-privileged applicants may challenge measures of general application: Case C-358/89 *Extramet Industrie v Council*, EU:C:1991:214 (anti-dumping); Case C-309/89 *Codorniu v Council*, EU:C:1994:197.

[50] P Craig (n 34), at p 131. [51] Ibid, at p 132.

[52] Case C-366/88 *France v Commission*, EU:C:1990:348, para 25.

[53] Case C-583/11 P *Inuit Tapiriit Kanatami and Others v Parliament and Council*, EU:C:2013:625, para 56, with references to Case 60/81 *IBM v Commission*, EU:C:1981:264, para 9, Case C-521/06 P *Athinaïki Techniki v Commission*, EU:C:2008:422; Case C-322/09 P *NDSHT v Commission*, EU:C:2010:701, para 45; and Joined Cases C-463/10 P and C-475/10 P *Deutsche Post v Commission*, EU:C:2011:656, paras 36–38.

[54] Case 60/81 *IBM v Commission*, EU:C:1981:264, para 9.

consistent case law of the Court any measure the legal effects of which are *binding on*, and *capable of affecting the interests of*, the applicant by bringing about a *distinct change in his legal position* is an act or decision which may be the subject of an action under Article 173 [263 TFEU] for a declaration that it is void. However, the *form* in which such acts or decisions are cast is, in principle, immaterial as regards the question whether they are open to challenge under that article. [emphasis added]

Likewise, in its ruling in *France v Commission* the Court stipulated that:[55]

... it must be held that the Communication constitutes an act intended to have legal effects of its own, distinct from those already provided for by the Treaty provisions on freedom to provide services, freedom of establishment and free movement of capital, with the result that an action for annulment will lie against it.

This means that although in theory, non-binding acts such as recommendations and opinions cannot produce legal effects for third parties, the relevant test, at least within a particular category of legal act, concerns substance and not form.

(a) Regulatory acts

A systematic reading of the criteria stipulated in Article 263 TFEU together with Articles 288, 290 and 291 TFEU combined with the previous case law by the European Courts, provides that a challengeable *regulatory act* might be either:

1. Any legally binding act including legislative, non-legislative, delegated, and implementing acts as long as they do not entail implementing measures;
2. Any legislative, non-legislative, delegated, or implementing act in the form of a regulation or decision that does not entail implementing measures, that is, not directives;
3. Any non-legislative, delegated, or implementing act in the form of a regulation or decision that does not entail implementing measures;
4. Any delegated or implementing act in the form of a regulation or decision that does not entail implementing measures;
5. Only delegated acts in the form of a regulation or decision that do not entail implementing measures; or
6. Only implementing acts in the form of a regulation or decision that do not entail implementing measures.[56]

As will be discussed further below, the first and second alternatives have been ruled out by the Court of Justice in its ruling in *Inuit*,[57] stating that a regulatory act is

[55] Case C-57/95 *France v Commission*, EU:C:1997:164, para 23.

[56] Cf. P Craig (n 34), at p 131.

[57] *Inuit* (n 53). For a comment see A Arnull, 'Arrêt "Inuit": la recevabilité des recours en annulation introduits par des particuliers contre des actes réglementaires' (2014) 22 Journal de droit européen 14; CF Bergström, 'Defending Restricted Standing for Individuals to Bring Direct Actions against

not a legislative act.[58] In addition, as Advocate General Wathelet and Advocate General Kokott have pointed out, decisions addressed to a Member State, that can shape a national legal system, can also be acts of general application.[59]

Yet, whichever of the other interpretations would be the correct one, the relaxation of the standing criteria would be rather limited. Nevertheless, in order to provide an answer to the questions posed, we need to further analyse these criteria.[60]

(b) Legislative acts

Adopting a systematic interpretation including Article 289(3) TFEU, and a functional approach, *legislative acts*, are acts adopted by a legislative procedure, be it the ordinary legislative procedure, or a special legislative procedure. As a result, legislative acts are defined in accordance with the procedure for their enactment. Legislative acts may include regulations and directives, and the General Court and the Court of Justice may deny standing if such a legislative regulation or directive is not of individual concern in accordance with the *Plaumann* criteria (see further Subsection (c)). This interpretation is supported by a teleological and a historical interpretation analysing the preparatory works of the Constitutional Treaty, which provided a systematic hierarchy of different kinds of acts.[61] Accordingly, a regulatory act is an act that is not at the same time a legislative act. Hence, neither the first nor the second alternative for defining regulatory acts that include legislative acts would be plausible.[62]

This analysis has been supported by the ruling in *Inuit*,[63] which confirmed the order by the General Court.[64] According to these cases, acts intended to produce

"Legislative" Measures' (2014) 10 EuConst 481; A Kornezov, 'Shaping the New Architecture of the EU System of Judicial Remedies: Comment on Inuit' (2014) 39(2) ELRev 251; P-A Van Malleghem and N Baeten, 'Before the law stands a gatekeeper—Or, what is a "regulatory act" in Article 263(4) TFEU?' (2014) 51 CMLRev 1187. See also the Opinion of Advocate General Kokott delivered on 17 January 2013 in Case C-583/11 P *Inuit Tapiriit Kanatami and Others v Parliament and Council*, EU:C:2013:21.

[58] See in particular *Inuit* (n 53), paras 58–61.

[59] Opinion of Advocate General Wathelet delivered on 29 May 2013 in Case C-132/12 P *Stichting Woonlinie and Others v Commission*, EU:C:2013:336, point 85, referring back to Opinion of Advocate General Kokott delivered on 21 March 2013 in Case C-274/12 P *Telefónica SA v European Commission*, EU:C:2013:204, points 21–9.

[60] See EU methods of interpretation, e.g. in K Lenaerts, and JA Gutiérrez-Fons, 'To Say What the Law of the EU Is: Methods of Interpretation and the European Court of Justice', EUI Working Papers AEL 2013/9.

[61] *Inuit* (n 53). For a comprehensive analysis, see P Craig (n 34), chap 2.

[62] For a critical analysis of the Court's 'interpreraive exercise' in this respect, see P-A Van Malleghem and N Baeten (n 57), at p 1202 ff.

[63] *Inuit* (n 53).

[64] Case T-18/10 *Inuit Tapiriit Kanatami and Others v Parliament and Council*, EU:T:2011:419, commented by S Peers and M Costa, 'Court of Justice of the European Union (General Chamber), Judicial review of EU Acts after the Treaty of Lisbon; Order of 6 September 2011, Case T-18/10 *Inuit Tapiriit Kanatami and Others v Commission* [Parliament and Council] & Judgment of 25 October 2011, Case T-262/10 *Microban v. Commission*' (2012) 8 EuConst 82. See further J Bast, 'New Categories of Acts after the Lisbon Reform: Dynamics of Parliamentarization in EU Law' (2012) 49 CMLRev 885.

binding legal effects may still be challenged by private parties, either if addressed to that person, that is, an individual act, or in relation to acts of general application including both legislative and regulatory acts that are of direct and individual concern to the applicant. In addition, the Court held that the new and less stringent admissibility rules where private parties are not obliged to satisfy the condition of individual concern, apply only to a more restricted category of acts, that is, regulatory acts. In this respect, the Court of Justice confirmed the view held by the General Court, that legislative acts are not covered by the concept of regulatory acts. As a result, the relaxation of the rules on standing in Article 263(4) TFEU will not benefit private applicants in cases such as *Unión de Pequeños Agricultores*,[65] where the Regulation in dispute would qualify as a legislative act under Article 289(3) TFEU.[66] Yet, acts of general application that are also regulatory acts can be challenged by private parties if the acts are of direct concern to the applicants and do not entail implementing measures. Hence, in cases such as *Jégo-Quéré* private parties may now be able to challenge regulations adopted under delegation, thus at least in theory remedying the previous situation.[67]

(c) Delegated acts

After Lisbon, a *delegated act* is an act adopted under the Article 290(1) TFEU procedure. In developing the above analysis, non-legislative acts are acts that are not the result of legislative procedures. Hence, a delegated act may be a regulation (normally),[68] a decision, or a directive adopted under this procedure, but as it is not a legislative procedure it therefore cannot be a legislative act. As a result, delegated acts are secondary regulations, directives, and decisions. In reality, such a delegated act will however often be legislative in nature, 'in the sense that they will lay down binding provisions of general application to govern a certain situation'.[69]

According to the Court of Justice in *Inuit*, private parties may initiate proceedings against acts that produce binding legal effects, both against individual acts addressed to a person, and against acts of general application. Acts of general application include both legislative acts, such as the contested act in the case, and regulatory acts. For legislative acts, the General Court and the Court of Justice still require the direct and individual concern tests to be met.[70] For regulatory acts, or non-legislative acts of general application such as delegated acts adopted

[65] Case C-50/00 P *Unión de Pequeños Agricultores v Council*, EU:C:2002:462.

[66] See Opinion of Advocate General Wathelet delivered on 29 May 2013 in Case C-133/12 P—*Stichting Woonlinie and Others v Commission*, EU:C:2013:336, who argued that a restrictive approach would lead to the paradox that the case of UPA that led to the reform of the Article would again make the appeal inadmissible (point 31).

[67] Case C-263/02 P *Commission v Jégo-Quéré & Cie SA*, EU:C:2004:210. See e.g. the discussion by S Balthasar, 'Locus Standi Rules for Challenges to Regulatory Acts by Private Applicants: the New Art 263(4) TFEU' (2010) 35 ELRev 542.

[68] P Craig (n 34), at p 131. [69] Ibid, at p 58.

[70] See, e.g. *Inuit* (n 53). In this case, the contested regulation was held to be legislative and not regulatory, and therefore still required the tests of individual and directly concerned to be met.

under Article 290(1) TFEU, the General Court and the Court of Justice may allow standing for private parties even if such a delegated regulation or decision is not of individual concern in accordance with the *Plaumann* criteria. In other words, a delegated regulation or decision may be challenged by directly affected private parties, if allowed *locus standi* by the Courts.

(d) *Implementing acts*

Article 291 TFEU recognizes a third category of legal act, the implementing act, that is an act adopted under Article 291(2–3) TFEU and the implementing regulation.[71] The same analysis as for delegated acts can be used for implementing acts. Hence, for regulatory acts, if including implementing acts adopted under this Article, the General Court and the Court of Justice may allow standing for directly affected private parties even if such an implementing regulation or decision is not of individual concern in accordance with the *Plaumann* criteria.

10.2.3 Implementing measures

What then is meant by implementing measures and which acts does this criterion exclude? A textual reading of Article 263 TFEU in combination with Article 288 TFEU provides that regulations are directly applicable and do not entail, in principle, discretionary implementing measures. Decisions are also directly applicable and a majority of them do not entail any measures to implement them. Directives on the other hand, by definition require implementing measures, which could be challenged on the national level. In this respect, the Court of Justice has emphasized that 'the opportunity open to individuals to plead the invalidity of a Community act of general application before national courts is not conditional upon that act's actually having been the subject of implementing measures adopted pursuant to national law'.[72]

This does not, however, mean that specific provisions of regulations or decisions never require uniform conditions for implementation, that is, implementing acts. It will, however, be for the General Court and the Court of Justice to elaborate on this further, where a teleological approach will be guiding. In this respect, the Court of Justice in *Telefónica v Commission* agreeing with Advocate General Kokott,[73] stated that

> the concept of a 'regulatory act which . . . does not entail implementing measures', within the meaning of the final limb of the fourth paragraph of Article 263 TFEU, is to be interpreted in the light of that provision's objective, which, as is clear from its origin, consists

[71] Regulation (EU) 2011/182 (n 29).

[72] Case C-491/01 *British American Tobacco (Investments) and Imperial Tobacco*, EU:C:2002:741, para 40.

[73] Opinion of Advocate General Kokott delivered on 21 March 2013 in Case C-274/12 P *Telefónica SA v European Commission*, EU:C:2013:204, points 40 and 41.

in preventing an individual from being obliged to infringe the law in order to have access to a court. Where a regulatory act directly affects the legal situation of a natural or legal person without requiring implementing measures, that person could be denied effective judicial protection if he did not have a direct legal remedy before the European Union judicature for the purpose of challenging the legality of the regulatory act. In the absence of implementing measures, natural or legal persons, although directly concerned by the act in question, would be able to obtain a judicial review of that act only after having infringed its provisions, by pleading that those provisions are unlawful in proceedings initiated against them before the national courts.[74]

10.2.4 Direct concern

In contrast to the continuous relaxation in relation to acts susceptible to review, after a slight relaxation of the initially harsh requirements to show direct and individual concern, for instance, in cases relating to anti-dumping, competition, and state aid,[75] the individual and direct concern tests seem to have become even stricter.

A measure is of direct concern to an applicant, if when it was adopted, it was substantially certain that it would affect the applicant.[76] As Advocate General Kokott has recently stated, according to settled case law, an applicant must be considered to be directly concerned if, 'first, the contested measure of the European Union directly affects his legal situation and, secondly, it leaves no discretion to its addressees, who are entrusted with the task of implementing it, such implementation being purely automatic and resulting from EU rules alone without the application of other intermediate rules'.[77]

Thus, problems of *direct concern* arise in situations where the application of a Union measure to the applicants depends on the exercise of discretion by a

[74] Case C-274/12 P *Telefónica v Commission*, EU:C:2013:852, para 27. Cf. Secretariat of the European Convention, Final Report of the Discussion Circle on the Court of Justice of 25 March 2003, CONV 636/03 para 21 where it was said that '[t]he addition of the words "without entailing implementing measures" aims to ensure that the extension of a private individual's right to institute proceedings would apply only to those (problematical) cases where the individual concerned must first infringe the law before he can have access to a court'. Cf. also the Opinion of Advocate General Wathelet in Case C-132/12 P *Stichting Woonpunt and Others v Commission*, EU:C:2014:100, point 73; and the ruling of the General Court in Case T-262/10 *Microban v Commission*, EU:T:2011:623, with comments by S Peers and M Costa (n 63); and by LW Gormley, 'Judicial Review—Reflections on the New Dawn after the First Judgments of the General Court' 2012(2) Europarättslig tidskrift 310.

[75] See, e.g. Case C-358/89 *Extramet Industrie v Council*, EU:C:1991:214 and Case C-309/89 *Codorniu v Council*, EU:C:1994:197. See A Arnull (n 9), at pp 7–10.

[76] A Arnull (n 9), with further references to Case 294/83 *Les Verts v Parliament*, EU:C:1986:166; Case 11/82 *Piraiki-Patraiki v Commission*, EU:C:1985:18; Case T-435/93 *ASPEC and Others v Commission*, EU:T:1995:79; Case T-442/93 *AAC and Others v Commission*, EU:T:1995:80.

[77] Opinion of Advocate General Kokott delivered on 21 March 2013 in Case C-274/12 P *Telefónica SA v European Commission*, EU:C:2013:204, point 59, with reference to Joined Cases C-463/10 P and C-475/10 P *Deutsche Post and Germany v Commission*, EU:C:2011:656, para 66 and the case law cited.

third party.[78] This discretion needs to be genuine, in which case those potentially affected are not directly concerned by the measure.[79] However, if the third party informs the applicant in advance of how it will use its discretion, the applicant is directly concerned.[80] Likewise, the discretion must not be entirely theoretical.[81] Accordingly, in *Société Louis Dreyfus & Cie*,[82] the Court of Justice, thereby reversing the General Court, said it was a purely theoretical idea that certain contracts could be fulfilled without Union financing. The applicants, who were importers under the contracts, were directly concerned by the Commission decisions not approving these contracts, without which Union financing would be denied. In other words, a person is directly affected by an act that neither requires or admits further acts by Union or national authorities, nor leaves room for discretion or real likelihood of its exercise, in its application to the person in question.

As pointed out by Advocate General Kokott,[83] there is no reason for interpreting the criterion of direct concern in the second and third limb of Article 263(4) TFEU differently. As Advocate General Wathelet argues, one might however ask whether the requirement of absence of implementing measures in the third limb is a condition of its own, or simply an explanation of direct concern.[84] In this respect, Wathelet cited Advocate General Kokott in *Telefónica v Commission*, where she had pointed out that the 'addition of "implementing measures"' was intended to ensure that the extension of the right to institute proceedings was restricted to cases where an individual 'must first infringe the law before he can have access to a court'.[85]

Agreeing with Kokott, Wathelet argued that an absence of measures implementing a regulatory act must be equal to a situation where the act produces its effect directly for individuals without requiring implementing measures. He therefore concluded that the condition linked to the absence of implementing measures is identical to the definition of direct concern.[86] A systematic interpretation, however, suggests that those two criteria would not both have been inserted had they not been intended to add something in comparison with leaving any one of them out.[87] Perhaps the

[78] See further A Ward, *Judicial Review and the Rights of Private Parties in EU Law* (Oxford University Press 2007), at p 317 *et seq*.

[79] For a typical example see, e.g. Case 333/85 *Mannesmann-Röhrenwerke v Council*, EU:C:1987:134.

[80] Case 62/70 *Bock v Commission*, EU:C:1971:108; For a case on the significance of a third party binding itself in advance see: Case C-30/95 *SCPA v Commission*, EU:C:1998:148.

[81] Case 11/82 *Piraiki-Patraiki v Commission*, EU:C:1985:18.

[82] Case C-386/96 P *Société Louis Dreyfus & Cie v Commission*, EU:C:1998:193.

[83] Opinion of Advocate General Kokott delivered on 21 March 2013 in Case C-274/12 P *Telefónica SA v European Commission*, EU:C:2013:204, point 59, with reference to her opinion in Opinion delivered on 17 January 2013 in Case C-583/11 P *Inuit Tapiriit Kanatami and Others v Parliament and Council* EU:C:2013:21, points 68 and 69.

[84] Opinion of Mr Advocate General Wathelet delivered on 29 May 2013 in Case C-133/12 P *Stichting Woonlinie and Others v Commission*, EU:C:2013:336, para 42.

[85] Opinion of Advocate General Kokott delivered on 21 March 2013 in Case C-274/12 P *Telefónica SA v Commission*, EU:C:2013:204, point 40.

[86] Opinion of Mr Advocate General Wathelet delivered on 29 May 2013 in Case C-133/12 P *Stichting Woonlinie and Others v Commission*, EU:C:2013:336, point 47 *et seq*.

[87] For a contrasting view on this point, see S Peers and M Costa (n 63), at p 96.

difference between the criteria lies in the second part of the direct concern test, that is, the requirement that it leaves no discretion to its addresses, who are entrusted with the task of implementing it, 'such implementation being purely automatic and resulting from EU rules alone without the application of other intermediate rules'.[88] Arguably, the first part of the direct concern test, that is, that the contested measure directly affects his legal situation, although phrased differently, lies closer to the criteria of absence of implementing measures. In other words, the direct concern test includes also a criteria referring to the (non)discretion of the addressee.

In *Telefónica*, the Court of Justice stated that the question whether a regulatory act entails implementing measures 'should be assessed by reference to the position of the person pleading the right to bring proceedings under the final limb of the fourth paragraph of Article 263 TFEU. It is therefore irrelevant whether the act in question entails implementing measures with regard to other persons'.[89]

When discussing the probable interpretation of the requirement that a regulatory act may not entail implementing measures, Advocate General Kokott distinguishes between abstract and specific legal effects of a legal act.[90] Two cases might therefore be envisaged where no implementing measure is foreseen by the Union legislature for a specific act, and some applicants may therefore be directly concerned by it, while at the same time a set of different applicants might not be so due to specific circumstances relating to their case. A regulation may for instance in practice need to be complemented by national measures in certain Member States due to national or local peculiarities. In such a case the applicants may therefore challenge the national or local measure before a national court, possibly reaching the Court of Justice through the Article 267 TFEU procedure. Although in line with the notion of a complete system of judicial remedies and procedures designed to ensure judicial review of the legality of Union acts,[91] such an order would still leave much to ask for from the private parties' point of view who might find it difficult to ascertain when to approach the Union courts or the national courts respectively. Hence, further guidance still needs to be provided by the CJEU, in the absence of which, practising lawyers may have to advise their clients to bring parallel cases 'both directly in the General Court and in national court seeking

[88] Opinion of Advocate General Kokott delivered on 21 March 2013 in Case C-274/12 P *Telefónica SA v European Commission*, EU:C:2013:204, point 59, with reference to Joined Cases C-463/10 P and C-475/10 P *Deutsche Post and Germany v Commission*, EU:C:2011:656, para 66 and the case law cited.

[89] Case C-274/12 P *Telefónica v Commission*, EU:C:2013:852, para 30, referring to the Opinion of Advocate General Kokott delivered on 21 March 2013 in Case C-274/12 P *Telefónica SA v Commission*, EU:C:2013:204, para 48.

[90] Opinion of Advocate General Kokott delivered on 21 March 2013 in Case C-274/12 P *Telefónica SA v Commission*, EU:C:2013:204.

[91] *Inuit* (n 53), para 92, with references to Case 294/83 *Les Verts v Parliament*, EU:C:1986:166, para 23; Case C-50/00 P *Unión de Pequeños Agricultores v Council*, EU:C:2002:462, para 40; Case C-131/03 P *Reynolds Tobacco and Others v Commission*, EU:C:2006:541, para 80; and Case C-59/11 *Association Kokopelli*, EU:C:2012:447, para 34. See further Section 10.2.6.

reference to the ECJ. If the "wrong" avenue of judicial review is chosen, the risk is that the client will find itself without a case and without a means of redress'.[92]

Further, from the point of view of private parties, the new rules make it decisive whether certain provisions, such as a prohibition to use fishing nets of a certain type, have been included in a basic act or not.[93] If so, these provisions can still not be challenged due to lack of individual concern, whereas the opposite could be the case if such provisions had been inserted in a non-legislative act that is of direct concern to the applicants. As pointed out by Barents, legal protection of individuals would become dependent on the form of the act in question, which would contradict the previous case law of the CJEU that only held the contents of the act decisive for the interpretation of the requirement of direct and individual concern, and not its form.[94]

10.2.5 Individual concern

The test of individual concern was established by the Court of Justice in its 1963 ruling in *Plaumann*.[95] Since then, it has consistently been held that persons other than the addressees only may claim to be individually concerned by a decision that affects them by reason of 'certain attributes which are peculiar to them or by reason of circumstances in which they are differentiated from all other persons, and by virtue of these factors distinguishes them individually just as in the case of the person addressed'.[96] Yet, *Plaumann* was not individually concerned by a decision addressed to Germany since he did not belong to a *fixed and identifiable group*.

The term 'person' in Article 263 TFEU has been held to cover at most a small group of persons. The Union courts have distinguished between open and closed categories. If the applicants could establish that they were affected because they were part of a closed class, both in theory and in practice, at the time when the measure was adopted, they would generally be individually affected by the measure.[97] Yet, if the applicants were part of a potentially open class this would be difficult.[98] Comparably, in cases where the class of persons affected by a measure is potentially an open one, individual concern will render it especially difficult to fulfil requirements of *locus standi*.

Yet, about twenty years after *Plaumann*, in *Piraiki-Patraiki*,[99] members of a *limited class of traders* identified or identifiable by the Commission were individually

[92] K Nordlander, 'Judicial Protection at EU level: Will the new standing test in Article 263(4) TFEU bring a complete system of legal protection?' (2012) 12 Europarättslig tidskrift 298, at p 302.

[93] Example borrowed from R Barents, 'The Court of Justice after the Treaty of Lisbon' (2010) 47 CMLRev 709, at p 725.

[94] Ibid.

[95] Case 25/62 *Plaumann v Commission*, EU:C:1963:17.

[96] *Inuit* (n 53), at para 72, with further references to Case 25/62 *Plaumann v Commission*, EU:C:1963:17; Case C-298/00 P *Italy v Commission*, EU:C:2004:240, para 36; and Joined Cases C-71/09 P, C-73/09 P and C-76/09 P *Comitato 'Venezia vuole vivere' v Commission*, EU:C:2011:368, para 52.

[97] Joined Cases 41-44/70 *International Fruit Company v Commission*, EU:C:1971:53, paras 21–22.

[98] See A Arnull (n 5), at p 43, with further references.

[99] Case 11/82 *Piraiki-Patraiki* (n 81), (three judges only).

concerned by a decision addressed to France that particularly affected them, although the decision as a whole did not apply to a *fixed and ascertainable group* of persons. The applicants who were found to be individually concerned had entered into contracts before the decision was adopted. These contracts could, however, not be executed as planned while the decision was in force.

The requirement of having to belong to a *closed circle of persons* has been relaxed in some cases concerning regulations. Most notably, in its rulings in *Extramet* and *Codorniu* the Court of Justice took an unusually liberal approach to the question of individual concern. These cases were thereby significant in more than this respect. Both cases were decided by the full Court, and they established that non-privileged applicants could challenge true regulations if they were directly and individually concerned. *Codorniu* was the last important ruling in relation to *locus standi* by the Court of Justice before the jurisdiction of Article 263 TFEU cases brought by non-privileged applicants was transferred to the General Court.

In other cases, however, the General Court has neither followed *Piraiki-Patraiki*,[100] nor the Court of Justice's liberal approach in *Codorniu*. Instead, the individual concern test seems to have become even more strict. In its ruling in *Buralux*,[101] which concerned the field of environment and a Council regulation on the movement of waste, the Court of Justice repeated the formula in *Plaumann* but did not find the applicants individually concerned, although they had concluded contracts before the regulation had been adopted that were to be executed while the regulation was in force. In addition, the applicants were practically the only undertakings who transported waste from Germany to France, now hindered to do so due to the regulation. Yet, the Court held that they were affected in the same way as anyone operating in the business of waste transfer between Member States. In contrast to *Piraiki-Patraiki*, it seems that the Court was of the opinion that the negative effects on the undertakings had not to be taken into consideration by the Council in its adoption of the act.[102]

Further, in the ruling in *Greenpeace*, the applicants were not found individually concerned by the contested decision. In contrast to *Plaumann*, the individual concern formula in *Greenpeace* is stated negatively. In other words, where 'the specific situation of the applicant was not taken into consideration in the adoption of the act, which concerns him in a general and abstract fashion and, in fact, like any other person in the same situation, the applicant is not individually concerned by the act'.[103]

After Lisbon these rules have been restated by the Court of Justice and private parties may be individually concerned by:

> a decision addressed to another person only if that decision affects them by reason of certain attributes which are peculiar to them or by reason of circumstances in which they

[100] For a recent reference see, e.g. Case C-132/12 P *Stichting Woonpunt and Others v Commission*, EU:C:2013:335, points 112–13.

[101] Case C-200/94 P *Buralux SA and Others v Council*, EU:C:1998:82 (heard by five judges).

[102] A Arnull (n 9), at pp 38–9.

[103] Case C-321/95 P *Stichting Greenpeace Council (Greenpeace International) and Others v Commission*, EU:C:1998:153, para 28.

are differentiated from all other persons and by virtue of these factors distinguishes them individually just as in the case of the person addressed.[104]

The Court further stated that:

> where the decision affects a group of persons who were identified or identifiable when that measure was adopted by reason of criteria specific to the members of the group, those persons might be individually concerned by that measure inasmuch as they form part of a limited class of traders and that that can be the case particularly when the decision alters rights acquired by the individual prior to its adoption.[105]

On the other hand, the Court has pointed out that:

> the possibility of determining more or less precisely the number, or even the identity, of the persons to whom a measure applies by no means implies that it must be regarded as being of individual concern to them as long as that measure is applied by virtue of an objective legal or factual situation defined by it.[106]

Accordingly, problems of *locus standi* for non-privileged applicants wanting to challenge EU measures are hard to overcome since the individual and direct concern tests now seem to have become even more strict. A narrow interpretation might, however, clash with demands put on the EU legal order by the EU Charter and the ECHR.

10.2.6 The EU Charter and the European Convention on Human Rights

During the years, many Advocate General Opinions have made reference to the EU Charter. For Instance, Advocate General Jacobs referred to the EU Charter at some length in his opinion of 21 March 2002 in the *UPA* case,[107] as a basis for changing the case law on standing for non-privileged applicants. On 3 May 2002, the General Court then referred to his opinion in its judgment in *Jégo-Quéré*.[108] In these cases, the General Court and Advocate General Jacobs referred to Articles 6 and 13 ECHR and Article 47 of the EU Charter in order to plead for a more liberal approach to the interpretation of the most problematic notion in Article 263 TFEU, that of individual concern. The General Court was of the opinion that the right to an effective remedy for everyone, whose rights and freedoms guaranteed by the law of the Union are violated, had been reaffirmed by Article 47 of the EU

[104] Case C-132/12 P *Stichting Woonpunt and Others v Commission*, EU:C:2014:100 para 57, with further references to Case 25/62 *Plaumann v Commission*, EU:C:1963:17, para 107; Case C-298/00 P *Italy v Commission*, EU:C:2004:240, para 36; *Inuit* (n 53), para 72; and Case C-274/12 P *Telefónica v Commission*, EU:C:2013:852, para 46.

[105] Case C-132/12 P *Stichting Woonpunt and Others v Commission*, EU:C:2014:100 para 59, with further references to Case C-125/06 P *Commission v Infront WM*, EU:C:2008:159, paras 71–72 and the case law cited.

[106] *Telefónica v Commission* (n 104), para 47.

[107] Opinion of Advocate General Jacobs delivered on 21 March 2002 in Case C-50/00 P *UPA v Council*, EU:C:2002:197.

[108] Case T-177/01 *Jégo-Quéré & Cie SA v Commission*, EU:T:2002:112.

Charter.[109] According to the General Court, the Article 267 TFEU procedure was not to be regarded as an adequate substitute for an Article 263 TFEU annulment action because it does not guarantee a right for an effective appeal.

Upon appeal, the Court of Justice based the right to an effective remedy before a court of competent jurisdiction, on the constitutional traditions common to the Member States and on Articles 6 and 13 of the ECHR.[110] Yet, this reference to Articles 6 and 13 ECHR and individuals' rights to effective judicial protection for the rights they derive from 'the Community legal order'[111] did not lead to any change in the standing criteria.[112] Instead, the Court focused on individuals' right to effective judicial protection before national courts and placed the onus for reform on the political agenda.[113] In contrast to the General Court and Advocate General Jacobs, the Court of Justice did not make reference to Article 47 of the Charter, which claims 'the existence of a right to effective judicial protection not only before national courts but also before EU Courts'.[114] Yet, the narrow interpretation of the Court of Justice has been followed in subsequent cases both by the General Court,[115] and the Court of Justice.[116]

With the entry into force of the Lisbon Treaty the EU Charter became legally binding upon the EU institutions and the Member States when implementing EU law.[117] Yet, in *Inuit*, the Court of Justice held that the EU Charter does not require that private parties should be granted unconditional access to bring direct annulment proceedings directly before the Union courts. Instead, the Court pointed out that 'judicial review of compliance with the European Union legal order is ensured by the Court of Justice and the Courts and tribunals of the Member States'.[118] Further, the Court emphasized that:

> the FEU Treaty has established, by Articles 263 and 277, on the one hand, and Article 267, on the other, a complete system of legal remedies and procedures designed to ensure judicial review of the legality of European Union acts, and has entrusted such review to the Courts of the European Union.[119]

[109] Ibid.

[110] Following its earlier judgments e.g. Case 222/84 *Johnston*, EU:C:1986:206, para 18.

[111] Case C-50/00 P *Unión de Pequeños Agricultores v Council*, EU:C:2002:462, para 39; Case C-263/02 P *Commission v Jégo-Quéré & Cie SA*, EU:C:2004:210, para 29.

[112] Cf. App No 45036/98 *Bosphorus Hava Yollari Turizm Ve Ticaret Anonim Sirketi v Ireland* (2005) indicating that the restrictive standing rules might be inconsistent with Article 6 ECHR, and Case C-229/05 P *PKK and KNK v Council*, EU:C:2007:32.

[113] P Craig (n 34), at p 129.

[114] M Eliantonio et al (n 12), section 2.9 at p 45, with further references.

[115] See, e.g. Case T-167/02 *Établissements Toulorge v Parliament and Council*, EU:T:2006:193; Case T-231/02 *Piero Gonnelli and Associazione Italiana Frantoiani Oleari (AIFO) v Commission*, EU:T:2004:105; Case T-292/02 *Confederazione Nazionale dei Servizi (Confservizi) v Commission*, EU:T:2009:188.

[116] See, e.g. *Inuit* (n 53), in particular paras 55, 70–3.

[117] See in particular Cases C-617/10 *Åkerberg Fransson*, EU:C:2013:105, and C-399/11 *Melloni*, EU:C:2013:107, and the many case reports on these cases, in particular D Ritleng, 'De l'articulation des systèmes de protection des droits fondamentaux dans l'Union. Les enseignements des arrêts *Åkerberg Fransson* et *Melloni*' (2013) RTDEur 267; and A Torres Pérez, 'Melloni in Three Acts: From Dialogue to Monologue' (2014) 10 EuConst 308.

[118] *Inuit* (n 53), para 90.

[119] *Inuit* (n 53), para 92, with reference to Case 294/83 *Les Verts v Parliament*, EU:C:1986:166, para 23; Case C-50/00 P *Unión de Pequeños Agricultores v Council*, EU:C:2002:462, para 40; Case

In addition, the Court of Justice continued (para 93):

> Accordingly, natural or legal persons who cannot, by reason of the conditions of admissibility stated in the fourth paragraph of Article 263 TFEU, challenge directly European Union acts of general application do have protection against the application to them of those acts. Where responsibility for the implementation of those acts lies with the European Union institutions, those persons are entitled to bring a direct action before the Courts of the European Union against the implementing measures under the conditions stated in the fourth paragraph of Article 263 TFEU, and to plead, pursuant to Article 277 TFEU, in support of that action, the illegality of the general act at issue. Where that implementation is a matter for the Member States, such persons may plead the invalidity of the European Union act at issue before the national courts and tribunals and cause the latter to request a preliminary ruling from the Court of Justice, pursuant to Article 267 TFEU (see, to that effect, *Les Verts* v *Parliament*, paragraph 23).

Hence, the Court stated that private parties have the right to challenge the legality of any decision or other national measure relative to the application to them of a European Union act of general application, by pleading the invalidity of that act in proceedings before the national courts. It is therefore for the Member States to establish a system of legal remedies and procedures that ensure respect for the fundamental right to effective judicial protection.[120]

However, in line with the principle of procedural autonomy, the Court of Justice stated that the Treaties did not intend to create new remedies before the national courts other than those already laid down by national law to ensure the observance of Union law. Only if there was no remedy making it possible, even indirectly, to ensure respect for the rights which individuals derive from Union law, or if the sole means of access to a court was available to parties who were compelled to act unlawfully, the situation might change. In line with this, the introduction of 'implementing measures' into the draft Treaty establishing a Constitution for Europe was indeed intended to ensure that 'the extension of the right to institute proceedings was restricted to cases where an individual "must first infringe the law before he can have access to a court" '.[121]

Accordingly, as Advocate General Jacobs has argued,[122] and Advocate General Kokott has reaffirmed,[123] an individual who can only challenge the validity of a

C-131/03 P *Reynolds Tobacco and Others v Commission*, EU:C:2006:541, para 80; and Case C-59/11 *Association Kokopelli*, EU:C:2012:447, para 34.

[120] On the interpretation of the concept of effective legal protection see, e.g. the discussion by R Barents, 'The Court of Justice after the Treaty of Lisbon' (2010) 47 CMLRev 709, at p 722 *et seq*, with further references.

[121] Opinion of Advocate General Kokott delivered on 21 March 2013 in Case C-274/12 P *Telefónica SA v European Commission*, EU:C:2013:204, point 40, citing Secretariat of the European Convention, Final Report of the discussion circle on the Court of Justice of 25 March 2003 (CONV 636/03), para 21.

[122] Opinion of Advocate General Jacobs in Case C-50/00 P *Unión de Pequeños Agricultores v Council*, EU:C:2002:197, point 43.

[123] Opinion of Advocate General Kokott delivered on 21 March 2013 in Case C-274/12 P *Telefónica SA v European Commission*, EU:C:2013:204.

Union act before the national courts by infringing the rules laid down by that act, thereby 'relying on the invalidity of that act as a defence in criminal or civil proceedings directed against him is not afforded an adequate means of judicial protection'.[124]

Nevertheless, according to Article 47 of the EU Charter, everyone whose rights and freedoms guaranteed by the law of the Union are violated has the right to an effective remedy and to a fair trial.[125] In relation to the ECHR, Articles 13 and 6 stress the importance of a fair trial and access to justice in the determination of one's civil rights and obligations. In this respect, the European Court of Human Rights (ECtHR) has stated that the ECHR is intended to guarantee rights that are practical and effective, such as the right to access to the Courts 'in view of the prominent place held in a democratic society by the right to a fair trial'.[126] Yet, as stated by Bast, the most decisive point might be whether 'the test of effective legal protection has to be met by the EU judiciary alone, or rather by a multilevel judiciary composed of Union and national courts'.[127]

Although access to the Courts is an important part of access to justice, *locus standi* is only a small part of this debate.[128] In addition, in its Opinion 2/13 on the draft agreement on EU accession to the ECHR,[129] the Court concludes that the agreement resulting from years of negotiations is *not* in compliance with EU primary law. The consequences of the Opinion are clearly far-reaching, possibly also for demands put on the EU legal order by the ECHR. Nevertheless, this may underline the importance of the EU Charter.

10.3 Main Obstacles and Remaining Incoherencies

10.3.1 Main obstacles met when challenging EU rulemaking

(a) Direct and individual concern

So far, private parties still have to show both direct and individual concern when challenging legislative acts. In addition, it now seems that irrespectively of whether a non-privileged applicant is part of a closed circle or not, at least in relation to measure of general application, individual concern can only be established if the

[124] Opinion of Advocate General Jacobs in Case C-50/00 P *Unión de Pequeños Agricultores v Council* [2002] ECR I-6677, point 43.

[125] For a comprehensive analysis, see, e.g. S Peers, T Hervey, J Kenner, and A Ward (eds), *The EU Charter of Fundamental Rights: A Commentary* (Hart Publishing 2014), on 'Article 47'.

[126] *Airey v Ireland* ECHR (1979), Series A, No 32; 2 EHRR 305, para 24.

[127] Bast (n 64), at p 899.

[128] C Harlow, 'Access to Justice as a Human Right: The European Convention and the European Union', in P Alston (ed), *The European Union and Human Rights* (Oxford University Press 1999), at p 189.

[129] Opinion of the Court of 18 December 2014, EU:C:2014:2454.

specific situation of the applicant had to be taken into consideration in the adoption of the act.

(b) A challengeable act

The Union courts' relaxation in their preconditions for access, and the consquence that a general legislative measure can be challenged by non-privileged applicants if it adversely affects their specific rights and they thereby are individually and directly affected, is not without importance. Besides the limited possibilities to challenge legislative acts that are of both individual and direct concern, since Lisbon regulatory acts that are of direct concern and do not entail implementing measures can also be challenged by non-privileged applicants. Yet, as pointed out by Barents, the new rules make it decisive whether certain provisions have been included in a basic act or not. As a result, legal protection of individuals would become dependent on the form of the act in question, which would contradict the previous case law of the CJEU that only held the contents of the act decisive for the interpretation of the requirement of direct and individual concern, and not its form.[130]

10.3.2 Remaining incoherencies concerning European Commission rulemaking

Besides the narrowly constructed criteria of direct and individual concern, the remaining questions concern the coherence of the terminology used in Articles 290 and 291 TFEU on the one hand and in Article 263 TFEU on the other. So far, this is far from clear, and further litigation may well be expected. Firstly, it remains to be seen which types of legal acts are in fact regulations within the meaning of Article 263(4) TFEU and therefore could be challenged directly before the General Court. Secondly, the CJEU needs to address the question whether the requirement of absence of implementing measures in the third limb of Article 263(4) TFEU is a condition of its own, or simply an explanation of direct concern.[131] Then, even if identified as two separate conditions, the correct interpretation of these and the relationship between them need to be elaborated upon by the CJEU. Thirdly, more cases need to be decided in order to establish whether the binding character of the EU Charter puts additional pressure on the Union courts to uphold judicial protection of private parties on the one hand, and the national courts on the other, and if so, which provisions and to what extent. Also within this field of law, the relationship between the EU Charter and the ECHR needs to be further assessed and established in order to ascertain whether there are additional demands put on the European judicial system, including how the interrelationship between the different courts should be developed and upheld.

[130] Example taken from R Barents, 'The Court of Justice after the Treaty of Lisbon' (2010) 47 CMLRev 709, at p 725.

[131] Opinion of Advocate General Wathelet delivered on 29 May 2013 in Case C-133/12 P *Stichting Woonlinie and Others v Commission*, EU:C:2013:336, point 42.

10.3.3 Possible ways around the main obstacles

(a) Preliminary rulings

Within the European Union, justice is largely administered through the national legal systems, which are responsible for the procedural rules. The fact that national rules on procedure may not be less favourable towards claims involving Union rights, whereas narrow standing rules before the Union courts do not hinder similar claims to be tried before national courts when the national procedural rules are more liberal than the Union's, may open up a 'window of opportunity' for litigation at the national level. In addition, the validity of Union measures can be ruled upon in a preliminary ruling, even when no national implementation measure has been adopted, as was the case in *BAT*.[132] In this particular case, the national court allowed the case which was mainly concerned with annulling an EU Directive, although clearly falling outside the jurisdiction of national courts and although there was no national implementation. Still, whether this will be a practical route much depends on the willingness of national courts to allow such challenges, and to make references. In this respect, national judges may be unfamiliar with complex EU grounds of review, which may place litigants at a practical disadvantage. In addition, preliminary references entail substantial delay and additional costs, and applicants are dependent on national rules on *locus standi*.

Nevertheless, the potential of the preliminary ruling procedure is linked to the benefit of national proceedings as such. Actions before national courts including a possible request for a preliminary ruling can be beneficial also for other reasons when private parties want to invoke or challenge EU law. Firstly, the applicants may be more familiar with domestic law and practices which may render it easier for them to advance their cause; secondly, not all cases need to be referred, as when the Court of Justice has already ruled on the matter or else when the interpretation of EU law is clear, saving time and costs; and thirdly, applicants may find it easier to take recourse to their national courts as well as national legal counsel. Further, at this level, private parties may be able to benefit compared both to industry and Member States, which with their comparably less limited resources may be equally at ease at the Union level.

(b) Developing possibilities to bring direct actions: towards participation and transparency

The narrow standing rights make it particularly difficult for private parties to fulfil requirements of *locus standi*. So far, successful cases tend to be limited to the vindication of economic or procedural rights and it seems that private parties with little or no influence upon the pre-adoption procedures are not likely to fulfil requirements of *locus standi*. Hence, in most cases that fall outside the fields of economic

[132] Case C-491/01 *Q v Secretary of State for Health, ex parte: British American Tobacco (Investments) Ltd and Imperial Tobacco Ltd*, EU:C:2002:741.

or competition law, private parties have to rely on the EU legislator to ensure that substantial rights are mirrored by procedural rights. From the point of view of most private parties, the paradox still remains though that 'the less democratic or popular participation provided for in relation to [EU] legislative or administrative procedures, the less danger there might be that an Article [263 TFEU] challenge will be admissible!'[133]

10.3.4 Final remarks

The Lisbon Treaty has created a new hierarchy of norms with legislative acts and non-legislative acts of general application, including delegated and implementing acts. The criteria for standing of private parties has consequently been changed accordingly, thereby meeting some of the critique for granting too limited access to the Union courts. At the outset, standing rules have therefore been adjusted to the current vision of the aim of the judicial system, where legislative acts should only be challengeable by private parties under very limited circumstances.

In contrast, whereas enhanced judicial control would increase the democratic legitimacy of Commission rulemaking, the Lisbon Treaty introduced some relaxed rules on stranding for private parties to challenge non-legislative acts. Although stronger scrutiny of non-legislative acts involving non-majoritarian institutions such as the Commission is welcome, it is still unclear how far the Lisbon changes allow for judicial protection for private parties in Commission rulemaking. The development, so far, shows that the Court of Justice is adopting a rather narrow interpretation of the Lisbon changes.

A narrow interpretation of the Article 263 criteria of regulatory acts, direct concern, and implementing measures might, however, clash with demands put on the EU legal order by the ECHR and the EU Charter. In contrast, a wider interpretation of the key concepts would increase democratic control of Commission rulemaking, enhance judicial protection of private parties, and meet the demands of the ECHR and the EU Charter. With EU accession to the ECHR further delayed, the external pressure is continuously rather weak. Nevertheless, even more lenient standing rights might be counterbalanced through narrow grounds for review, and few available remedies. In the years to come, legal battles will most probably include inter-institutional battles concerning internal power struggles, rather than allowing any leeway for private parties.

The way chosen by the CJEU so far is to make use of the entire judicial system where direct access to the Union courts is only one possibility. Hence, the important point seems to be that the limited purpose of the new wording of Article 263(4) TFEU is to prevent private parties from having to breach the law in order to have access to judicial protection. In such cases, a direct legal remedy before the Union courts is now foreseen when regulatory acts directly affect the legal situation of private parties without requiring implementing

[133] J Shaw, 'Citizens' Rights and Access to Law', in: H-W Micklitz and N Reich (n 5), at p 252.

measures. If, however, implementing measures are in place, legal remedies are meant to be available as a corollary of a plea of illegality under Article 277 TFEU, or via a request for a preliminary reference from a national court under Article 234 TFEU. Given the remaining obstacles for private parties, judicial protection may however be both incidental and difficult to foresee, thereby not living up to current demands for effective judicial protection.

In particular, the legal uncertainty surrounding the Lisbon criteria of 'no implementing measures' and how this criteria should be interpreted and distinguished from the direct concern test has contributed further to an unclear and unsatisfactory situation, thereby diminishing rather than increasing effective judicial protection, be it before the Union courts primarily, or divided between the different courts within the European Union. Then, even if one accepts that there is a choice between securing effective legal protection before the CJEU alone or before a multilevel judiciary including both Union and national courts, from a more theoretical viewpoint, one must question why legal redress in relation to the validity of Union acts should be sought at all before national courts, which do not have any jurisdiction on these matters.

11

The Making of Delegated and Implementing Acts

Legitimacy beyond Institutional Balance

Joana Mendes

11.1 Introduction

The Lisbon system of delegated and implementing acts has enough ingredients to feed constitutional disputes and debates that are core to the Union's legal and political system. Articles 290 and 291 TFEU embody, firstly, a new system of sources that purports to ensure flexibility of the EU lawmaking process and to further democracy, anchored on the enhanced role of the European Parliament.[1] Secondly, they establish a new distribution of powers between the European Parliament, the Council, and the Commission in the making of non-legislative acts. Thirdly, Article 291 TFEU clarifies a vertical delimitation of Union and Member State executive competences that, depending on how it is practiced, may solidify a model of executive federalism.

The discussions around these provisions that have taken place during the last decade—roughly since the distinction was first presented in the Constitutional Treaty in 2004—have focused on the consequences of the new scheme to the relative powers of the EU institutions involved.[2] At issue has been, firstly, how to adjust the scheme of comitology to the specifications of Article 291 TFEU—a question that depended mostly on the Comitology Regulation and on how it is implemented—and, secondly, how to re-establish the institutional balance between the Commission, the Parliament, and the Council in the light of Article 290 TFEU—a point that remains largely open and at the core of institutional struggles.[3]

[1] Based on the formal controls envisaged in Article 290 TFEU and on its role as a co-legislator under Article 291(3) TFEU. On the respective weaknesses, see Section 11.2.

[2] At the inception, see Final Report of Working Group IX on Simplification of 29 November 2002, CONV 424/02 (henceforth, 'Final Report').

[3] Resolution of 25 February 2014 on follow up on the delegation of legislative powers and control by Member States of the Commission's exercise of implementing powers (2012/2323(INI)—henceforth, 'Resolution of 2014 on delegated acts'); Initiative to complement the Common Understanding on

Yet, Articles 290 and 291 TFEU do not exhaust the constitutional framing of delegated and implementing acts. Even if one chooses to analyse the new system through an institutional and functional lens, these are acts of the Union subject to the principle of democracy fleshed out in Articles 9 to 12 TEU.[4] The institutions' margin of autonomy in defining procedures for the adoption of delegated and of implementing acts is limited by the normative standards that emerge from the Treaty provisions on democracy.[5] This chapter takes this argument further in a two-fold way. Firstly, it explains why procedures should also structure the relationships between the institutions, bodies, offices, and agencies of the Union, on the one hand, and citizens and interest representatives, on the other, and why they should be designed to be also a source of democracy of delegated and implementing acts. Secondly, it shows that this external dimension of procedures has been hitherto neglected, in a way that is arguably incongruous with the current Treaty and with the rationale of enhancing the democracy of non-legislative acts of the Union, which also justified the distinction between delegated and implementing acts.[6]

The chapter starts by pointing out the shortcomings of the controls envisaged in Articles 290 and 291 TEU from a perspective of democracy (Section 11.2). Next, it explains the insufficiencies of approaching procedures from a purely interinstitutional perspective. Such perspective fails to address procedures as a means to rationalize and lend legitimacy to public action (Section 11.3) and as a means to structure the Union's actions in accordance with constitutional principles (Section 11.4). In this view, procedural rules that structure the public authority of the Union need to be designed and justified *also* in the light of the provisions on democracy that shape the way its institutions, bodies, offices, and agencies relate to the citizens and interest representatives (Section 11.4.1). While there are important risks in making participation of interest representatives a source of democratic legitimacy, procedures can create the conditions (non-existent at present) to make participation a complementary source of democracy (Section 11.4.2). The chapter concludes with a critical analysis of the resolution on a Law of Administrative Procedure of the European Union (Section 11.4.3).[7] The Parliament's resolution makes no reference to procedural rules that would guide the making of acts of general application. A critical look at this choice will discuss the reasons that may explain this silence and confront it with the lack of legal-normative grounds that could justify

Delegated Acts as regards the consultation of experts, Council Doc 6774/14 of 21 February 2014 (henceforth, 'Council Initiative 2014').

[4] The argument is premised on arguments I have made in two previous articles: there is a constitutional link between Articles 290 and 291 and 11 TEU (J Mendes, 'Delegated and Implementing Rulemaking: Proceduralisation and Constitutional Design' (2013) 19 ELJ 22); Article 11 TEU has normative legal consequences (J Mendes, 'Participation and the Role of Law after Lisbon: A Legal View on Article 11 TEU' (2011) 48 CMLRev 1849).

[5] J Mendes, 'Delegated and Implementing Rulemaking' (n 4).

[6] Final Report of Working Group on Simplification (n 2) shows that enhancing democracy was also one of the rationales of the Lisbon system of non-legislative acts of the Union. See also Chapter 1 by Carl Fredrik Bergström in this volume (Section 1.1).

[7] Resolution of 15 January 2013 with Recommendations to the Commission on a Law of Administrative Procedure of the European Union (2012/2024(INI)).

ignoring rulemaking procedures. While the fate of this resolution is not certain in the current legislative term, the debate on the possibility to adopt such a law remains open.[8] The inclusion or exclusion of rulemaking from a future law on the EU administrative procedure remains therefore a relevant issue.

11.2 Controls and Democratic Legitimacy

11.2.1 Delegated acts—in the shadow of democracy

The controls envisaged in Article 290 TFEU are the main tools to ensure the democratic legitimacy of delegated acts.[9] They are crucial to the operation of the Lisbon system of non-legislative acts, which was intended to ensure the flexibility of the lawmaking process in a way that would not be detrimental to Union's democracy.[10] As underlined by the Parliament, the correct application of the Treaty is a condition to ensure a 'sufficient level of democratic legitimacy of delegated acts'.[11]

In accordance with the dual representative democratic basis of the Union (Article 10(2) TEU), the Parliament and the Council, firstly, define explicitly the 'objectives, content, scope, and duration of the delegation of power' (Article 290 (1) TFEU) and, secondly, retain controls over the exercise of delegation, either by using powers of revocation and veto (Article 290 (2) TFEU), or by establishing other controls.[12] The former allows the legislator to frame the delegation in considerably strict terms, although the exactness of this framing arguably hinges on the actual possibility of determining what are the 'essential elements of an area'.[13]

[8] In January 2015, Members of the European Parliament have called on the Commission 'to adopt binding rules and table a legislative proposal on administrative procedure in the EU institutions' (see press release at http://www.europarl.europa.eu/news/en/news-room/content/20150109IPR06319/html/European-Ombudsman-transparency-a-key-concern-for-citizens-in-2013).

[9] On how far the rationale of democracy can explain the choices of Article 291 TFEU, see Section 11.2.2.

[10] The rationales behind the distinction between two types of non-legislative acts have been stressed often times in the debates and disputes arising from Articles 290 and 291 TFEU. They may be part of the 'noisy interferences' that surround the origins of the new categorization of non-legislative acts of the Union (Opinion AG Villalón in C-427/12 *Commission v Parliament and Council (Biocides)*, EU:C:2013:871, para 21). They are, nevertheless, an important aspect thereof, in particular because of the difficulties in interpreting the wording of these provisions.

[11] Resolution of 2014 on delegated acts (n 3), recital A.

[12] On the real possibilities of establishing additional controls, see C Blumann, 'À La Frontière de La Fonction Législative et de Fonction Exécutive: Les "Nouveaux" Actes Délégués', in *Chemins d'Europe. Mélanges En l'Honneur de Jean-Paul Jacqué* (Dalloz 2010), at pp 134–5.

[13] According to C Blumann, 'it is difficult to imagine a stricter framework' which 'underlies the relative suspicion that *a priori* weights over the mechanism of delegation' (ibid, 133–4—see however Article 80(1) of the German Grundgesetz: 'The content, purpose and scope of the authority must be stated in the statue that delegates authority to issue secondary legislation'). For a sceptical view of the constraining degree of these controls, see P Craig, *The Lisbon Treaty. Law, Politics, and Treaty Reform* (Oxford University Press 2010), p 267. See also, M Chamon, 'How the concept of essential elements of a legislative act continues to elude the Court' (2013) 50 CMLRev 849; see, further, Chapter 7 by Dominique Ritleng and Chapter 4 by Kieran Bradley in this volume.

However, this construction has important weaknesses. Leaving aside for the moment the question—equally relevant for issues of legitimacy—of how far the definition of objectives, content, scope, and duration of the delegation is capable of structuring the power of discretion the Commission exercises under Article 290 TFEU, the following remarks will point out the weaknesses of the controls: specifically, the weaknesses of the Parliament in exercising those controls, as portrayed in recent analyses and confirmed by official documents. The weaknesses are both structural and practical.

Firstly, the powers to revoke and veto are radical powers. Formally, at least, they do not entail the possibility of introducing modifications in the envisaged delegated acts, although they may cast a shadow over their preparation (i.e., the Commission may work to avoid the exercise of the controls envisaged in Article 290(2) TFEU).[14] Due to the political implications and the practical difficulties entailed in the exercise of these controls, they are likely to be applied parsimoniously, to an extent that may amount to lack of effective control.[15] Timely access to information, lack of 'personal and technical resources', and short time frames to exercise oversight have been revealed to be a problem.[16]

Secondly, the Parliament is not on equal footing with the Council in triggering the controls of Article 290(2) TFEU, given the demanding voting majority required (majority of its component members).[17]

Thirdly, the Commission's resort to expert committees—despite their formal absence in the adoption of delegated acts—tends to exclude the European Parliament, which, in addition, might not have the means to know who is being consulted and how.[18] The Committee of Constitutional Affairs of the Parliament has recently 'urged' the Commission to involve the Parliament adequately in the preparation of delegated acts, which is a sign of the institutional difficulties it has been having in accessing the respective procedures, in particular in accessing to the Commission's expert meetings.[19]

[14] The Guidelines of the Commission on delegated acts confirm this point (see Commission, Implementation of the Lisbon Treaty—Delegated Acts—Guidelines for the Services of the Commission, para 100 and 102 (henceforth 'Commission Guidelines of 2011')). See also P Craig (n 13), pp 63–4, 262; M Keading and A Hardacre, 'The European Parliament and the Future of Comitology After Lisbon' (2013) 19 ELJ 382, at pp 396, 401, although based on a study of the regulatory procedure with scrutiny.

[15] T Christiansen and M Dobbels, 'Delegated Powers and Interinstitutional Relations in the EU after Lisbon: A Normative Assessment' (2013) 36 West European Politics 1167, at p 1173. The study undertaken by the European Economic and Social Committee on delegated acts confirms the rare use of objection and revocation (Information Report of the Section for the Single Market, Production and Consumption on Better Regulation: Implementing acts and delegated acts, Rapporteur: Pegado Liz, Brussels, 31 July 2013, paras 4.13, 4.15 (see also 1.3.8 of the Appendix II).

[16] Resolution of 2014 on delegated acts (n 3), paras 10, 12, and 15.

[17] K Lenaerts and M Desomer, 'Towards a Hierarchy of Legal Acts in the European Union? Simplification of legal instruments and procedures' (2005) 11 ELJ 744, at p 755; C Blumann (n 12), pp 127–44 at p 136; D Ritleng, 'La Délégation du Pouvoir Législatif de l'Union Européenne', in *Chemins d'Europe. Mélanges En L'honneur de Jean-Paul Jacqué* (Dalloz 2010) pp 559–76, at p 572.

[18] See T Christiansen and M Dobbels (n 15) 1166, at p 1173.

[19] Resolution of 13 March 2014 on the implementation of the Lisbon Treaty with respect to the European Parliament, 2013/2130(INI), 13 March 2014—Strasbourg, paras 34 and 35. See also the

Fourthly, the difficulties in determining when an act should be an implementing act or a delegated act supplementing non-essential elements of a legislative act have been solved by bargaining between the two co-legislators.[20] In this process, the Parliament may sacrifice its advocacy for delegated acts in exchange for accommodation by the Council on substantive points of legislative acts.[21] This possibility may not diminish the legitimacy of the legislative process, but it opens the way to matters that would otherwise fall under the controls of Article 290 TFEU (hence, under parliamentary control) being decided via comitology procedures, where the Parliament has very little to say. The European Parliament's position in *Biocides* confirms that, at least, there are limits to the Parliament's favourable reading of the scope of Article 290 TFEU.[22] In addition, the judgment in *Biocides* indicates that, within quite broad limits, the Court will be deferential to the use the Parliament and the Council decide to make of their powers. In fact, the Court stressed the discretion of the legislator without referring this time to the need to abide by objective criteria amenable to judicial review.[23] The fact that the Court explains in detail why it considers that the provision at stake in this case justifiably gives the Commission powers under Article 291 TFEU is not inconsistent with the deferential approach of the Court.[24]

Resolution of 2014 on delegated acts (n 3), para 13. These difficulties are also mentioned in the Report of the Economic and Social Committee on implementing and delegated acts (n 15), para 1.9 (however, this report also indicates that the EP has access to the committees of experts with an observer status; this status prevents the EP from having an input in the experts' conclusions, but allows the EP to communicate 'its concerns unofficially' to the committees and to establish 'beneficial and valuable contacts'—see point 1.3.7. of Appendix II to the information report).

[20] See the Resolution of 2014 on delegated acts (n 3), para 3; Secretary General of the Commission, 'Note for the Attention of Directors General and Heads of Service on Delegated and Implementing acts—further guidance', SEC(2012) 537, Brussels, 14.09.2012, at pp 2–3.

[21] T Christiansen and M Dobbels have reported this possibility, but specify that these are 'initial observations' (T Christiansen and M Dobbels, 'Non-Legislative Rule Making after the Lisbon Treaty: Implementing the New System of Comitology and Delegated Acts' (2013) 19 ELJ 42). The extent to which this is effectively happening is still unknown and impacts on the argument being made here. The Commission mentions negotiations regarding delegated and implementing acts as a practice to be avoided, because it impacts on its institutional prerogatives (Secretary General of the Commission, Note for the Attention of Directors General and Heads of Service on Delegated and Implementing acts—further guidance, SEC(2012) 537, Brussels, 14.09.2012 pp 2–3).

[22] Judgment in C-427/12 *Commission v Parliament and Council (Biocides)*, EU:C:2014:170, where the Commission has contested the freedom of the legislator to choose between a delegated and an implementing act (para 31).

[23] Compare the *Biocides* case, para 40 with the *Schengen Borders Code* case (Case C-355/10 *Parliament v Council*), para 67. Note that AG Villalón in the *Biocides* case had both stressed the need for judicial review over this question and emphasized its limits (Opinion (n 10), paras 70–2), upholding that the legislator has 'full discretion' to choose between delegated and implementing acts (para 77).

[24] See, in particular, para 48, 49, and 51 of the judgment. Note also how quickly the Court considers that, in the case at hand, the power conferred on the Commission 'may be considered reasonable for the purposes of ensuring uniform conditions' of implementation (para 52). This may indicate reasons to be sceptical about the relevance of this condition in limiting the power of the Union to adopt implementing acts (see the contrasting views of R Schütze, '"Delegated" Legislation in the (new) European Union: A Constitutional Analysis' (2011) 74 MLR 661, at p 691 and J Bast,

In sum, the way these controls were designed, the lack of resources of the Parliament, and the existing indications on their operation (in particular, the institutional bargaining) ground reasons to be sceptical about the effectiveness of parliamentary control over delegated acts.[25] However, the political significance of the matters decided via their adoption—public health, consumer safety, security—stresses how important compliance with the provisions of the Treaty and with the principle of democracy is.[26] In particular, their political relevance ought to place the legitimacy of the procedures followed for the adoption of these acts at the core of the discussions on the legitimacy of the Union.

One may argue that, even if the controls of the Parliament may turn out to be too weak to uphold the democratic legitimacy of delegated acts, the controls that the Council (or the Member States via expert committees) may exercise would still preserve it. One of the sources of democracy of the Union—the one that relies on the representation of Member States in the Council (Article 10(2))—would subsist unchanged by the possible weaknesses of the Parliament. Yet, that is equally problematic: in the face of those weaknesses, the duality in which the Union representative democracy relies no longer holds for the adoption of acts under the ordinary legislative procedure.[27] The democratic legitimacy of delegated acts grounded on representative democracy is no longer 'beyond dispute'.[28]

11.2.2 Implementing acts—out of the radar of democracy

The sources of democratic legitimacy of implementing acts are more difficult to trace back to a model of representative democracy. Given that the Union is exercising a competence that primarily belongs to the Member States, the Parliament has only minimal control over the adoption of implementing acts—a right to scrutiny that adds to a right to be informed—as does the Council (in formal terms at least).[29] Control over the adoption of these acts rests in the Member States via the

'New Categories of Acts after the Lisbon Reform: Dynamics of Parliamentarization in EU Law' (2012) 49 CMLRev 885, at pp 909–10).

[25] Note also that, as non-legislative acts, delegated acts are not subject to the scrutiny of national parliaments, under the protocol on subsidiarity (Protocol No 2 on the Application of the Principles of Subsidiarity and Proportionality, OJ 2012 C 326/206).

[26] Report of the Economic and Social Committee on implementing and delegated acts (n 15), point 1.1.2, Annex II p 15.

[27] The prevailing view seems to be that the EP does not have a right of revocation or objection when an act is adopted by the Council in consultation with the EP (see, for example, Article 96 Council Decision (EU) 2013/755 of 25 November 2013 on the association of the overseas countries and territories with the European Union (Overseas Association Decision), OJ 2013 L 344/1). Defending this view as only applicable to acts that only require consulation of the EP (but not to acts that require its consent), see the Commission Guidelines of 2011 (n 14), at pp 20–1.

[28] Final Report (n 2) p 8.

[29] Formally the Council has the same rights to information and scrutiny of the Parliament (Articles 10 and 11 of Regulation (EU) 2011/182 of the European Parliament and of the Council of 16 February 2011 laying down the rules and general principles concerning mechanisms for control by Member States of the Commission's exercise of implementing powers, OJ 2011 L 55/13). Yet, doubts have been expressed on whether the Appeal Committee is in fact a 'Council in disguise'

comitology procedures defined in the Comitology Regulation. 'Control' is the term used in Article 291(3) TFEU, although the degree in which comitology committees are embedded in the Union's institutional set up may weaken the purported function of control.[30] Be that as it may, an argument cannot be made that the democratic legitimacy of implementing acts rests in the Member States' role in comitology procedures, based on the formal accountability of national governments to the respective parliaments. Seeking links of democratic accountability between national officials sitting in comitology committees and the citizens' representatives in national parliaments is searching for, and relying on a very thin, formalistic and remote thread of democratic legitimacy.[31] At the same time, arguing that the democratic legitimacy of implementing acts is reinforced by the fact that, under Article 291(3) TFEU, the Parliament participated for the first time in the design and functioning of comitology procedures not only suffers from a similar formal myopia,[32] but also fails to address the legitimacy of the functioning of the system put in place by the Comitology Regulation.

But, taking one step back, the very question of the democratic legitimacy of implementing acts seems to be misplaced. The democratic concerns underlying the new system of non-legislative acts—present when setting up the category of delegated acts—seem to halt at the moment one moves across the 'grey area' between the two categories of acts and enters the purported realm of implementing acts. Having formally carved out the delegation of legislative power, and formally withdrawn it from the realm of comitology, the world of implementing acts seems to be purely run by concerns on how to distribute and structure the exercise of executive power.[33] We are no longer tackling a power that belongs originally to the EU legislator, the matter being mainly to define the modalities according to which the original holders of that power (the Member States) participate in, rather than control, the exercise of that function at the Union level, and the ensuing adjustments to the powers of the Union's institutions. In these equations, democracy seems to be no longer a concern. Remaining legitimacy issues either become a matter of doctrinal elaboration on the functioning of the system, or are tackled via making

(T Christiansen and M Dobbels (n 15), at p 1168). Underlying the legal differences between the old and the new regime, see C Blumann, 'Un Nouveau Depart Pour La Comitologie: Le Règlement No 2011/182 Du 16 Février 2011' (2011) 47 Cahiers de Droit Européen 23, at pp 46–8 (and 36–9, on the relative position of the Council and the Parliament in the Comitology Regulation).

[30] C Blumann (n 29), at p 31, who underlines that the committees are strongly enmeshed in the Union institutional setting. 'Control' by Member States is also the way the institutions view the function of committees under Article 291 TFEU (see, e.g. Council Initiative 2014 (n 3), at p 5).

[31] It would rely on the effective parliamentary scrutiny of those government officials that, by sitting in comitology committees, act in a European function. The legitimacy of comitology committees has fed vivid discussions prior to the entering into force of the Lisbon Treaty (see, e.g. C Joerges and J Neyer, 'From Intergovernmental Bargaining to Deliberative Political Processes: the Constitutionalisation of Comitology' (1997) 3 ELJ 273). The analysis above brackets these discussions to focus on a normative analysis of the Treaty framework and the institutional practice so far.

[32] For a critical view of the effective role the Parliament had in defining the content of Regulation (EU) 2011/182, see T Christiansen and M Dobbels, 'Comitology and Delegated Acts after Lisbon: How the European Parliament Lost the Implementation Game' (2012) 16 European Integration online Papers (EIoP) Article 13.

[33] See further Chapter 2 by Jean Paul Jacqué in this volume.

the committee proceedings transparent through the comitology register.[34] While such registers are valuable, even assuming that all the information specified in the Comitology Regulation is systematically available, they are limited in giving access to the functioning of the system. The register may give *ex-post* access to information on decision-making, but it does not give access and voice to institutional and non-institutional actors outside the comitology system during decision-making.[35] The democratic principles of Articles 9 to 12 TEU seem to be far away from the regime of implementing acts based on Article 291 TFEU. And, in fact, one will struggle if, as attempted above, one proposes to read it in the light of the prevalent paradigm of democracy within the EU—representative democracy.

Indeed, Article 291 TFEU coveys more strongly than Article 290 TFEU that what is mainly at issue is how to manage a sharing of power (mainly vertically, but also with important horizontal implications). The fact that this provision has been perceived hitherto as dealing with executive power has arguably blocked considerations of democracy from the conception of the regime of Article 291 TFEU. That Article 291 TFEU would refer to matters of executive nature was the original conception of the Working Group on Simplification of the European Convention, whose members also acknowledged the pitfalls of distinguishing legislative and executive matters.[36] The Commission and the Parliament, in particular, have also resorted to this distinction when seeking to delimit their respective scope of action in the scheme of Articles 290 and 291 TFEU.[37] Recently the Court, in *Biocides* seems to have avoided a functional delimitation between the scopes of the two provisions based on a legislative-executive classification. The Advocate General had attempted to define the scope of '*pouvoir d'exécution*' ('*potestad ejecutiva*' in the original Spanish version) as referring to a concrete application of a 'defined and finished norm' that does not require further normative specification.[38] The Court

[34] Article 10 of the Comitology Regulation. On the transparency of the register before current legal framework, see G Brandsma, D Curtin, and A Meijer, 'How Transparent Are EU "Comitology" Committees in Practice?' (2008) 6 ELJ 819 (an empirical study of the register in 2005).

[35] Access is furthermore covered by the exceptions of Article 4(3) of Regulation (EC) 2001/1049 of the European Parliament and of the Council, regarding public access to European Parliament, Council and Commission documents, OJ 2001 L 145/43.

[36] Final Report (n 2), p 8, stressing the problems with delegating to the Commission 'the more technical or detailed aspects of the legislation *as if they were implementing measures, subject to the control of Member States*' (emphasis added) as a justification to creating the category of delegated acts. On the importance of the work of the European Convention for the interpretation of the Lisbon Treaty provisions that originated there, see G Garzón Clariana, 'Les actes délégués dans le système du droit de l'Union européenne' (2011) 12 ERA Forum, p 107 (stressing the continuity between Article I-36 of the Constitutional Treaty and Article 290 TFEU, ibid, at pp 117–18).

[37] More recently, the EP reiterated that under Article 290 TFEU the Commission exercises 'a power which is intrinsic to the legislator's own role' (Resolution of 2014 on delegated acts (n 3), Recital A). According to the Commission, under Article 290 'the legislator delegates *its powers* to the Commission in the interests of efficiency' while under Article 291 'its power is purely executive' (Commission Communication, 'Implementation of Article 290 of the Treaty on the Functioning of the European Union', COM(2009) 673 final, at p 3).

[38] Opinion of AG Villalón (n 10), paras 26, 63, 47, 78. The obvious difficulties of drawing that line—which have fed many of the discussions around Articles 290 and 291—may explain, at least in part, the Court's position in this judgment.

has, more ambiguously, referred to the 'addition of further detail' to the content of a legislative act, which takes place within the 'normative framework laid down by the legislative act itself'.[39] The problem lies, of course, in the difficulty of defining where begins the phase of 'regulation' that does not entail a normative development of a given legal regime, which could be 'implementation' (*exécution*) in the sense of Article 291 TFEU and not 'supplementation' in the sense of Article 290 TFEU.

It would then seem advisable to leave aside the legislative-executive distinction as a basis to delimit the scopes of Articles 290 and 291 TFEU. The problem, however, remains, since Articles 290 and 291 TFEU do require a functional delimitation between 'implementing' and 'supplementing' a legislative act. The Court suggested that implementing a legislative act would mean 'only' adding 'further detail' within a 'normative framework laid down by the legislative act itself'. This formula is ambiguous enough and fitting with the Court's dictum: the functional delimitation between Articles 290 and 291 TFEU is a matter of legislative discretion, where the Court will have little to say except perhaps in more extreme cases in which it would be able to establish a 'manifest error of assessment'. The message seems clear: whichever criterion of delimitation one may end up having, this is a matter for the institutions involved to decide.

If the main issue is in fact how to re-establish and stabilize the interinstitutional collaboration in exercising the non-legislative power of the Union, one should take a step back and query whether democracy is at all a suitable normative angle of analysis of acts adopted under Articles 290 and 291 TFEU.

11.3 A Matter of Institutional Collaboration Only?

Even the more legitimacy-laden delegated acts can be interpreted as mainly establishing a new scheme of collaboration between the Parliament, the Council, and the Commission in the exercise of the legislative function of the Union.[40] This

[39] *Biocides* case (n 22), paras 40 and 52, and para 49. The second defining characteristic is the purpose of acts adopted under Article 291, i.e. to ensure uniform conditions of implementation (para 40), which the Court rather quickly determined was verified in this case (para 53). The avoidance of the legislative-executive classification is more easily observable in the English translation of the judgment. The Court followed the Treaty terminology, which is more neutral in English (implementing power and implementing act) than in other languages that convey more strongly the executive-legislative terminology—'compétences d'exécution' (Article 291(2)) and 'actes d'exécution' (Article 291(4)); 'competenze di esecuzione' and 'atti di esecuzione' (respectively); 'competências de execução' and 'atos de execução' (respectively). But note that in the original French version, the Court does use the more loaded expression '*pouvoir* d'exécution' instead of 'competences d'exécution' that figures in Article 291 (*Biocides* case, paras 39, 40, and 53).

[40] Opinion of AG Villalón (n 10), para 36. This is also the prevailing view voiced by the Parliament, the Council, and the Commission: see the Resolution of 2014 on delegated acts (n 3), where the EP underlines Article 290 as a 'valuable means of rationalisation of the legislative process, which was its initial rationale in order to avoid micro-management and a heavy and lengthy co-decision procedure' (para 7); similarly, according to the Council, delegated acts are 'an important tool to guard the efficiency of the Union's decision-making processes as it avoids an overburdening of the legislator' (the Council Initiative 2014 (n 3), at p 2). In the same sense, see Commission Communication,

perspective repositions the problem. Irrespective of a rationale of democracy that may have inspired the distinction, the crux of the matter undoubtedly has been to re-establish the institutional balance under the new Treaty configuration. Democracy may at best be an effect of such re-balancing.[41] It is eventually downgraded to an argument that the Parliament and the Council (holders of direct legitimacy under Article 10 TEU) may invoke when setting the limits they wish to place on the exercise of the Commission's powers.[42] This is indeed the lens one is led to take when moving away from the interpretation of the Treaty provisions in the light of their roots (flexibility and democracy),[43] and looks instead at the institutional acts that have sought to flesh out Articles 290 and 291 TFEU.[44]

The existing rules that concretize Articles 290 and 291 TFEU have one common feature: more remotely (e.g. the traits of comitology that represent a continuation of the previous regime) or more directly, they are the result of a power struggle between the institutions.[45] They are directed at delimiting the respective realm of action and influence of the Council, the Parliament, and the Commission in the system of non-legislative acts introduced by the Lisbon Treaty. The Comitology Regulation contains a wealth of procedural rules that constrain several aspects of the operation of comitology committees with the main purpose of stabilizing the relationships between the institutions when they resort to Article 291 TFEU. It mainly shapes the new comitology system in accordance with this Treaty article, that is, establishing a shared executive power between the Union and the Member States.[46] Similarly, the main purposes of the Common Understanding on Delegated Acts were to ensure the 'smooth' exercise of delegated powers and the control of the European Parliament and the Council over the ensuing acts.[47] The Common Understanding was specifically intended to streamline the adoption

Implementation of Article 290 of the Treaty on the Functioning of the European Union, COM(2009) 673 final, at p 3.

[41] Admittedly, separating democracy from power-sharing between the institutions of the Union is, to a certain extent, artificial. The horizontal distribution of functions and the vertical allocation of executive power has important implications for democracy in the Union.

[42] See, e.g. Resolution of 2014 on delegated acts (n 3), recital A.

[43] 'Their roots' refers to the Final Report (n 2) p 2; on the relevance of a teleological and historical interpretation, see also n 10 and n 36.

[44] See Council, 'Common Understanding on Delegated Acts', Brussels, 4 April 2011, 8640/11—PE-L 40, INST 192, and Regulation (EU) 2011/182, of the European Parliament and of the Council, Laying down the rules and general principles concerning mechanisms for control by Member States of the Commission's exercise of implementation powers, OJ 2011 L 55/13. See also the documents cited in n 3, which underline flexibility and efficiency as the main rationales of delegated acts, and, indirectly of the Lisbon system of non-legislative acts (note that the Parliament does attach importance to the need to ensure a correct application of the Treaty that will 'guarantee a sufficient level of democratic legitimacy for delegated acts' (recital A)).

[45] See, in particular, Chapters 2, 3, and 9, in this volume, by Jean Paul Jacqué, Paolo Ponzano, and Paul Craig respectively.

[46] See in detail the analysis of Blumann, 'Un Nouveau Depart' (n 29). It is important to note that the Standard Rules of Procedure for Committees contain rules on third parties and experts' attendance of committee meetings, access to documents, and data protection that go beyond a purely interinstitutional dimension (Articles 5(1), 7, 11, 13, and 14; OJ 2011 C 206/11).

[47] See Common Understanding (n 44), at p 2.

of delegated acts after the first institutional clashes on whether and to what extent national governmental experts and European Parliament experts should be consulted.[48] The more recent initiative to complement the Common Understanding on Delegated Acts addresses the consultation of experts and confirms the centrality that controversies surrounding this issue retain.[49]

Yet, even if one holds that Articles 290 and 291 TFEU are predominantly about re-defining the powers of the institutions, the legitimacy of delegated and implementing acts can hardly rely only on institutional balancing. If the procedures in place are mainly directed at ensuring a mix of institutional controls that satisfies the expectations of each institution under Articles 290 and 291 TFEU, they ignore important functions that are relevant to ensure the legitimacy of public acts. Procedures rationalize public action. They channel information and balance competing substantive interests, thereby enhancing the material justice and quality of the decisions adopted and allowing scrutiny of the choices made.[50] The specific weight of these functions will depend on the type of public action at issue (e.g. adjudication—whether administrative or judicial—or rulemaking—whether legislative or administrative) and procedures will vary significantly accordingly.

One may argue that, in order to fulfil these functions, procedures need not be formalized. This has been the predominant view in EU law and practice when it comes to non-legislative rulemaking. Outside comitology, rulemaking procedures are left to sparse and scattered sector provisions occasionally defined by the legislator. The Commission and the EU agencies make sure that the functions of procedures mentioned above are fulfilled without the need to be formally constrained by legal rules.

However, an assessment of the current procedure for the adoption of delegated acts hardly confirms this view. The making of delegated acts is at present largely in the hands of the Commission.[51] No formal procedural rules structure the respective process, except in the few instances where the legislator has determined

[48] See G Garźon Clariana (n 36), at pp 122–4 on the procedure for the adoption of delegated acts. T Christiansen and M Dobbels (n 21), at p 50. On the institutional disputes regarding the consultation of experts, see the chapters by Paul Craig (Chapter 9) and Kieran Bradley (Chapter 4) in this volume.

[49] Council Initiative 2014 (n 3). See also Chapter 5 by Thomas Christiansen and Mathias Dobbels in this volume.

[50] E Schmidt-Assman, 'Pluralidad de estructuras y funciones de los proeedimentos administrativos en el Derecho alemán, europeo e internacional', in J Barnes (ed), *La Transformación del Procedimento Adminsitrativo* (Editorial Derecho Global 2008), at p 77. In national doctrine these remarks are usually made regarding administrative acts, but they are of broader relevance. Think of the problems raised by the informal meetings between the Parliament, the Council, and Commission (trialogues) in the making of legislative acts.

[51] The Commission has defended this state of affairs, by stressing, inter alia, that Article 290 TFEU is 'sufficient in itself' (Commission Communication, Implementation of Article 290 of the Treaty on the Functioning of the European Union', COM(2009) 673 final, at p 2) and Commission Guidelines of 2011 (n 14). This statement has institutional consequences: the imbalances in the position of the Parliament, pointed out above, stem also from the lack of formal procedures that make visible what the Commission is doing when making delegated acts.

specific and sparse requirements in the enabling act.[52] The only general rules are those specified in the Common Understanding. They refer to the consultation of experts and the transmission of information to the Council and the European Parliament.[53,54] But the Commission has so far refused to be bound by any rules that would, inter alia, specify the extent to which it should take into account the views of the experts consulted, or that would identify the experts the Commission would be bound to consult.[55] This refusal is due to the Commission's resistance to put in place a system that would resemble comitology, which the Commission rightly deems incompatible with the Lisbon Treaty.[56] Nevertheless, this refusal hinders the transparency of public action and the scrutiny of the acts adopted.[57]

The interinstitutional controversy on how to consult experts has narrowed down the debate on the legitimacy of procedures to an exclusive focus on how the experts of Member States or of the Parliament can participate in the making of delegated acts. Thereby, it has silenced other equally relevant aspects of procedural legitimacy, in particular the issue of how to ensure the consideration of a plurality of views that is able to enhance the material justice and the quality of the final decision. In doing so, the current debate has ostensibly ignored another crucial dimension of procedures: their external dimension, which structures the relationships between the makers of legal acts and the outer sphere composed of legally affected persons and of citizens in general.

Procedures structure the relationships between the makers of legal acts, legally affected persons, and citizens in a two-fold way. They channel, in a visible way, the action of the various bodies and actors whose contributions are needed to reach an outcome. They allow access points along the way, be it in the form of access to information or access to decision-making. From a procedural protection

[52] See, e.g. Article 10(3) of Directive (EU) 2010/30, of the European Parliament and the Council (labelling of energy consumption), OJ 2010 L 153/1.

[53] The Framework Agreement on the relations between the European Parliament and the European Commission further specifies that the Commission may invite Parliament's experts to attend the expert meetings (point 15 and Annex I, OJ 2010 L 304/47).

[54] These are the rules that have been at the core of the interinstitutional disputes.

[55] Commission Guidelines of 2011 (n 14), para 82, (p 21); Note for the Attention of Directors General and Heads of Service of 14 September 2012, Delegated and Implementing Acts – Further Guidance, SEC(2012)537, Brussels, at p 5, where the Secretariat General specified that 'one should refrain from including provisions on consultations in the basic act. Consultation requirements cannot be made part of a conferral of powers.... They cannot be made essential procedural requirements...' and classified this as a non-negotiable point. See also Letter from M Šefčovič, Vice-President of the European Commission, enclosed in Cover Note, Initiative to complement the Common Understanding on Delegated Acts as regards the consultation of expert, 7792 2014 INIT, Brussels, 17/3/2014.

[56] Commission Guidelines of 2011 (n 14), para 86.

[57] The Commission publishes explanatory memoranda where it explains the steps it took in the preparation of the delegated act. This practice has been specified in the Commission Communication of 2009 (Annex), and reiterated in the Commission Guidelines of 2011 (n 14), para 124. But the terms of these explanatory memoranda are too concise to ensure transparency and scrutiny. In relation to procedures, often they do not go beyond stating that meetings were held with expert groups or with representatives of stakeholders, that these meetings allowed an exchange of views on the draft, and that observations and comments made orally in these meetings were taken into account in the final draft.

perspective, the latter are particularly important in adjudicatory procedures, but should not be exclusively a concern of adjudicatory procedures.[58]

This external dimension is insufficiently heeded in the rules that guide the making of delegated and of implementing acts. The very limited way in which the current procedures are open to non-institutional or non-Member State actors is incapable of structuring adequately, in the sense indicated above, the relationship between the authors of delegated and implementing acts, on the one hand, and interested parties and citizens, on the other. In the context of delegated acts, the Commission does consider the possible inclusion of 'stakeholders'. In the Commission's view, readily endorsed by the Council, the consultation of interested persons should be held after the meetings with the experts groups.[59] Moreover, both types of consultation preceded the internal service consultations, there being the possibility of consulting again the same experts (but not interested parties).[60]

The sequence of consultations is designed to ensure the institutional prerogatives of the Council and of the Commission. Crucially, the terms of consultation are fully determined by the Commission, to protect its institutional prerogatives vis-à-vis the Council (expert groups) and vis-à-vis the possible over-legalization and judicialization of consultation of interested third parties. The Council and the Parliament are trying to change this situation, but only in what concerns their respective experts.[61] The situation is different in the making of implementing acts, but only regarding the consultation of experts, which is obviously mandatory under the Comitology Regulation. The Standard Rules of Procedure for Committees do envisage that the chair of the committees (a Commission representative) '*may* decide to invite representatives of other third parties or other experts' as observers, who, in any event, cannot be present nor participate in the voting of the committee. Further, these rules specify that a simple majority of the component members of the committee may object to the participation of third parties or experts.[62] The only exception to this situation is when the enabling act specifically determines the consultation of interested parties or of other experts.[63] But, even then, the decisions on when, who, and how to consult are largely left in the hands of the Commission. Admittedly, the broader perspective on the legitimacy of delegated and implementing acts adopted here is not a concern of the institutions. But it is questionable whether this state of affairs is normatively defensible under the current constitutional framework, as will be argued below.

[58] J Mendes, *Participation in EU Rulemaking. A Rights-based Approach* (Oxford University Press 2011), chap 5.

[59] Commission Guidelines of 2011 (n 14), para 96, Council Initiative 2014 (n 3), para 4.

[60] Commission Guidelines of 2011 (n 14), para 103.

[61] Council Initiative 2014 (n 3), para 4 (the reference to stakeholders merely endorses the stated practice of the Commission—see also the standard clauses suggested by the Council in the same document). Resolution of 2014 on delegated acts (n 3), para 13.

[62] Article 7(3) and (4) of the Standard Rules (n 46), emphasis added.

[63] See Article 7(1) of the Standard Rules. For examples of consultation during the making of delegated acts, see n 52.

11.4 Procedures and Democratic Legitimacy

11.4.1 Procedures: concretizing democracy as a founding principle

From a formal legal perspective, the principle of democracy as enshrined in Articles 9 to 12 TEU ought to frame the exercise of authority in the Union.[64] While the principle of democracy is not an innovation of the Treaty on European Union, the revision made by the Lisbon Treaty gave it a normative density unknown before. These Treaty norms provide the normative framework that ought to shape the relationships between the EU institutions and bodies, on the one hand, and the EU citizens, representative associations, and civil society in general, on the other. The Treaty now determines that these relationships should be established both via procedures and institutional design based on representative democracy, and via procedures and mechanisms of participatory democracy.

It follows in particular from Articles 9, 10(3) and 11 TEU that the legitimacy of the Union's actions does not rely anymore purely in a combination of the different institutions representing the 'Union interest', the Member States, and the citizens.[65] This normative consequence may be an 'irritant' in a polity that evolved via power struggles between institutions and between institutions and the Member States. But it is one that, mindful or not, the Member States chose and to which they gave constitutional 'dignity'. If citizens have the right to participate in the democratic life of the Union (Article 10(3) TEU), the mechanisms that ensure citizens' representation via the Parliament need to be effective and as open as possible (Article 10(3) TEU). In addition, even if subject to an institutional choice of 'appropriate means', there need to be mechanisms that give citizens and representative associations a voice 'in all areas of Union action' (Article 11(1) TEU) in equal terms (Article 9 TEU). While participatory mechanisms established outside legal procedures are important tools to flesh out the provisions of Article 11 TEU, to deny the legal implications of this provision means denying the normative shift introduced by Article 11 TEU.[66]

Article 9 TEU, first sentence, is perhaps the most obscure of these provisions. More than recognizing that the Union respects the principle of equality, it specifies that Union citizens ought to receive equal attention from the Union's institutions, bodies, and offices. The legal meaning of 'attention' is far from clear. The 'shall' used in the English version indicates that this could

[64] On democracy as a founding principle, see A von Bogdandy, 'Founding Principles', in A von Bogdandy and J Bast (eds), *Principles of European Constitutional Law* (Hart Publishing 2010), at pp 11–54.

[65] This statement only takes into account the procedures where the Commission, the Council, and the Parliament intervene.

[66] J Mendes, 'Participation and the Role of Law after Lisbon' (n 4).

be a specific legal command. If this is the case, it is diluted in other official languages, which emphasize that Union citizens *benefit from*—rather than 'shall receive'—equal attention.[67] Nevertheless, irrespective of more concrete interpretations that Article 9 TEU may allow, it is safe to conclude, firstly, that this provision implies that the Union establishes relationships with its citizens, and, secondly, that equality ought to shape these relationships. Even if these relationships may not be established 'in all its activities', the external effects of delegated and implementing acts make it hard to deny that Article 9 TEU would apply to acts of the Commission adopted in lieu of the legislator under the scheme of Article 290 TFEU and to acts of the Commission or of the Council adopted because uniform conditions of implementation require Union action. By the same token, it is difficult to envisage how the actions of the Union under Article 290 and 291 TFEU would be excluded from the scope of application of Articles 10(3) and 11 TEU.

Procedural rules are an important means to shape the relationships between the citizens and the institutions in a way that complies with the determinations of Articles 9, 10(3), and 11 TEU. These provisions establish normative parameters that are directly relevant to designing decision-making procedures. Participation, equality, and transparency ought to shape the making of the acts of the Union. The encompassing way in which those provisions are drafted grounds the presumption that the making of delegated and implementing acts is no exception. The relevance of constitutional principles in defining procedural rules is not new in national legal systems, where procedures have been seen as a means to bridge constitutional determinations and administrative actions. That the administrative procedure ought to concretize constitutional principles by incorporating elements such principles require is accepted in Germany—whose constitution does not contain explicit norms on the administrative procedure—and in Spain and in Portugal—where norms on the administrative procedure are part of the written constitution.[68] Arguably, this constitutional reading of procedures is equally valid in the European Union.[69] In what concerns the principle of democracy, and insofar as openness is a dimension of democracy, Article 15(3) TFEU lends textual support to this interpretation, by specifically determining the way the Union's institutions, bodies, offices, and agencies ought to '*conduct their work*'.

[67] Cf. the French, Italian, Portuguese, and Spanish versions.

[68] On this approach in the German legal system, see E Schmidt-Assman (n 50), at pp 81–6. From a Spanish perspective—albeit in a general analysis of the procedure detached from the Spanish constitutional precepts—J Barnes, 'Reforma e innovación del procedimiento', in J Barnes (ed), *La Transformación del Procedimento Adminsitrativo* (Editorial Derecho Global 2008), 11–69, at p 16. Similarly, regarding the US, see GE Metzger, 'Ordinary Administrative Law as Constitutional Common Law' (2010) 110 Columbia Law Review 479.

[69] D Curtin, H Hoffman, and J Mendes, 'Constitutionalising EU Executive Rulemaking Procedures: A Research Agenda' (2013) 19 ELJ 1. It applies to the making of both delegated and implementing acts J Mendes, 'Delegated and Implementing Rulemaking' (n 4). See also n 50.

11.4.2 Participatory procedures and representative democracy

Depending on how they are designed, procedures can be a complementary source of democracy that straddles representative and participatory democracy. This can be achieved by procedures that accommodate the participation of citizens and interest representatives. Undoubtedly, those that will use the opportunities of participation will be mostly interest representatives—that is, interest groups of various kinds—and the most powerful groups may benefit from formal access points to the procedure, given in particular the possibilities of litigation that they may open. How their participation in decision-making can be a source of democracy is thus far from obvious. Particularly when considering Union decision-making procedures, the risks of conflating interest representation and participatory democracy are too important to be overlooked.[70] The relationships established between the Commission, in particular, and interest representatives throughout the process of European integration, as well as the rhetorical use of the participation of civil society made by the Commission since its 2001 White Paper on Governance, recommend care, at the very least, when approaching participation from a perspective of democracy.[71] A minimum degree of caution prevents one from relying on current practices to make a claim of democracy. They serve different purposes.[72] In addition, no matter what one's normative perspectives may be, one should acknowledge that participation under Article 11 TEU is bound to rely largely (if not completely) on marshalling interest-specific input. Nevertheless, the caution required when viewing participation as a potential source of democracy is precisely a reason to uphold rather than to dismiss the role of procedures. Procedures will have the function of channelling participation in a way that could ground a claim of democratic legitimacy. How then may participatory procedures be a source of democracy?

A claim that participation in Union decision-making could be a source of democracy depends on the verification of at least two premises. Voice ought to be given to those interested in participating, irrespective of the policy preferences of decision-makers. Participants ought to have equal opportunities of influencing outcomes.[73] Formal equality before the law may not address the power imbalances between different groups, but it potentially gives access to interest representatives that may be excluded from behind-the-scenes lobbying. Arguably, access (voice) and justification (equal treatment) are the core procedural issues on which hinges the normative shift from participatory governance to participatory democracy that Article 11 TEU entails.[74] Voice and equal treatment are likely to upset the

[70] See P Allott, 'European Governance and the Re-branding of Democracy' (2002) 27 ELRev 60, and B Kohler-Koch, 'Post-Maastricht Civil Society and Participatory Democracy' (2012) 34 Journal of European Integration 809.

[71] For an overview, see J Mendes (n 58), chap 3.

[72] On the difference between participation from a governance perspective and from a perspective of democracy, see J Mendes, 'Participation and the Role of Law after Lisbon' (n 4).

[73] J Mendes, 'Participation and the Role of Law after Lisbon' (n 4), at p 1862.

[74] Ibid, at p 1866.

participatory arrangements created with the purpose of ensuring 'evidenced-based policy-making'.[75] If designed accordingly, procedures are capable of ensuring the fulfilment of these conditions. Only then could participation in the making of delegated and implementing acts be considered a complementary source of their democratic legitimacy.

Furthermore, these acts, whether amending and supplementing non-essential elements of a legislative act, or implementing it, are subordinate to the 'essential' choices made in their 'parent' act. As such, they ought to further those choices. This means pursuing the range of public interests that the 'parent' act defined as legally protected.[76] Procedures ought to link the choices made in delegated and implementing acts back to the legal framework within which they are enacted. Participation—duly channelled by appropriate procedures—would be a means of ensuring that the decision-maker has a proper representation of the legally protected interests affected by its decisions. Thus, one criterion to assess the pertinence of the comments received via a participatory procedure would be the extent to which they contribute to a better representation and composition of the interests the legislator set as goals in a given area. From this perspective, participation of persons concerned or of the public may enhance representative democracy: it frames the choices of the Commission (or of the Council, in the exceptional cases of Article 291 TFEU) according to the law.

Participation needs to entail a moment of justification of the choices made in view of the legally protected interests the Commission (and the Council in its executive function under Article 291 TFEU) is bound to pursue. The justification of the balancing of competing interests is made in the light of the legislative mandate. Justification makes choices accessible not only to those who participated in the procedure, but also to the legislator, and, eventually, to the Courts. Therefore, participation may aid both Parliament's (and Council's) oversight and judicial review of delegated and implementing acts. Its contribution to enhancing the role of the Parliament is particularly relevant regarding the adoption of delegated acts: the information gathered by participants could be used by the Parliament to strengthen its control over the Commission's choices, thus balancing the weaknesses of the existing controls that were pointed out above.[77] The timing of participation (i.e. the moment in which it would occur in the procedure) is crucial in this respect. It would need to be reconciled with the timing of the controls the Parliament has under Article 290 TFEU. From this perspective, it seems adequate that the consultation of interested parties takes place before the consultation of experts groups (provided that there are efficient ways for parliamentary involvement in these groups), as the Commission and the Council have proposed.[78] However, the

[75] Commission Staff Working Document, 'Review of the Commission Consultation Policy', SWD(2012) 422 final, Strasbourg, 12.12.2012, at p 3. Pointing out the absence of equal participation and indicating this absence as a reason not to consider participation in the EU, as currently practiced, as a source of democracy, see B Kohler-Koch (n 70), at pp 818–20.

[76] Similarly, see J Mendes (n 58), at p 17.

[77] I am grateful to Jürgen Bast for a discussion on this point.

[78] See n 59.

period in which the Parliament or the Council can object—generally two months, renewable for another two—may need to be extended.[79] This sort of advocacy coalition between the Parliament and interest representatives qualifies the general claim that procedures support legislative control.[80] Participation by citizens and interests representatives in the making of delegated and implementing acts would allow the legislator to follow the process of making of rules and possibly influence their development.[81] In the case of implementing acts, participation would not be formally instrumental to parliamentary control, but it would enhance the possibility of public scrutiny, equally relevant under the principle of democracy.

Portraying procedures as a source of participatory democracy capable also of enforcing the choices made by the representative institutions of the Union does not mean that democracy is the only, or the prevailing principle that ought to guide the design of procedures. Far from it. As mentioned above, procedures rationalize public action. They do so in ways that need to go beyond strictly democratic concerns. Certainly, the making of delegated and implementing acts will need to draw its legitimacy also from the technical expertise the procedure allows to gather. Technical expertise is crucial to determine, for example, what is needed to adapt the annexes of a legislative act to scientific progress, or the possible obstacles to the uniform application of a legal act in the different Member States. There are trade-offs between competing sources or types of legitimacy.[82] The balancing of these trade-offs is bound to determine specific procedural designs. But what the considerations above stress is that procedures have the ability to further democratic legitimacy and that, under the current Treaty framework, democratic legitimacy ought at least to be considered when designing the procedures for the making of delegated and implementing acts.

Democracy-based participation entails costs and imbalances that need to be accommodated or accepted as a consequence of a constitutionally informed choice. As a result, which specific procedural rules are appropriate to accommodate democratic concerns is not an easy question to answer. Procedural rules, in addition, need to give leeway to the Commission, the Council (where pertinent) and the agencies to adjust constitutional and legislative requirements regarding procedures to the regulatory contexts in which they operate. Be that as it may, in the light of the above, within the current constitutional framework, choices on procedures ought not to be in the full discretion of decision-makers. It ought

[79] This is in any event a general problem—see Report of the Economic and Social Committee on implementing and delegated acts (n 15), Annex II, point 1.3.5. Note that the Treaty does not specify a given time period for objection, which should be determined by the legislator (Article 290(2) TFEU).

[80] M McCubbins, R Noll, and B Weingast, 'Administrative Procedures as Instruments of Political Control' (1987) 3 Journal of Law, Economics and Organization 243; and E Schmidt-Assmann, *Teoria General Del Derecho Administrativo como Sistema* (Marcial Pons 2003), at pp 27ss, and 359ss.

[81] S Rose-Ackerman, S Egidy, and J Fowkes, 'The Political Economy of the Law of Lawmaking: The United States in Comparative Perspective', Paper Prepared for the *Conference on Comparative Administrative Law and Regulation*, George Washington University Law School, 31 January–1 February, 2014, Washington DC, at p 7, referring to procedures in general.

[82] Ibid, at p 3.

not be fully in the hands of the Commission to decide on the priority it should give to consultations with national experts vis-à-vis consultations with interest representatives, nor the ways through which it decides to consult interest representatives.[83] The Commission's preferences should be framed by the procedural constraints that follow from the Treaty provisions on democracy and need to be justified also in their light.

11.4.3 The silence of the Parliament

If procedures can aid the European Parliament in overseeing the actions of the Commission when making delegated and implementing acts, and enhance public scrutiny, the minimum view of the Parliament on a law on the administrative procedure is difficult to understand. By a resolution of 2013, the Parliament requested the Commission to make a legislative proposal for a regulation on a European Law of Administrative Procedure. The Parliament's recommendations regarding the content of this proposal are, in substance, limited to codifying general principles and procedural rules applicable to individual decision-making.[84] Both the principles and the rules proposed have long been established in the case law and have been restated in the Code of Good Administrative Behaviour of the European Ombudsman.[85] The Parliament is completely silent regarding procedural rules that could guide the making of non-legislative acts.

No legal-normative reason justifies this silence. The legal basis for such an act (Article 298 TFEU) does not exclude the establishment of procedural rules on the making of non-legislative acts. An argument drawing on the 'quasi-legislative' nature of delegated acts is weak, given the difficulties in defining the borderline between the two categories of acts and the fact that, as mentioned above, whether the Commission is given delegated and implementing powers is mainly a result of the political bargaining between the institutions. From a formal perspective delegated acts are non-legislative acts. There is also no legal reason why the openness, efficiency, and independence of European administration should be attributes of the EU administration only when adopting individual decisions, or that would merit being specified in procedural rules only in this ambit.

[83] See above text accompanying nn 59–61.

[84] Resolution of 15 January 2013 with Recommendations to the Commission on a Law of Administrative Procedure of the European Union (2012/2024(INI)), Annex, recommendations 3 and 4. The other recommendations pertain to the objective and scope of the regulation to be adopted (Recommendation 1), to the relationship between the regulation and sectoral instruments (Recommendation 2), to the review and correction of own decisions (Recommendation 5), to the form and publicity to be given to the regulation (Recommendation 6).

[85] The Code is available at http://www.ombudsman.europa.eu/en/resources/code.faces#/page/1. The legislative proposal requested would not make the Ombudsman's Code binding. The content of the Code partially overlaps with principles and rules of judicial origin, but it also covers principles and rules that are not binding and that would remain non-binding if an act like the one the Parliament envisaged were to be adopted (e.g. the duty of officials to be service-minded, correct, and courteous).

True, the right to good administration of the Charter of Fundamental Rights is restricted to the relationships that the EU administration establishes with EU citizens via the adoption of individual decisions.[86] But, as significant as it may be, in particular since the Charter has become legally binding, Article 41 of the Charter is a codification of the Court's case law. While the protection of good administration as a fundamental right is restricted to individual decision-making, most procedural rights that Article 41(2), (3), and (4) enshrines either have a 'mirror' outside this type of procedures, or ought to be extended to general rules.[87] A patent exception is the right to be heard. However, both the procedural protection of rights and legally protected interests and the principle of democracy would justify establishing participation rights in lawmaking procedures of the EU administration.[88] Article 41 is not an obstacle to enshrining procedural rules on transparency and participation, which would remain outside the scope of a fundamental right to good administration.

Furthermore, if efficiency and independence do not have democratic connotations, the same is not true for openness. The reference to an 'open administration' stresses the relationships between the EU administration and the EU citizens, third country nationals, and legal persons. Article 298 TFEU should hence be read in the light of the provisions on democracy of the TEU. By requiring that there be an open administration, Article 298 TFEU makes clear that openness is not only an attribute of the legislative activities of the Union (stressed in Article 15 TFEU). Openness ought to pervade also those regulatory activities and institutional practices that shape the EU outside formalized procedures and contribute to shaping the EU polity (Article 15(1) TFEU).

The Parliament's silence regarding non-legislative acts can be explained (but not justified) by a different set of reasons. First, national laws on the administrative procedure largely lack rules on rulemaking by administrations. This fact may have influenced the choice of the Parliament. In favour of that choice, one may argue that the eventual coherence of a possible EU law on the administrative procedure with its national counterparts could facilitate the Council's support to the Parliament's proposal. Nevertheless, the absence of rules on administrative rulemaking in most national laws on the administrative procedure makes them obsolete, rather than commendable.[89] In addition, most national constitutions do not include provisions on openness of the administration and on participation as

[86] Article 41 of the Charter of Fundamental Rights of the European Union (OJ 2007 C 303/1).

[87] The right of access to documents mirrors the right of access to the file, despite its different rationales; the duty to give reasons is generally applicable to all legal acts of the Union (Article 296, second paragraph); the right to damages is also not restricted to individual decisions (Article 340 TFEU), the same applies to the right to address the institutions in one of the languages of the Treaty and to receive an answer in the same language (not restricted either by Article 41(4) of the Charter, or by Article 20(d) TFEU).

[88] From a rights-based perspective, see for arguments and conditions under which such rights should be established J Mendes (n 58), chap 5 and chap 9; from a perspective of democracy, see J Mendes, 'Participation and the Role of Law after Lisbon' (n 4).

[89] J Barnes (n 68), at pp 19–23.

a source of democratic legitimacy that ought to inform administrative procedures. Also from the perspective of rights' protection, the sheer significance of the use of general rules by contemporary administrations—including the EU administration—impoverishes a law on the administrative procedure that focuses only on individual decision-making.[90] Secondly, the Commission, traditionally resistant to the type of rules proposed by the Parliament, is more likely to favour (if at all) a minimum version of an EU law on the administrative procedure. Hence, the probability that the Commission would favour the submission of a legislative proposal following the Parliament's resolution could be increased.[91] However, if the resolution of the Parliament were to be the template of a future Commission proposal, a future law on the administrative procedure of the European Union would have missed a crucial share of what the EU administration does—making delegated and implementing acts. A final reason that may explain, but does not justify, the silence of the Parliament would be lack of sufficient political interest in controlling lawmaking by the Commission. But, if this is the case, the Parliament would be denying its constitutional role of overseeing the observance of the Commission's exercise of delegated powers and its legal right of scrutiny over the implementation of legislative acts adopted via the ordinary legislative procedure.

11.5 Conclusion

The procedures that guide the making of delegated and implementing acts have been conceived from a predominantly interinstitutional perspective. The re-arrangement of the powers of the EU institutions in the making of these acts prevailed in the provisions of the Comitology Regulation, and it is at the core of the disputes still involving the making of delegated acts. One may question whether democracy is indeed a suitable normative angle of analysis of these acts. Without denying that institutional collaboration and the stabilization of interinstitutional relations is at the heart of the Lisbon system of delegated and implementing acts, in the current constitutional framework, the legitimacy of

[90] J Mashaw, 'Administrative Due Process: The Quest for a Dignitary Theory' (1981) 61 Boston University Law Review 889, at p 896.

[91] Under Article 225 TFEU the Commission is not bound to follow the Parliament's request. As the European Parliament stressed recently, although the Commission usually complies with the formal requirement to reply to Parliament's requests, it fails on 'substantial follow-up'. The problem seems to be serious enough, given that the Parliament has invoked the need for a Treaty revision that would force the Commission to follow up on its proposals, thereby directly challenging the Commission's formal exclusive power of initiating legislation that has been at the core of the Union method since the outset of the Communities (see Report on the implementation of the Lisbon Treaty with respect to the European Parliament (2013/2130(INI)), A7-120/2014, 17.2.2014, Committee on Constitutional Affairs, Rapporteur: Paulo Rangel, paras 28 and 29). In this case, the Commission purported to follow the Parliament's recommendation (see 'Follow up to the European Parliament resolution with recommendations to the Commission on a Law of Administrative Procedure of the European Union, adopted by the Commission on 24 April 2013', available at http://www.europarl.europa.eu/oeil/popups/ficheprocedure.do?lang=en&reference=2012/2024%28INL%29#tab-0).

these acts cannot rely purely on the role that the institutions play in the respective procedures. Firstly, thus far, their democratic legitimacy is not sufficiently ensured via the controls envisaged in the Treaty and via the procedures that were established as a result of Articles 290 and 291 TFEU. Secondly, viewing procedures from a purely interinstitutional perspective ignores that procedures should rationalize public action by channelling information, weighing competing interests, and allowing scrutiny of the choices made. The exclusive focus of the current institutional debate on the role of the experts of Member States and of the Parliament in the making of delegated acts silences these equally relevant aspects of legitimacy. Thirdly, the current institutional approach to the making of delegated acts (but also the current provisions on the making of implementing acts) ostensibly ignores that procedures are a means of structuring the relationships between decision-makers and the 'outer' sphere: those legally affected by the legal acts of the Union and the citizens. This is a dimension that cannot be ignored in the current constitutional framework, given that Articles 9, 10(3), and 11 TEU establish normative parameters that ought to shape the relationship between the institutions and the citizens. Therefore, as it presently stands, an interinstitutional perspective on procedures ignores the constitutional declinations of the principle of democracy as enshrined in the Treaty on European Union.

Procedural rules that structure the public authority of the Union need to be justified *also* in the light of the provisions on democracy that shape the way its institutions, bodies, offices, and agencies relate to the citizens and interest representatives that voice the concerns of the persons affected by the legal acts of the Union. The making of delegated and implementing acts is no exception, in particular given the political significance of the matters that can be decided via their adoption. While there are risks in making participation of interest representatives a source of democratic legitimacy, they need to be heeded, and, to the extent possible, tackled via procedures. Provided that minimum conditions of voice and equality are fulfilled, participation through suitably designed procedures can be a complementary source of democracy of non-legislative acts. Participation channelled through suitable procedures can favour the weighing of the competing public interests that the legislator mandates the Commission to pursue. Participatory procedures should then be designed as a means of linking the substantive choices made in delegated and implementing acts to the legislative framework that they supplement, amend, or implement. They would also support legislative control of the choices made in the enactment of delegated and implementing acts. Finally, in view of the Treaty, openness, which such procedures would favour, also ought to be an attribute of the rules adopted by the EU administration.

PART V

THE GENERAL CONCLUSIONS

12

Patterns and Findings: Five Central Themes

Carl Fredrik Bergström and Dominique Ritleng

12.1 The Constitutional Narrative

There seems to be a full consensus among our authors that the centrepiece of the reform of the system for delegation of powers to the European Commission can be found in a specification of what type of legal acts such delegation may give rise to: from the undefined acts resulting from the exercise of general 'powers of implementation'—the interpretation of which had become very wide—to a new distinction between two subcategories of non-legislative acts: 'delegated acts' (Article 290 TFEU) and 'implementing acts' (Article 291 TFEU). But it is less clear exactly why they think so.

The view embraced by several authors focuses on the objectives of the reform—the underlying intentions or the core assumptions—and they all appear to agree that the narrative underpinning the reform is that of making a better 'separation of powers' (in both a horizontal and a vertical sense). This in turn was also linked to a belief that EU democratic legitimacy would be enhanced, at least in its representative dimension (Chapters 3, 5, 8, and 11). According to such a 'constitutional' narrative the adoption of *normative* delegated acts is tantamount to acting within the domain of the EU legislature and in compliance with a model of executive federalism (Chapter 2) where the responsibility for implementation of EU legislative acts is, in principle, in the hands of the Member States (save for specific conferrals of powers on the Commission to adopt *executive* implementing acts). In consequence, the mechanisms for control over the adoption of both delegated and implementing acts have been designed to uphold a horizontal and vertical separation of powers. Article 290(2) TFEU ensures supervision by the two arms of the EU legislature and it is presupposed that consultations of committees with experts representing the national administrations can no longer be required. Article 291(3) TFEU, in contrast, systematically subjects the exercise by the EU 'executive' of implementing powers to such committees, as 'mechanisms for control by Member States'.

Notwithstanding their apparent consensus with regard to the underlying constitutional narrative of the reform, our authors differ on what this implies. The most common view is that the new subcategories of non-legislative acts are—or at least ought to be—mutually exclusive, and, therefore, that it must be possible to make a sharp division between them, but without suggesting that this is easy (Chapters 2, 3, and 9).

In sharp contrast to that view one author boldly challenges the assumption that the conceptual distinction between the new types of subcategories of non-legislative acts embodies also a difference in nature between delegated and implementing acts (Chapter 8). Instead it is argued that there is legal room for a substantial overlap as regards the scope of application of delegated and implementing acts and, therefore, that situations can be conceived of where the specific power to be conferred on the Commission will satisfy the legal preconditions of both Articles 290 and 291 TFEU. In those situations, it is said, the EU legislature will be able to choose whatever form of delegation it considers most appropriate for its purposes and, by implication, which of the two different mechanisms for control it finds best suited to the case in hand. Perhaps most provokingly, this not only implies that the legislature is permitted to make delegations of powers which enables the Commission to adopt implementing acts which 'supplement' and perhaps even 'amend' legislative acts but also that the Lisbon Treaty did not establish any hierarchical relationship between delegation of (normative) powers to adopt delegated acts and delegation of (executive) powers to adopt implementing acts.

Clearly, our authors' focus on the constitutional narrative of the reform largely reflects much of the reasoning in the *travaux préparatoires* of Articles 290 and 291 TFEU. But the *travaux préparatoires* also stated a very practical ambition that the reform should 'encourage the legislator to look solely to the essential elements of an act and to delegate the more technical aspects to the executive' (an ambition for which delegated acts would become a new type of instrument 'accompanied by strong control mechanisms' which would guarantee that the legislator would be able to retrieve, as it were, its power to legislate).[1] That ambition fits well into the historical development where the need to 'seek to distinguish between major and minor issues' and make extensive use of delegation of powers has consistently been advanced in response to perceived inefficiency within the EU legislature (Chapters 1 and 4). Somewhat surprisingly, that dimension of the reform—whether it has created preconditions for more extensive delegation than before—is something that our authors have only dealt with haphazardly. In other words, much more attention has been given to the implications of the distinction between the new subcategories of non-legislative acts—delegated and implementing acts—than to the question of their combined effect on the relationship between non-legislative and legislative acts.

[1] Final Report of Working Group IX on Simplification of 29 November 2002, CONV 424/02 (at http://european-convention.europa.eu), at p 9. Cf. Section 1.3.

12.2 The Practical Operation

Even if the old system for delegation of powers—characterized by a generous delegation of increasingly wider powers of 'implementation' combined with strict requirements for consultation of comitology committees—was always contested for interinstitutional reasons, as a regulatory machinery it was highly effective or, perhaps better, productive. Against that background some of our authors address the question, more or less ambitiously, of how successful the new system has been, judging from its operation. Most notably in that regard the conclusion is drawn (Chapter 5) that the new system has worked well and, in terms of practice, does not seem to differ so much from the old: the adoption of legislative acts has not been slowed down in any noticeable way, there have been few rejections of (draft) delegated acts,[2] nor have there been any moves to recall the powers to adopt them. Importantly the conclusion is also drawn that the involvement of groups of 'national experts' has continued to function as providing 'cooperative venues' for meetings between the Commission and the national administrations, not only within the process for adoption of implementing acts but also within the process for adoption of delegated acts.

The initial observation that much time has been needed to bring the new system for delegation of powers into motion is confirmed by our authors. Immediately after the entry into force of the Lisbon Treaty, the institutional machinery for adoption of binding legal acts was not proceeding at normal speed. Even though the new provisions in primary law were in place the negotiations went on for numerous practical arrangements. It was not until 2011 that the 'rules and general principles' were adopted which should constitute the system for supervision of implementing acts.[3] Parallel to that an informal 'common understanding' was presented with the ambition of settling the routines for delegated acts.[4]

It has been submitted that reflections of the problems with which the institutional machinery was initially beset can be found in the number of legal acts adopted since the introduction of the reform (Chapter 1). During 2010, the first year after the reform, the number of legislative acts adopted subject to the ordinary legislative procedure was remarkably low; only 35 regulations, 16 directives, and 8 decisions. Four years later, in 2014, the corresponding numbers were 88 regulations, 47 directives, and 13 decisions. An even more striking illustration can be found in the number of non-legislative acts resulting from delegation of powers. During 2010, the first year after the reform, there were no implementing acts or delegated acts adopted by the Commission (but 45 implementing acts adopted by

[2] During the legislative period 2009–14 the European Parliament only objected to a delegated act once (the same was true for the Council).

[3] Regulation 182/2011 of the European Parliament and of the Council of 16 February 2011 laying down the rules and general principles concerning mechanisms for control by Member States of the Commission's exercise of implementing powers, OJ 2011 L 55/13.

[4] Common Understanding on Delegated Acts, Council Doc 8753/1/11 of 14 April 2011.

the Council).[5] The year after, in 2011, 975 implementing acts (790 regulations, 21 directives, and 164 decisions) and 3 delegated acts (3 regulations) were adopted by the Commission. Over the following years the numbers rose steadily and in 2014, 1,032 implementing acts (703 regulations, 13 directives, and 316 decisions) and 138 delegated acts (111 regulations, 26 directives, and 1 decision) were adopted by the Commission.[6]

It is observed (Chapters 1 and 9) that the low number of implementing and delegated acts adopted during the first years after the reform—and the increase—must be seen in the light of all those non-legislative acts which were simultaneously being adopted by the Commission in exercise of powers conferred upon it in legislative acts adopted before the entry into force of the Lisbon Treaty. In 2010 there were 1,495 such acts (1,123 regulations, 68 directives, and 304 decisions). This shows that regulatory productivity was not low during 2010, but rather that the new system for delegation of powers had not yet entered into operation (in comparison, in 2008 the numbers of non-legislative acts adopted by the Commission in exercise of powers conferred upon it in legislative acts were 1,139 regulations, 54 directives, and 374 decisions).[7]

It is obvious that there are still reasons to be cautious when drawing conclusions about the operation of the new system for delegation of powers. For example, it is suggested (Chapter 5) that a low incidence of conflict within the process for adoption of delegated acts could also be interpreted as evidence of remaining deficiencies in the new framework and raises concerns with regard to whether the EU legislator(s) have the administrative resources, the necessary time, and the required political will to engage with post-delegation supervision on a regular basis.

Importantly, a relatively large proportion of non-legislative acts are still being adopted by the Commission in exercise of powers conferred upon it in legislative acts adopted before the entry into force of the Lisbon Treaty, that is, under the rules of the old system (Chapters 1 and 9). In 2014 there were 243 such regulations and 21 such directives. A closer look at those non-legislative acts reveals that they are often the result of a delegation of powers to 'supplement' or 'amend' the content of legislative acts, combined with binding requirements for consultation of comitology committees (typically PRAC).[8] After the reform, when a delegation of such powers is made, it falls within the field of application of Article 290 TFEU. This means that the resulting acts will be designated delegated acts (and that it is not possible to uphold the old requirements for consultation of comitology

[5] The 45 implementing acts adopted by the Council in 2010 consisted of 36 regulations and 9 decisions.

[6] In 2010 the Council adopted 82 implementing acts (39 regulations and 43 decisions).

[7] In 2008 the Council adopted 124 implementing acts (75 regulations and 49 decisions).

[8] For an example see Commission Directive (EU) 2014/18 of 29 January 2014 amending Directive (EC) 2009/43 of the European Parliament and of the Council as regards the list of defence-related products, OJ 2014 L 40/20, with a legal basis in Article 10 of Directive (EC) 2009/43 of the European Parliament and of the Council of 6 May 2009 simplifying terms and conditions of transfers of defence-related products, OJ 2009 L 146/1.

committees). The obvious reason why the old system is still kept alive and for the lack of any agreement, thus far, on an 'omnibus' alignment is found in the ongoing conflict over the governments' insistence that the Commission shall continue to comply with requirements for consultation of comitology committees or similar groups of 'national experts' (Chapters 4 and 9, cf. Section 12.6).

12.3 The Institutional Implications

Even if the new system for delegation of powers appears to be functioning well, in terms of operation and regulatory productivity, the effects on the EU institutional system and the balance of powers are still far from clear. For the more general evaluation of how the new system for delegations of powers has affected the positions of the institutions involved and the institutional balance, a point of departure is typically taken in the popular description of the European Parliament being the real winner. It appears to be readily admitted that the European Parliament has now succeeded in its long fight for 'real equality' with regard to the responsibility for delegation of powers to the Commission and for supervision of the exercise of those powers under both Articles 290 and 291 TFEU (Chapters 3 and 4). The arguments put forward pertain to the granting of co-responsibility in the supervision over legislative delegation, shared power in the design of arrangements for the adoption of implementing acts, and formal exclusion of the Council from control of the exercise of implementing powers. Further support for that conclusion is found in the empirical assessments, which confirm that the European Parliament is now exercising an influence—over both delegation and post-delegation supervision—which it was not able to exercise before (Chapters 5 and 6). But beyond that many doubts are expressed, not only about the European Parliament being the real winner (Chapter 4) but whether there is any real winner at all (Chapter 9).

For the European Parliament, the hope was real equality with the Council and the excision of comitology committees from Article 290 TFEU. The reality is that it has formal equality with the Council but that the 2011 Common Understanding on Delegated Acts has brought committees or 'groups' of national experts back into the area (Chapters 2, 4, and 9). Furthermore, despite the formal exclusion of the Council from the new Comitology Regulation, the reality appears to be somewhat different: the committees are composed of national representatives, their voting rules mirror those of the Council itself, and there will inevitably be close linkages between the national views as expressed in the Council and Coreper, and the national views expressed through the comitology committees (Chapter 9); the Appeal Committees which shall meet 'at the appropriate level' can be seen as the Council in all but name (Chapters 2 and 4). Then, there is the additional fact that so much rulemaking occurs via Article 291 TFEU, where the European Parliament has now less input under the new Comitology Regulation than it had before (Chapters 4 and 9).

For the Commission, the ambition was to be unfettered from the constraints of comitology committees within the area of Article 290 TFEU, thereby reinforcing its executive autonomy (albeit subject to control by the EU legislature). The reality is that national input was retained through the 2011 Common Understanding, and that it will be further enhanced if the 2014 revisions come into effect. In addition, the new Comitology Regulation places as many constraints on the Commission as existed previously (Chapters 2 and 9), or, it is argued, even greater constraints (Chapter 3).

Finally, from the perspective of the Council, the initial loss was the demise of comitology committees from Article 290 TFEU, although it has since been seeking to recover ground through the 2011 Common Understanding, and if the 2014 revisions come into effect a new regime of groups of national experts will come ever closer to the old regime of comitology committees (Chapters 4 and 9, cf. Section 12.6).

12.4 The Unsolved Problems

The regulatory efficiency of the new system for delegation of powers and the pragmatism which some authors find in the institutions' behaviour (Chapters 2, 3, and 4)—and, as a result, a general situation which is now more stable than before—must be weighed against some specific points on which it is clear to everyone that a fundamental difference of opinion has persisted. These points concern, most obviously, the constitutional rationale for the new system for delegation of powers, the mechanisms for control over the process for adoption of delegated acts, and the tension between the governments' continuous insistence on consultation of comitology committees or similar groups of 'national experts' and the claim that the new preconditions established in primary law (Article 290 TFEU) have finally unfettered the Commission from such constraints (cf. Section 1.2).

The general framework for legal acts introduced by the Lisbon Treaty established a new system for delegation of powers and new preconditions for post-delegation supervision of the exercise of these powers. But to bring the new system into motion additional measures have been required. Most obvious among those measures was the adoption of 'the rules and general principles concerning mechanisms for control by Member States of the Commission's exercise of implementing powers' which according to Article 291(3) TFEU were required in advance (the new Comitology Regulation). Parallel to that the 2011 Common Understanding on Delegated Acts was presented, with the objective of settling the routines for application of Article 290 TFEU. Importantly, empirical assessment draws our attention also to components of the new system which have taken shape in a more covert or invisible way, in the course of its application: informal types of procedures, acts, and actors which do not fit neatly into the rules now established in primary law (Chapter 6).

In spite of the operation of the new system a relatively large proportion of the non-legislative acts which ought to be adopted in the form of delegated acts are still adopted in what is, after the reform, an atypical form (neither 'delegated' nor 'implementing' acts), under the rules of the old system. This is possible because delegation clauses in old legislative acts, adopted before the reform, have not yet been adjusted to the new system. A traditional solution to this type of problem has been to make the necessary alignment of old legislative acts through the adoption of a new 'omnibus' legislative package. The Commission did indeed make such proposals, which were not approved by the Council and finally withdrawn. The reason for the Council's opposition is that it seeks sufficient guarantees for systematic consultation of national experts during the preparation of delegated acts and, pending that, prefers not to shift the old acts to the new system (Chapters 4 and 9). At the time of concluding our study, modifications of the arrangement for application of Article 290 TFEU are under active consideration—in revisions to the Common Understanding or, possibly, an interinstitutional agreement—but the solutions discussed have been miles apart (Chapters 4 and 9 but cf. Sections 5.4 and 12.6).

Another type of problem, linked to that above, concerns the lack of a precise dividing line between 'delegated' and 'implementing' acts in primary law. This leaves much room to the EU legislator to decide, on a case-by-case basis, when delegation of powers should envisage the adoption of delegated or implementing acts. All our authors acknowledge the fundamental significance of problems relating to the dichotomy between delegated and implementing acts and the room left by the law for wrestling between the two arms of the EU legislator. The conclusion is also drawn that it is unclear how far the EU legislator gives systematic considered thought as to whether delegated or implementing acts should be used, and insofar as it does so the choice can be affected as much if not more by political considerations as by the analytical nature of the distinction between the two types of act (Chapters 4 and 9). The Council has shown and expressed a reluctance to resort to delegation owing to insufficient guarantees about the proper consultation of national experts during the preparation of delegated acts (Chapter 4) whereas, as exemplified by the ruling in *Biocides*, the European Parliament has sometimes sacrificed its advocacy for delegated acts in exchange for accommodation by the Council on substantive points of legislative acts (Chapters 3 and 11). Several authors specifically address the fact that this opens the way for challenges before the Court of Justice and, thus, important judicial development.

Lastly, the new system for delegation of powers has emerged from discussions which—whether focusing on the constitutional narrative or the response to perceived inefficiency—have failed to address any participatory dimension. Also, as the new system has been set into motion the interests of the institutions involved and, indeed, the national administrations have prevailed. This can be seen in the provisions of the Comitology Regulation and, indeed, in the interinstitutional attempts to settle the routines for adoption of delegated acts. In response to that, one of our authors sets out the grounds for concerns that the new system for delegation of powers does not envisage—let alone structure—the relationships between its decision-takers and the outer sphere: those affected by the delegated and implementing acts and the public (Chapter 11). This is in spite of those normative parameters which are now laid down in Articles 9, 10, and 11 TEU, which should be used to shape the relationships between the citizens and the institutions, also in the drafting of delegated and implementing acts. Therefore it is suggested that, since Articles 290 and 291 TFEU do not exhaust the constitutional framing of delegated and implementing acts, procedural rules should be adopted by the EU legislature which can secure participation, equality, and transparency within the process for adoption of non-legislative acts.

12.5 The Judicial Development

The current absence in primary law of a sharp distinction between delegated and implementing acts has called for authoritative guidance from the Court of Justice, not least to prevent, to the extent possible, the (re)emergence of endless institutional conflicts. Those of our authors who have addressed this seem to agree that the Court has declined the invitation (Chapters 2–5, 7–9, and 11). They find support for that conclusion most notably in the ruling in *Biocides*, where the Court granted the EU legislature a degree of discretion in its choice between Articles 290 and 291 TFEU and subjected that choice to a review limited to manifest errors of assessment. Irrespective of the answers to the question of whether the solution is well-grounded or not—something on which our authors differ—the distinction between delegated and implementing acts will continue to depend on the choices made by the EU legislator on a case-by-case basis (Chapters 3, 4, 8, and 9). But beyond that, the Court has clarified, in its later ruling in *EURES*, that Article 290 TFEU excludes the use by the Commission of its powers to implement under Article 291 TFEU to 'amend or supplement' legislative acts (Chapters 4 and 7).[9] That does not mean that 'implement' cannot be anything similar and substantially overlapping to supplement legislative acts and a resulting 'grey zone' (Chapters 3, 4, 8, and 9). But it does mean that it is difficult to maintain that the Commission may use its powers to implement also to 'amend' legislative acts, since that is a rather precise notion (and, indeed, an activity which is not so difficult to identify).

While the distinction between delegated and implementing acts has given rise to difficulty, the borderline between the legislative domain and the non-legislative also seems uncertain. The notion of the 'essential elements of an area'—which appeared earlier in the ruling in *Köster*—has now made its way into the text of Article 290 TFEU, to designate what the EU legislature itself is bound to establish in its legislative acts and, hence, what is 'genetically' excluded from a legislative delegation. It has been queried whether the new legal context of the legislative domain might now change its meaning. But as regards the content of the notion of 'essential elements of an area' this does not appear to be the case (Chapter 7). In the absence of any definition in primary law it has been incumbent upon the Court of Justice to specify what should be deemed an 'essential element'. The pre-existing case law did not offer any precise guidance on that point but in its

[9] Case C-65/13 *Parliament v Commission (EURES)*, EU:C:2014:2289, para 45.

recent ruling in *Schengen Borders Code* the Court endeavoured to provide the EU legislature with a more detailed indication on how to assess whether an element is essential or not.[10] From this ruling it emerges that an element is essential when it entails policy choices or when it interferes to a certain extent with fundamental rights. Those of our authors who discuss this differ, slightly, in their answers to the question of whether the criteria will really prove helpful (Chapters 4 and 7). But in any event, the application of the criteria will require a case-by-case assessment and the case law suggests that the remaining indeterminacy of the notion, if any, will not stop the Court from exerting a strict scrutiny of the observance of the legislative domain.

A completely different matter examined by one of our authors (Chapter 10) concerns the new preconditions in Article 263 TFEU for private parties' standing to bring direct actions before the Court of Justice, challenging the legality of 'a *regulatory act* which is of direct concern to them and does not entail *implementing measures*' (emphasis added). In particular, how those terms interrelate to the new typology of legal acts and to what extent Articles 290 and 291 TFEU have been allowed to influence their interpretation are examined. The conclusion drawn is that the judicial development with respect to private parties' standing under Article 263 TFEU has been adjusted in accordance with a current understanding of the overall aim of the EU judicial system. Accordingly, it will not be possible for private parties to challenge legal acts adopted by the EU legislature in any different circumstances than before and, therefore, such acts are not covered by the new notion of 'regulatory' acts. Instead that notion falls somewhere within the confines of 'non-legislative' acts. It is also argued that, if interpreted generously, the new preconditions for private parties' standing to bring direct actions for annulment of non-legislative acts involving non-majoritarian institutions such as the Commission could increase the (participatory) democratic legitimacy of executive rulemaking. But so far the Court has preferred to stick to a narrow interpretation and to place emphasis on the central role of national courts within the EU judicial system (and private parties' standing to bring indirect actions). Therefore, even if there is still much room for further development with respect to the relationship between Article 263 TFEU and the new typology of legal acts, the important battles before the Court of Justice will have to be fought by institutions and governments, not by citizens.

Finally, the judicial establishment of another system for delegation of powers from the EU legislature—to EU agencies—should be observed (Chapters 1, 7, and 9). The choice made by the Court of Justice not to position such delegation within the legal framework set out in Articles 290 and 291 TFEU but instead to itself design an analogous regime which will exist in parallel to those provisions and independent from their legal confines has far-reaching implications.[11] Most obviously, these concern the place of agencies' legal acts within the EU hierarchy of norms and

[10] Case C-355/10 *Parliament v Council*, EU:C:2012:516.

[11] Case C-270/12 *United Kingdom v Parliament and Council*, EU:C:2014:18.

the nature of agencies' executive powers in relation to those of the Commission. It remains to be seen how far the Court will allow delegation of powers to agencies to depart from the original system in Articles 290 and 291 TFEU. But it is important to note that the Court has already rejected the chance to demonstrate its support for the idea that the EU constitutional framework for legal acts builds on a distinction between non-legislative acts that are either *normative* or *executive* in nature. Irrespective of that, the new case law on EU agencies demonstrates that there is an inevitable need for the Court to clarify the relationship between the different notions of 'executive powers' which are now in operation within the EU rulemaking machinery—and decide if they should be brought closer together or strongly kept apart.

12.6 A New System?

The overall judgments which our authors pass on the new system for delegation of powers range from those which are rather enthusiastic, emphasizing that it is working well (Chapter 5), that there is now a more stable situation with regard to executive rulemaking (Chapter 2), and in better keeping with a democratic model based on separation of powers (Chapter 3), to those which are profoundly critical, questioning if the distinction between delegated and implementing acts will have any real utility (Chapter 9), if it may even contain new seeds of conflict (Chapter 4), and, indeed, if democracy is really a suitable angle of analysis (Chapter 11). Clearly, the pattern corresponds to the focus of each study and the different perspective from which each author observes the same object of study. But the doubts about the constitutional, technical, or theoretical consistency of the new system for delegation of powers are generally shared, and, at the same time, there is no one who seriously contests that it is functioning more efficiently than before. The question we ourselves would like to focus on is the one which we placed at the centre of the aim of this book: has the new system really affected the old doctrine of delegation of powers and, if so, how?

The old doctrine of delegation of powers was founded in the case law of the Court of Justice and its landmark ruling in *Köster*. In that ruling the Court explained that 'the legislative system' of the treaties established a conceptual distinction between, on the one hand, acts directly based on the treaties which lay down the 'essential elements' of the matter to be dealt with and, on the other hand, derived acts intended to ensure their 'implementation'.[12] According to the Court, the legal preconditions for such a 'delegation of powers' was reflected then by Article 155 EEC, stating only that the Commission should exercise the powers of implementation which the Council conferred upon it in its legal acts. And that, said the Court, also

[12] Case 25/70 *Einfuhr- und Vorratsstelle für Getreide und Futtermittel v Köster, Berodt & Co*, EU:C:1970:115, paras 6 and 9. Cf. also paras 13–19 and the Court's assessment of the question relating to 'the delegation of powers' to the Commission.

permitted the Council to determine any requirements—for example, consultation of comitology committees—to which it would want to subject such delegation of powers to the Commission. Throughout the entire period leading up to the entry into force of the Lisbon Treaty, the Court managed to uphold its doctrine with an impressive coherency and the doctrine continued to shape the understanding of delegation of powers which was reflected in the choices made by the legislature and, indeed, in the reasoning of those responsible for reform of the treaties. The Court, in return, confirmed its readiness to accept the manner in which the legislature—for most of that period the Council alone—put the doctrine of delegation of powers into practice, and the coherency with which it managed to uphold the doctrine was combined with an impressive flexibility, with respect to all that which could be fitted into the notion of 'implementation'. Perhaps most strikingly, the Court proved itself prepared to accept that the legislature could make a delegation of general powers of implementation 'without having to specify the essential components of the delegated power' and that powers of implementation could be used to adopt 'normative acts which supplement or amend certain non-essential elements of a legislative act'.[13] Clearly, such flexibility fitted well into a political context where the need to make increasingly more use of the doctrine of delegation of powers was permanently advanced as a standard solution to a perceived inefficiency within the legislature.

The answer to the question of whether the new system of delegation of powers has really affected the old doctrine which emerges from the different pieces of our study appears to be 'no'. The constitutional, technical, and theoretical significance of the changes to that system was predicated on a clear distinction between the new subcategories of delegated and implementing acts. To many of our authors these acts were intended to be fundamentally different in nature. To some of our authors they were not intended to be fundamentally different in nature but still different in function (offering fundamentally different mechanisms for control). From both perspectives the reality has taken a different turn. Firstly, the tolerance which has—again—been declared by the Court of Justice with respect to the choices made by the legislature has blurred the borderline and undermined the constitutional relevance of the distinction between delegated and implementing acts. Secondly, the unwillingness of the governments to unfetter the Commission from their constraints, which has—again—been demonstrated, has led to the reintroduction of requirements for comitology committees into the process for adoption of delegated acts and, thus, the start of a new life cycle of the committees. At the time of writing these last lines we note that the insistence within the Council on enhanced consultation of 'groups of national experts' finally appears to have been digested by the Commission (not through the reluctant concession to the Council's revisions of the 2011 Common Understanding on Delegated Acts but within the

[13] Case C-156/93 *Parliament v Commission*, EU:C:1995:238, paras 18–24; Case C-240/90 *Germany v Commission*, EU:C:1992:408, paras 35–42; and Case C-427/12 *Commission v Parliament and Council (Biocides)*, EU:C:2014:170. See further Section 1.2.

Commission's own ambitious proposal for an interinstitutional agreement).[14] This return to regular business is bound to deprive the distinction between delegated and implementing acts of much of its functional relevance.

But in spite of such evidence that the new system is not so new when compared with the old, there are other developments to anticipate, beyond those which were most obviously reflected in our authors' expectations. Before the reform, the constitutional framework for legal acts and its preconditions for delegation of powers were only vaguely stated in primary law. This meant that every fundamental change was in the hands of the Court, and pending such change, there was little room for anyone else to make any constitutional improvement. Even if there is still much resemblance between the provisions in primary law and the doctrine established by the Court, the system for delegation of powers is now committed to important constitutional guarantees which are independent of the Court. This can be seen, in particular, in Article 290 TFEU. In comparison to the situation before the reform, where the Court had permitted the legislature to make a general delegation of powers of implementation 'without having to specify the essential components of the delegated power', the legislature is now compelled to define, explicitly, '[t]he objectives, content, scope and duration of the delegation of power'. This offers the European Parliament guarantees which it has never been given before and this will undoubtedly make it easier to 'encourage the legislator to look solely to the essential elements of an act and to delegate the more technical aspects to the executive' (cf. section 12.1). The same can obviously be said about the new mechanisms for control by the legislature over delegated acts, and this independently of the use—or not—of comitology committees.

The most central feature of the general framework for legal acts in primary law can be found in the conceptual distinction between legal acts classified as either legislative or non-legislative acts. At first glance, that distinction, like the doctrine of delegation of powers, is not so new but appropriately reflects 'the legislative system' which the Court of Justice had already identified in *Köster* (based on a distinction between 'acts directly based on the treaties' and 'derived acts' intended to ensure their implementation). But after a closer look, the conclusion is unavoidable that the logic of the legislative system introduced by the Lisbon Treaty is more refined or, at least, more complicated. This is particularly so because many of those acts which the Court previously treated as legislative are now formally branded non-legislative acts.

Most importantly, it has been noted that the number of non-legislative acts adopted by the Council which have their basis directly in primary law is remarkably high.[15] In 2014 there were 58 regulations, 0 directives, and 331 decisions adopted as non-legislative acts (compared with 88 regulations, 48 directives, and 22 decisions adopted as legislative acts, of which all but 1 directive and 9 decisions

[14] Commission Communication of 19 May 2015 Proposal for an Interinstitutional Agreement on Better Regulation, COM(2015) 216 final. See in particular Annexes 1 and 2. See also Section 5.4.

[15] See Section 1.4.

were subject to the ordinary legislative procedure). This provokes a number of questions, many of which fall outside the immediate focus of our current study. But some are central for us. Firstly, what would be the rationale for a delegation of powers to supplement or amend the content of such non-legislative acts? To the extent this has been considered in this study the conclusion seems to be that a delegation of powers to supplement or amend the content of non-legislative acts which have their basis directly in primary law cannot fall within the field of application of Article 290 TFEU and, therefore, must be regarded as a delegation of implementing powers (but not necessarily within the field of application of Article 291 TFEU). Secondly, what would be the permitted scope of those powers which are subject to delegations in non-legislative acts which have their basis directly in primary law? Before the reform, the notion of 'essential elements' was designed to manifest the absolute border between that which had to be specified in acts having their basis directly in primary law and that which was permitted to regulate in derived acts.[16] The new legal context created by Articles 290 and 291 TFEU gives reason to wonder if the notion of 'essential elements' now restricts only the EU legislature's right to make delegations in legislative acts. Those of our authors who have addressed that issue are inclined to consider that it will continue to apply also to delegations in non-legislative acts that have their basis directly in primary law (Chapters 7 and 8).

[16] Case 25/70 *Einfuhr- und Vorratsstelle für Getreide und Futtermittel v Köster, Berodt & Co*, EU:C:1970:115, paras 6 and 9. Cf. also paras 13–19 and the Court's assessment of the question relating to 'the delegation of powers' to the Commission.

Bibliography

MONOGRAPHS

Achenbach, J von, *Demokratische Gesetzgebung in der Europäischen Union* (Springer 2014)

Arnull, A, *The European Union and its Court of Justice* (Oxford University Press 2006)

Barnard, C and Peers, S, *European Union Law* (Oxford University Press 2014)

Bast, J, *Grundbegriffe der Handlungsformen der EU* (Springer 2006)

Bergström, C F, *Comitology—Delegation of Powers in the European Union and the Committee System* (Oxford University Press 2005)

Bergström, M, *Advocacy Groups and Multilevel Governance: The Use of EC Law as a Campaigning Tool*, Doctor of Laws Thesis defended at the European University Institute on 13 June 2003

Cooley, A and Spruyt, H, *Contracting States: Sovereign Transfers in International Relations* (Princeton University Press 2009)

Craig, P, *The Lisbon Treaty: Law, Politics and Treaty Reform* (Oxford University Press 2010)

Craig, P and de Burca, G (eds), *The Evolution of EU Law* (Oxford University Press 2011)

Curtin, D, *Executive Power of the European Union* (Oxford University Press 2009)

Curtin, D and Egeberg, M (eds), *Towards a New Executive Order in Europe?* (Routledge 2009)

Gautier, Y, *La délégation en droit communautaire*, PhD thesis (Université de Strasbourg 1995)

Harlow, C and Rawlings, R, *Pressure through Law* (Routledge 1992)

Héritier, A, *Explaining Institutional Change in Europe* (Oxford University Press 2007)

Héritier, A, Moury, C, Bischoff, C S, and Bergström, C F, *Changing Rules of Delegation: A Contest for Power in Comitology* (Oxford University Press 2013)

Joerges, C and Vos, E (eds), *EU Committees: Social Regulation, Law and Politics* (Hart Publishing 1999)

Locke, J, *Second Treatise of Civil Government* (1690)

Mayer, O, *Le droit administratif allemand*, Bibliothèque internationale de droit public (Giard and Brière 1903–6)

Maurer, H, *Droit administratif allemand* (LGDJ 1994)

Mendes, J, *Participation in EU rulemaking. A rights-based approach* (Oxford University Press 2011)

Micklitz, H-W, *The Politics of Judicial Co-operation in the EU: Sunday Trading, Equal Treatment, and Good Faith* (Cambridge University Press 2005)

Möllers, C, *Gewaltengliederung* (Mohr Siebeck 2005)

Northcote Parkinson, C, *Parkinson's Law or The Pursuit of Progress* (John Murray 1958)

Peers, S, Hervey, T, Kenner, J, and Ward, A (eds), *The EU Charter of Fundamental Rights: A Commentary* (Hart Publishing 2014)

Rieckhoff, H, *Der Vorbehalt des Gesetzes im Europarecht* (Mohr Siebeck 2007)

Ross, A, *Theorie der Rechtsquellen* (Scientia 1929 reprint 1989)

Savino, M, *I comitati dell'Unione europea: La collegialità amministrativa negli ordinamenti composite* (Giuffrè 2005)

Schmidt-Assmann, E, *Teoria General Del Derecho Administrativo como Sistema* (Marcial Pons 2003)

Schütze, R, *European constitutional law* (Cambridge University Press 2012)

Schwarze, J, *European Administrative Law* (Sweet and Maxwell 1992)

Tremeau, J, *La réserve de loi. Compétence législative et constitution* (Presses universitaires d'Aix-Marseille 1997)

Ward, A, *Judicial Review and the Rights of Private Parties in EU Law* (Oxford University Press 2007)

Weiß, W, *Der Europäische Verwaltungsverbund* (Duncker & Humblot 2010)

Wilde, O, *The Importance of Being Earnest: A Trivial Comedy for Serious People* (Leonard Smithers 1899)

ARTICLES, CHAPTERS, AND PAPERS

Adamantopoulos, K, 'Access to Justice in the European Courts for Consumers', in H-W Micklitz and N Reich (eds), *Public Interest Litigation before European Courts* (Nomos 1996)

Alemanno, A and Meuwese, A, 'Impact assessment of EU Non-Legislative Rulemaking: The Missing Link in "New Comitology"' (2013) 19 ELJ 76

Alemanno, A, 'The Biocides Judgment: In Search of a New Chemistry of the Principle of EU Institutional Balance', at: http://europeanlawblog.eu/?p=2336

Alfe, M and Christiansen, T, 'Institutional Tensions in the Evolution of Comitology', in T Christiansen and B Vaccari (eds), *21st Century Comitology: The Role of Implementation Committees in the Wider European Union* (EIPA 2009)

Alfé, M, Brandsma, G J, and Christiansen, T, 'The Functioning of Comitology Committees in Practice', in T Christiansen and B Vaccari (eds), *21st Century Comitology: The Role of Implementation Committees in the Wider European Union* (EIPA 2009)

Allott, P, 'European Governance and the Re-branding of Democracy' (2002) 27 ELRev 60

Arnull, A, 'Private Applicants and the Action for Annulment under Article 173 of the EC Treaty' (1995) 32 CMLRev 7

Arnull, A, 'Challenging Community Acts—An Introduction', in H-W Micklitz and N Reich (eds), *Public Interest Litigation before European Courts* (Nomos 1996)

Arnull, A, 'Private Applicants and the Action for Annulment since *Codorniu*' (2001) 38 CMLRev 7

Arnull, A, 'The Principle of Effective Judicial Protection in EU law: An Unruly Horse?' (2011) 36 ELRev 51

Arnull, A, 'Arrêt "Inuit": la recevabilité des recours en annulation introduits par des particuliers contre des actes réglementaires' (2014) 22 Journal de droit européen 14

Baldwin, R and Hawkins, K, 'Discretionary Justice: Davis Reconsidered' (1984) PL 570

Balthasar, S, 'Locus Standi Rules for Challenges to Regulatory Acts by Private Applicants: the New Art 263(4) TFEU' (2010) 35 ELRev 542

Barents, R, 'The Court of Justice after the Treaty of Lisbon' (2010) 47 CMLRev 709

Bast, J, 'Legal Instruments and Judicial Protection', in A Von Bogdandy and J Bast (eds), *Principles of European Constitutional Law* (Hart Publishing 2011)

Bast, J, 'New Categories of Acts after the Lisbon Reform: Dynamics of Parliamentarization in EU Law' (2012) 49 CMLRev 885

Baudrez-Toucas, M, 'Italie. Les décrets législatifs' (1987) 3 RFDA 732

Bergström, C F, 'Defending Restricted Standing for Individuals to Bring Direct Actions against "Legislative" Measures' (2014) 10 EuConst 481

Bergström, C F, 'Shaping the New System for Delegation of Powers to EU Agencies: *United Kingdom* v. *European Parliament and Council (Short Selling)*' (2015) 52 CMLRev 219

Bering Liisberg, J, 'The EU Constitutional Treaty and Its Distinction between Legislative and Non-Legislative Acts—Oranges into Apples?' Jean Monnet Working Paper 01/06 NYU School of Law

Biondi, A, 'Effectiveness Versus Efficiency: Recent Developments on Judicial Protection in EC Law' (2000) 6 European Public Law 311

Blom-Hansen, J, 'The EU Comitology System: Taking Stock Before the New Lisbon Regime' (2011) 18 JEPP 607

Blumann, C, 'Actes législatives et mesures d'exécution dans le projet de Constitution pour l'Europe', in J Andriantsimbazovina et al, *Les dynamiques du droit européen en début de siècle: études en l'honneur de Jean Claude Gautron* (Editions A Pedone 2004)

Blumann, C, 'À La Frontière de La Fonction Législative et de Fonction Exécutive: Les "Nouveaux" Actes Délégués', in *Chemins d'Europe. Mélanges En L'honneur de Jean-Paul Jacqué* (Dalloz 2010)

Blumann, C, 'Un Nouveau Depart Pour La Comitologie: Le Règlement No 2011/182 Du 16 Février 2011' (2011) 47 Cahiers de Droit Européen 23

Bogdandy, A von, Arndt, F, and Bast, J, 'Legal Instruments in European Union Law and their Reform: A Systematic Approach on an Empirical Basis' (2004) 23 YEL 91

Bogdandy, A von, 'Founding Principles', in A von Bogdandy and J Bast (eds), *Principles of European Constitutional Law* (Hart Publishing 2010)

Bouwen, P and Fischer, J, 'Towards a Stronger EU Surveillance of Macroeconomic Imbalances: Rationale and Design of the New Procedure' (2012) 51 Reflets et perspectives de la vie économique 21

Bradley, K, 'Comitology and the Law: Through a Glass, Darkly' (1992) 29 CMLRev 693

Bradley, K, 'The European Parliament and Comitology: On the Road to Nowhere?' (1997) 3 ELJ 230

Bradley, K, 'Alien Corn, or the Transgenic Procedural Maze', in R van Schendelen (ed), *EU Committees as Influential Policymakers* (Ashgate 1998)

Bradley, K, 'Institutional Aspects of Comitology: Scenes from the Cutting Room Floor', in C Joerges and E Vos (eds), *EU Committees: Social Regulation, Law and Politics* (Hart Publishing 1999)

Bradley, K, 'The institutional law of the European Union in 1999' (2000) 19 YEL 547

Bradley, K, 'Halfway House: The 2006 Comitology Reforms and the European Parliament', in D Curtin and M Egeberg (eds), *Towards a New Executive Order in Europe?* (Routledge 2009)

Bradley, K, 'Powers and Procedures in the EU Constitution: Legal Bases and the Court', in P Craig and G de Burca (eds), *The Evolution of EU Law* (Oxford University Press 2011)

Bradley, K, 'Legislating in the European Union', in C Barnard and S Peers (eds), *European Union Law* (Oxford University Press 2014)

Bradley, K, 'The European Parliament', in T Tridimas and R Schütze (eds), *Oxford Principles of European Union Law* (Oxford University Press 2015)

Brandsma, G J, Curtin, D, and Meijer, A, 'How Transparent are EU "Comitology" Committees in Practice?' (2008) 14 ELJ 819

Brandsma, G J and Blom-Hansen, J, 'Negotiating the Post-Lisbon Comitology System: Institutional Battles over Delegated Decision-Making' (2012) 50 JCMS 939

Cananea, G della, 'The European Union's Mixed Administrative Proceedings' (2004) 68 Law and Contemporary Problems 197

Cano, M and Mestre, J, 'Espagne. La délégation législative' (1987) 3 RFDA 725

Chayes, A, 'The Role of the Judge in Public Law Litigation' (1976) 89 HarvLRev 1281
Chamon, M, 'How the concept of essential elements of a legislative act continues to elude the Court' (2013) 50 CMLRev 849
Christiansen, T, 'Administrative Fusion in the European Union—Reviewing 10 Years of Comitology Reform', in U Diedrichs, A Faber, F Tekin, and G Umbach (eds), *Europe Reloaded: Differentiation or Fusion?* (Nomos 2010)
Christiansen, T and Dobbels, M, 'Comitology and Delegated Acts after Lisbon: How the European Parliament Lost the Implementation Game' (2012) 16 European Integration online Papers (EIoP) Article 13
Christiansen, T and Dobbels, M, 'Delegated Powers and Inter-Institutional Relations in the EU after Lisbon: A Normative Assessment' (2013) 36 West European Politics 1159
Christiansen, T and Dobbels, M, 'Non-Legislative Rule Making after the Lisbon Treaty: Implementing the New System of Comitology and Delegated Acts' (2013) 19 ELJ 42
Craig, P, 'Legality, Standing and Substantive Review in Community Law' (1994) 14 Oxford Journal of Legal Studies 507
Craig, P, 'Standing, Rights and the Structure of Legal Argument' (2003) 9 European Public Law 493
Craig, P, 'Delegated Acts, Implementing Acts and the New Comitology Regulation' (2011) 36 ELRev 671
Craig, P, 'Institutions, Power, and Institutional Balance', in P Craig and G De Búrca (eds), *The Evolution of EU Law* (Oxford University Press 2011)
Curtin, D, Hoffman, H, and Mendes, J, 'Constitutionalising EU Executive Rulemaking Procedures: A Research Agenda' (2013) 19 ELJ 1
Driessen, B, 'Delegated Legislation after the Lisbon Treaty: an Analysis of Article 290 TFEU' (2010) 35 ELRev 837
Eberhard, H, 'Das Legalitätsprinzip im Spannungsfeld von Gemeinschaftsrecht und nationalem Recht' (2008) 49 Zeitschrift für Öffentliches Recht 63
Eliantonio, M, Backes, C, van Rhee, C H, Spronken, T, and Berlee, A, *Standing Up for Your Right(s) in Europe, A Comparative Study on Legal Standing (Locus Standi) before the EU and Member States' Courts* (Intersentia 2013)
Elsmore, M J and Obolevich, V, 'Thank You for Not Smoking: the Commission's Proposal for a new Tobacco Products Directive—Legally Sound, but Does It Hit the Spot?' (2013) 38 ELRev 552
Fabbrini, F and Granat, K, '"Yellow Card, but No Foul": The Role of the National Parliaments under the Subsidiarity Protocol and the Commission Proposal for an EU Regulation on the Right to Strike' (2013) 50 CMLRev 115
Farrell, H and Héritier, A, 'Formal and Informal Institutions Under Codecision: Continuous Constitution-Building in Europe' (2003) 16 Governance 577
Farrell, H and Héritier, A, 'Interorganizational Negotiation and Intraorganizational Power in Shared Decision Making' (2004) 37 Comparative Political Studies 1184
Farrell, H and Héritier, A, 'A Rationalist-institutionalist Explanation of Endogenous Regional Integration' (2005) 12 JEPP 273
Garzón Clariana, G, 'Los actos delegados en el sistema de fuentes de derecho de la Unión Europea' (2010) 37 Revista de Derecho Communitario Europeo 721
Garzón Clariana, G, 'Les actes délégués dans le système des sources du droit de l'Union Européenne' (2011) 12 ERA Forum 105

Gormley, L W, 'Public Interest Litigation', in: D O'Keeffe, and A Bavasso (eds), *Judicial Review in European Union Law: Liber Amicorum in Honour of Lord Slynn of Hadley, Vol. I* (Kluwer Law International 2000)

Gormley, L W, 'Public Interest Litigation in Community Law' (2001) 7 European Public Law 51

Gormley, L W, 'Judicial Review—Reflections on the New Dawn after the First Judgments of the General Court' (2012) 12 Europarättslig tidskrift 310

Griller, S and Orator, A, 'Everything under Control? The "Way Forward" for European Agencies in the Footsteps of the Meroni Doctrine' (2010) 35 ELRev 3

Gueguen, D, 'Unifying Comitology—Omnibuses Meet Brick Wall of Member State Opposition' *Europolitics* 25 July 2014

Gueguen, D, 'Court of Justice Keeps Low Profile on Secondary Legislation', *Europolitics* 21 March 2014

Haibach, G, 'The History of Comitology', in M Andenas, and A Türk (eds), *Delegated Legislation and the Role of Committees in the EC* (Kluwer 2000)

Hardacre, A and Kaeding, M, 'Delegated and Implementing Acts: The New Comitology' EIPA Essential Guide, 5th edn, September 2013

Harlow, C, 'Towards a Theory of Access for the European Court of Justice' (1993) 12 YEL 213

Harlow, C, 'A Special Relationship? American Influences on Judicial Review in England', in I Loveland (ed), *Lessons From America* (Clarendon Press 1996)

Harlow, C, 'Access to Justice as a Human Right: The European Convention and the European Union', in P Alston (ed), *The European Union and Human Rights* (Oxford University Press 1999)

Hedemann-Robinson, M, 'Article 173 EC, General Community Measures and *Locus standi* for Private Persons: Still a Cause for Individual Concern?' (1996) 2 European Public Law 127

Heijer, M den and Tauschinsky, E, 'Where Human Rights Meet Administrative Law: Essential Elements and Limits to Delegation' (2013) 10 EuConst 513

Héritier, A, 'Policy-making by Subterfuge: Interest Accommodation, Innovation and Substitute Democratic Legitimation in Europe—Perspectives from Distinctive Policy Areas' (1997) 4 JEPP 171

Héritier, A, 'Institutional Change in Europe: Co-decision and Comitology Transformed' (2012) 50 JCMS 38

Hofmann, H, 'A Critical Analysis of the New Typology of Acts in the Draft Treaty Establishing a Constitution for Europe' (2003) 7 European Integration Online Papers (EIoP) No 9

Hofmann, H and Türk, A, 'The Development of Integrated Administration in the EU and its Consequences' (2007) 13 ELJ 253

Hofmann, H, 'Legislation, Delegation and Implementation under the Lisbon Treaty: Typology Meets Reality' (2009) 15 ELJ 482

Jakab, A, 'Probleme der Stufenbaulehre' (2005) 91 Archiv für Rechts- und Sozialphilosophie 333

Joerges, C and Neyer, J, 'From Intergovernmental Bargaining to Deliberative Political Processes: the Constitutionalisation of Comitology' (1997) 3 ELJ 273

Justus Lipsius, 'The 1996 Intergovernmental Conference' (1995) 20 ELRev 235

Kaeding, M and Hardacre, A, 'The European Parliament and the Future of Comitology after Lisbon' (2013) 19 ELJ 382

Kennedy, D, 'Form and Substance in Private Law Adjudication' (1976) 89 HarvLRev 1685

Kohler-Koch, B, 'Post-Maastricht Civil Society and Participatory Democracy' (2012) 34 Journal of European Integration 809

Kornezov, A, 'Shaping the New Architecture of the EU System of Judicial Remedies: Comment on Inuit' (2014) 39(2) ELRev 251

Kottmann, M, 'Plaumanns Ende: Ein Vorschlag zu Article 263 Abs' 4 AEUV (2010) 70 Zeitschrift für ausländisches öffentliches Recht und Völkerrecht 547

Kröll, T, 'Delegierte Rechtsakte und Durchführungsrechtsakte und das institutionelle Gleichgewicht der Europäischen Union' (2011) 66 Zeitschrift für Öffentliches Recht 253

Lane, R, 'Locus Standi', in J Monar et al (eds), *Butterworths Expert Guide to the European Union* (Butterworths 1996)

Lenaerts, K, 'Some Reflections on the Separation of Powers in the European Community' (1991) 28 CMLRev 11

Lenaerts, K and Verhoeven, A, 'Towards a Legal Framework for Executive Rulemaking in the EU? The Contribution of the New Comitology Decision' (2000) 37 CMLRev 645

Lenaerts, K and Gerard, D, 'The Structure of the Union According to the Constitution for Europe: The Emperor is Getting Dressed' (2004) 29 ELRev 289

Lenaerts, K and Desomer, M, 'Towards a Hierarchy of Legal Acts in the European Union? Simplification of Legal Instruments and Procedures' (2005) 11 ELJ 744

Lenaerts, K and Gutiérrez-Fons, J A, 'To Say What the Law of the EU Is: Methods of Interpretation and the European Court of Justice', EUI Working Papers AEL 2013/9

Liisberg, J, 'The EU Constitutional Treaty and its Distinction between Legislative and Non-Legislative Acts', in B Olsen and K Sorensen (eds), *Regulation in the EU* (Thomson 2006)

Lindseth, P L, 'The Paradox of Parliamentary Supremacy: Delegation, Democracy and Dictatorship in Germany and France, 1920s–1950s' (2003–4) 13 Yale Law Journal 1341

Lindseth, P L, 'The "Law-Regulation Distinction" and European Law Integration: Reflections on the German Jurisprudence from the 1960s to the Present' (2010) 4 Jus politicum

Mashaw, J, 'Administrative Due Process: The Quest for a Dignitary Theory' (1981) 61 Boston University Law Review 889

McCubbins, M, Noll, R, and Weingast, B, 'Administrative Procedures as Instruments of Political Control' (1987) 3 Journal of Law, Economics and Organization 243

Mendes, J, 'Participation and the Role of Law after Lisbon: A Legal View on Article 11 TEU' (2011) 48 CMLRev 1849

Mendes, J, 'Delegated and Implementing Rule Making: Proceduralisation and Constitutional Design' (2013) 19 ELJ 22

Metzger, G E, 'Ordinary Administrative Law as Constitutional Common Law' (2010) 110 Columbia Law Review 479

Moloney, N, 'The European Securities and Markets Authority and Institutional Design for the EU Financial Market—A Tale of Two Competences: Part (1) Rulemaking' (2011) 12 European Business Organization Law Review 41

Möllers, C and von Achenbach, J, 'Die Mitwirkung des Europäischen Parlaments an der abgeleiteten Rechtsetzung der Europäischen Kommission nach dem Lissabonner Vertrag' (2011) 46 Europarecht 39

Nettesheim, M, 'Article 173 of the EC Treaty and Regulations: Towards the Development of Uniform Standing Requirements', in H-W Micklitz and N Reich (eds), *Public Interest Litigation before European Courts* (Nomos 1996)

Nordlander, K, 'Judicial Protection at EU level: Will the New Standing Test in Article 263(4) TFEU Bring a Complete System of Legal Protection?' (2012) 12 Europarättslig tidskrift 298

Peers, S and Costa, M, 'Accountability for Delegated and Implementing Acts after the Lisbon Treaty' (2012) 18 ELJ 427

Peers, S and Costa, M, 'Court of Justice of the European Union (General Chamber), Judicial review of EU Acts after the Treaty of Lisbon; Order of 6 September 2011, Case T-18/10 *Inuit Tapiriit Kanatami and Others v Commission* & Judgment of 25 October 2011, Case T-262/10 *Microban v Commission*' (2012) 8 EuConst 82

Ponzano, P, 'Executive and Delegated Acts: the Situation after the Lisbon Treaty', in S Griller and J Ziller (eds), *The Lisbon Treaty—EU Constitutionalism without Constitutional Treaty* (Springer 2008)

Ponzano, P, 'La Nouvelle Comitologie et les Actes Délégués', Mscr, Workshop RSCAS, EUI, Florence, 11/12 February 2010

Pünder, H, 'Democratic Legitimation of Delegated Legislation—A Comparative View on the American, British and German law' (2009) 58 ICLQ 353

Rasmussen, H, 'Why is Article 173 Interpreted against Private Plaintiffs?' (1980) 5 ELRev 112

Ritleng, D and David, E, 'Les actes de l'Union', in V Constantinesco, Y Gautier and V Michel (eds), *Le Traité établissant une Constitution pour l'Europe, analyses et commentaires* (Presses Universitaires de Strasbourg 2005)

Ritleng, D, 'La Délégation du Pouvoir Législatif de l'Union Européenne', in *Chemins d'Europe. Mélanges En L'honneur de Jean-Paul Jacqué* (Dalloz 2010)

Ritleng, D, 'La loi', in J B Auby (ed), *L'influence du droit européen sur les catégories du droit public* (Dalloz 2010)

Ritleng, D, 'De l'articulation des systèmes de protection des droits fondamentaux dans l'Union. Les enseignements des arrêts *Åkerberg Fransson* et *Melloni*' (2013) RTDEur 267

Ritleng, D, 'The Dividing Line between Delegated and Implementing Acts: the Court of Justice Sidesteps the Difficulty in *Commission* v. *Parliament and Council (Biocides)*' (2015) 52 CMLRev 243

Robinson, G, 'The Making of Administrative Policy: Another Look at Rulemaking and Adjudication and Administrative Procedures Reform' (1970) 118 UPaLRev 485

Roederer-Rynning, C and Schimmelfennig, F, 'Bringing Codecision to Agriculture: a Hard Case of Parliamentarization' (2012) 19 JEPP 951

Rose-Ackerman, S, Egidy, S, and Fowkes, J, 'The Political Economy of the Law of Lawmaking: The United States in Comparative Perspective', Paper Prepared for the *Conference on Comparative Administrative Law and Regulation*, George Washington University Law School, January 31–February 1, 2014, Washington DC

Rrapi, P, 'L'incompétence négative dans la QPC: de la double négation à la double incompréhension' (2012) 34 Nouveaux Cahiers du Conseil constitutionnel 5

Schmidt-Assman, E, 'Pluralidad de estructuras y funciones de los proeedimentos administr-ativos en el Derecho alemán, europeo e internacional', in J Barnes (ed), *La Transformación del Procedimento Adminsitrativo* (Editorial Derecho Global 2008)

Schusterschitz, G and Kotz, S, 'The Comitology Reform of 2006: Increasing the Powers of the European Parliament Without Changing the Treaties' (2007) 3 EuConst 68

Schusterschitz, G, 'Komitologie und Binnenmarkt: Von der Komitologiereferom 2006 zum Vertrag von Lissabon', in W Schroeder (ed), *Europarecht als Mehrebenensystem* (Facultas WUV 2008)

Schütze, R, 'Constitutional Limits to Delegated Powers', in A Antoniadis et al (eds), *The European Union and Global Emergencies* (Hart 2011)

Schütze, R, '"Delegated" Legislation in the (New) European Union: A Constitutional Analysis' (2011) 74 MLR 661

Shapiro, D, 'The Choice of Rulemaking or Adjudication in the Development of Administrative Policy' (1965) 78 HarvLRev 921

Shaw, J, 'Citizens' Rights and Access to Law', in H-W Micklitz and N Reich (eds), *Public Interest Litigation before European Courts* (Nomos 1996)

Stacey, J and Rittberger, B, 'Dynamics of Formal and Informal Institutional Change in the EU' (2003) 10 JEPP 858

Stein, E and Vining, J, 'Citizen Access to Judicial Review of Administrative Action in a Transnational and Federal Context', in F R Jacobs (ed), *European Law and the Individual* (North Holland 1976)

Stelkens, U, 'Article 291 AEUV, das Unionsverwaltungsrecht und die Verwaltungsautonomie der Mitgliedstaaten' (2012) 47 Europarecht 511

Stewart, R B, 'The Reformation of American Administrative Law' (1975) 88 HarvLRev 1668

Torres Pérez, A, 'Melloni in Three Acts: From Dialogue to Monologue' (2014) 10 EuConst 308

Türk, A, 'The Development of Case Law in the Area of Comitology', in T Christiansen and B Vaccari (eds), *21st Century Comitology: The Role of Implementation Committees in the Wider European Union* (EIPA 2009)

Tusseau, G, 'La législation déléguée', in M Troper and D Chagnollaud (eds), *Traité international de Droit constitutionnel, Vol 2* (Dalloz 2012) 605

Van Malleghem, P-A and Baeten, N, 'Before the Law Stands a Gatekeeper—Or, What is a "Regulatory Act" in Article 263(4) TFEU?' (2014) 51 CMLRev 1187

Vesterdorf, B and Lundgaard Hansen, K, 'Søgsmålsret ved fællesskabsdomstolene. Et forhindringsløb for sagsøgerne?' *Ugeskrift for Retsvæsen* 1996

Vidal-Naquet, A, 'L'état de la jurisprudence du Conseil constitutionnel sur l'incompétence négative' (2015) 46 Nouveaux Cahiers du Conseil constitutionnel 7

Vírgala Foruria, E, 'Los actos no legislativos en la Constitución europea' (2006) 6 Revista de Derecho Constitucional Europeo 279

Voermans, W, 'Delegation is a Matter of Confidence' (2011) 17 European Public Law 313

Voermans, W, Hartmann, J M R, and Kaeding, M, 'The Quest for Legitimacy in EU Secondary Legislation' (2013) 2 The Theory and Practice of Legislation 5

Vos, E, 'The Fall of Committees?', in J W de Zwaan et al (eds), *The European Union: An Ongoing Process of Integration* (TMC Asser Press 2004)

Weiler, JHH, 'Epilogue: "Comitology" as Revolution—Infranationalism, Constitutionalism and Democracy', in C Joerges and E Vos (eds), *EU Committees: Social Regulation, Law and Politics* (Hart Publishing 1999)

Wessels, W, 'Comitology: Fusion in Action. Politico-administrative Trends in the EU System' (1998) 5 JEPP 209

Witte, B de, 'Simplification and Reorganization of the European Treaties' (2002) 39 CMLRev 1255

Witte, B de, 'Legal Instruments and Law-Making in the Lisbon Treaty', in S Griller and J Ziller (eds), *The Lisbon Treaty—EU Constitutionalism without Constitutional Treaty* (Springer 2008)

Xhaferri, Z, 'Delegated Acts, Implementing Acts and Institutional Balance Implications Post-Lisbon' 2013 (20) Maastricht Journal of European and Comparative Law 557

Ziller, J, 'National Constitutional Concepts in the New Constitution for Europe' (2005) 2 ECLR 452

Ziller, J, 'La constitutionnalisation de la Charte des droits fondamentaux et les traditions constitutionnelles communes aux Etats membres', in N De Grove-Valdeyron and M Blanquet (eds), *Liber amicorum – Mélanges en l'honneur du professeur Joël Molinier* (LGDJ 2012)

Index

Accountability 53, 140, 144, 162, 176, 183, 239
Advisory (committee) procedure 32–34, 41, 45, 165, 176, 189–190, 193, 202
Agencies 13–17, 48, 79, 81, 96, 100–101, 148, 177, 193–202, 213–214, 234, 243, 247, 250, 254, 265–266

Charter of fundamental rights 1, 153, 205, 225–226, 228–229, 231, 252
Citizens 3, 11, 26, 139–140, 207, 234–235, 239, 244–248, 250, 252, 264–265
Comitology 5–6, 8–9, 13, 21–22, 26–29, 31–35, 37–38, 40–48, 51–53, 56–60, 62–63, 66–68, 70, 72–78, 82–84, 87–91, 93–102, 111, 114, 138–139, 141–142, 144, 151, 159–163, 165–166, 170, 174–176, 185–187, 189–193, 195, 197–198, 202, 211–213, 233, 237, 239–240, 242–245, 253, 259–263, 267–268
Committee(s)
  General 5, 6, 8, 11, 13, 26–27, 30, 32–34, 37–38, 40–42, 44–47, 52–53, 58–59, 64, 66, 68, 73–74, 82–83, 87, 90–91, 96, 98–103, 105, 108, 110–114, 117, 121, 159–160, 162, 165, 175–176, 186–188, 190–193, 195, 197–199, 202, 236, 238–240, 242, 245, 257, 259–262, 267–268
  Advisory 32–34, 41, 45, 165, 176, 189–190, 193, 202
  Appeal 34–35, 46, 53, 74–75, 91, 99–103, 193, 261
  Examination 33–35, 46, 52, 74, 76, 100–101, 160, 193
  Management 32–34, 40–41, 45–46, 52, 59, 160, 175, 187, 189, 193
  Regulatory 8–9, 13, 33–34, 41–42, 45–46, 58, 76, 160, 175, 187, 189, 193, 260
Common understanding 12, 44, 50, 66–68, 81–82, 90–91, 97–99, 103, 125, 163–165, 173, 176, 188–191, 193, 202, 211, 242–244, 259, 261–263, 267
Competence(s) 3, 15, 24–27, 29, 31–32, 38, 43, 48, 53, 106–107, 117, 122, 133–135, 142, 149, 177, 213, 233, 238
Consultation 5–6, 8, 12–13, 31, 38, 44, 50–51, 54, 59, 66–67, 70, 81–83, 95–99, 165, 187–191, 243–245, 249, 251, 257, 259–263, 267
Coreper 46, 75, 100, 113, 193, 261

Delegated acts 9–13, 16, 27, 29, 30, 35, 37, 40, 43–44, 47–54, 56, 63, 65–70, 72, 77–79, 81–84, 87–88, 90–92, 94–99, 102–103, 107–108, 110–111, 113, 115, 117–129, 138–143, 145, 149, 160, 162–167, 169–170, 173, 175–176, 178–180, 182–184, 186–192, 194–198, 210–212, 214, 216, 218–219, 233–245, 249–251, 253–254, 257–263, 267–268
Delegation of power(s) 4–17, 38, 43, 47, 58, 61, 64, 71, 77, 80, 83, 88, 92, 98, 111, 117, 125, 133, 136, 141–142, 147, 176, 182, 187, 212, 235, 257–263, 265–269
Direct action(s) 2, 208, 227, 230, 265

Essential elements 7–10, 17, 28–33, 43, 48, 50, 52, 58–61, 65–66, 77, 79–81, 87, 107, 118–119, 122–123, 127–129, 133–145, 147–155, 162, 169, 175–176, 178–181, 185, 210, 212, 235, 237, 249, 258, 264, 266–269
Examination (committee) procedure 33–35, 46, 52, 74, 76, 100–101, 160, 193
Executive
  Acts 16, 21–22, 25, 28, 43, 118, 166, 175, 258
  Delegation 43, 107, 127, 139
  Federalism 25, 233, 257
  Power 5–6, 10, 14–17, 21–29, 31–32, 36–37, 40, 42–45, 52–53, 73, 107, 133–136, 141, 146, 148, 162, 175, 190, 194, 202, 233, 239–242, 249, 257–258, 262, 266, 268
  Rulemaking 21, 27, 35, 159, 166, 265–266
Experts 5, 11–12, 31, 38, 44, 50–51, 55, 66–68, 81–84, 90, 94–97, 99–100, 103, 134, 165, 186–191, 196–197, 202, 206, 211, 234, 236–238, 243–245, 249–251, 254, 257, 259, 261–263, 267

Federalism 25, 233, 257

Hierarchy of norms 1, 3, 22, 81, 143, 157–159, 161, 163, 165–172, 174, 209–210, 217, 231, 265

Implementation 4–8, 10, 12, 21–29, 31–35, 37–39, 42, 46–50, 53, 59, 67, 70–73, 75, 79, 87–90, 94–95, 102–103, 113–114, 119, 134–138, 140–141, 144, 147, 150–153, 159–161, 166, 170–171, 174, 176–177, 179–180, 187, 192, 198, 213, 219–220, 222, 227, 230, 241, 247, 253, 257, 259–260, 266–268

Implementing acts 9–12, 14–16, 23, 29–30, 35, 37–38, 40, 44–45, 47–52, 54–57, 63, 67–68, 70–72, 75, 77–81, 83, 87–88, 90, 92, 94, 96, 98–99, 102–103, 107–108, 110, 115, 117–121, 123–128, 138–139, 143–146, 148, 153–154, 158–163, 165–167, 169–172, 173–187, 190–194, 197–199, 201–202, 210–214, 216, 219, 231, 233–234
Implementing measures 42, 53, 57–58, 63, 72, 75, 78, 80, 100, 137, 149, 159, 161, 183, 205, 213–214, 216, 218–222, 227, 229, 231–232, 265
Indirect action(s) 208, 265
Institutional balance 11, 15, 17, 31, 35, 60, 137, 139, 144, 147, 171, 177, 233, 235, 242, 261
Interinstitutional agreement(s) 82, 89, 91, 103, 163, 263, 268

Judicial protection 158, 205–207, 209, 213, 220, 226–229, 231–232
Judicial review 1–2, 14–15, 17, 48–49, 60, 62–63, 65, 71, 79–80, 102, 143–144, 155, 168, 179–181, 194, 206–208, 220, 222–223, 226, 237, 249
Judicial standing 2, 22, 158, 205–209, 217–219, 223–226, 228, 230–231, 265

Legal act(s) 1–4, 6, 8–12, 14–15, 38, 47, 136, 138, 146, 169, 209, 214, 229, 244, 254, 257, 259, 262, 265–266, 268
Legislative act(s) 1–4, 7–13, 16–17, 21, 23, 25–33, 37–44, 47–49, 51–53, 55, 59–61, 63, 65, 69, 71–72, 77, 79–81, 89–90, 116–117, 122–124, 129, 134, 136–147, 149–150, 153–154, 157–158, 162–164, 166–171, 174–185, 187–189, 194–198, 202, 210, 212–218, 228–229, 231, 237, 241, 249–250, 253, 257–260, 263–264, 267–269
Legislative procedure
  Ordinary 2–3, 8, 10, 12–13, 53, 57, 63–65, 73, 89–90, 92, 112, 115–116, 120, 123, 128, 145–146, 175, 192, 210, 212, 217, 238, 253, 259, 269
  Special 2–3, 44, 65, 69, 73, 146–147, 175, 210, 217
Legislator(s)/Legislature 3–5, 7, 9–11, 13, 15, 17, 22–24, 27–32, 34, 37–40, 42–44, 46–53, 56–57, 60–61, 63–65, 68–69, 75, 77, 79–80, 83, 88, 90, 95, 98, 107, 111, 113, 118, 123, 126–127, 129, 133–137, 139–149, 151–154, 157, 162, 164, 167–168, 171, 177–182, 194, 201, 210, 212, 222, 231, 235, 237, 239, 243, 247, 249–250, 254, 257–258, 260, 262–265, 267–269
Legitimacy 3, 17, 52–53, 64, 73, 88, 97, 139–140, 144, 147, 157, 164, 170, 205, 231, 233–239, 241–251, 253–254, 257, 265

Management (committee) procedure 32–34, 40–41, 45–46, 52, 59, 160, 175, 187, 189, 193

Non-legislative act(s) 1–4, 7, 9–10, 12–13, 21, 43, 55, 77, 122, 147, 157–158, 164, 166, 168, 174–175, 205, 207, 210, 212, 214, 218, 223, 231, 233–235, 239, 242, 251–252, 254, 257–260, 262, 264–266, 268–269

Participation 57, 67, 72, 74–75, 83, 118, 145–147, 210–211, 230–231, 234, 245, 247–250, 252, 254, 264
PRAC, *see* Regulatory (committee) procedure with scrutiny
Publication 2, 14

Regulatory acts 2, 71, 158, 176, 205, 210, 213–214, 216–222, 229, 231, 252, 265
Regulatory (committee) procedure 8, 33–34, 41–42, 45–46, 58, 76, 160, 175, 187, 189, 193
Regulatory (committee) procedure with scrutiny 9, 13, 46, 58, 76, 160, 260
Right to object 10, 62–64, 66, 68, 70, 82, 87, 90, 96, 98–99, 102, 107, 117, 121, 127, 162, 164, 188, 212, 250
Right to revoke 10, 29–30, 63–64, 68, 70, 83, 87, 90, 96, 98, 102, 107, 111, 117, 121, 127, 162, 164, 176, 182, 187, 191, 212, 235–236, 238
Rules of procedure 74, 245

Safeguard (committee) procedure 35, 40, 45
Separation of powers 2–3, 6, 22–24, 27, 52, 133, 136, 139, 146, 157, 161, 164, 166, 257, 266
Statement of reason 14, 74
Subsidiarity 2, 29, 116–117, 120–123, 126, 128

Transparency 47, 51–52, 67, 83, 97, 162, 188, 190, 230, 240, 244, 247, 252, 264

The manufacturer's authorised representative in the EU for product safety is Oxford University Press España S.A. of el Parque Empresarial San Fernando de Henares, Avenida de Castilla, 2 – 28830 Madrid (www.oup.es/en or product.safety@oup.com). OUP España S.A. also acts as importer into Spain of products made by the manufacturer.

www.ingramcontent.com/pod-product-compliance
Lightning Source LLC
LaVergne TN
LVHW011916200926
848484LV00002B/639
* 9 7 8 0 1 9 8 7 0 3 2 3 5 *